EUROPE

ASIA

AFRICA

INDIAN

OCEAN

EASTERN HEMISPHERE

The World in Turmoil, 1914-1944

A survey of contemporary world history from the beginnings of the First World War through the Teheran Conference, with a section on postwar planning

THE

WORLD

IN

TURMOIL

1914-1944

By T. Walter Wallbank
and Alastair M. Taylor

University of Southern California

SCOTT, FORESMAN AND COMPANY

CHICAGO   ATLANTA   DALLAS   NEW YORK

Preface

T HE WORLD IN TURMOIL: 1914-1944 is a concise but world-wide contemporary history covering the beginnings of the First World War, the war itself, the unsettled peace, the Second World War, and postwar planning. While observing the limits of conciseness, the authors have attempted to provide a clear and comprehensive treatment of the vital historical backgrounds of today and tomorrow.

Following the accepted viewpoint, the authors have dealt with the present struggle as part of an unfolding historical movement which had its genesis in the latter part of the 19th century, provoked the First World War, continued to operate in the "Long Armistice" from 1919 to 1939, and again precipitated world war in 1939. In the narrative the earlier events are discussed with a minimum of detail. The story broadens as events carry the reader into the First World War and the interval between two wars. The rise of Communism, Fascism, Nazism, the failure of the League of Nations and collective security, the events leading to Munich are given full treatment. Three chapters are utilized to cover four years of the world at war and another to project attention upon the problems of a world returning to peace.

This study is global. In addition to an examination of European developments there is unusually complete coverage on the British Dominions, the United States, Latin America, the Orient. One full chapter is devoted to Far Eastern Affairs from 1919 to 1939, and the Orient—including its home fronts—is naturally covered in the later chapters on the war.

Though not economic determinists, the authors have paid careful attention to the importance of economic factors in contemporary history whenever they have been particularly prepotent—for example, reparations and war debts, the great depression of 1930-1933, and the operation of such techniques of economic nationalism as devaluation of currency, high tariffs, and quota systems.

Postwar problems and their solution lie in the realm of speculation and quite frequently in that of controversy. Yet students are vitally interested in the emerging shape of the civilization they are helping to save; and they need whatever guidance history courses can give them as they move toward the decisions of tomorrow. A chapter on postwar planning therefore appears here. To justify the inclusion of such material the authors have taken pains not to tilt a lance for or against any particular plan or proposal relating to the postwar world and have confined their efforts to elucidation rather than persuasion.

W HILE ASSUMING complete responsibility for all facts and interpretations throughout the book, the authors wish to express their thanks to the following persons for valuable assistance at the points indicated: to Professor S. William Halperin of the University of Chicago, Chapters 1 through 9; to Mr. Francis J. O'Malley of Notre Dame

University, Chapters 1 through 6; to Professor Ross Berkes of The University of Southern California, the material on Latin America in Chapter 4; to Professor H. F. MacNair of the University of Chicago, the material on China, Japan, and the Pacific Islands in Chapter 5; to Professor G. V. Bobrinskoy of the University of Chicago, the material on India in Chapter 5; to Mr. Carroll Binder, Foreign Editor of *The Chicago Daily News*, Chapters 7 through 9; and to Professor E. A. Wolfram of St. John's College, the preparation of the Chart of Contemporary Events, through 1942.

We express our thanks also to the following persons for various kinds of work on the book: to Mr. R. M. Chapin, Jr., who besides drawing under special assignment the maps for Chapters 1 through 6, gave discriminating attention to the best possible ways to dramatize and clarify certain important geographical impressions; to Mary Herrick Porter for the large amounts of research for the maps in Chapters 1 through 6; to Mr. Chapin and the publishers of *Time* for permission to use in Chapters 7 through 9 maps that appeared in their columns during the past year; to Mr. Barney Moore for the initial drawings for Chapters 1 through 6; and to Miss Winifred Pawliger for the initial drawings for Chapters 7 through 9.

Finally, we express our appreciation to the following publishers from whose books quotations have been made. Such quotations are indicated in detail in the Bibliography beginning on page 270: D. Appleton-Century Company, New York; Carnegie Endowment for International Peace, New York; The Christian Science Publishing Company, Boston; F. S. Crofts & Co., New York; The Curtis Publishing Company, Philadelphia; Doubleday, Doran and Company, New York; Editorial Publications, Inc., New York; L. B. Fischer, New York; Foreign Affairs, New York; Foreign Policy Association, New York; Harcourt, Brace and Company, New York; Harper & Brothers, New York; Harvard University Press, Cambridge; Henry Holt and Company, New York; Houghton Mifflin Company, Boston; International Publishers, New York; Alfred A. Knopf, New York; J. B. Lippincott Company, Philadelphia; The Macmillan Company, New York; Methuen and Company, London; Newsweek, New York; New Zealand Legation, Washington, D. C.; W. W. Norton & Company, New York; Oxford University Press, New York and London; Oskar Piest, New York; Simon and Schuster, New York; Soviet Russia Today, New York; Time, Inc., New York; University of California Press, Berkeley; The University of Chicago Press, Chicago; D. Van Nostrand Company, New York; The Viking Press, New York.

T. W. W.
A. M. T.

Los Angeles, California
December 15, 1943

Table of Contents

Preface. v

PART ONE

From Sarajevo to Manchukuo 1

CHAPTER 1 . . . . Explosion in Europe. 5
POLITICS, DIPLOMACY, AND WAR: 1870-1918

Chronology. 4
Economic Progress
  and World Interdependence. 6
The Causes of the Great War. 9

The Coming of the Great War (1871-1914). .14
The First World War. 20
The United States and the War. 23
Summary. 28

CHAPTER 2 . . . . .A Quest for World Order. 31
THE SETTLEMENT; WORLD ECONOMY: 1918-1933

Chronology. 30
Making the Peace. 32
Organization and Function
  of the League of Nations. 38
The League of Nations in Action. 43
Problems of Security and Disarmament. 45

Problems of Reconstruction
  and Economic Stability. 53
Tariff Barriers and the War Debts. 55
Depression and Economic Nationalism. 56
Capitalism on Trial. .58
Summary. 60

CHAPTER 3 . . . . .New Patterns in Statecraft. 63
COMMUNISM, FASCISM, NATIONAL SOCIALISM: 1917-1939

Chronology. 62
Communism in Russia. 64
Mussolini and Italian Fascism. 74

Efficient Turkish Dictatorship. 79
The Rise of Hitler's Third Reich. 81
Summary. 89

CHAPTER 4 . . . . .Democracy on Trial. .93
COUNTRIES OF THE ESTABLISHED ORDER: 1919-1939

Chronology. 92
The Period of French Reconstruction. 94
Czechoslovakia, Poland, Hungary,
  and Yugoslavia. 96
Austria, Rumania, Bulgaria, and Spain. 98

Great Britain and the British Empire. 102
The United States. 107
Latin America (1919-1939). 112
Summary. 118

CHAPTER 5 . . . . .The Orient Astir. .121
INDIA, CHINA, JAPAN, OCEANIA: 1900-1939

Chronology. 120
India Seeks to Rule Herself. 122
The Great Powers in Eastern Asia. 126
China Tries to Change. 132

Japan Expands. 139
Japan Prepares for a "New Order". 142
The Pacific Situation: 1939. 146
Summary. 148

PART TWO

Ordeal of Our Time   149

CHAPTER 6 . . . . A World Divided 153

BACKGROUNDS FOR WAR; THE SECOND WORLD WAR: FIRST PHASES

Chronology 152
Fascism Triumphant in Abyssinia
  and Spain 154
Milestones to Munich 157
Hitler Looks toward Poland 161
Blitzkrieg over Europe 164
The United States and the Spreading War . .172
The War Encircles the Globe 177
Summary 190

CHAPTER 7 . . . . Since Stalingrad 193

THE SECOND WORLD WAR: 1942, 1943

Chronology 192
The War in Retrospect: 1939-1942 193
Crest of Axis Power 194
Emergence of Allied Strength 201
Pattern for Victory 210
Cairo and Teheran: New Unity 218
Summary 219

CHAPTER 8 . . . . On the Home Fronts .221

PRODUCTION, POLITICS, ECONOMICS: 1942, 1943

Chronology 220
The United States 221
Great Britain 225
Canada 228
Australia, New Zealand,
  and South Africa 231
Latin America 234
Russia 236
China 239
Italy 241
Germany 243
Japan 244
Summary 246

CHAPTER 9 . . . . Preparing for Tomorrow 249

THE TRANSITION; PEACE AIMS

Chronology 248
The First Steps 249
The Period of Transition 251
Reduction of the Hazard of War 255
Perfection and Encouragement
  of Democracy 260
Advancement of Colonial Peoples 260
Freedom from Want 261
Improvement of International Economic
  Cooperation 263
Summary 264

Chart of Contemporary Events 266
Bibliography, Footnotes, and Acknowledgments 270
General Index 281

List of Maps

1. Explosion in Europe

Europe: 1871.........................12
Balkans: 1914 (Inset)...................12
Background for War—World War I.......17
The Schlieffen Plan....................21
Nations in World War I.................27

2. A Quest for World Order

The Mandate System...................34
The Peace Settlements.................35
Trouble Spots in Postwar Europe.........39
Postwar Europe.....................48-49

5. The Orient Astir

Asia.................................123
Foreign Holdings in China.............137

6. A World Divided

Prelude to War.......................160
The World at War.................178-179

7. Since Stalingrad

The Atlantic Supply Routes.............194
War in the Pacific....................195
The Big Push........................196
The U. S. Attacks....................200
The Mediterranean Area..............202
Russian Seesaw......................206
Counterattack in the Aleutians..........209
Plowing Water in China...............210
Routes to Berlin......................211

List of Illustrations

1. Explosion in Europe

The Horseless Carriage Versus the Horse (engraving)........................*The Bettmann Archive*   7
Raven Hill: The Boiling Point...   13
Trench Warfare..*Brown Brothers*   23
Fighter Planes..*Kaufmann-Fabry*   24
Airplane of World War I..*Acme*   25

2. A Quest for World Order

"Etiquette for America" (cartoon)..   42
It Is for Peace That This Hammer Works (cartoon)...   51

3. New Patterns in Statecraft

Organization of Russian Government (diagram)..   68
Russian Agricultural Students......................................*Ewing Galloway, N. Y.*   70
Cotton Farmers in Turkestan...*Acme*   71
Vaccinating Russian Peasants..*Acme*   72
Turkestan Factory Girl...*Ewing Galloway, N. Y.*   73
Monumental Bust of Mussolini...*Acme*   77
Mussolini and the Stork (cartoon)..   78
Reclamation of Pontine Marshes...................*By Burton Holmes from Ewing Galloway*   79
Statue of Kemal Ataturk, Ankara, Turkey.........................*By Ewing Galloway, N. Y.*   80
Famous Berlin Outdoor Cafe.....................................*By Ewing Galloway, N. Y.*   82
Hitler Reviews Troops in Nuremberg......................................*Acme*   85

Chancellor Hitler Greets President Von Hindenburg..*Acme* 86
Organization of German Government (diagram).. 86
Fire in the Reichstag...*Acme* 87
Nazi Youth Practices Hurling Grenades...*Acme* 88
Hitler Addresses May Day Crowd in Berlin...*Acme* 89

4. Democracy on Trial

Léon Blum and French Popular Front Ministry..*Acme* 95
Ignace Jan Paderewski...*Acme* 97
Karl Marx Hof in Vienna...*Acme* 99
Apartment Houses, Stockholm...*Acme* 101
Election Posters in Barcelona, 1933...*Acme* 102
Premier Ramsay MacDonald and Aristide Briand...*Acme* 103
Organization of English Government (diagram).. 104
Grain Elevator, Quebec, Canada.................................*By Ewing Galloway, N. Y.* 105
Emptying Barrels of Whiskey in the Prohibition Era.....................................*Acme* 108
Organization of the United States Government (diagram)................................. 109
New Yorkers Welcome Admiral Byrd...*Acme* 110
Tennessee Valley Authority Dam...............................*Tennessee Valley Authority* 111
Political Criticism in Mexico..*Acme* 113
Brazil Improves Production of Coffee...*Acme* 114
Oil Refineries at Curaçao, Dutch West Indies..*Acme* 116
Avenue 18th of July, Montevideo, Uruguay.........................*By Ewing Galloway, N. Y.* 117

5. The Orient Astir

Gandhi Calls on the Viceroy..*Acme* 123
Principal Bazaar Street in Delhi, India..*Acme* 124
War Production in India..*Acme* 125
Dutch Oil Wells in Borneo...*Acme* 129
Tapping a Rubber Tree in Sumatra..*Acme* 130
Rice Fields in Netherlands East Indies...*Acme* 131
Farming in the Philippines...*Acme* 132
Morrison Street in Peiping, China...*Acme* 135
Jawaharlal Nehru, Madame Chiang Kai-shek, and General Chiang Kai-shek..................*Acme* 137
Tea-vendor's Stand in Canton, China..*Acme* 138
Japanese Women Campaign for Civic Rights...*Acme* 140
Japanese Colony in Manchukuo..*Acme* 143
Chinese Flee the Invading Japanese..*Acme* 144
Hitler Receives the Japanese Ambassador...*Acme* 147

6. A World Divided

Haile Selassie Arrives at Geneva..*Acme* 154
Soldiers of the Spanish Loyalist Army..*Acme* 156
Men and Women Soldiers in Spain...*Acme* 156
Signs of the Times in Vienna...*Acme* 158
Prime Minister Chamberlain Reviews Hitler's Storm Troops...............................*Acme* 159
German Night Patrol...*Acme* 162

Nazi Army Invades Holland...*Acme* 166
German Tanks and Guns..*Acme* 167
London Bombed..*Acme* 168
British Fighting Planes..*Acme* 170
America First Meeting...*Acme* 173
German Prisoners in Russia..*Acme* 177
Nazi Tank Stalled by Mud...*Acme* 180
U.S.S. Arizona Afire after Pearl Harbor Attack.........................*Acme* 183
American Bombers Patrol the Atlantic..................................*Acme* 184
Curtiss Commando...*Acme* 186
United States Aircraft Production...................*From Ewing Galloway, N. Y.* 188

7. Since Stalingrad

Street Fighting in Stalingrad...*Sovfoto* 197
Scuttling of the French Fleet...*Acme* 203
Singsong in North Africa..*British Combine* 204
United States Marines on Guadalcanal..................................*Acme* 208
Hunting for Snipers in Messina..*Acme* 212
Occupation of Kiska...*Acme* 214
Leaders of the Quebec Conference..................*National Film Board of Canada* 215
Amphibious Landing in Italy...*Acme* 217

8. On the Home Fronts

"Our Chief Pressure Groups" (diagram).....*(From "Government Under Pressure," by Donald C. Blaisdell, published by the Public Affairs Committee, Incorporated, New York City.) Graphic Associates for Public Affairs Committee* 222
Newsman in England...*British Combine* 227
United States-Canadian Cooperation.................*National Film Board of Canada* 230
The Alaska Highway................................*National Film Board of Canada* 230
Australian "Cub Pack" Collecting Scrap................................*Acme* 232
New Zealanders in Slit Trenches.......................................*Acme* 233
Latin American Conference...*Pix* 235
Soviet Women in Ammunition Plant....................................*Sovfoto* 237
Chinese Troops Fording a River..*Acme* 240

9. Preparing for Tomorrow

"A Platform Is No Good without Steps" (cartoon)..................*St. Louis Star-Times* 250
"Some Jobs for the United Nations Relief Organization" (diagram)...*(From "Rebuilding Europe—After Victory," by Hiram Motherwell, published by the Public Affairs Committee, Incorporated, New York City.) Pictograph Corporation for Public Affairs Committee* 252
Posting the AMG Proclamation in Sicily................................*Acme* 254

1870 TO 1939

PART ONE

From Sarajevo to Manchukuo

CHAPTER 1

Explosion in Europe

CHAPTER 2

A Quest for World Order

CHAPTER 3

New Patterns in Statecraft

CHAPTER 4

Democracy on Trial

CHAPTER 5

The Orient Astir

FROM SARAJEVO TO MANCHUKUO

B Y THE END OF THE NINETEENTH CENTURY the culture and power of Europe had made themselves felt all over the world. European culture was spread over the entire Western Hemisphere: the United States, Canada, Mexico, Central and South America. It permeated South Africa and was basic in Australia and New Zealand. Nor did Europe's influence stop there. Major European powers had staked out vast territorial claims in Africa, Asia, and Oceania. For purposes of prestige, strategy, and trade (as well as the more sincere objectives of the missionary) they had painted the map all colors. The nineteenth century was a period of aggressive imperialistic expansion, but the European justified his actions by maintaining that he had taken up the "white man's burden"—he was bettering the lot of backward peoples by giving them the benefits of European civilization.

But Europe was soon to reveal to the rest of the world that its pretentions to superiority of culture were based on fallacious grounds. From 1870 on, the major European powers entered into a suicidal rivalry among themselves. The stakes were high: colonial possessions, lucrative world markets, and prestige at the conference table. In this hotly contested race they jockeyed for better positions and to gain them were not above indulging in shady tactics. Finally the race narrowed down to two principal contestants, the Triple Alliance—composed of Germany, Austria, and Italy, and the Triple Entente—made up of Great Britain, France, and Russia. After many years of "incidents" in which war was only narrowly averted, the great struggle known as the First World War exploded in Europe. At tremendous cost and after the United States had entered the war, the Germans, Austrians, and their followers were defeated.

Now followed a futile quest for world order. The Treaty of Versailles (1919) was designed to make the world safe for democracy, but it left unsettled some major problems, accentuated others, and was phrased in such a manner as to give demagogues in the defeated countries a chance to warp its limitations into an excuse for violent revision. At the same time, as part of the new framework of the war settlement, the League of Nations was established. This institution, chiefly the offspring of Woodrow Wilson's idealism, was the first real attempt in world history to create an international agency for the settlement of differences among nations and to ensure world peace.

Meanwhile, certain countries had started to experiment with new patterns of government. The corrupt and reactionary régime of the czars in Russia first revealed its incompetence during the Russo-Japanese war of 1905. Russian reverses in the First World War convinced the people that a drastic change was essential. The outcome was the Revolution of 1917 and the resulting Communist government. Later a new socialistic order was established.

Soon after the war another important experiment in government began with the triumph of Mussolini's philosophy of Fascism. This ideology established strict governmental regulation over capital and labor for purposes of national planning and building up Italy's power.

Early in the thirties Germany accepted a brand of Fascism with the rule of Hitler and his National Socialist party. Hitler too believed in national planning, pledged himself to wipe out the Treaty of Versailles, and undertook to make Germany the supreme power in Europe.

THE DEMOCRATIC NATIONS had won the First World War, and the attendant treaty was of their shaping. While Great Britain and France accepted the League of Nations (the United States refused to do this) with its program for peace, in reality they appeared little interested in trying to change the *status quo*. Democracy in the twenties and thirties became complacent and static, for it did little to rectify many economic and social maladjustments, and it neglected to prepare defense against the aggressive ideologies bent upon its destruction.

The failure of western civilization in the twentieth century to live up to its self-proclaimed ideals of the nineteenth caused profound reverberations all through Asia. Despite the obvious fact that western science and invention had put in the hands of the white race the most powerful weapons and industrial techniques, the European had "lost face" in the eyes of the Asiatic. The Indians saw in British rule not the political emancipation which it had promised them but only imperialistic exploitation. The Chinese attempted to enlist western support in their struggle for national unity and independence but saw their efforts thwarted time and again by the unwillingness of the occidental powers to relinquish vested interests. The Japanese were swift to see the value of adopting western technology as a means of reorganizing the political and economic life of their country. But they also knew that the occidental nations were not invincible; Japan's smashing defeat of Russia in 1905 convinced them of that. Therefore, their statesmen planned through the decades of the twentieth century how best to drive the western powers out of Asia and build up a vast Japanese-controlled empire.

In 1931 Japan started upon its program of conquest, inaugurating a series of events which threw the entire world into further turmoil, which was to culminate in the Second World War.

1870-1914	**Events Leading up to World War I**	
	Non-political international cooperation	
1856	European Danube Commission	
1864	International Red Cross	
1868	International Telegraphic Union	
1874	Universal Postal Union	
1888	International Copyright Union	
1899-1907	Hague Peace Conferences	
1877-1878	Russo-Turkish war in Balkans	Treaty of San Stefano
1878	Congress of Berlin	Reduces Russian war gains
1884-1885	Berlin Conference	Made rules for partition of Africa
1873	Bismarck's Three-Emperors' League	With Russia and Austria-Hungary
1879	Bismarck makes Dual Alliance with Austria	
1881-1887	Three Emperors' League revived	
1882	Italy joins alliance, making it the Triple Alliance	
1887-1891	Reinsurance Treaty between Germany, Russia	Tries to keep both Austria, Russia allies
1889	First Pan American Conference	Three more conferences held before War
1894	Franco-Russian alliance	
1898	Fashoda incident	British-French rivalry in upper Nile
1899	Boer War in South Africa	British victory
1894	Sino-Japanese War	
1902	Anglo-Japanese alliance	
1903	Berlin-to-Bagdad railway	Germany seeks hegemony in Near East
1904-1905	Russo-Japanese War	
1904	Entente Cordiale	France and Great Britain
1907	Triple Entente	Great Britain, France, Russia
1908	Austria annexes Bosnia-Herzegovina	With approval of Germany
1911	Second Moroccan crisis	Bargain made by France, Germany
1911-1912	Turco-Italian War	Libya gained by Italy
1912-1913	First and Second Balkan wars	Balkan countries quarrel over spoils
1914	Assassination of Austrian archduke	By Serbian nationalists
	Austria's ultimatum	Clever Serbian reply
	Austria declares war on Serbia	Russian mobilization
1914-1918	**The First World War**	
	Allies: France, Great Britain, Russia, Japan	
	Central Powers: Germany, Austria-Hungary, Turkey	
1914	Battle of the Marne saves France	Germans advance on Paris
1915-1918	Trench warfare	Little large-scale movements
1915	Rout of Russians on eastern front	Battle of Tannenberg, German victory
	Italy joins Allies	Secret Treaty of London
	U. S. helps finance war, sends materials	
	Sinking of Lusitania	Stirs United States against Germany
	Bulgaria joins Central Powers	
1916	Battles of Verdun and Somme	Huge Allied losses
	Rumania joins Allies	Soon forced to capitulate to Bulgaria
1917	Russian revolution	Treaty of Brest Litovsk with Germany
	United States entry into war	U-boat campaign immediate cause
1918	Wilson's Fourteen Points	
	German offensive	Allied counterattack
	Germany collapses, asks armistice	

CHAPTER 1

Explosion in Europe

Few periods in history have been graced with so much promise, worth-while accomplishment, and consequent optimism as the last half of the nineteenth century in Europe. In the span of one century Europe's population had more than doubled to reach a figure of over four hundred million in 1910. Europe was now, more than ever, the center of the world, the richest area in material wealth, and the most fruitful in artistic and intellectual achievement. The spread of public-school systems made illiteracy less prevalent; the expansion of public libraries and the publication of inexpensive books and periodicals made literature the property of the people; and applied science blessed the life of civilized man with such new inventions as the telephone, the telegraph, the modern locomotive, and gas illumination. Governments also showed more solicitude for their peoples. "It seemed as if statesmen had now at last learned the lesson that politics is the art of human happiness."[1]

In increasing number laws protecting the workers from industrial accidents and assuring them adequate medical service and support during unemployment found their way onto the statute books. A kind of cultural internationalism pervaded Europe, with music, art, and literature transcending political boundaries. In the field of government, too, the omens were promising. The franchise was broadened, parliamentary government began to crowd out aristocratic plutocracy, and everywhere political liberty was on the march. The progress of industry made the nations increasingly interdependent as strands of railroads, cables, and shipping bound the world into a single unit. Science and business appeared to be heralding the approach of the world community in which cooperation and not conflict would prevail among nations. Yet, despite numerous instances of cooperation between nations, there was a lamentable absence of idealism, justice, and generosity in their dealings with one another. Fundamental forces were at work making the nations more bellicose and selfish. If men could be said to have reached a position just lower than the angels in their intellectual and scientific attainments, their tactics in international relations fell considerably short of this mark.

This chapter reveals what happened because nations knew and accepted no laws higher than their own narrow interests. Our discussion surveys the forces working for world cooperation, the fundamental causes of the conflict of 1914, the diplomatic history of western Europe from 1871 to 1914, the operation of the system of rival alliances, and the First World War. In this connection attention is also given to the factors that brought the United States into the conflict in 1917.

Economic Progress and World Interdependence

The new industrialism and its results. The story of our day starts with industrialism. Industrial changes began to transform life in England in the latter part of the eighteenth century and later revolutionized economic life in many other parts of the globe. As the nineteenth century drew to a close, a new phase of the Industrial Revolution, even more intense and breath-taking than its predecessor, took place. New machines for production, new instruments for transportation, and new devices for communication made the inventions and discoveries of Arkwright, Stephenson, Fulton, and Morse seem old-fashioned and inefficient. This new phase began to gather force shortly after 1850 and was most evident in the United States and Germany. In the United States the rapid progress of the new industrialism was characterized by the introduction of mass-production methods. In Germany the rapid advance of industry was assisted especially by the skillful utilization of chemistry. While Germany and the United States made the most phenomenal industrial advances, progress was also recorded in such countries as France, Belgium, Sweden, Japan, and Great Britain.

The new industrialism brought about many changes, of which the following may be singled out as of major importance: (1) Machinery became more complicated and more automatic in its operation. (2) Parts for machine-made goods became standardized so that repairs could be obtained cheaply and readily by the consumer. (3) New forms of power were developed, especially electricity and oil. (4) Products of nature were created artificially by chemical processes, and even products heretofore unknown to nature were likewise developed. Perfumes, flavoring extracts, fats, explosives, fertilizers, and many other things now came out of test tubes.

(5) Great new industries began to compete with the textile industry and other giants that had been born earlier. Shortly before the American Civil War drilling for oil was perfected in the United States. This was the beginning of an amazing industry that soon developed large refineries, transportation systems, factories to manufacture by-products, and great corporations to guide the many manufacturing processes connected with petroleum. Rubber is another example. As early as 1825 rubber had been used to waterproof textiles, but its extensive industrial application was not possible until the process of vulcanization was discovered in 1839. In Ireland in 1888 J. B. Dunlop hit upon the principle of the pneumatic tire, a discovery which created a tremendous demand for rubber shortly thereafter. The appearance of horseless carriages in the latter part of the nineteenth century led to the development of yet another great new industry. By the first decade of the twentieth century it was apparent that the automobile would soon radically change older modes of transportation and at the same time become one of the most important of all industrial enterprises.

(6) Another major result was the creation of ever larger business organizations, some of which were corporations capitalized at more than one billion dollars, having annual sales totaling the same amount. Capitalism by 1900 had already passed through two basic stages

Inevitably the old horse-drawn lorry had to try to show up its competitor, the new steam-driven passenger vehicle. The "self-acting steam omnibus" is getting the better of it in this London race.

of development—commercial in the fifteenth, sixteenth, and seventeenth centuries and industrial in the eighteenth and nineteenth. Now it was entering the third stage—finance capitalism, in which the banker and financier rather than the manufacturer became the dominant figure. To create and operate huge industrial organizations required larger sums of capital than the manufacturer could ordinarily provide. Hence these sums had to be secured from great investment banks or financial houses. More and more the control of industry came into the hands of the financiers.

Increase in productivity. All these new changes in the economic life of men and nations brought significant results with them. There was an enormous increase in industrial productivity. The new automatic machines, for example, enabled one man to turn out 500 pounds of nails daily. In 1780 the output had been only five pounds. In the eighteenth century the daily output of one man in a coal mine had been one half a ton. Now it was four tons. In 1865 the production of iron by the main industrial nations was nine million tons. In 1910 it had reached sixty-six million tons, and in the same period the output of coal increased from 180 million tons to one billion and a quarter.

This increase in industrial productivity brought about a need for new markets and new sources for raw materials. These demands

in turn gave rise to a vast network of international communication and transportation. Telephone, telegraph, and cable linked the many countries of the world and facilitated business transactions. Transcontinental railroads, canals, and fleets of cargo vessels carried a stream of the ever more numerous commodities around the globe. In 1860 world trade was worth slightly more than seven billion dollars; in 1913 it was worth nearly forty-two billion.

Economic interdependence. It seemed as if the world would soon become one great integrated business unit in which the people would be held together by bonds of common economic interdependence. An era of world economy seemed just around the corner. New inventions increased industrial efficiency. Although there was a noticeable trend in the direction of higher tariffs, up to the First World War tariffs were relatively low and consequently no serious detriment to the flow of goods across national boundaries. People were still fairly free to move about and came by the millions from Europe to the New World. This movement tended to ease Europe's economic problems and at the same time assisted in the development of the countries of the New World. International trade was based on a stable world monetary system, the gold standard. There was little tinkering with national currencies, and world trade profited thereby. Moreover, in this era of economic expansion, the world was relatively peaceful. Investors did not hesitate to invest capital all over the world. These investments, for the time being at least, brought profitable returns to the capitalists, who lived for the most part in the industrialized countries, and helped develop the resources of other areas, mainly in economically backward countries.

International cooperation. Despite the fact that national boundaries divided the world into some sixty independent political units, there was some measure of international cooperation. A habit of political collaboration apparently was developing among the European powers. Ever since the Congress of Vienna, the great powers had frequently conferred among themselves whenever the peace of the continent was jeopardized. This practice of consultation, called the concert of Europe, had helped on several occasions to keep the peace. Following the revolt of the Belgians, a conference met at London in 1831 to work out a suitable arrangement for Belgian independence. A congress met in Geneva in 1864 to organize the international Red Cross. Again in 1868, at St. Petersburg, and in 1874, at Brussels, conferences took place to secure more humane agreements regarding the conduct of war.

The Congress of Berlin in 1878 averted war between Russia and her opponents, Great Britain and Austria. The Berlin Conference of 1884-1885 drew up rules regulating the partition of Africa, and in 1906 on the initiative of the United States a conference was held at Algeciras to prevent the French and Germans from coming to blows over Morocco. In 1912-1913 the European powers met in London to work out terms for ending the Balkan wars. In the Western Hemisphere the first Pan American Conference, consisting of eighteen countries, assembled in 1889 at Washington, D.C. Matters of common economic interest were discussed as well as problems pertaining to the maintenance of peace in the Western Hemisphere. Before the First World War other conferences were held at Mexico City (1901), Rio de Janeiro (1906), and Buenos Aires (1910).

The examples just given deal only with cooperation among nations in the realm of international politics. Although nations continued to retain their national identities, there was ample recognition among them of the fact that the forces of industrialism and modern science were pushing them in the direction of a world community in other fields as well. In 1865 a conference met at Paris to discuss the coordination of telegraph lines and the problem of rates. This resulted in the establishment of the International Telegraph Union, formed by twenty countries, which created a permanent office in Switzerland in 1868. The Universal Postal Union was set up in 1874 to facilitate the handling of mail all over the world. In 1886 an international copyright union was formed. It drew up an agreement for the protection of authors which was subsequently ratified by nineteen nations. During the period from 1880 to 1914 there were similar agreements regarding cables, weights and measures, and the protection of birds. One of the most important examples of international cooperation was the formation and operation of the European Danube commission. This commission, established in 1856, policed the lower Danube, kept boat facilities in order, and established rates for river commerce. In the interests of international commerce and cooperation, Rumania, through which the lower Danube flowed, surrendered a portion of its sovereign right to police and control "its own river."

The idea of international cooperation became apparent in the minds and actions of peoples as well as governments. World-wide religious movements and scientific congresses and societies appeared, and a world parliamentary union was formed. In general, men were being drawn together on the basis of universal needs and desires, particularly in matters which were nonpolitical in character.

The movement for peace. Moreover, there was a consistent interest in the maintenance of peace, although the desire for it was perhaps stronger among the people than it was among their governments. Starting in England as early as 1816, the peace movement had grown steadily until by the end of the century it was a vigorous and powerful movement. Alfred Nobel, a Swedish manufacturer, devoted much of his fortune to the advancement of peace, and an American philanthropist, Andrew Carnegie, subsidized internationalism by building a "temple of peace" at The Hague. In this edifice, in 1899 and in 1907, two great peace conferences were held in an attempt to achieve some limitation in armaments. This aim was not achieved, but the conferences established a court of international arbitration and agreed to certain rules for the humane conduct of warfare. Many individuals wrestled with the problem of the elimination of war, and many writers devoted their attention to this subject. One book which made a deep impression in 1898 maintained that war would mean the end of civilization. *The Great Illusion*, which was the work of Norman Angell, declared that the world was becoming so unified and its economic structure so sensitive that the shock of war would bring disaster to victors and vanquished alike—in short, that in modern war there could be no complete victory for either side.

The Causes of the Great War

The forces of antagonism. At the same time that some forces were working to bring about closer cooperation between nations and peoples, other forces were operating to bring about distrust and rivalries. These forces of antagonism finally proved to be more potent than those working for cooperation, and Europe and most of the world with it were plunged into war in 1914. Back of this great conflict were some six basic causes: (1) the national-state system and power politics, (2) militarism, (3) the system of rival alliances, (4) secret diplomacy, (5) economic imperialism, and (6) the emotion of nationalism.

National states and power politics. Organized under the national-state system, Europe in 1914 consisted of some twenty independent political units which recognized no authority higher than their own. International law had no force behind it adequate to guarantee its continuous enforcement, although the rules of international law were obeyed for the most part if they did not clash with a nation's fundamental interests. It was the aim of the governments in Europe, as elsewhere, to advance national interests. Questionable methods were frequently employed and ethics ignored because each state was answerable to no higher authority. In fact, all nations regarded war as an instrument of national policy to be used in obtaining their ends when peaceful methods failed.

Often departing from ethical standards, subordinated to no higher law, and always ready to utilize force, the nations of the world lived in a system of "international anarchy." Power became an end in itself. In the nineteenth century, the operation of the "concert of Europe" and the growth of an active sentiment for international peace camouflaged the fact that power politics were as strong as ever. Great Britain and France, for example, discussed the possibility of carving up the Turkish empire on several occasions; on the eve of the First World War Germany and Great Britain were making plans to divide the Portuguese colonial empire; and France, Great Britain, and Italy in 1906 made an agreement looking to the division of Abyssinia. The undignified scramble for Chinese territory in the last decade of the nineteenth century was merely another reflection of power politics.

Militarism. When war is the ultimate arbiter in international affairs, armed forces become extremely important. Bismarck showed his neighbors in three wars leading up to the unification of Germany what could be done with an efficient fighting force. The German army was based on the conscription of all the nation's manpower, and this practice was likewise prevalent in the rest of Europe. Only Great Britain, protected by its fleet, refused to introduce conscription. The latter part of the nineteenth century saw Europe being transformed into an armed camp. From 1870 to 1910 about one billion dollars was spent yearly on arms. In 1913 the figure had reached nearly two billion dollars.

With the growth of these huge national armies, augmented by the most scientific equipment, war became a science. Trained specialists were needed by the thousands, a complex system of mobilization had to be worked out, and intricate plans had to be laid for conquest or against invasion. This condition gave rise, more than ever before, to a powerful class of professional soldiers or militarists. Some thinkers in Europe, influenced by the concept of the survival of the fittest, developed a kind of neo-Darwinian theory in which they saw war as the instrument for weeding out the decadent and exalting the strong nations. One organization in Germany announced:

"War is the noblest and holiest expression

of human activity. For us, too, the glad hour
of battle will strike. Still and deep in the
German heart must live the joy of combat,
and the longing for it. Let us ridicule to the
utmost the old women in breeches, who fear
war and deplore it as cruel and revolting. No!
War is beautiful."[2]

Such sentiments were found in nearly all
European states; no one nation had a complete
monopoly of militarism. Germany, however,
seemed to be the most blatantly militaristic.
Here the adulation of war was most intense
and the prestige of the Prussian military clique
most elevated. "Eternal peace is a dream,"
declared Moltke, one of Germany's military
heroes, "for war is part of God's world ordi-
nances. . . . In war, the noblest virtues flourish
that otherwise would slumber and decay. The
experience of war stays with a man, and steels
him all his life."[3] Nations increased their
armaments so as to be reassured that their
neighbors would not be tempted to attack
them. Meanwhile these neighbors had interpreted the increase not as a defensive but as
an offensive measure which left them no alternative but to increase their own armaments.
Thus the armament race began, and the
faster it went, the higher tension and distrust
mounted.

Rival alliances. Living in this "international anarchy," where no nation could trust
its neighbors, no state felt strong enough to
rely upon its own military resources for protection. Nations whose interests ran along
parallel lines joined together so that in union
they could command more fighting power.
But this, in turn, provoked nations outside
the alliance to form a union capable of
matching strength with strength. The creation of two great rival alliances was a feature
of European diplomacy after 1871 (see map,
page 17), but it did not offer any more security to the states involved. In fact it made
the prospects of war more horrible because it
was now unlikely that any conflict between two
nations in Europe could be localized. Immediately—as members of two opposing alliances—
the aid of their allies would be invoked, and
the whole continent would be at war. This is
what happened in the summer of 1914.

Secret diplomacy. Another basic cause of
the war and one closely connected with the
system of alliances was the practice of secret
diplomacy. The two rival diplomatic com-
binations were vitally concerned in weakening
each other's ranks. And since allies in the
same alliance did not always completely trust
each other, there were often rumors that attempts were being made to wean one state
away from its diplomatic friends. While the
majority of people remained ignorant of
what was going on, jockeying for power,
threats and intimidations, and offers of gifts,
often involving the territory of another power,
went on unrestrained. The activities of spies,
secret reports, and unscrupulous methods employed by the foreign offices of Europe poisoned the atmosphere and heightened the
tension.

Economic imperialism. The tremendous increase in industrial productivity and the expansion of world trade between 1870 and 1914
have already been noted. At the same time a
contest developed between business groups of
rival nations over the lion's share of the new
riches. To the extent that industry and finance
now controlled their governments or were influential in the formation of policy, various
nations competed among themselves to secure
economic advantages for their respective
groups. *Laissez faire* and the absence of governmental interference in business began to decline in the last decades of the nineteenth century. Governments now began to raise their
tariffs and to use their diplomatic power and
even the force of arms to secure control of
areas rich in essential raw materials or valuable as markets for manufactured goods. Thus
laissez faire gave way to a new kind of mer-
cantilism in which governments acted as aggressive champions for their own business interests. One of the most significant features
of this neo-mercantilism was economic imperialism, which mainly concerned the struggle for the control of the backward or colonial
areas of the world.

Economic imperialism brought many nations to the verge of war. Great Britain and
Germany had serious disputes over the partition of Africa in the 1880's. These nations
also nearly came to blows over Samoa in 1889,
and German support of the Boers in South
Africa, involving as it did an obstacle to British plans of control in this region, also caused
much ill will between Great Britain and Germany. Another serious clash of British and
German imperialism took place in Asia Minor.
Here in 1903 German capitalists had secured

from Turkey the right to construct a railroad connecting Constantinople with Bagdad and thence to the Persian Gulf (see map, page 17). Forming a junction at Constantinople with German controlled railroads that led north to the Baltic Sea, the Berlin-to-Bagdad railroad would have enabled German businessmen to control a great corridor from the Baltic through middle Europe down into Mesopotamia to the Persian Gulf. The German scheme created much alarm in British political and financial circles. The British government was also fearful that access to the Persian Gulf might enable Germany to threaten the security of India. Although the British government was able to block completion of the railway, for several years the Berlin-to-Bagdad railroad scheme was a serious source of friction between Great Britain and Germany.

Great Britain and Russia also had their differences, mainly in the Balkans and Afghanistan. Great Britain sought to prevent Russian domination of the Straits and encroachment in the vicinity of the Indian northern frontier. From 1880 to 1900 Great Britain and France were rivals in southeast Asia and in Africa, where France envisaged an empire stretching from the Atlantic to the Red Sea. Such an empire would give her control of the headwaters of the Nile and seriously interfere with Great Britain's program of creating a continuous stretch of British territory from the Cape to Cairo. British and French armies almost came to blows along the upper Nile in 1898, but a battle was averted when France gave way.

There were several other occasions on which various powers found themselves blocked by others, but before the First World War the most serious crises concerned the control of Morocco. On two occasions (1905 and 1911) German and French rivalry very nearly brought Europe into open conflict (see page 16).

In some cases war did occur. In 1894 Japanese designs upon the Asiatic mainland brought about war with China, and in 1899 Great Britain became engaged in war with the Boer republics of South Africa. Japan and Russia fought over Manchuria in 1904-1905, and Italy wrested Tripoli from Turkey after the war of 1911-1912 (see map, page 17).

The emotion of nationalism. In the opinion of many people the most important funda-

mental cause of the First World War was nationalism. National pride and inflated patriotism became a new religion, the emotional adjunct to power politics. Nationalism fattened on the acquisition of colonies, took pride in the defeat of enemies, and refused to believe that a nation could ever be wrong. History, as taught in schools, was frequently distorted in order to glorify a nation's past achievements and gloss over its shortcomings. National self-glorification became the objective of numerous writers in various countries who exalted their own particular country's culture and often heaped ridicule and odium on that of others.

The polyglot Balkans. Notwithstanding the unification of Germany and Italy, Europe still contained many danger spots in 1914, submerged peoples having strong nationalistic aspirations. They were numerous and they were active in the Balkans. In 1914 nationalism in this area had grown acute enough to bring on the war. Nowhere else in Europe was the connection between power politics, secret diplomacy, and instability in international relations better illustrated.

The Balkan peninsula in 1815 was ruled mainly by the Turkish empire. The Turks were only a minority ruling caste, the great majority of the people being Christian Slavs. In Austria-Hungary a similar situation obtained. Under the *Ausgleich,* the agreement that created the dual monarchy of Austria-Hungary, a number of national groups, principally Slavic peoples, were ruled by the Austrian Germans and the Hungarians. More nationalities were found in the Balkans than anywhere else in Europe, most of them cherishing nationalistic aspirations. These aspirations were aggravated by the interests of the great powers in the Balkans.

In the nineteenth century the geography of the Balkan area made it of supreme strategic importance in power politics. Since the days of Peter the Great the dominant policy of Russia had been to obtain warm-water ports, for many of her harbors are frozen in winter. Peter the Great had bequeathed his country a window on the Baltic, but this of itself did not solve the problem, for here again ice hinders shipping at certain periods of the year. The logical place for Russia to secure a good exit to the outside world was in the south via the Black Sea (see map, page 17). But this body of water is connected with

In 1871 the long historical trend toward the growth of national states was apparently ended with the unification of Germany and Italy. The map of Europe looked complete. Then the trend began to reverse itself. Out of the old Turkish empire appeared the Balkan states (see inset); after the First World War the trend to more and smaller states continued (see page 35).

the Mediterranean by two narrow straits, the Bosporus and the Dardanelles, and these were under Turkish control. It was the policy of Russia, therefore, to weaken and even dismember Turkey so that she could obtain the Straits. But again the factor of geography intruded itself. Most Englishmen as individuals detested the corrupt rule of the sultans, but the British government supported Turkey in the nineteenth century for reasons of national self-interest. If Russia obtained the Straits, she would become a naval power in the eastern Mediterranean. This, so the British diplomats argued, would menace the safety of the Suez Canal, which had become of prime strategic importance to Great Brit-

ain. Perhaps no other area in the world presents a better example of the influence of geography upon history, and more specifically on political strategy, than does the Straits.

Russia in the Balkans. The discontent of the various submerged nationalities in the Balkans gave Russia an excellent opportunity to interfere in this region in the nineteenth century. The first people to escape from Turkish thralldom were the Greeks; they won freedom in 1829. Some twenty-five years later the Rumanians gained a measure of self-government. Disguising her interest in obtaining the Straits, Russia began to pose as the protector of her brother Slavs in the Balkans. Following 1870 numerous nationalist revolts occurred throughout the peninsula. These were put down with great ferocity by the sultan, Abdul Hamid, and Russia thereupon in 1877 declared war on Turkey. Gaining a complete victory, Russia forced upon her defeated foe the Treaty of San Stefano (1878). This gave additional territory and complete independence to the Serbians, Rumanians, and Montenegrins, and it further provided for the creation of a large Bulgarian state under the thumb of Russia.

This arrangement was not to the liking of the two other most interested powers, Great Britain and Austria. Threatening war, these nations forced Russia to agree to a congress, held at Berlin in 1878, where Russia's peace treaty was reëxamined. Bulgaria was reduced in size and the two important Turkish provinces of Bosnia and Herzegovina were given to Austria, whose aim was to push her control in the direction of the Aegean Sea. While Russia's ambition of domination of the Balkans had been thwarted, she was permitted to retain certain towns in the Caucasus and also a strip of Rumanian territory. The Congress of Berlin left a legacy of hatred. The Serbians were enraged at the action of Austria, the Bulgarians resented having their new state whittled down, and Irredentist movements flourished all over the peninsula. Irredentism, a term used by the Italians to refer to their "unredeemed Italy" still under Austrian rule, generally refers to a nation's desire to secure territory inhabited by people of the same nationality and under alien rule.

Germany and Austria in the Balkans. It soon became clear that both Germany and Austria were determined to extend their influence in the Balkans. German motives were largely economic. The Germans envisaged a great continuous economy stretching from the Baltic to the Persian Gulf. The Austrian concern in the Balkans was primarily defensive. Austria-Hungary was a polyglot empire containing millions of Slavs. If Serbia, egged on by Russia, should extend an Irredentist movement into the southern part of the Austrian empire, many Slavs might be lost and ultimately the operation of nationalism would result in the destruction of the whole empire. The Austrians were thus determined that Pan-Slavism, of which the Greater Serbia movement was a manifestation, should be checked before it became too dangerous.

Raven Hill's cartoon, "The Boiling Point," represents the great powers—among them Austria, Germany, and England—attempting to retain their influence in the troublesome Balkans. The picture was printed in "Punch."

Hence they acquired Bosnia and Herzegovina outright in 1908 (see map, page 17).

Balkan wars (1912-1913). Following the Russo-Turkish War of 1877-1878 Balkan affairs continued to give much worry to the European diplomats, and, in fact, a European war was narrowly averted in 1908 and 1913. In 1912, under the leadership of the famous Greek prime minister Venizelos, an alliance was formed by Greece, Bulgaria, Serbia, and Montenegro for the purpose of waging war on Turkey.

War followed, in which the allies were completely successful, and a conference was held at London to arrange the peace. Here the allies illustrated the viciousness of power politics as they began to quarrel over the spoils. Bulgaria's claims ran counter to those of Greece. Serbia wanted Albania because the territory would give her access to the sea, but this desire clashed with Austria-Hungary's ambition of pushing back Slav expansion. Denied Albania, Serbia demanded as compensation territory that Greece and Bulgaria wanted. Finally the erstwhile allies began to fight each other. Greece, Serbia, and Montenegro fought Bulgaria, and, to complicate this second Balkan war, vanquished Turkey and Rumania joined in to see what spoils they could obtain.

In 1913 the second war came to an end, but no permanent solution had been found for the Balkan problem. The Serbians had been prevented by Austria from obtaining Albania. Backed by Russia the Serbs began to carry on active propaganda among the Slavs in Austria to undermine their loyalty to the dual monarchy of Austria-Hungary. Russia was more determined than ever to try to obtain the Straits. This resolution ran counter to German interests, whose Berlin-to-Bagdad railway project in turn caused the British much alarm. The Bulgarians nourished a bitter hatred against Serbia, Greece, and Rumania. Truly the Balkans in 1914 were a witches' cauldron of international discord.

Other national groups. There existed also numerous nationalistic sore spots in Europe outside the Balkans. As has been indicated, the Italians wanted to free their kinsmen from Austrian rule. In France the spirit of revenge was directed toward the reincorporation of Alsace-Lorraine in the French domain, and in Austria Poles, Czechs, Slovaks, Croats, and Slovenes all yearned for freedom. Danes, Finns, and Irish in other parts of Europe also represented discontented nationalities, waiting for the hour of deliverance.

The Coming of the Great War (1871-1914)

The isolation of France. Following its defeat by Germany in 1870-1871, France was isolated diplomatically for twenty years. Bismarck fully realized that France would hope some day to defeat Germany and regain her lost provinces in Alsace-Lorraine, and he therefore determined to prevent France from obtaining any allies. "As long as France has no alliances," Bismarck observed, "she is not dangerous to Germany."[4]

In 1873 Bismarck made an alliance with Russia and Austria-Hungary known as the Three Emperors' League. By this agreement in the event of threat of war the signatories agreed to consult "in order to determine a common course of action." Germany and Russia specifically promised mutual support in case of attack. In 1877 the Russo-Turkish War occurred, and, following the demands of Austria and Great Britain, Russia was forced to agree to a European conference on the Balkan problem to be held at Berlin. Up to this point Bismarck had had few diplomatic worries. Great Britain was following the policy of "splendid isolation," Russia and Austria were the allies of Germany, and Italy was unimportant. But at the Congress of Berlin (1878) Bismarck was forced to choose between supporting the claims of Austria or those of Russia in the Balkans.

Bismarck's diplomacy. Bismarck chose to support Austria because he apparently believed that it was impossible to have both countries as close allies and because he trusted Austria more than Russia. The Germans in Vienna were his kinsmen, whereas he was somewhat suspicious of Slav loyalty, and in any event Austria was too close to Germany for comfort in any capacity other than as an ally. Furthermore Bismarck was afraid that supporting Russia would alienate Great Britain and cause her to make an alliance with Austria. Russia for her part was resentful over Bismarck's support of Austria's Balkan ambitions at the Congress of Berlin. The year after the Congress of Berlin (1879), Bismarck negotiated the Dual Alliance with the Austrian government. Three years later in 1882 a new partner was secured, Italy, thus bringing into operation the Triple Alliance (see map on page 17). By its terms the three powers promised not to enter into any alliance against each other. Further, it was provided that in the event of an unprovoked French attack upon either Italy or Germany both allies would wage war on France. And if any member or members of the alliance were attacked by two or more great powers, all three allies were pledged to make war.

The choice of Austria as a close ally in preference to Russia did not mean that Bismarck was reconciled to the loss of the latter's friendship. In 1881 the Three Emperor's League was renewed and continued to 1887, when rivalries between Austria and Russia in the Balkans made it impossible for these two powers to be in the same group. Bismarck therefore negotiated a separate alliance with Russia called the Reinsurance Treaty. Many diplomats pondered how Germany could at one and the same time be the ally of Russia and Austria, and Bismarck's tactics were described as "keeping five balls in the air at once."

The Franco-Russian alliance. Under the masterful hand of Bismarck Germany retained hegemony over the European continent from 1871 to 1890. In 1890, however, young William II, the new German kaiser, dismissed the old chancellor who had served so long, and German foreign policy now passed into his hands. The kaiser allowed the Reinsurance Treaty to lapse, thus permitting Russia to seek new allies, and France, isolated and smarting from her diplomatic impotency, immediately began to woo Russia. In 1891 a French naval squadron visited Russia, and the czar agreed to a military alliance which, however, did not go into effect until 1894. Russia was badly in need of loans for construction of the Trans-Siberian railway and for military purposes. Millions of French francs went to buy Russian bonds, and France received what she had wanted for twenty years, a strong military ally.

England's position. The diplomatic history of the next seventeen years (1890-1907) concerns the development of a great alliance system including Great Britain, France, and Russia, to offset the Triple Alliance of Germany, Austria, and Italy (see map, page 17). The most important nation in this development was Great Britain. As long as she followed her policy of "splendid isolation," Germany's Triple Alliance and the Russo-French combination were fairly equally matched. But if Great Britain were to join the Russians and the French, the balance of power would shift at once and make this combination supreme. In the 1890's Great Britain began to question the wisdom of having no allies. At this time she was engaged in active and sometimes bitter colonial rivalry with Russia and France. In 1898 in the Fashoda incident Great Britain and France narrowly averted war when the rival expeditions of General Kitchener and Colonel Marchand both claimed the region of the upper Nile. Again, during the Boer War all the great powers in Europe were anti-British. Only the supremacy of England's fleet effectively discouraged the development of an interventionist movement.

More and more, Great Britain became disquieted by her policy of diplomatic isolation.

It was this circumstance which explained British overtures to Germany in 1898 and again in 1901. The exponent of Anglo-German friendship and concord was Joseph Chamberlain, the father of Neville Chamberlain, late prime minister of Great Britain. The Germans were not favorably impressed by the offer of a British alliance and interpreted it as a sign of British weakness. Most important: (1) Germany felt strong enough to be able to dispense with allies; and (2) she believed she could get an alliance on her own terms.

Meanwhile Anglo-German relations steadily grew worse. The Germans were jealous of the great empire the British had built up before Germany had succeeded in attaining national unity. The kaiser himself contributed to Anglo-German misunderstanding by his bellicose and threatening speeches. The British, on the other hand, were alarmed at the tremendous strides made by German industry. The new naval program, more than anything else, made Germany and Great Britain enemies. Great Britain's dependence upon the outside world for most of her food supply had always made command of the seas an indispensable feature of her defense strategy. The British had no quarrel with the size of the German army, but when the German Reichstag in 1900 passed a naval law providing for the construction by 1920 of a fleet strong enough to jeopardize Great Britain's naval supremacy, England was seriously alarmed.

The Entente Cordiale (1904). Rebuffed by Germany, England turned elsewhere for friends. In 1902 she made a treaty of alliance with Japan, and two years later England and France settled their outstanding differences. This rapprochement was made possible, in some degree, by the popularity in France of Edward VII and his enthusiasm for all things French. An Entente Cordiale between these two countries thus ended England's traditional policy of isolation and brought her into the diplomatic combination pitted against Germany's Triple Alliance. Great Britain's desire to settle all outstanding differences with France and Russia was accentuated by alarming developments in her relations with Germany. In 1905 Great Britain began the construction of a new type of warship, the dreadnought, which rendered all existing ships largely obsolete by its heavy armor and twelve-inch guns. The advent of this new type of battleship enabled the Germans to carry on the naval race on equal terms with their British rivals, as all existing ships were now outmoded. The British suggested a naval holiday to the German government, but the kaiser and his admiral, von Tirpitz, were determined to push their naval building program. Two years after laying the keel of the dreadnought, Great Britain settled its problems with Russia, thereby establishing the Triple Entente. Great Britain made no definite military commitments in her agreements with France and Russia. She retained theoretically her freedom of action but, for all this, was now part of the alliance system.

Diplomatic crises: 1905-1914. For a decade before the First World War, from 1905 to 1914, Europe experienced a series of crises. In each of these diplomatic duels both sides managed to come out without losing too much prestige and without going to war. France thought her safety and economic interests demanded the exclusion of German interests in Morocco, Austria wanted a free hand in the Balkans—an objective resolutely opposed by Russia—Germany resented Great Britain's opposition to her economic penetration into the Near East, and England was determined to maintain her naval supremacy against Germany in the North Sea. With each new crisis war seemed inevitable, but the diplomats somehow managed to control the machinery of diplomacy. But it was almost certain that a crisis would soon be precipitated, unleashing forces that could not be stopped.

The first Moroccan crisis (1905). The first serious diplomatic crisis concerned Morocco, a backward area under an independent sultanate. By obtaining control of this territory France would have a stretch of contiguous dependencies from the north Atlantic across the north African coast to Tunisia. The German government thought it saw in the Moroccan question a chance to weaken the Anglo-French Entente. Russia had just suffered a decisive defeat by Japan and could not be expected to assist her ally France. Carefully timing his moves, the German chancellor arranged for the kaiser to visit the Moroccan port of Tangier, where he declared that all powers

must respect the independence of the country. The French were forced to give up their immediate plans for taking over Morocco and agree to Germany's suggestion that an international conference be called at Algeciras (1906) to discuss the matter. At this meeting the German hope that a rift might appear between the British and French did not materialize. On the contrary, all the nations in attendance—even Italy—supported France rather than Germany. Only Austria remained at the side of Germany. It was agreed that Morocco should still enjoy its sovereignty but that France and Spain should be given certain rights to police the area.

European tension. The events at Algeciras and the British agreement with Russia the following year (1907) filled the Germans with dread. The diplomatic hegemony enjoyed by Germany under Bismarck was completely gone. Italy could not be trusted. Germany had no friend except her ally, Austria. The Germans spoke of this situation as the encirclement policy. In 1908 another crisis occurred, this time in the Balkans, where Austria annexed the two provinces of Bosnia and Herzegovina (see map, page 17). Serbia was furious at this incorporation of what she considered her Slavs in the Austro-Hungarian empire. The Russian government moved to throw its armed might in support of Serbia but was forced to back down when it became apparent that full German support had been pledged to Austria. If Algeciras had been a defeat for Germany, Austria and Germany had managed to secure a victory for the Triple Alliance in 1908.

In 1911 the scene shifted back to Morocco again, where France had sent an army "to maintain order." Germany countered by dispatching the gunboat *Panther* to the Moroccan port of Agadir. Russia was still weak from her defeat at the hands of the Japanese, but Great Britain came out with the plain warning that all her power was at the disposal of France. It was now Germany's turn to back down, although this was done without loss of prestige. A diplomatic bargain was struck. France got a free hand in Morocco in return for which Germany was given grants of French holdings in equatorial Africa.

Following the second Balkan war in 1913 (see pages 13 and 14) Europe faced the future with uncertainty and dread. One German general remarked, "There is a smell of blood in

Triple Alliance

Triple Entente

Naval Race   1907

1894

GREAT
BRITAIN

1907

GERMANY

1879

1882

AUSTRIA-
HUNGARY
annexes
BOSNIA-HERZEGOVINA
1908

1882

FRANCE

ITALY

takes

Sarajevo
1914

Balkan Wars, 1912-1913

RUSSIA

wants
the Straits

German projected
railway to Bagdad

Algeciras
Conference
1906

Tangier
1905

MOROCCO
1912

ALGERIA
(French)

TUNISIA
(French)

takes

British route to India

Suez
Canal

Agadir
1911

BACKGROUND
FOR WAR

TRIPOLI
1912

R. M. Chapin

the air." The American statesman, Colonel House, then touring Europe, reported: "Everybody's nerves are tense; it only needs a spark to set the whole thing off."

Assassination of the archduke. This fateful spark came on June 28, 1914, when the Archduke Francis Ferdinand, the heir to the Austrian throne, and his wife were assassinated in the town of Sarajevo in Bosnia.

This deed was the work of a young Bosnian student, Gavrilo Princip, who was inspired by the Greater Serbia propaganda. He and his two associates had received assistance from high Serbian officers, and although the direct complicity of the Serbian government has not been proved, nevertheless it seems unlikely that it could have been ignorant of the plot. Count Berchtold, the Austrian foreign minister, believed that the assassination justified crushing, once and for all, the anti-Austrian propaganda and terrorism emanating from Serbia. Austria could take no action, however, without securing the support of its ally, Germany. Berchtold thereupon prepared a letter to the kaiser and succeeded in getting the Austrian emperor's signature. This letter, received by the kaiser, declared:

"The crime against my nephew is the direct

consequence of the agitation carried on by Russian and Serbian Pan-Slavists, whose sole aim is to weaken the Triple Alliance and shatter my empire. . . . The aim of my government must henceforth be to isolate and diminish Serbia."[5]

The German emperor was genuinely moved by this appeal. The news of the assassination had shocked him deeply, and he viewed the Bosnian terrorists as little more than fanatical savages. William decided to assure the Austrian government of his full support. Berchtold thus obtained a "blank check" from Germany. Austria was Germany's only reliable ally. Everything possible must be done to prevent her from being weakened by such forces as Serbian terrorism. Germany agreed with Austria that military action against the Serbs was necessary. Vienna wanted only a local Austro-Serb war, and Germany favored quick action to forestall intervention. But the possibility of Russian intervention was not ignored by the German and Austrian governments.

The Austrian ultimatum. The Austrian foreign minister proceeded with his plans of subjugating Serbia. On July 23 an Austro-Hungarian ultimatum was presented to Serbia. The terms were harsh. All anti-Austrian activities in Serbia must cease, textbooks unfriendly to Austria could not be used in the schools, and the assistance of Austro-Hungarian officials was to be accepted in putting down any "revolutionary movement directed against the territorial integrity of the Dual Monarchy." Furthermore it was demanded that all officials in the Serbian army and governmental service "guilty of propaganda" against the Austrian government should be removed. The ultimatum, which was intended to be turned down, contained ten demands in all, and Berchtold demanded unconditional acceptance within forty-eight hours. In answer, on July 25, the Serbians penned a very clever reply. Only two demands were accepted in their entirety, and most of the others were neatly sidestepped by diplomatic qualifications. This reply was announced as unsatisfactory, and mobilization of the armed forces in the Austro-Hungarian empire was ordered.

Russia, meanwhile, was following developments in the Balkans closely. She realized that, if the Austrians succeeded in humbling Serbia, Russian prestige in this area would suffer tremendously. Even before the Austrian ultimatum had been presented, Sergei Sazonov, the Russian foreign minister, had plainly told the Austrian representative at St. Petersburg that "Russia would not be indifferent to any attempt to humiliate Serbia; Russia could not permit Austria to use menacing language or military measures against Serbia."[6] The French in the meantime assured the Russians of their full cooperation and urged strong support for Serbia.

Grey's peace efforts. Sir Edward Grey, the British foreign minister, began his efforts to maintain peace as early as July 20, before the ultimatum to Serbia had been served. He advised negotiations between the Russians and Austrians to avoid the problem of dangerous demands upon Serbia. On July 24, Grey proposed that England, France, Germany, and Italy should agree to exercise a "moderating or mediating influence" simultaneously in St. Petersburg and Vienna. The Germans agreed, but the French opposed the plan, saying they would collaborate if Germany first exerted pressure on Vienna. A third peace proposal came from Grey on July 26, but this had no more success than its predecessors. While the diplomats worked for peace, Berchtold was fearful that Serbia would escape from his clutches. On July 27 he succeeded, thanks in part to falsehood, in convincing the emperor that war was the only way out, and the following day a formal declaration of war was announced against Serbia.

Russian mobilization. Berchtold's decision made a general European conflict almost inevitable, but there was still the hope that Germany could restrain its ally. The kaiser had been satisfied with Serbia's reply to the Austrian ultimatum. The German chancellor, Bethmann-Hollweg, urged Austria to negotiate with Russia. As the possibility of a general European war loomed, several frantic telegrams were sent by Berlin to Vienna. The German ambassador was instructed to tell Berchtold, "As an ally we must refuse to be drawn into a world conflagration because Austria does not respect our advice."[7] At this critical stage, when German pressure on Austria might have opened a path to peace, an event took place which wrecked any further attempts at negotiation. This was the Russian mobilization on July 30.

Up to this time Bethmann-Hollweg, the

German chancellor, had sought peace, but the mobilization of Russia caused an abrupt halt to his efforts. The significance of mobilization in modern warfare must be understood to appreciate the import of the Russian action. Modern armies constitute millions of men. To call out the reserves to join their regiments, to hand out equipment, and to reach previously assigned strategic positions is a task requiring several days and careful timing. To allow a dangerous rival to mobilize before you do would be to enable him to inflict defeat before your mobilization was complete. In the case of Germany the mobilization question was especially vital, because in the event of war with Russia and France she would be confronted with enemies on two fronts. The best plan seemed to be to launch a lightning attack against France, crush her, and then turn to meet Russia, who could ordinarily be expected to mobilize rather slowly (see map, page 21). To allow Russian mobilization to proceed would jeopardize this strategy, called the Schlieffen Plan.

World war. Faced by the Russian action, the German government decided upon war July 31. Ultimatums were sent to Russia and France demanding from the former cessation of mobilization and from the latter a pledge of neutrality. Failing to receive satisfactory replies, Germany declared war on Russia August 1 and on France August 3. On August 2 an ultimatum was delivered by the German ambassador in Brussels announcing Germany's intention of sending troops through Belgium. The Belgian cabinet refused to grant permission for this transit and appealed to Russia, France, and Great Britain for aid in protecting her neutrality.

The position of Great Britain during these momentous days had been obscure. She was under no definite obligation, by the agreements of 1904 and 1907, to furnish military aid to her allies. Sir Edward Grey was in an embarrassing position. A majority in the cabinet were not in favor of war. But the news of the German ultimatum to Belgium turned the tide in favor of entering the war on the side of France and Russia. The invasion of Belgium, declared Lloyd George, "set the nation on fire from sea to sea. . . . Before then the cabinet was hopelessly divided. After the German ultimatum to Belgium the cabinet was almost unanimous." It should

not be thought that Great Britain entered the war because Belgium was invaded. The basic reason was the maintenance of the balance of power and the protection of the buffer states of Belgium and Holland along the English Channel and North Sea. "In this crisis of British policy," declares a recent volume produced by a group of British scholars, "Belgian neutrality was wholly subordinate to the wider issues, the ambitions of Germany and the fate of France. . . . Great Britain would not have remained neutral even if Belgium had not been violated."[8] Sir Edward Grey sent an ultimatum to Germany demanding that Belgian neutrality be respected. This Germany refused to do, and on August 4 Great Britain declared war.

Italy refused to carry out her engagements under the Triple Alliance on the basis that Germany and Austria were not waging a defensive war and remained neutral for the time being. In the latter part of August Japan joined the Allies, and in October Turkey, fearing the designs of Russia, threw in her lot with the Central Powers, Germany and Austria.

The responsibility for the war. During the terrible years between 1914 and 1918 when hatred ran high, the two sides accused each other of bringing on the war. The Allies charged that Germany was guilty of provoking the conflict. The structure of the Treaty of Versailles, as we shall see later, rested in large part on the "war guilt" of Germany. Scholars and laymen alike in the Allied countries sincerely believed when the Treaty was first written that Germany was completely responsible for the war. As a more realistic perspective developed in the light of new evidence, it became increasingly clear that the problem was more complex than had been originally thought. Today, most historians agree it is next to impossible to try to explain the war in terms of any one great power's actions. Rather, all the major participating nations must own, in some measure, responsibility for the outbreak of the First World War.

It is conceivable that inspired statesmanship, the right kind of leadership, and a good measure of luck might have avoided war in 1914. It is also conceivable that certain of the European powers must bear more of the responsibility for the outbreak of the conflict than other nations. Yet even if we were to grant all this, it is foolish to try to apportion the blame for the tragedy, because it was inherent in the prevailing order of international anarchy. As J. W. Swain says: "When once the Archduke Francis Ferdinand had been assassinated, nothing could be done. The French seizure of Morocco, the Agadir crisis, the Turco-Italian War and the Balkan wars, chauvinism, militarism, and preparedness, political demagogues and heroic newspaper editors had brought Europe to such a state of excitement that the insane act of three ill-balanced youths could set the world on fire."[9] War came in 1914 because it was the logical outcome of the political arrangements and ambitions of the time.

The First World War

Strategy in 1914. Both sides anticipated a quick victory in 1914. Allied strategy was to launch two simultaneous offensives—one by the French against Alsace, the other by the Russians against East Prussia. The German high command put their trust in the famous Schlieffen Plan (see map). This was a brilliantly conceived maneuver designed to crush the French armies. A great enveloping movement was to be launched through Belgium. Wheeling through France, the German armies would outflank the French and push them against Alsace-Lorraine, where they would be met by another German army. Hemmed in on both the east and west, capitulation must take place. With France smashed, the main German forces would then be transported to East Prussia, where a relatively small German army had been given the task of holding the Russians at bay. The reinforcements then would fall on the Russians and destroy their forces, and the war would be over.

Battle of the Marne. In the west the German strategy unrolled with clocklike precision. Belgian resistance was smothered by the fire of immense siege artillery. A small British expeditionary force tried unsuccessfully to halt the German onrush in Belgium. Meanwhile disaster had overtaken the French, whose offensive against Alsace fizzled out. Nearer and nearer the German forces came to the French capital. At the beginning of September they were within twenty-five miles of Paris. At this moment the German high command made a fatal blunder. Somewhat weakened by the dispatch of troops to East Prussia to meet a Russian attack, the German command directed its east flank to pass to the east of Paris. The original plan had been to encircle Paris from the west. This tactic left the right flank of the German forces exposed, a fact not lost to Joffre, the French commander, and his advisers. On September 5, Joffre decided to initiate a bold counter-offensive, and so began the Battle of the Marne. For five days a titanic battle raged, but in the end the Germans had to retreat, and France was saved. A race to the sea followed, the object being to reach the important ports along the English Channel. The Channel ports were saved, and by December 1914, the western front had been stabilized. A huge system of trenches stretched from the English Channel to Switzerland. Open warfare now ceased, and trench warfare replaced it until the last few months of the conflict in 1918.

The eastern front. On the eastern front, the Russian armies had little trouble in overrunning East Prussia. It seemed likely that the Russian "steam roller" might smash its way to Berlin. At this moment Paul von Hindenburg was brought from retirement and made head of the German forces in Prussia. In the Battle of Tannenberg (August 26-31) the Germans surrounded and dispersed one Russian army under General Samsonov, who committed suicide. Hindenburg then turned his attention to the other Russian army and inflicted a severe loss. While the Battle of the Marne was raging, the Russians under General Brusilov launched a successful offensive against the Austrians at the same time that an Austrian attack on Serbia was being repulsed.

The Dardanelles campaign. The year 1915 dawned with both the Allies and the Central Powers supremely confident of the outcome of the war. The aim of the Allies was to widen Germany's battle front and reëstablish communication with Russia. The entrance of Turkey on the side of Germany had closed the Dardanelles to Allied shipping, and much needed munitions and other supplies could now be sent to Russia only via Archangel, a port ice-locked much of the year. Therefore Great Britain tried to force the Dardanelles,

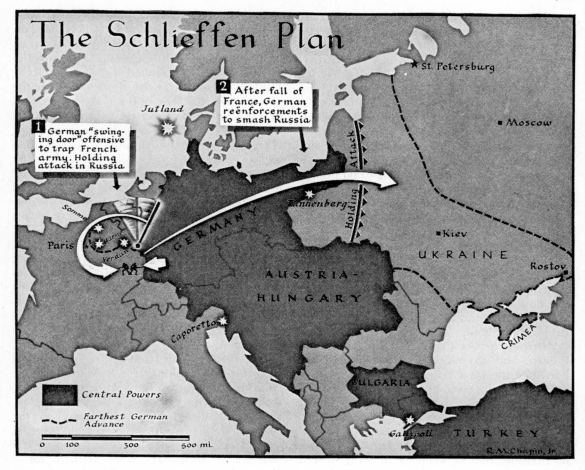

The Schlieffen Plan

1 German "swinging door" offensive to trap French army. Holding attack in Russia

2 After fall of France, German reënforcements to smash Russia

Central Powers

--- Farthest German Advance

0   100   300   500 mi.

R.M.Chapin, Jr

a plan attributed largely to Winston Churchill. Other objectives of this campaign were to lessen the possibility of attack on Egypt and Suez, to isolate Turkey, and to win over the Balkan neutrals. The campaign was a series of blunders and ghastly failures. As if to furnish the Turks with advance information regarding their intentions, the Allies sent a naval squadron to make a preliminary attack in November 1914 and followed this up by a determined naval attack in March. In the engagement three battleships were sunk, and the Allies withdrew. We know now that at this moment the Turkish batteries were practically out of ammunition. Had the attack been pressed, the Straits must have fallen.

During the latter part of April Australian and New Zealand troops forced a landing on the Gallipoli peninsula (see map above). In the face of machine-gun nests and concealed barbed wire, the "Anzacs" waded ashore from small boats and charged up the beach, suffering tremendous losses. For the remainder of the year the British troops clung to their precarious foothold but were finally evacuated in January 1916.

Italy joins the Allies. The attempt of the Allies to widen Germany's battle front brought Italy into the war. From December 1914 to April 1915, both sides wooed Italy. The Allies were successful because in the secret Treaty of London they made the most generous promises, including a promise to turn German-speaking people in the southern Tyrol over to Italy after the war ended. As the British statesman Balfour remarked, "This is the sort of thing you have to do when you are engaged in war." Italy entered the war on what she believed was the winning side in 1915 in spite of her earlier commitments to the Triple Alliance. The entrance of Italy on their side was the only victory achieved by the Allies in 1915. Everywhere else there was a series of melancholy defeats.

German successes in 1915. The Germans, on the other hand, went from victory to victory. They carried out a terrific offensive against the Russian forces in May 1915, in which 700,000 shells paved the way for the infantry attack. The Russian trenches simply melted away. Soon the czar's army was in rapid retreat, which quickly degenerated into a rout. More than 1,200,000 were killed and wounded. The Germans captured nearly 900,000 prisoners. Russia never fully recovered from this debacle. On all sides criticism began to grow against the government, and the morale of the nation began to break down.

Serbia was the next victim. The conquest was made all the easier because Bulgaria entered the war on the side of Germany and Austria-Hungary in September 1915. Serbia was now surrounded by enemies and thus unable to prevent them from completely overrunning her land.

Attrition before Verdun. To all Germans, French, and British who went through the horror of the First World War, the year 1916 was made unforgettable by the blood baths of the Somme and Verdun. It was the Allied strategy to restrict attacks on the western front to intermittent nibbling and to concentrate upon the naval blockade. This policy of attrition, that is, steady weakening, would in the end result in starvation in Germany. Germany, on the other hand, resorted to another kind of attrition and applied it to France. The plan was to concentrate a gigantic attack on Verdun. This move would attract hundreds of thousands of French troops, terrible losses would result, and French morale would be steadily worn down. All during the spring and summer of 1916 the Germans pounded the forts of Verdun with thousands of shells and threw wave after wave of infantry against the French positions. In the face of these attacks the French stubbornly resisted. The cry of the French *poilu* was "Ils ne passeront pas!" ("They shall not pass!") The result of this fighting around Verdun was attrition for both sides. The Germans alone suffered the loss of 300,000 men.

The Somme. To ease the tremendous pressure against Verdun and also to discourage the Germans from sending fresh troops against Russia, the British army began a great offensive along the Somme on the western front. For seven days a tornado of artillery fire battered and wrecked the German trenches; then on the morning of July 1, as the shrill whistles of British officers sounded the zero hour, the English troops advanced slowly through the wire toward the German lines. A terrible blast of machine-gun fire met the attackers, and by the end of the day 60,000 British troops had been killed or wounded, more casualties than had been suffered in whole wars waged by Great Britain in the past. In spite of these heart-breaking losses the attack was continued until heavy rains in October made further efforts impossible. The British had gained a few square miles of territory at the cost of over 400,000 killed and wounded.

Russia and Rumania, 1916. A bright spot for the Allies in the midst of all this gloom was the thrust of the Russian commander Brusilov, who in June 1916 struck the Austrian lines with the force of a thunderbolt, capturing 300,000 prisoners. The assistance of German troops and the lack of war materials, however, halted the Russian drive before it destroyed the Austrian armies. The Russian offensive had one important result. Rumania was convinced that the German cause was hopeless. In August she threw in her lot with the Allies and successfully launched an invasion against Hungary. Her success, however, was short-lived. Bulgarian and German forces simultaneously attacked the Rumanian armies, which proved to be quite inferior, and Rumania was forced to capitulate. Vast stores of oil and grain, urgently needed by the Central Powers, were obtained.

Allied offensives, 1917. The tremendous cost of the fighting in men and materials became apparent early in 1917, especially in Russia and Germany. On the western front, however, the French and British were approaching the height of their fighting strength. Military conscription in Great Britain had enabled her to train and equip an army of two million men. This force during April and May carried out a successful offensive against German positions. In April the French army also made a large-scale attack. The new French commander in chief, General Nivelle, who had succeeded Joffre, confidently expected an audacious attack to break the German lines. The attack was a complete failure. Thousands of French lives were lost. The army was thoroughly disgusted by the failure of their leader, and ten divisions mutinied rather than continue what they considered useless slaughter. This disaster forced the British army to take over large sections of the front which had hitherto been defended by various units of the French army.

The meaning of modern war. In the First World War, as in the Second, the burden was carried not only by the soldiers in the field but by entire nations. From the vigorous young men in the trenches to the women at work in the munitions factories ran a continuous link touching the lives of practically every adult in a nation at war. Old women knitted socks and sweaters for the soldiers, scientists put aside their research to work on new gases or explosives, men too old for active military service worked behind the lines in labor battalions, and even school children were ex-

pected to till school gardens to help produce the necessary food.

On the western front there was enacted a drama of horror never before witnessed by man. In a line of trenches almost 600 miles long two opposing bodies of troops faced each other. Between the trenches was no-man's-land, crisscrossed with barbed wire and spotted with craters where lay the dead. During the day the soldiers crouched in their dugouts, using periscopes to peer over the parapets, for sharpshooters were a constant menace. At night, while the men tried to gain a little fitful sleep, the sentries peered anxiously into the darkness on the watch for raiding parties. Machine-gun fire, the menace of gas, the flame thrower, the risk of attack from marauding airplanes, the sudden death from the salvo of big guns—these became the lot of the soldiers in the trenches.

The United States and the War

The policy of the United States. After Italy entered the war on the side of the Allies, America was the only great power remaining neutral. The outbreak of the war came as a staggering surprise to most Americans, who had little understanding and knowledge of the conditions in Europe. The overwhelming

sentiment in this country was for peace. On August 4, 1914, President Wilson announced the neutrality of the United States and declared that the people "must be impartial in thought as well as in action." The events of the next two years showed that this was no easy task.

A type of combat new in its day—trench warfare—characterized a large part of the fighting in the First World War. The tank, looking thin by comparison with present-day models, was also introduced.

A German airplane boils black smoke as it plunges toward earth, shot down by an Allied fighter. Along with the new tanks, such machines were the forerunners of the total, mechanized warfare that was to develop in twenty short years.

Our economic stake in the Allied cause. As the war got under way, it became apparent that the British blockade would permit our trade and commerce to be carried on with the Allies only, and it was not long before our factories and farmers were producing munitions and food exclusively for Great Britain and France. Our industry expanded and began to enjoy a prosperity dependent upon the continuance of Allied purchases. During 1915 and 1916 about one and a half billion dollars of Allied bonds were sold in America. "... to those who sponsored and participated in these loans, whose financial reputation and whose principal and interest depended upon the continued solvency of the debtor nations, it was not a matter of indifference which side won the war."[10] The financial stake of the United States in the Allied cause has in recent times received much attention. But careful students point out that, although this certainly influenced our final decision to go to war, "the financial community as a whole . . . favored American

neutrality rather than American participation; for neutrality afforded Wall Street all the profits of war without the compensating sacrifices and taxation. And there is not a shred of evidence to support the allegation that Wilson was at any time influenced by the financial 'stake' in his relations with Germany. . . ."[11]

The German U-boat campaign. The immediate cause of the entry of the United States into the war on the side of the Allies was undoubtedly the German submarine campaign. At the outbreak of hostilities, Great Britain immediately imposed a tight naval blockade against Germany. Neutral ships were brought into British ports for examination, and the list of contraband goods was expanded despite the existing rules of international law. For the first nine months of the war it was the British blockade, more than anything else, that evoked protests from our state department. During this period we had little trouble with Germany. But the kaiser's government was getting desperate as a result of the pressure of

Great Britain's blockade. There was only one method of retaliation—the submarine. The German government, therefore, announced unrestricted submarine warfare in February, 1915. On May 1, 1915, the *Gulflight* was torpedoed with the loss of several of her American crew. On May 7, 1915, came the horrible disaster of the sinking of the *Lusitania*, one of the largest and most luxurious liners of the Cunard line. The *Lusitania* had on board a large number of civilian passengers, and, in addition, it is generally recognized that she was carrying ammunition. However, it is still debated whether she was armed. Sunk by a torpedo in the Irish Sea, she went to the bottom with the loss of over one thousand lives, including more than one hundred Americans. Public opinion in America never recovered from the horror of this tragedy.

In March 1916, the unarmed French steamer *Sussex* was sunk without warning, and several Americans were killed. Following this act, an ultimatum demanding the cessation of the submarine campaign was sent by the government of the United States to Germany. In reply the Germans made pledges that in the future merchant vessels would not be sunk without warning and that provision would be made for the safety of passengers and crew. President Wilson had apparently won an important diplomatic victory.

American entry into the war. In the fall of 1916, Wilson was reëlected to the presidency. One of the important claims made during the campaign was that "he kept us out of war." This claim, however, was soon swept away by the force of events. In January of the next year another crisis in our diplomatic relations with Germany appeared with the renewal of submarine warfare. In February diplomatic relations were broken off. The discovery of German plots to embroil Mexico in a war against us added more fuel to the fire. Finally, on April 2, 1917, the President asked Congress to declare war against Germany. Resolutions to this effect passed both houses, and on April 6, 1917, war was declared.

If the immediate cause of our entry in the war was unrestricted submarine warfare, there were less obvious but nevertheless potent factors that motivated public opinion in America to war on the side of the Allies. It should not be overlooked that, by and large, American opinion from 1914 was favorable to France, Great Britain, and their allies. There was the strong tradition of friendship for France because of that country's help to the struggling American colonies during the Revolutionary War. Hence "Colonel Stanton's 'Lafayette we are here' was something more than dramatics." Despite the fact that there had been much "twisting of the British Lion's tail" in America since the days of the Revolution and the War of 1812, there persisted strong cultural links between the two Anglo-Saxon peoples. There was similarity of language, literature, law, and political institutions.

In the case of Germany American opinion had been profoundly shocked by the invasion of Belgium in 1914 and the sinking of the *Lusitania*. Even before the war German-American relations had been none too cordial. The German government had, unlike Great Britain, refused to sign one of Secretary of State Bryan's arbitration treaties. Many Americans were disgusted with the "sabre-rattling" speeches of the kaiser and found little to their liking in the mode of government in the German empire. In 1914 it was virtually inconceivable that we would ever join Germany against France and Great Britain, but it was not unthinkable that we might eventually join the cause of the Allies.

The Wilsonian blueprint for peace. Whatever the cause—our economic stake, our common traditions, the U-boat campaign—America was now fighting on the side of the Allies. President Wilson was convinced that America was fighting for national security, justice,

Despite its flimsiness, the "orange crate" airplane of World War I (here dropping a torpedo) proved that air power would be all-important in future wars.

honor, and democracy in the world. The conflict, in his words, was "a war for freedom and justice and self-government amongst all the nations of the world, a war to make the world safe for the peoples who live upon it and have made it their own, the German people themselves included."[12] In January 1918 President Wilson therefore enunciated his famous Fourteen Points as the basis for a lasting peace. These provided for:

1. Open covenants openly arrived at.
2. Freedom of the seas in peace and in war alike.
3. The removal of all economic barriers and the establishment of an equality of trade conditions among all nations.
4. Reduction of national armaments.
5. A readjustment of all colonial claims in which the interests of the population concerned must have equal weight with the claims of the government whose title is to be determined.
6. The evacuation of Russian territory and the independent determination by Russia of her own political development and national policy.
7. The evacuation and restoration of Belgium.
8. The evacuation and restoration of France and the return of Alsace-Lorraine.
9. A readjustment of the frontiers of Italy along national lines.
10. Self-determination for the peoples of Austria-Hungary.
11. Evacuation of Rumania, Serbia, and Montenegro and access to the sea for Serbia.
12. Self-determination for the peoples under Turkish rule and freedom of the Dardanelles under international guarantees.
13. The independence of Poland, with free access to the sea guaranteed by international covenant.
14. The formation of a general association of nations under specific covenants for the purpose of affording mutual guarantees of political independence and territorial integrity to great and small states alike.

This program represented the Wilsonian blueprint for a new and just world order. The spell of his idealism and the challenge of his speeches caused a great welling of idealism in America. No matter what causes had operated to bring America in, she was now fighting, in the words of her President, "to make the world safe for democracy."

Allied weakness in 1918. American help was needed desperately. In March 1917 a revolution in Russia deposed the czar. For a few months the new government endeavored to carry on the war, but in November it was overthrown by the Bolsheviks under Lenin. In December the Bolsheviks agreed to negotiate a separate peace with Germany and in March 1918 were forced to sign the Treaty of Brest Litovsk, a harsh settlement. The Russians agreed to cede 500,000 square miles of territory and nearly 70,000,000 people (see map, page 35). The Allies had already suffered a severe blow in the fall of 1917 when the Italians had been crushed at the battle of Caporetto. Only the arrival of British and French troops saved Italy from collapse.

Ludendorff's last effort. While the United States mobilized its tremendous resources in manpower and materials, the German government decided the war must be won at any cost before American aid became effective. General Ludendorff, freed from the necessity of fighting on the Russian front, transferred every available man to France and launched in March 1918 what he hoped would be a knockout blow against the British fifth army. Carrying all before them, the German shock troops, outnumbering the British four to one, made a large dent in the Allied line. A breakthrough, however, was not achieved. Another blow was made by Ludendorff against the British in another sector. Again impressive gains were made but not the rout which the German command had expected. A third desperate offensive was launched against the French forces, but fresh American troops thrown into the struggle halted the advance. Ludendorff now made a last supreme effort. Launching a "Peace Drive" against the French, Ludendorff declared, "If my offensive succeeds, we have won the war." By this time, however, the German troops had suffered heavy losses since they had assumed the offensive in March. The Allies created a unified command of all their armies under General Foch, Great Britain sent every available man to France, and American troops were now arriving in large numbers. Between March

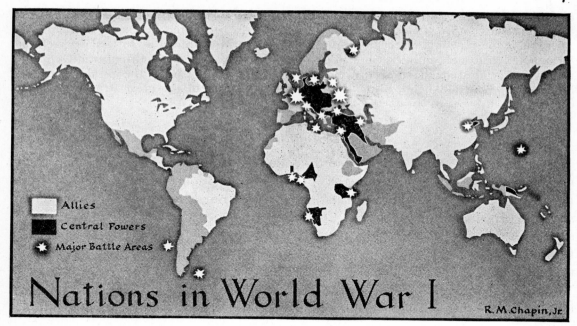

Allies
Central Powers
★ Major Battle Areas

Nations in World War I

R.M.Chapin, Jr

and July 1918 more than one million landed in France. The advantage in manpower and equipment was now with the Allies, and Ludendorff's "Peace Drive" failed after an advance of some three miles.

German collapse and armistice. Hardly had the German drive been halted when Foch counterattacked on July 18. For three weeks the Second Battle of the Marne raged. Outnumbered and without adequate supplies, the Germans had to retreat to their Hindenburg Line, the position held before they began their great offensive in March. Foch gave no respite. With fresh American troops in France the reinvigorated Allied armies advanced along the whole Hindenburg Line. The German line bent, broke, and then fell back in rapid retreat. By the end of October the German forces had been pushed out of most of France, and Allied armies were advancing through Belgium.

On October 1, Hindenburg notified the kaiser that Germany must sue for peace. Three days later the German chancellor sent a note to President Wilson requesting peace. The President's reply notified the German government that peace was impossible as long as the autocratic régime in Germany existed. The German chancellor tried to retain the monarchy by introducing certain liberal reforms, but it was too late. Revolution broke out in many parts of the country, and on November 9 the kaiser abdicated, and the republic was proclaimed. On November 5 Wilson had already notified the German government of the willingness of the Allies to initiate peace negotiations. Two days later, German delegates entered the Allied lines and were given the armistice terms by General Foch, the supreme Allied commander. Then at five o'clock on the morning of November 11, in a dining car in the Compiègne Forest, the two German delegates signed the terms of the armistice. At eleven o'clock the same day hostilities were halted. The world was now at peace, confronted with the task of binding up its wounds and removing the scars of conflict. All over the world the news of the armistice was received with an outburst of unrestrained joy.

While Germany was staggering under the relentless pounding of Foch's armies, her allies were suffering even greater misfortunes. Bulgaria surrendered on September 30, Turkey capitulated a month later, and Austria gave up the struggle against Italy on November 3.

Ramifications of the war. Only the barest sketch of the great war has been given. It was a world war fought on land, sea, and in the air. To study this conflict adequately we should have had to describe the Japanese conquest of the German colony in China, to follow the activities of South African and Indian troops in their capture of German colonies in Africa, note the expeditions sent from Australia and New Zealand against the German colonies in the Pacific, study the successes of British forces led by General Allenby in the Turkish empire and the escapades of the romantic Lawrence of Arabia, and, finally, follow the many sea battles that reached a climax in the great naval encounter at Jutland between the high-seas fleets of Great Britain and Germany. There were few parts of the world where some manifestation of the great struggle had not occurred.

Summary

The progress of the second phase of the Industrial Revolution promised a new era of economic prosperity for the world. The closest cooperation between nations was demanded to ensure the harmonious operation of an increasingly integrated world economic structure. In spite of the retention of old political boundaries and the idea of national sovereignty, the great powers recognized this fact in some measure. In the political field attempts were made to eliminate the danger of war, and attention was given to technical and economic problems through the formation of several international unions. To a certain extent, peoples as well as nations banded together to solve national and international problems, although most of these attempts were concerned with nonpolitical matters.

These cooperative efforts could not cope with other forces that made for international rivalry and war. The national-state system, power politics, secret diplomacy and its rival alliances, militarism, economic imperialism, and emotional nationalism finally led Europe to war in 1914 and most of the world with it as well.

The immediate cause of the 1914 conflict was nationalism in the Balkans. Serbian Irredentism menaced the existence of the polyglot Austrian empire. Russia backed Serbia because this move suited her designs in the Near East. In turn Russia received the support of France because France hoped to compel Germany to cede her the "lost provinces." Germany was committed to back Austria, who was her only reliable ally. Great Britain tried to remain aloof from the system of alliances but was finally drawn in. She could not afford to see Germany triumph, because German success would alter the European balance of power to the detriment of Great Britain.

The war became a world conflict fought on land, sea, and in the air and inaugurated what we now refer to as "total war." The distinction between soldier and noncombatant tended to become nonexistent. The immediate cause of America's entry into the war was the submarine campaign, but behind this cause were a strong tie with Great Britain and France, tactless German diplomacy, an economic stake in an Allied victory, and finally the realization that a German victory would endanger American security. Although there are many conflicting opinions on why the United States entered the war, the people themselves believed that they had embarked on a great crusade "to make the world safe for democracy."

In the first years of the war—1914-1916—Germany appeared likely to win. Even the entrance of Italy on the side of the Allies in 1915 did not add greatly to Allied strength. Although British and French forces had begun to make impressive gains by 1917, the help of the United States was desperately needed when the German U-boat campaign at last precipitated American entry into the war early the following year. By October 1918 the Germans had been pushed out of France; a month later they surrendered to the Allies.

The Peace Settlement

1918	Personnel of the peace conference	Wilson, Lloyd George, Clemenceau
1919	Treaty of Versailles (involves compromises)	Germany humiliated
	Treaty of St. Germain with Austria	Carves up Austro-Hungarian empire
	Treaty of Sèvres with Turkey	Turkey refuses harsh terms
1923	Treaty of Lausanne	Turkey obtains more favorable terms
	Treaty of Trianon with Hungary	Loses territory, people
	Treaty of Neuilly with Bulgaria	Did not suffer as much as Hungary

The League of Nations

1919	Covenant adopted	Headquarters at Geneva, Switzerland
	Organization—Assembly, Council, Secretariat	Permanent, non-permanent members
1920	The World Court	Located at The Hague
	The International Labor Organization	Governing Body and Labor Office
	Membership—forty-two nations	Rose to 65 in 15 years
	U. S. refuses to join League	Wilson's collapse
1921-1927	Boundary settlements	Vilna controversy
1922-1928	Resettlement of refugees of Greco-Turkish War	
1923	Corfu incident	War averted at cost of League prestige
1924	Aland affair	Victory for League
	Financial assistance to Austria and Hungary	

Security and Disarmament

1922-1927	French system of alliances	Known as Little Entente
	With Poland, Czechoslovakia, Rumania, Yugo-slavia	Directed against Germany
1922	Washington Conference	5:5:3 ratio
1923	French occupation of the Ruhr	Result of reparations dispute
1924	Dawes' plan for reparation	
1925	Locarno Treaties	Guaranteed Rhine
1927	Geneva Conference	
1928	Kellogg-Briand Pact	Renunciation of war as instrument of national policy

Tariff Barriers and War Debts

1922	Fordney-McCumber tariff in U. S. makes war debt payment difficult	Highest rates ever in U.S.
	Smoot-Hawley tariff causes retaliatory tariffs in other countries	Rates raised to almost highest in world
1929	Young Plan for reparations payments	Bank of International Settlements established

Depression and International Finance

1929	Stock market crash in U. S.	Ended wild speculation
1931	Hoover moratorium on debts	
1931-1933	Great Britain and United States go off gold standard	World trade becomes barter
1932	Lausanne conference	Reparations practically canceled
1932-1934	War debt payments cease	Finland continues to pay
1932	Germany stops reparations payments	
	Great Britain goes off free trade	Enacts high tariff
1932	Ottawa Imperial Economic Conference	Principle of imperial preference
1933	World economic conference in London	
1934	U. S. reduces gold content of dollar	Other countries also devalue currency

CHAPTER 2

A Quest for World Order

Laying down its arms in 1919, the world looked to the Peace Conference to repair the damage of the conflict. The war had lasted for 1565 days. During this time over sixty million men had donned uniforms. About nine million of these were killed, twenty-two million were wounded, and, in addition, about ten million civilians lost their lives as a direct or indirect result of the war. Furthermore, billions of dollars' worth of property had been used up or destroyed by the warring armies. The statesmen at the conference had two basic tasks. The first was to reverse the trend toward international anarchy that had brought on the First World War. It was imperative to remove or at least lessen such factors as nationalism, secret diplomacy, economic imperialism, and militarism—all of which had helped to bring war in 1914. The second task was to repair the extensive economic damage wrought by war and to endeavor to continue the world's economic progress. This problem demanded the reduction of barriers to world trade and cooperation among the nations in solving their mutual economic problems.

This chapter records the attempts to perform these tasks during the postwar decade. It will be seen that the peace was not based on President Wilson's Fourteen Points, as the Germans hoped, and that vindictiveness and selfish national interests conspired from the beginning to defeat Wilsonian idealism. One result of the Great War, however, was the establishment of a league of nations. For the first time, the world was to have a powerful agency, composed of representatives from nearly all the nations existing, to compel states to arbitrate their differences, protect nations from aggression, and endeavor to eliminate the various causes that had in the past brought on wars. Some attention will be given to the League of Nations, its achievements and its failures, and the reader will see why and how both national and international efforts to achieve security and disarmament were unsuccessful.

Problems of postwar economic reconstruction form the last half of the chapter. The impossible financial burden of reparations placed on Germany and the failure of the Allied nations to come to some agreement regarding inter-Allied debts revealed themselves as serious obstacles in the path of reconstruction, and with them appeared an increase of tariffs, a contraction of international trade, and a world depression in 1930. In general the world was no more successful in its search for economic prosperity than it was in the quest for political security.

Making the Peace

The armistice terms. The armistice terms accepted by Germany on November 11, 1918, compelled her to evacuate Alsace-Lorraine, Luxemburg, Belgium, and the northern part of France. Within a month Allied troops were to occupy the German territory west of the Rhine. A large number of units of the German fleet were to be surrendered, locomotives, trucks, and other equipment turned over, and all Allied prisoners released. While these terms were being carried out by the new German government that had taken over after the kaiser's abdication, delegates from the Allied nations from all over the world were converging on Paris, where the greatest Peace Conference in the world's history was to be held.

Personnel of the conference. The thirty-two Allied powers all sent delegations, some numbering more than a hundred, which included statesmen and experts of various kinds, secretaries, and clerical help. The vanquished nations—Germany, Austria-Hungary, Turkey, and Bulgaria—were not accorded representation. At the conference Woodrow Wilson, David Lloyd George, and Georges Clemenceau dominated the proceedings. Wilson, in a number of truly great speeches, had already formulated the hopes and aspirations of a war-weary world, and in the eyes of the peoples of Europe he was a veritable Messiah. However, it soon became apparent after his arrival in France in December 1918 that he would be unable to prevent his ideals and promises from being sabotaged. Wilson's idealism was challenged not only by the Allied statesmen in Paris but back home in America as well, where certain factions in Congress were preparing to repudiate his program for a more just and a better ordered world. Wilson was preëminently the scholar and idealist, and so thoroughly convinced was he of the validity of his own ideas that he often refused to consider the possibility of merit in those of his opponents. A farseeing "armchair statesman," handicapped by a cold and imperious personality, Wilson had little chance of holding his own against the wily Lloyd George and the cynical Clemenceau.

Lloyd George, the prime minister of Great Britain, came to the conference just after a triumphant victory at the polls in which the electorate had been promised the "hanging of the kaiser" and the "squeezing of the German lemon until the pips squeaked." He was determined to destroy the commercial and naval power of Germany, to acquire the German colonies, and to compel Germany to pay a large share of the cost of the war. Lloyd George was not a scholar, but he was a consummately clever politician who could use the arts of diplomatic bargaining with rare skill. His greatest asset was an engaging personality that thawed many a stubborn opponent.

The strongest personality of the conference was an old man of seventy-seven years. Clemenceau was the sole survivor of the French Assembly that had protested against the loss of Alsace-Lorraine in 1871. His one burning ambition was to secure conditions ensuring the security of France in the future. The "Old Tiger" was shot in the chest by a madman during the peace negotiations, but so strong was his desire to live that he quickly rallied after the shooting and, for a time, dominated the conference from his bedside.

Pre-armistice peace principles. The Germans had not surrendered unconditionally, but only with the understanding that the peace would follow in the main the Fourteen Points and in general coincide with the speeches of Wilson. In February 1918, the President had announced "There shall be no annexations, no contributions, no punitive damages," and on July 4 he had said that every question must be settled "upon the basis of the free acceptance of that settlement by the people immediately concerned." Some of the Allies saw the question of the peace in a different light, and before the armistice was signed, three reservations to the Fourteen Points were made by the European Allied powers. One sprang from Great Britain's attitude toward the freedom of the seas, another came from the demand that Germany must be made to pay for all damage done to Allied civilians, and the third appeared because of the dissatisfaction of the peoples of Austria-Hungary with mere autonomy within the Hapsburg empire. Subject to these reservations the victorious Allies were pledged to work out a peace based on Wilsonian principles.

The conference. With two hundred newspaper men reporting the conference, the statesmen assembled in their first plenary meeting on January 18, 1919, the anniversary of the date on which the German empire had been proclaimed in Paris in 1871. It became evident at once that little progress could be made if business was carried on in the full conference. The Council of Ten was therefore set up. It consisted of the two ranking delegates of the five great powers—the United States, Great Britain, France, Italy, and Japan. Soon this was narrowed down to the Big Four, minus Japan, and when the Italian delegates went back to Rome after a quarrel with Wilson, the Big Three carried on the work of the conference. The lesser powers counted for little, although their representatives often delivered long addresses before the Council of Ten, "who for the most part sat in bored silence."

The League Covenant. The first difficulty in the peace conference arose over the question of a league of nations. As early as March 1918 a draft plan had been prepared in England, and drafts were later prepared by Colonel House, the close personal friend and adviser of Wilson, and General Smuts, the premier of the Union of South Africa. In Paris a special committee was assigned to draw up a definite scheme. Wilson was insistent that the first work of the conference must be to agree upon a covenant of a league of nations and that this must be made a part of the peace treaty. After much disagreement the Covenant was approved by the full conference in April 1919. In order to gain support for his league idea, Wilson had to give way on other matters. This compromising meant a partial repudiation of his Fourteen Points, but he felt that it was better to have an imperfect treaty incorporating the League than a perfect one without it.

Redrawing German boundaries. Redrawing German boundaries was another task of the conference (see map, page 35). Alsace-Lorraine was turned over to France without question, in accordance with one of the Fourteen Points. Three districts formerly belonging to Germany were given to Belgium, after a dubious plebiscite conducted by Belgian officials, and another plebiscite gave half of Schleswig back to Denmark. Clemenceau and General Foch were determined that a buffer state consisting of the German territory west of the Rhine should be established under the domination of France. In the eyes of the American and British representatives, such a crass violation of the principle of self-determination would only breed future wars, and a compromise was therefore offered Clemenceau, which he accepted. The territory in question was to be occupied by Allied troops for a period of from five to fifteen years, and, further, a zone fifty kilometers east of the Rhine was to be demilitarized. In addition, Wilson and Lloyd George agreed that the United States and Great Britain would guarantee France against aggression, and two treaties were drawn up and signed. Although Clemenceau also claimed the Saar Basin, a rich coal area, this was not given outright to France but placed under the administration of the League instead. The French were given the ownership of the mines to compensate for the destruction of their own in northern France. It was agreed, however, that after fifteen years a plebiscite would be conducted to determine whether the region wished to continue under League supervision, become part of France, or return to Germany.

Along Germany's eastern frontier the creation of the Polish Corridor raised grave problems. Large sections of German territory in

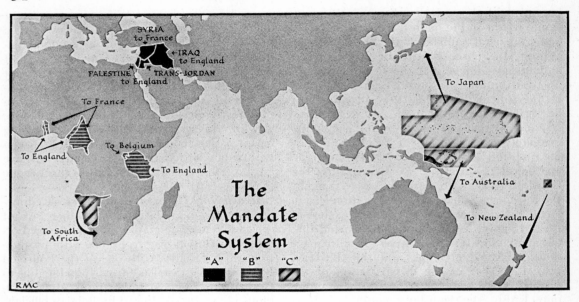

The Mandate System

"A"   "B"   "C"

RMC

which there were Polish majorities but also a goodly number of Germans were turned over to Poland (see map, page 39), and Danzig, a German city, was handed over to the League for administration. Although many Germans were turned over to Poland by this arrangement, the land in question had been taken from Poland by Prussia in the eighteenth century. A section of Silesia was likewise given to Poland, but only after a plebiscite, and a small section of East Prussia was placed in 1923 under the control of Lithuania. All in all, Germany lost 25,000 square miles inhabited by some six million people.

The mandate system. A curious mixture of idealism and revenge determined the allocation of the German colonies and certain territories belonging to Turkey. Because outright annexation would look too much like unvarnished imperialism, it was suggested that the colonies be turned over to the League which in turn would give them to certain of its members to administer (see map above). The colonies were to be known as mandates, and praiseworthy precautions were taken that the mandates would be administered for the well-being and development of the inhabitants. Once a year the mandatory powers were to present a detailed account of their administration to the permanent mandates commission of the League.

"A" mandates, such as Syria, Palestine, and Iraq, were regarded as territories able to achieve full statehood in the not too distant future. "B" mandates, such as most in central Africa, represented peoples whose progress had not reached a point where admission to statehood was possible for a long time to come. "C" mandates, in southwest Africa and the South Pacific islands, were regarded as locations where size, proximity to the mandatory power, or remoteness from civilization made control by others the best safeguard of the natives' rights and welfare. The mandate system, as such, was a step forward in colonial administration, but Germany nevertheless had been deprived of all her colonies on the excuse that she could not rule them justly or efficiently.

Reparations. Germany had accepted the armistice terms with the understanding that she was to pay for all damage done to the civilian population of the Allies. At the conference the British and French delegates went much further by demanding that Germany pay the total cost of the war including the pensions. The American representatives maintained that such a claim was contrary to the pre-armistice Allied terms and succeeded in arriving at a compromise. It was agreed that Germany was not to pay the entire cost of the war, except in the case of Belgium, but only for war damages which included damage to civilians and the cost of pensions. These payments, called reparations, were exacted on the ground that Germany was responsible for the

The Peace Settlements

Lost by:

Germany

Russia

Austria-Hungary

Bulgaria

Trouble Spots

100 mi.

10,000 sq. mi.

100 sq. mi.

R. M. Chapin, Jr.

war. In fact, the war guilt clause (Article 231) in the Treaty of Versailles said explicitly:

"The Allied and Associated Governments affirm and Germany accepts the responsibility of Germany and her allies for causing all the loss and damage to which the Allied and Associated Governments and their nationals have been subjected as a consequence of the war imposed upon them by the aggression of Germany and her allies."

Although the Allies were in complete agreement that Germany should be made to pay, they were completely unable to decide on the sum. Some demands ran as high as two hundred billion dollars. Finally they decided to let a committee fix the amount and report to them not later than May 1921. In the meantime Germany was to commence payments which were to total the equivalent of nearly five billion dollars by the time the reparations committee's report was ready.

Other Allied demands. Germany was required to hand over all her merchant ships over 1600 tons and fifty per cent of all those between 1000 and 1600 tons and in addition to construct for the Allies one million tons of new shipping. Vast amounts of equipment, tools, and machinery were also to be delivered by Germany to the Allies, and over twenty-two million tons of coal were to be given to France, Belgium, and Luxemburg over a ten-year period. In matters regarding Germany's fighting strength, the demands were even more drastic. Germany was permitted a standing army of only 100,000 men, the size of her fleet was drastically reduced, possession of military airplanes was forbidden, and her munitions plants were to be placed under close supervision. The treaty also provided that the kaiser was to be tried by a tribunal "for a supreme offense against international morality and the sanctity of treaties," and over 800 German officials were cited for trial for war atrocities. But the kaiser fled to Holland after the German revolution, and when that country refused to surrender him, no further steps were taken by the Allied governments, who had inserted the clause providing for the punishment of the kaiser largely for home consumption.

German reaction to the Treaty. The German delegation came to Paris in April 1919 to receive the Treaty of Versailles. Up to this time they had been given no official informa-

tion as to its terms. In addressing the German delegates Clemenceau declared:

"You have before you the accredited plenipotentiaries of all the small and the great powers united to fight together in the war that has been so cruelly imposed upon them. The time has come when we must settle our accounts. You have asked for peace. We are ready to give you peace."[1]

In receiving the Treaty on May 7, Brockdorff-Rantzau, the German foreign minister and head of the German delegation, replied:

"It is demanded of us that we shall confess ourselves to be the only ones guilty of war. We are far from declining any responsibility, . . . but we energetically deny that Germany and its people . . . were alone guilty. In the last fifty years the imperialism of all the European states has chronically poisoned the international situation. You will find us ready . . . with a firm intention . . . of repairing . . . any wrong that may have been committed— principally the wrong to Belgium, and to show to mankind new aims of political and social progress. . . . Only if the gates of the League of Nations are thrown open to all who are of good will can the aim be attained, and only then the dead of this war will not have died in vain."[2]

During the 1920's and the early 1930's the majority of scholars were inclined to agree with the German complaint that the terms of the peace made at Versailles were unnecessarily severe. The course of Nazi imperialism in the Second World War, however, has tended to cause a revaluation of the Treaty of Versailles. The following quotation is characteristic of this new attitude:

"After all the Peace Treaty was less catastrophic than [German] nationalism likes to portray it. Certainly it was a punitive peace, garnished with many senseless humiliations which operated as constant irritants; but it was not a Punic Peace, such as Imperial militarism, gone stark mad, tried to impose on temporarily defeated Russia and Rumania in Brest Litovsk and Bucharest (1917-1918) or as Nazi militarism, as briefly, we hope, forced upon Czechoslovakia and Poland (and other conquered countries). The Peace settlement of 1919 left intact Germany's national unity and allowed the defeated nation to work out its own internal solution without manifest interference."[3]

The Treaty of Versailles signed. After obtaining the Treaty the German government balked at what it considered its outrageous terms. The menace of Allied invasion gave it no alternative but to sign, and the government therefore instructed its delegates to accept the Treaty for Germany "without abandoning her view in regard to the unheard of injustice of the conditions of the peace." On June 28, on the anniversary of the assassination of Archduke Francis Ferdinand and in the Hall of Mirrors at Versailles where the German empire had been proclaimed in 1871 by the victorious hosts of Bismarck, the ceremony of signing the Treaty was carried out.

During the last stages of the conference Lloyd George apparently began to realize how unfair some of the clauses in the Treaty really were. Another statesman, General Smuts, was outspoken in his criticism of the Treaty. On May 30 the general sent Wilson a communication in which he declared, "I think we should all give the gravest consideration to the question whether our Peace Treaty is within the four corners of your speeches of 1918. Frankly I do not think this is so, and I think the Germans make out a good case. . . . All the one-sided provisions . . . and all the pinpricks, with which the Treaty teems, seem to me to be both against the letter and the spirit of your Points."[4]

Other World War treaties. Treaties were also concluded with the rest of the Central Powers. In the case of Austria-Hungary these legalized the nationalist movements of Czechs, Poles, and Slavs and transformed the empire into the states of Austria and Hungary (see map, page 35). By the treaty of Saint Germain Austria was reduced from 116,000 to 32,000 square miles and in population from 28,500,000 to 6,000,000. *Anschluss,* or union of the Germans in Austria with their kinsmen in the new German republic, was forbidden. The disposition of former Hapsburg territory at the conference created a serious controversy. Italy, taking her stand on the secret Treaty of London, wanted the Adriatic as an Italian lake. In order to achieve this the cession of a slice of the Dalmatian coast and especially the port of Fiume was necessary. This city, however, was the natural port for the newly created state of Yugoslavia and had not been promised to Italy in 1915. Wilson declared that the Italian claim was

in flat contradiction to the principle of self-determination, and a controversy ensued which nearly wrecked the Peace Conference. The question of Fiume was finally settled in 1924 by direct Italo-Yugoslav negotiations. Austria also ceded to Italy the south Tyrol district containing 250,000 Germans, an arrangement likewise violating the principle of self-determination. Hungary by the Treaty of Trianon lost territory to Czechoslovakia, Yugoslavia, and Rumania (see map, page 35). Under these arrangements one third of the Hungarian population was placed under foreign rule (see map, page 39). The motto of Hungary following the peace was "No, no, never!"

The Treaty of Sèvres with Turkey required Turkey to give up Arabia, Palestine, Mesopotamia, and Syria and to relinquish control of the Straits, which were to be demilitarized and internationalized. After these terms had been announced an English paper declared, "After five hundred years the Turkish power disappears for all practical purposes." But Turkey refused to accept the terms, and under its great leader Kemal Ataturk succeeded in obtaining more favorable terms by the Treaty of Lausanne in 1923. The Balkans thus continued to be full of international discord as they were before the war.

The Treaty of Neuilly cut off Bulgaria from the Aegean Sea (see map, page 35), imposed an indemnity, and provided for compulsory demilitarization. Bulgaria lost nearly one million of her subjects but did not suffer so severely as Hungary in the loss of land.

The gap between aims and achievements. Such was the general outline of the settlement worked out by the victorious Allies at Paris. The possibility of a permanent peace foundered on the rocks of secret treaties and national interests, and on the whole the peace settlement was inadequate and unrealistic. In the signing of the treaties, "the statesmen had not been equal to the grandeur of events." Nevertheless in evaluating what the Allies did to their foes, one must also consider what the victorious Germans meted out to Russia in the Treaty of Brest Litovsk. Of the great powers who drafted the Treaty of Versailles, the United States alone received no concessions of territory and asked no reparations, but only the payment of loans made during the war.

Results of the war. Out of the conflict democracy seemingly emerged stronger than ever before. In 1914 there had been only two important republics in Europe (France and Switzerland); after the peace settlement there were seventeen. Wilson's insistence upon the self-determination of nations had resulted in an almost universal victory for the principle of national self-determination. For five hundred years larger nations had swallowed their weaker neighbors. In 1750 there were some 350 independent states in Europe. By 1815 this number had been decreased to about sixty, and in 1914 there were only about twenty. Enthusiastic adoption of the principle of self-determination at the Peace Conference, however, reversed this process of unification, and the peace treaties of 1919 increased the number of states in Europe by nearly fifty per cent. While many people welcomed the emancipation of the heretofore submerged nationalities, others were disturbed at what they described as the "Balkanization of Europe."

Moreover the peacemakers at Versailles had not been able to liberate all Europeans from alien rule. The Italians had been given Yugoslavs and Germans, the Poles had within their frontiers a large number of Germans and Russians, nearly a million Bulgars had been distributed among Bulgaria's neighbors, and three million Magyars (Hungarians) had been detached from Hungary (see map). The political frontiers of Europe coincided better than ever before with racial boundaries in 1919, but there were exceptions that in time became sources of infection in Europe and which German leaders later used to advantage.

The war also radically altered the political balance of power. France, not Germany, now enjoyed undisputed political dominance on the continent. After 1919 it was France's desire to maintain the status quo as laid down in the Treaty of Versailles. From a world viewpoint, the war weakened the relative strength of Europe as a whole in comparison with other areas in the world. After 1919 the United States became recognized as the strongest and wealthiest of all nations. The countries of South America and the self-governing dominions of the British Empire assumed a new importance in world affairs. Japan also came out of the First World War with increased influence and prestige, and an appetite for imperial expansion.

Organization and Function of the League of Nations

Development of the League idea. The League of Nations came into existence in the spring of 1919. At that time Sir Eric Drummond was given $500,000 to employ a staff and proceed with the task of building the machinery of the League. Soon the League Secretariat and library were established in a large hotel in Geneva, Switzerland. People all over the world followed these events with keen interest, for this was the first time that such an ambitious scheme in international cooperation had been launched.

The actual organization of the League of Nations was novel, but the idea of such a body had been in the minds of idealists and prophets for hundreds of years. In ancient Palestine the Jewish prophet Isaiah had already prophesied a day when "Nation shall not lift up sword against nation, neither shall they learn war any more." At the close of the Middle Ages, Dante, the Italian scholar and poet, in his work *De Monarchia* (1313) outlined a plan for a united Europe under one benevolent ruler. About the same time the French scholar Pierre Dubois proposed a plan for the abolition of war by means of a league and an international court. Hugo Grotius (1583-1645), Hollander noted as the founder of international law, discussed methods for utilizing arbitration in international disputes in his treatise *On the Law of War and Peace*. Another landmark in the development of the league of nations idea was William Penn's suggestion, in 1603, that Europe should have a general parliament with arbitration powers. In 1786 the noted English political philosopher Jeremy Bentham published his *Plan for an Universal and Perpetual Peace*. This work suggested the formation of an international court of justice, the limitation of arms, and the abolition of secret diplomacy. The great German philosopher Immanuel Kant, who ushered in the philosophical idealism of the early nineteenth century, wrote two important tracts on the problem of war and peace. Believing that despotic rulers often caused wars, this thinker advocated that democratic government should supersede absolut-

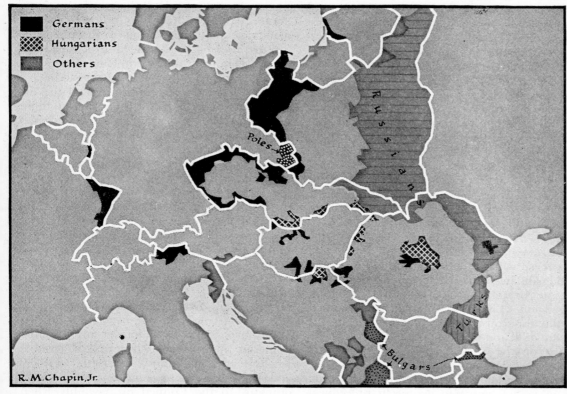

Germans
Hungarians
Others

R. M. Chapin, Jr.

TROUBLE SPOTS IN POSTWAR EUROPE—THE SUBMERGED MINORITIES

ism, standing armies be abolished, and the nations federated into one large group.

During the nineteenth century the peace movement grew rapidly. In 1828 William Ladd formed the American Peace Society. Twelve years later he wrote an important work entitled *Essay on a Congress for the Adjustment of International Disputes without Resort to Arms.* By 1914 there were about 150 peace organizations in the world. During the Great War many of these groups in England and America discussed the possibility of creating some kind of international league following the termination of hostilities. A committee appointed by the British government worked out an elaborate plan for a league of nations. To this scheme were also added the ideas of Woodrow Wilson and General Smuts of South Africa. The British and American contributions were finally merged into a third draft which, with certain changes, became the Covenant of the League of Nations. The Covenant, the constitution of the League, consisted of a preamble and twenty-six articles.

Organization of the League. The three principal organizations of the League of Nations as set up by the Covenant were the Assembly, the Council, and the Secretariat. The first body contained representatives of every member state and held annual sessions at Geneva, usually on the second Monday in September. The Assembly determined the budget of the League, admitted new members, elected the judges of the World Court in co-operation with the Council, and might consider "any matter within the sphere of action of the League or affecting the peace of the world." The Assembly could not make any important decisions without the unanimous consent of its members, and every nation represented in the Assembly had one vote. The public was admitted to plenary sessions of the Assembly upon presentation of cards which might be secured upon request.

The Council of the League of Nations as originally planned was to consist of five permanent and four nonpermanent members, the former representing the great powers (Great

Britain, France, the United States, Italy, and Japan) and the latter the smaller states. Changes were later made in the rules regulating the membership of the Council, so that the permanent members came to number five (without the United States) and the nonpermanent members, nine. In 1936 two nonpermanent seats were added, and the withdrawal of Japan, Germany, and Italy between 1935 and 1939 left the number of permanent members of the Council at three—Great Britain, France, and Russia. After 1929 the Council held four regular meetings each year, usually at Geneva. The general scope of the powers of the Council corresponded to that of the Assembly, except that the former was given more specific duties. Among these were the reduction of arms, the study of the annual reports submitted by the nations holding colonial mandates, and the formulation of measures to be taken to protect any state from aggression. Like the Assembly, the Council might also consider "any matter within the sphere of action of the League or affecting the peace of the world." Each member state represented on the Council had only one representative and one vote. The rule of unanimity prevailed here also except in procedural matters. A smaller body which met more frequently than the Assembly, the Council dealt with most of the emergencies that occurred in international affairs.

The Secretariat represented the civil service of the League. At the head of this permanent staff was the secretary-general, who was assisted by one deputy and three undersecretaries. The personnel of the Secretariat, numbering about 700, constituted the first example in history of an international civil service whose loyalty was pledged to no single nation but to the interests of all nations in common. In 1938 the head of the Secretariat was Joseph Avenol, a Frenchman, assisted by two deputies, one Spanish and the other Italian. The undersecretary-general was British, and a citizen of Uruguay held the post of legal adviser. The chiefs of the principal departments of the Secretariat consisted of two Englishmen, two Italians, an American, a South African, a Dutchman, a Pole, a Swede, a Greek, a Frenchman, and a Dane. The Secretariat handled a tremendous amount of correspondence. All treaties made by members of the League had to be registered with the Secretariat, and its fifteen departments had charge of the many matters of administrative routine arising from mandates, questions relating to disarmament, health problems, the protection of racial minorities, and any other problems, general or special, which the League was considering.

The World Court. In addition to the Assembly, the Council, and the Secretariat, there were two other important bodies which derived from the Covenant of the League. The first of these was the Permanent Court of International Justice, commonly referred to as the World Court. Empowered by article XIV of the League Covenant, a committee drew up a draft for an international court in 1920. Adopted unanimously by the Assembly, the plan provided for a permanent court consisting of eleven judges chosen for nine-year terms. Later the number of judges was raised to fifteen. The Hague was selected as the site of the tribunal. Unlike the court of the first Hague peace conference in 1899, the new World Court was not one of arbitration. Its main purpose was to "interpret any disputed point in international law and determine when treaty obligations had been violated," and it was also competent to give advisory opinions to the Council or Assembly when they asked for them. By 1937 forty-one states had agreed to place before the Court all disputes to which they were a party concerning the interpretation of treaties, questions on international law, problems arising from breaches of international obligations, and the question of reparations arising from such breaches.

The International Labor Conference. The second international body stemming from the Covenant was the International Labor Conference. Pledged "to secure and maintain fair and humane conditions of labor for men, women, and children," this institution consisted of three organizations: the general conference, the governing body, and the international labor office. The general conference was similar in organization to the League Assembly. Each member state sent four representatives to its annual meetings. Two of these four represented the government of the sending state, one represented the employers, and one represented labor. Each delegation voted individually. The most important work of the general conference was in passing recommendations called "draft conventions" relating to working hours, forced labor in colonies, workmen's compensation, labor organization, and many other allied problems. These conventions were then presented to the various governments represented in the International Labor Conference for ratification.

The governing body, which met every three months, and the International Labor Office were similar to the League Council and the Secretariat in organization and function. The governing body was composed of thirty-two members, sixteen representing the governments, eight the employers, and eight the workers. The International Labor Office had a permanent staff which was responsible for research and investigation in labor problems and for the publication of important findings.

Purposes of the League. Some attention has been given to the organization of the League of Nations because, in 1920, it was the first time in history that a carefully planned scheme for the encouragement of international cooperation had been established. Following the Great War the world stood in dire need of such an agency. Misery and confusion were prevalent in Europe. In Poland the peasants were faced with famine, in Russia typhus and cholera stalked through the land, and even the victorious French were faced with the immense task of restoring their devastated regions. At one time more than seventy-five million people were dependent on supplies given by the Allies, mainly the United States. The political scene also reflected chaos. In 1920 Russia and Poland fought a bitter war. The new Russian government was also fighting desperately to eject the pro-czar "White Russian" armies from the country. Greek armies invaded Turkish Asia Minor, civil war caused turmoil in India and Ireland, and in Hungary a Rumanian army had just crushed a strong Communist movement. It was these facts General Smuts had in mind when he declared, "Unemployment, starvation, anarchy, war, disease, and despair stalk the land . . . a large part of Europe is threatened with disaster and decay."

The postwar world, especially Europe, obviously presented serious problems. But it was generally felt that political anarchy and economic confusion rife in certain areas of the globe would gradually be removed by the constructive efforts of the League of Nations. Before tracing the achievements and failures of the League in the decade following the Great War it will be useful to see just how the framers of the League intended it to operate as an agency of international reconstruction. Its purposes may be thought of as fourfold: (1) to prevent war and punish aggression, (2) to organize peace, (3) to assume certain duties connected with the operation of the peace treaties, and (4) to stimulate international cooperation for the removal of economic and social evils and for general humanitarian and cultural purposes.

Preventing war. By Article x of the League Covenant, the member states agreed "to respect and preserve as against external aggression the territorial integrity and existing political independence" of all states belonging to the League. Other articles enjoined the members to accept arbitration in the case of international disagreements, to accept any verdict reached by arbitration, and not to embark on war in defiance of the verdict of the Council.

In answer to any nation embarking on such a belligerent course, Article xvi specifically required the members "immediately to subject it to the severance of all trade or financial relations." The imposition of these "economic sanctions" on an aggressor could also be made more drastic by a decision of the Council recommending military or naval measures against the wrongdoer.

Organizing peace. The second main purpose of the League was to carry on positive activities for peace. The World Court was to be used as a judicial agency to which states could bring their differences. The menace of secret treaties was to be removed by the rule that all League members were to present their treaties to the Secretariat, which was then to arrange for their publication. A very far-seeing clause in the Covenant (xix) recognized that there were certain features in the postwar settlements made at Paris that would sooner or later have to be changed. The Assembly, therefore, "from time to time" was "to advise the reconsideration by members of the League, of treaties which have become inapplicable and the consideration of international conditions whose continuance might endanger the peace of the world." Finally, in its positive and long-term efforts for peace, the League was to strive for arms limitation. The members were, in the words of the Covenant, to "recognize that the maintenance of peace re-

The United States' extreme isolationist sentiment of the twenties is reflected in this cartoon by Herbert Johnson. "Hm, please close the gate on your way out!" was the title given to it when it appeared in the "Saturday Evening Post."

quires the reduction of national armaments to the lowest point consistent with national safety."

Other duties of the League. Certain duties connected with the operation of the peace treaties represented a third type of League activity. It was to conduct plebiscites in Schleswig, East Prussia, and Silesia and to be responsible for the administration of the Free City of Danzig; it was to govern the Saar territory for a period of fifteen years, at which time a plebiscite was to be held. It also acted as a supervising body for the mandate system. Each year the nations administering mandates were to present to a permanent mandates commission of the League a full account of their administration of the mandated areas.

The fourth basic purpose of the League was to carry on international humanitarian activities and encourage all types of intellectual and social welfare cooperation among nations.

To this end special agencies were established as part of the League machinery, such as an economic and financial organization. Other agencies were created in the interests of health, intellectual cooperation, and the opium evil.

United States' refusal to join the League. In 1919, the year of its establishment, the League, with its high purposes and comprehensive machinery, constituted a most promising agency for improving the status of mankind everywhere. At the very outset, however, the League suffered a blow when the United States refused to enter its membership. During the war Americans took pride in the world-wide acclaim of President Wilson's proposals for a new world order. But the peace settlement as finally worked out pleased few people. Chauvinists found it too lenient, and liberals found it too harsh. Republicans, seeking to discredit Wilson, agitated against it. Returning to the United States in July 1919, President Wilson immediately pressed the Senate for a ratification of the Treaty of Versailles, carrying with it membership in the League of Nations, of course. A strong group of isolationists in the Senate successfully blocked ratification. In desperation, and faced with the wreckage of all his visions of a new world united in a common effort to outlaw war, President Wilson toured the country in September 1919, appealing to the people to support the League of Nations. Not yet fully recuperated from his exertions at the Peace Conference, Wilson could not stand the heavy strain of his whirlwind campaign. He suffered a complete physical collapse and was stricken with paralysis, and with his collapse the opportunity to build a new world order disappeared. Although the retiring President appealed to the nation from his sickbed to make the presidential campaign of 1920 a "solemn referendum" on the question of the League, the election was in no sense clear-cut on this issue. Harding, the Republican candidate, both praised and criticized the League in one and the same breath. As one historian has said, "His masterly obfuscation of the issue was perhaps his supreme intellectual achievement."[5]

Following the Republican victory at the polls in 1920, Wilson lived in retirement until his death in 1924. One cannot help feeling the deep anguish and bitterness in his few last public utterances. Speaking over the radio in November 1923, Wilson declared:

"The only way in which we can worthily give proof of our appreciation of the high significance of Armistice Day is by resolving to put self-interest away and once more formulate and act upon the highest ideals and purposes of international policy. Thus, and only thus, can we return to the true traditions of America."

These words, in most part, fell upon deaf ears. The chaos in international affairs that was to come in the 1930's and the coming of World War II were hidden in the future. Following the easy slogan "Back to normalcy," the mass of Americans lapsed into complacent isolationism and optimistic economic prosperity.

United States' cooperation with the League. The cooperation of the United States with the League was not, however, denied completely. During the postwar period American observers at Geneva followed the deliberations of the Council and Assembly and kept their government at Washington informed. Many of the important conferences held under League auspices, such as those on disarmament, were attended by official representatives from the United States. The United States began to cooperate with the advisory opinion committee as early as 1923 and took a vigorous part in the activities dealing with the protection of women and children. Membership was also accepted in the International Labor Conference, and representatives from the United States made valuable contributions to its work. In February 1939, in a note to the League, the United States said in part: "The League, however, has been responsible for the development of mutual exchange and discussion of ideas and methods to a greater extent and in more fields of humanitarian and scientific endeavor than any other organization in history. The United States Government is really aware of the value of this type of general interchange and desires to see it extended."[6]

The League of Nations in Action

Growth of the League. The refusal of the United States to join the League of Nations was a serious impediment to the successful functioning of the new body. Despite this handicap, however, the membership of the League increased rapidly. In 1920 the original membership was forty-two nations. In 1921 three Baltic states joined, in 1922 Hungary, in 1923 the Irish Free State and Abyssinia, in 1926 Germany. Later, in 1932, Mexico joined the League. Russia entered in 1934. The roster of League membership in 1935 reached the total of sixty-two states.

The Aland Islands affair. The record of the League from 1920 to 1930 was neither a dismal failure nor a complete triumph. In the matter of attempting to prevent war, the League achieved some outstanding successes in certain international disputes and failed miserably in others. The Aland Islands affair can be cited as an example of the former. Lying between Sweden and Finland, the Aland Islands dominate the entrance to the Gulf of Bothnia. These islands and Finland once belonged to Sweden but came under Russian rule in 1809. In 1917, when Russia collapsed, Finland became an independent state and extended her control over them. The following year, Sweden recognized the independence of Finland and made no objection to Finnish control. The Alanders, however, are mainly Swedish and commenced an agitation for union with Sweden. Two unofficial polls showed that a large majority of the inhabitants were not content to remain under Finnish rule. The movement for union with Sweden grew rapidly, and open revolt seemed imminent. The arrest of many of the agitators by the Finnish authorities angered Swedish opinion, and prospects of war became lively.

In June 1920 the League investigated the dispute, and in the spring of 1921 the Council gave its decision. Accepted by both Sweden and Finland, the decision permitted Finland to retain its sovereignty over the Aland Islands. The inhabitants were given local self-government, the use of Swedish in the schools was guaranteed, and the islands were demilitarized. The settlement without recourse to war was indeed a notable achievement of the League.

Boundary settlements. Many of the disputes presented to the League of Nations for settlement concerned boundary problems raised by the peace treaties. After an inconclusive plebiscite in Silesia, the Council assumed the task of determining the boundary between Poland and Germany in this area. Following the investigation of a committee appointed by the Council, the larger part of the area was turned over to Germany, although the most valuable economic resources were awarded to Poland.

In 1921 a serious boundary dispute occurred between Yugoslavia and Albania. Yugoslavian troops crossed into Albanian territory, and there was danger of another Balkan war. The League threatened to impose an economic blockade on the aggressor, whereupon Yugoslavia agreed to accept the boundary line drawn by a delimitation committee of the League.

Two additional boundary disputes were brought to the attention of the League. A serious disagreement in 1924 between Great Britain and Turkey over Mesopotamia, rich in oil, was settled successfully by the action of the Council, and in 1925 the menace of war between Greece and Bulgaria was likewise removed.

When the disputants were small powers, the League was generally able to enforce its decision. When the dispute concerned a major power, the League was not so successful. The success obtained by the League in the British-Turkish dispute was not a conclusive test of its strength because the verdict had been favorable to a great power—Great Britain.

The Corfu incident. Perhaps the most significant test of the League's power in the decade following the Peace Conference was the Corfu incident of 1923, involving Greece and Italy. An international commission had been sent to the Balkans to settle the Greco-Albanian boundary line. During its labors four Italian members of the commission were killed in Greek territory by unknown assailants. Mussolini immediately dispatched a stiff ultimatum to Greece demanding a full apology, a salute to the Italian flag, an inquiry by Greece with the assistance of an Italian official, and the payment of a large reparation. Mussolini had been dictator of Italy at this time for less than a year and saw in the outrage an opportunity to obtain national glory and a diplomatic triumph for the Fascist régime. Greece refused to accept all the terms of the ultimatum, denouncing the demands as "outraging the honor and violating the sovereignty of the State," and appealed to the League. Mussolini thereupon ordered an Italian naval squadron to the Greek island of Corfu to bombard the harbor. Fifteen civilians were killed and many wounded, and Italian marines landed and took possession of the port. Mussolini let it be known that Italy would refuse to be bound by any action taken by the League.

Confronted by this defiance on the part of a great power, the League sought to escape from a serious situation by turning the dispute over to a council of ambassadors. This non-League body ordered a commission to investigate the controversy. In September 1923 the commission presented its report to the council of ambassadors without having discovered who had been guilty of the murders. The council then ordered Greece to pay Italy the sum of 50,000,000 lire. This amount was duly paid, and the Italian forces evacuated Corfu. War had been averted, but many members of the League Assembly were indignant over the handling of the whole affair because the League had allowed Italy to defy it. And many suspected that the evidence obtained by the commission of investigation did not warrant the imposition of such a large indemnity upon Greece. This failure of the League to function successfully in a dispute involving a major power in 1923 was a portent of what was to happen in the period of international anarchy following 1930.

Other League political activities. The effectiveness of the League as a peace agency following the Great War is debatable, but certain of its activities deserve only the highest praise. It supervised the exchange and repatriation of nearly half a million prisoners of war. More than a million Greek refugees expelled as a result of the Greco-Turkish War of 1922 were saved from starvation by the League. By 1928 it had been instrumental in erecting 76,000 houses in Greece for these refugees and settling 143,000 families in the land. Several important loans were floated by Greece under League auspices.

Following the war, Austria and Hungary were faced with financial bankruptcy. In 1922 it became evident that Austria was in danger of imminent economic collapse. Responding to an appeal for assistance, the Council immediately investigated the situation. In October 1922 the League announced that the governments of Great Britain, France, Italy, and Czechoslovakia would guarantee a loan of $135,000,000 to Austria, that a special bank to handle Austrian currency would be set up, and that during the period of the rehabilitation of Austrian finances the various measures recommended by the League to attain this end would be supervised by a commissioner-general who was to be a League official. Valuable assistance was also afforded Hungary. A fifty million dollar loan was obtained, and a special League official was sent to Hungary to supervise certain features of Hungarian finance. Other examples of the League of Nations' financial activities were foreign loans arranged for Bulgaria to enable her to take care of 200,000 refugees, loans to Estonia to assist her in placing her currency on a gold basis, and financial aid to the Free City of Danzig.

Of importance also in assisting the economic reconstruction of war-worn Europe was its work in administering the region of the Saar Basin and the Free City of Danzig. In the Saar until 1926 a pro-French commission created resentment and discontent among the inhabitants. Upon the insistence of Great Britain the situation was investigated, and a Canadian was appointed by the League to head the commission responsible for the administration of the Saar. From this point on, conditions in the Saar improved, and the German inhabitants relaxed their criticisms. In the Free City of Danzig a popular assembly of 120 members and a senate of 22 members were established by the League to administer the city. The port facilities of Danzig were placed under the administration of an equal number of Poles and German Danzigers.

Nonpolitical efforts of the League. More successful than its work in the political field were the League's efforts in the fields of health, humanitarian, and intellectual activity. The health organization at Geneva concerned itself in perfecting hygienic techniques to decrease epidemics in the various nations. Studies of the cause and control of such diseases as smallpox, anthrax, cancer, and tropical maladies were stimulated by the League. The League also investigated the existence of slavery in certain sections of the world, sought to control the traffic in dangerous drugs, and stood ready to offer assistance when great disasters brought suffering and destruction to any portion of the world's population. It published books and periodicals dealing with national and international problems of all kinds, broadcast important information, particularly in the field of health, from its own radio station, and generally was of extreme usefulness in its own technical work. The budget for all its activities, which was subscribed to principally by the members, was more than six million dollars a year.

Problems of Security and Disarmament

The search for security. Following the First World War there was a universal desire of nations for security. France hoped that she could make herself strong enough with the aid of allies and the League to discourage Germany forever from attacking her. Great Britain still retained her faith in a great navy to protect her. Germany was determined to build up her power again so that she could regain her former prestige. In central Europe new states such as Czechoslovakia and Poland, apprehensive of Germany and Russia, also sought to obtain security for themselves. Poland feared Germany and Russia from the start, while Czechoslovakia was worried about Hungarian revisionism immediately after 1920. Despite this common desire of all nations for security it soon became evident that what one nation regarded as security for herself was invariably considered by others as a menace to them.

German response to Versailles. What was the German conception of security? It could hardly be expected that she would remain content with an inferior role in Europe after having been the strongest military power on the continent from 1871 to 1914. Her population was a third larger than that of either France or Great Britain, and her industry was more efficient than that of any country in Europe with the exception, in certain instances, of Great Britain. She was resolved to break the iron ring of unfriendly powers that had been established at Versailles, to rearm, to cancel reparations, to get back her colonies, and to obtain some of the territory—such as the Saar Basin, Danzig, and the Polish Corridor—taken away from her in 1919. Germany never ceased believing that the Treaty of Versailles was unjust, and this belief helped shape her foreign policy to gain strength enough to force a revision of its clauses. When the Treaty was first presented to Germany in 1919, Philipp Scheidemann, the chancellor, declared:

"This treaty is, in the view of the German government, unacceptable, so unacceptable that I am unable to believe that this earth could bear such a document without a cry issuing from millions and millions of throats in all lands, without distinction of party: 'Away with this murderous scheme.'"

Middle Europe's dissatisfaction. In 1920 the attitude of Hungary, Bulgaria, Turkey, and Austria coincided in general terms with the German view. They, too, interpreted security as the right to rearm and regain some of the territory that had been taken away from them. Bulgaria and Hungary, especially, were determined to get back land that had gone to build up the new state of Yugoslavia and enlarge their old rival Rumania. In addition, Hungary had also been forced to cede territory to Czechoslovakia. Turkey was fairly content.

Of all the defeated nations, she alone (as will be shown in Chapter 3) had been able to defy the harsh peace terms imposed on her and obtain much fairer treatment in a new agreement. Austria was not so bellicose and bitter as Germany over her peace terms. But there were many Austrians who believed that their country's destiny lay in union with Germany. Furthermore, there were some in Austria who wanted to restore the House of Hapsburg and secure a union with Hungary.

Fear in France. If Germany and her former allies interpreted security as the right to break the peace terms of 1919, France believed that security meant a rigid enforcement of these same terms. The plain truth was that France was afraid. During the past half century German armies had tramped on French soil on two occasions. The disparity between the population of Germany and that of France gave the French great concern as they contrasted their thirty-nine million people with the sixty-two million across the Rhine. As Wilson once said, "France feels an almost superstitious awe of Germany." In view of these conditions, security in French eyes was to be achieved only by keeping Germany disarmed and surrounded by powerful neighbors allied to France.

The new and enlarged states of Europe were the logical allies of France. They, too, feared an Austro-German union and the menace of a rearmed Germany. Czechoslovakia had a few million Germans within her borders. Poland had been rebuilt out of areas previously seized by Russia, Germany, and Austria-Hungary. Rumania had absorbed a large number of Hungarians.

Great Britain's isolation. After the war Great Britain tended to return to the "splendid isolation" she had maintained throughout most of the nineteenth century. Her task had been accomplished when she had joined France and Russia in preventing Germany from becoming too powerful. Now Germany's naval might had been destroyed and her commercial menace to the British Empire removed. Great Britain, therefore, was not greatly concerned with her security. Protected by her great fleet, her far-flung empire and world commerce had little to fear, and as a great industrial power she was anxious that central Europe and Germany should achieve a measure of economic prosperity as soon as possible in order to furnish her with a market for manufactured goods.

Italy's jealousy. Italy was torn by conflicting diplomatic purposes. It was to her interest to uphold the Austrian treaty settlements of 1919, for Austria now constituted a convenient buffer state between Italy and Germany. But many features of the peace settlement nettled the Italians. They were angry with their former allies for not giving Italy a greater share of the spoils and were especially jealous of France's claims in the Mediterranean. During the postwar decade, then, Italy tried to run with the hare and hunt with the hounds. She usually sided with her former allies but was not averse to associating herself with Germany at times.

Thus it was that each of the nations gave a different meaning to "security." In their attempts to achieve it they sometimes acted alone and sometimes made alliances against those they feared. On several occasions they attempted to negotiate directly with their rivals. In the end none of the methods employed produced enduring results in spite of the pacts, alliances, and conferences inside and outside of the framework of the League.

French efforts to weaken Germany. In 1919 France in her quest for security had two objectives: to make Germany pay the costs of the war and to render Germany incapable of challenging the Treaty of Versailles. The first aim, discussed at length later in this chapter, led France to occupy the German territory of the Ruhr in 1923. This action brought about very strained relations between France and Germany during 1923 and 1924. The second aim led France to secure from Great Britain and the United States in June 1919 a guarantee that these two nations would aid France in the event of German aggression. Upon the return of Wilson to the United States, however, the American Senate refused to ratify this pact, whereupon the British also withdrew their ratification.

Overwhelmed by this blow to their hopes, the French set about obtaining allies on the continent. In 1920 a defensive alliance was made with Belgium. Overtures were then made to Poland. This country owed much to France. In 1920 General Weygand and a group of French military experts had helped save Poland from the Bolshevik armies, and at Paris in 1919 France had supported Polish claims in Silesia. After a preliminary agreement in 1921, France and Poland concluded an outright military alliance in 1922 directed against any future danger from Germany. This agreement was buttressed by large French loans and by the assistance of military experts from France.

After the visit to Paris of President Thomas Masaryk and Foreign Minister Benes of Czechoslovakia a treaty was signed with France in 1924. This pact pledged the signatories to take concerted measures in the event of a union between Germany and Austria or an attempt on the part of either Germany or Hungary to restore their ruling houses. Not content with these allies, the French foreign office negotiated similar pacts of alliance with Rumania in 1926 and with Yugoslavia in 1927. These smaller states not only made pacts with France but during 1920 and 1921 also made treaties of mutual assistance among themselves. This diplomatic bloc was known as the Little Entente, and its power rested upon extensive French loans and military collaboration. In place of the perilous diplomatic equilibrium created by the Triple Alliance and the Triple Entente in the years prior to 1914, the new system of alliances dominated by France now tipped the scales heavily in favor of the French (see map, pages 48-49).

The Locarno Conference and conciliation. For five years following the peace settlements, Europe was little more than an armed camp. In 1925 conditions suddenly improved in international affairs. Aristide Briand came to the foreign office in France. Gustav Stresemann held the same position in Germany, and in Great Britain foreign affairs were now handled by Sir Austen Chamberlain. All of these men believed in pursuing a policy of conciliation in European affairs. Stresemann had been a bitter foe of France during the war, but he was now eager to try cooperating with his former enemies. British statesmen for some time had been deploring France's harsh attitude toward Germany, and Briand in Paris was now ready to offer the olive branch to Berlin. In the spring of 1925 Stresemann proposed to Briand that France, Germany, Great Britain, and Italy should guarantee the existing Franco-German and German-Belgian frontiers and agree to settle their differences by arbitration and that Germany and her neighbors should conclude treaties of arbitration. This proposal paved

POSTWAR EUROPE

French alliances
encircling Germany

R.M.Chapin, Jr.

the way for a conference held during October of the same year in the little Swiss town of Locarno. For the first time since 1919 the distinction between conquered and conqueror seemed forgotten, and the German delegation was cordially received. Referring to previous conferences, a German statesman at Locarno said, "They treated us decently but never permitted us to forget that we were Huns."[7]

After twelve days of negotiation five treaties emerged from the conference, the most important being a treaty of mutual guarantee. Signed by Germany, Great Britain, Belgium, France, and Italy, this agreement guaranteed the existing frontiers along the Rhine (this was a reaffirmation of the provision in the Treaty of Versailles), provided for a demilitarized German zone fifty kilometers east of the Rhine, and pledged France, Germany, and Belgium not to invade or resort to war against each other except under certain specified conditions. In case of the violation of these pledges the nations signing the treaty agreed to assist the injured party. There were also four arbitration treaties and two bilateral treaties of guarantee.

The Locarno agreements heralded a new era in European affairs. Germany accepted an invitation to join the League of Nations, and there were good grounds for believing that the hatreds of the past war were now on the wane. In referring to the Locarno agreements, Briand eloquently declared:

"Peace for Germany and for France: that means that we have done with the long series of terrible and sanguinary conflicts which have stained the pages of history. We have done with black veils of mourning for sufferings that can never be appeased, done with war, done with brutal and sanguinary methods of settling our disputes. True, differences between us still exist, but henceforth it will be for the judge to declare the law. . . . Away with rifles, machine guns, cannon! Clear the way for conciliation, arbitration, peace!"[8]

The Kellogg-Briand Pact. Three years after the meeting at Locarno an event occurred which seemed to register another triumph for peace and international good will. This was the appearance of the Kellogg-Briand Pact, a general plan for the renunciation of war. Getting the nations of the world to agree to outlaw war was first initiated as a practical movement by a Chicago lawyer whose ideas

were presented for the first time in the *New Republic* in March 1918 and whose program to outlaw war secured the support of many eminent men in America.

In April 1927 Briand made a speech in Paris proposing that war be renounced or outlawed between France and the United States. Encouraged by several prominent Americans, Briand sent the draft of a treaty incorporating these ideas to Washington. Mr. Kellogg, then secretary of state, persuaded Briand to make the treaty cover all the great powers. After several months of negotiation, the representatives of fifteen states gathered at the Quai d'Orsay (the location of the French foreign office) to sign the pact. In 1932 President Hoover announced that the treaty had been signed by sixty-two nations. While the Kellogg-Briand Pact (August 27, 1928) had its origin in the movement for the outlawry of war, it merely provided for the renunciation of war as an instrument of national policy. Moreover, there were no provisions for enforcing the agreements made in the pact.

Disarmament proposals. Article VIII of the League's Covenant plainly stated that it was the intention of the members to reduce arms to the lowest point consistent with security. It further empowered the Council of the League to formulate plans for disarmament. The Article also condemned the manufacture of munitions by private enterprise and declared that, as a means of avoiding suspicion and fear, the various members of the League should keep each other informed of their armament plans. The question of disarmament was raised in 1922, but any progress in this direction was blocked by the passage of a resolution stating that no disarmament would be possible until the members were guaranteed security and protection from attack. Thereupon the League attempted to provide security for its members, and when this failed, it tried once more to achieve results by a direct method of limitation. The Council, as stipulated in the Covenant, created a permanent advisory commission on armaments whose members were mainly military experts. These specialists floundered in a maze of military technicalities and made little progress.

When the sixth Assembly of the League met in 1925, it was the common feeling at Geneva that something had to be done about disarmament. Germany had been disarmed in

"It is for peace that this hammer works," read the caption on this French cartoon published in postwar times. The Frenchman (probably Briand) smashes his guns while the English (personified by Sir Austen Chamberlain, left) and the Germans (represented by Stresemann) wait their turn.

1919 with the understanding that other nations would follow suit. The Assembly therefore requested the Council to make a preparatory study of the problem to pave the way for an international conference on disarmament. A preparatory commission was consequently set up to meet at Geneva in 1926.

At the end of a year's study, Great Britain and France each presented a draft convention to serve as a basis for further discussion at meetings of the commission. These tentative proposals for disarmament clashed on nearly every vital point. In counting soldiers France objected to the inclusion of trained reserves, while states which depended on volunteer armies maintained that reserves should be counted as part of a nation's military power. After much wrangling over this question of "When is a soldier not a soldier?" the Commission was again divided on problems relating to naval limitation. The United States and Great Britain wanted total-tonnage restriction, plus a definite tonnage limit for each type of ship. This was opposed by France and Italy. Soviet Russia proposed complete disarmament, a position supported by Germany and Turkey. This proposal did

not get very far because the English delegates were suspicious of the Russian government's sincerity. Germany, in the meantime, became more and more rebellious. She had already been disarmed, and she demanded to know why her neighbors could not agree to reduce their armaments. Finally, in 1930 a general scheme for an international disarmament conference was adopted, but so many reservations were made that few people hoped for much in the way of accomplishment when the conference convened.

Progress in the direction of naval disarmament was a little more encouraging. At the end of the war a naval race between Great Britain and the United States was in prospect. Up to this time England had followed the policy of maintaining a fleet equal to the combined navies of the next two naval powers. Following the war she accepted naval parity with the United States, whom she regarded as a friendly power. Differences of opinion, however, still persisted. In 1921, the same year that Great Britain dropped her two-power standard, President Harding called a conference at Washington to consider the problem of disarmament and that of the Pacific.

The Washington disarmament conference. The Washington Conference was a dramatic event in international relations. Apparently without any warning, Secretary of State Charles Evans Hughes dramatically proposed that Great Britain, Japan, and the United States should together scrap seventy-nine capital ships. The United States would have made the greatest sacrifice, thirty of these vessels being hers. This proposal was too radical for adoption, but it served as an effective means of getting the discussion started. In all, seven treaties were signed at the conference, two of which concerned naval armaments. The total tonnage of aircraft carriers and capital ships was limited for the United States, Great Britain, Japan, Italy, and France, in such a way as to make the ratio of naval strength in this class of vessel 5:5:3:1.67:1.67. The powers agreed to a ten-year naval holiday in capital ships and agreed further that no battleship was to be built unless it replaced a vessel twenty years old.

Hence the Washington Conference registered a definite advance in naval disarmament. The largest type ships were kept down to a reasonable limit, but much was left undone. France refused to discuss the limitation of submarines, and no limit was placed upon the building of smaller type naval units, such as light cruisers and destroyers.

The Geneva and London conferences. In 1927 President Coolidge called another conference to convene at Geneva. France and Italy refused to take part in the deliberations. At this conference a serious dispute occurred between the United States and Great Britain on the question of cruisers. Having few naval bases, the United States pressed for the limitation of cruisers, which in her opinion ought to be of a large type. With bases all over the world, England maintained that she ought to have small cruisers upon which there should be no limitation in number.

In 1930 another naval conference met in London. This meeting was signalized by a bitter dispute between France and Italy, wherein Italy was unsuccessful in securing naval parity with France. The United States, Great Britain, and Japan settled the problem of relative cruiser strength among themselves, and agreements were also made as to tonnage in cruisers and submarines. That the work of the conference did not rest upon too

firm a foundation is apparent from the appearance of the famous "escalator clause," in the treaty. This gave any one of the signatories the right to increase its tonnage of any class of ships in the event it believed that its security demanded such action.

Europe's "high period." The years from 1925 to 1929 have been called Europe's diplomatic high period. Germany entered the League, economic prosperity appeared to be returning to Europe, the frontier along the Rhine was settled by the Locarno agreement, and the nations of the world renounced war. These achievements in postwar international affairs were primarily the work of three men: Gustav Stresemann, German foreign minister from 1923 to 1929; Aristide Briand, French foreign minister almost continuously from 1925 to 1930; and Sir Austen Chamberlain, foreign minister of Great Britain from 1924 to 1929. Stresemann echoed the sentiments of all these statesmen when he said, "Each one of us must first be a citizen of his own country —a good Frenchman, a good Englishman, a good German—as a member of his own nation, but each one also is a citizen of Europe, linked together by the great conception of civilization which imbues our continent."

Undercurrents of trouble. The promise of Europe's high period, however, was not fulfilled. There were many straws in the wind in 1930 indicating that progress in the direction of international amity and cooperation was only superficial. Germany loudly and repeatedly protested against the failure of her neighbors to disarm and simultaneously proceeded to rearm secretly. She had also expected that Locarno and her entry into the League would mean changes in the Treaty of Versailles. France, however, thought that German acceptance of Locarno meant that Germany had resigned herself to the terms of Versailles. Nothing could have been further from the truth.

When the Kellogg-Briand Pact was signed, the nations of the world were lauded for their change of heart. A careful examination of the treaty hardly justifies such enthusiasm. The pact was a declaration only. It contained no provisions for its enforcement. So many informal reservations were made by the various nations as to render it meaningless. Wars of self-defense were not renounced or wars in fulfillment of obligations under a military alliance. Further, such states as Great Britain and the United States both retained freedom of action to exercise force in maintaining their vital interests in certain regions of the world. The United States, for example, would not permit the Kellogg-Briand Pact to interfere with the Monroe Doctrine. Hence a nation could interpret almost any war as being either defensive or related to its vital interests.

By 1930 it was apparent that in the field of politics the statesmen of the world had fallen far short of the expectations of the war-weary world of 1919 and that neither security nor disarmament was in sight.

Problems of Reconstruction and Economic Stability

The cost of the war. The most obvious of the economic consequences of the First World War was the tremendous cost. In 1918 the average daily cost was $224,000,000, or about ten million dollars every hour in the day. The total cost was estimated to be $337,000,000,000. The significance of this sum is not so much in the fact that it had been spent but rather that it had been invested in destruction rather than in the creation of equipment capable of producing wealth.

The shift to a peace economy. The armistice found the world's commercial and industrial structure geared to a war basis. There was an urgent need for getting back to a peacetime economy, which meant the production of peacetime goods instead of munitions, the demobilization of millions of soldiers, and their absorption in the business structure.

It was not easy to return to the prosperous and stable world economy that had been operating before 1914. The conflict had brought about many changes in world trade. Europe in particular had suffered a serious decline in its share of the world's commerce because of war blockades, the reduction of purchasing power on the part of consumers, the loss of shipping and other transportation facilities, and the capture of overseas markets during the war by the United States, Latin America, and Japan. This loss was keenly felt by Germany and Great Britain.

The huge increase in the public debt was a further economic consequence of the war. Germany's national debt increased twenty times between 1913 and 1918 and that of France and Great Britain also mounted, although to a lesser extent. These increases were accompanied in many nations by the circulation of large amounts of paper money not backed by adequate reserves. Tension sprang up between economic groups in the various nations. War profiteers were particularly detested by the people, and labor unions that frequently had made important gains in wages during the war were determined not to give up these advantages when it ceased. For a brief period many of these economic problems were obscured by an artificial postwar boom from 1919 to 1920. The peak of prosperity was reached in 1920. It was followed by a diminution of world trade and industrial activity. Strikes, unemployment, and other industrial problems multiplied, and for the next five years the nations, particularly in Europe, tried to extricate themselves from this economic morass.

The statesmen at Paris had paid little heed to matters of economics. The existence of world economic unity and interdependence had been forgotten or disregarded in the preoccupation with political matters. National boundaries were multiplied by the creation of new states and soon became obstacles to the flow of goods. Moreover, impossible economic burdens were placed upon Germany, one of the world's most important industrial nations.

German reparations. The Treaty of Versailles stipulated that Germany was to pay a preliminary sum of about five billion dollars. In the meantime, the reparations commission was to determine what the total reparations payments should be. By 1921 Germany claimed she had paid, in money and goods, the equivalent of the preliminary sum demanded in the treaty. The Allied powers answered that less than half of the necessary payment had been made. As a means of bringing pressure upon Germany, three of her cities were added to the area of Allied occupation, and a customs wall was erected around the Rhineland in order to obtain additional payments from Germany. The reparations commission (in 1921) fixed the total German reparations as $32,000,000,000. The reparations payments were apportioned among the various Allied nations, France being given 52 per cent and the British Empire 22 per cent.

In August 1921, Germany made a payment of $250,000,000. This reacted disastrously upon her currency system. It was commonly believed that the reparations were impossibly high and that higher tariffs the world over were keeping out German goods. Furthermore Germany had already lost many of her most important economic resources. In 1922 some relief was granted her by the Allies, and she then asked them to extend this relief until the end of 1924. The alarming economic conditions prevailing in central Europe, and Germany in particular, caused Lloyd George to support this idea. Great Britain believed that her own economic difficulties could not be removed until prosperity was reëstablished in Germany.

The French, however, were outraged at Germany's request. They estimated that France had been spending $5700 a minute to restore her devastated regions and pay war pensions while Germany had been paying reparations at the rate of only $381 a minute. The French believed that Germany was able to pay and was deliberately seeking to escape her obligations. Raymond Poincaré, the French prime minister, thought that although France had won the war there was a danger she might lose the peace.

France invades the Ruhr. Searching for a justification to employ force in compelling Germany to make the full reparations payments, Poincaré discovered that the Germans had not delivered to France the stipulated number of telegraph poles as laid down in the Versailles Treaty. Germany was likewise in arrears in the matter of coal and cattle deliveries. This default was termed microscopic by the British, who impolitely referred to Poincaré as "Monsieur Shylock." Undeterred by this British opposition, French, Belgian, and Italian troops marched into the Ruhr district of Germany in January 1923. A sorry state of affairs then ensued. The Germans were scandalized by having French black colonial troops quartered in their towns. The French were determined that the inhabitants should work the industries and mines of the Ruhr for the benefit of France. Defying the French army of occupation, the Germans went on a general strike. All economic life stopped, and many German officials were thrown into prison by the French authorities. Nothing hardened the resolve of Germans to revise the Treaty of Versailles more than this invasion of the Ruhr.

During the winter of 1923-1924 France endeavored to establish a separatist state in the Rhineland which the Germans called a "revolver republic." Subsidized by the French, political agitators were shipped into the Ruhr from all parts of Germany and encouraged to carry on a separatist movement which, if successful, would create a buffer state between Germany and France.

The chaotic conditions in the Ruhr gave the *coup de grace* to the German economic system. The currency completely collapsed. Inflation skyrocketed the marks into the stratosphere. In January 1923, one American dollar was worth 8695 marks; in November of the same year it took 6,666,666,666,667 marks to equal one dollar! Public opinion all over the world was shocked at Poincaré's strong-armed tactics in the Ruhr, and Great Britain was particularly critical. The French, meanwhile, were learning that they "could not dig German coal with French bayonets." Following the fall from power of Poincaré in 1924, the French government signified its desire to settle its difficulties with Germany, whose leaders were equally anxious to negotiate.

The Dawes Plan for reparations. An international committee of economic experts was accordingly set up under the chairmanship of the American banker Charles Dawes to examine the whole reparations problem. In the fall of 1924 the Dawes Plan came into operation. No figure was set for the total reparations bill, but the individual payments were decreased and extended over a longer period. A large loan was also floated to aid Germany's economic recovery. On her part Germany ended her currency inflation, and the French reciprocated by evacuating the Ruhr.

The war debt problem. The adoption of the Dawes Plan and the evacuation of the Ruhr eased the tension in Europe. Germany recommenced her reparations payments, made possible only by huge loans from abroad, chiefly America. Referring to the Dawes Plan, James Ramsay MacDonald optimistically declared, "Now we are agreed. Satan only can divide us."

This soon proved to be a vain hope. The reparations burden continued to be denounced by Germans as excessive, and there were many in Europe who shared this view. But the Allied powers would not reduce German payments unless the United States reduced their obligations to her, known as the war debts. During and after the war more than ten billion dollars had been loaned by the government of the United States to the Allies for the prosecution of the war and for purposes of reconstruction. Great Britain, who owed the United States over four billion dollars, had also extended credit to her European allies amounting to more than ten billion dollars. She therefore proposed in 1922 that there should be a general cancellation of all war debts. To this proposal the United States would not agree, but between 1923 and 1925 a series of debt settlements, involving in certain instances generous reductions of interest but not of principal, was made with the debtor European nations. The total amount to be paid to the United States by her debtors was $22,188,000,000.

The question of the war debts proved to be one of the most serious problems in post-war international relations. The Allied powers contended that reparations and war debts were inseparably connected.

They felt that, if Germany's reparations payments were reduced, a similar reduction should be made in the debts owed to the United States. Our stand on the debt question, whether wise or not, undoubtedly made France determined to exact the full reparations bill from Germany. Most Americans were apparently not interested in this phase of the question and accepted Coolidge's comment, "They hired the money, didn't they?"

Tariff Barriers and the War Debts

The disappearance of free trade. During the nineteenth century in spite of the growth of tariffs one could still speak of a world economy in which free trade existed throughout much of the British empire and in which people, goods, and capital moved in comparative freedom over national frontiers in other parts of the world.

Immediately after the war, barriers, mainly in the form of tariffs, began to appear as obstacles to international trade. Instead of buying manufactured goods or commodities where they could be produced most cheaply, nations tried to manufacture or grow them at home even though the cost was greater. They strove for self-sufficiency, or what the economists call autarchy. Those who had suffered from an inability to secure vital foodstuffs and other materials from old sources of supply now determined not to find themselves in the same predicament again. The search for national political security in postwar Europe was accompanied by an attempt to found economic nationalism as well.

The old freedom of international trade was also hampered by the gradual weakening of the international gold standard. During the war many nations had been forced to go off the gold standard. Paper currencies of doubtful value were created, and stability was never completely regained for any great period.

The effect of rising tariffs and other barriers on world trade was particularly strong in the general interplay of international finance and more especially in the problem of reparations and war debts. This happened largely because of the revolution in the relative position of the great powers as debtors or creditors in the field of international finance. Before 1914 France, England, and Germany were all creditor nations with billions of dollars invested over the world, but the United States was a debtor nation to the extent of five billion dollars. After the war the United States became a creditor nation. Germany also changed her position, in this case from creditor to debtor, when the reparations payments were imposed upon her. For the former allies of the United States, outside perhaps of Great Britain, to pay their war debts from accumulated capital (that is, investments made abroad, or gold and silver) was not possible. The only other course available was to sell goods. The United States, however, did not want foreign goods to compete with those produced in her own factories.

United States tariffs. The revolution in the world creditor-debtor situation demanded a shift in trade relationships in order that the debtors could obtain funds to meet their heavy obligations. Unfortunately this shift was not made. Tariffs were raised, and the United States—the greatest creditor nation—led the movement. In 1922 our moderate Underwood Tariff Act was superseded by the Fordney-Mc-Cumber Tariff Act, which levied the highest tariff rates in our history. This act had three results, according to most economists: it fostered monopolies at home, it made it difficult for our former allies to pay their war debts, and it brought on tariff reprisals from other countries. Between 1926 and 1930 fifty-seven important tariff revisions were made by the nations of the world, and in most instances the rates were raised. The climax came in 1930 when, contrary to the advice of President Hoover, objections from the American Bankers Association, and a vigorous protest from 1028 American economists, Congress enacted the Smoot-Hawley Tariff Act, which was described by a League of Nations committee as the highest in the world with the single exception of Spain. Within two years twenty-five nations retaliated with discriminatory tariffs against us and against each other, and world trade steadily decreased in volume. In particular, American foreign trade seriously declined.

It should be noted that economists and other groups which opposed the Smoot-Hawley Tariff Act were not attacking the principle of protection in the United States. Although in theory free trade might be a desirable goal for the nations of the world to try ultimately to achieve, under existing circumstances some protection was considered essential. What was criticized was the mounting rate of the tariff in the United States, a great creditor nation.

During the 1920's our former allies paid their war debt installments to us, the funds for this purpose being obtained mainly from German reparations payments. Germany, in turn, was able to meet her reparations payments only because millions of dollars from the United States and Great Britain had been made available in private loans. In view of our high tariff, it was only this economic ring-around-the-rosy that kept reparations and war-debt payments going.

In 1929 Germany's creditors set up the Young Plan to supersede the Dawes Plan. The new plan, which was to run until 1988, provided that Germany should pay a principal sum of $8,800,000,000. The experts who drew up the new schedule of payments believed that Germany would have no difficulty in meeting her obligations thereafter. But within two years the whole world was reeling from the impact of the worst depression of all time, in which the entire structure of reparations and war debts collapsed. Nevertheless, one significant organization developed out of the Young Plan—The Bank for International Settlements. It acted as a channel for the payment of reparations and distribution to the various governments, and although this function ceased when the payments ceased, it continued to serve as a means whereby central banks in various countries could cooperate.

Depression and Economic Nationalism

The collapse of world economy. By 1926 there were signs of a forthcoming collapse of the world economy. Following the economic depression of 1920-1921 in Europe there had been some improvement, but by 1926 unemployment began to be widespread in many European countries. Throughout the world production was in excess of demand, and an alarming glut developed in the wheat, rubber, tin, and copper markets. The condition of the United States was an outstanding exception to the general trend. Prices increased, consumer demand kept pace with supply, and business confidence was unbounded. A wave of optimistic speculation occurred on the stock market. From February 1928 to September 1929 the value of stocks on the New York Stock Exchange increased fifty-one billion dollars.

As long as prosperity existed in the United States, the forces of economic disaster in the rest of the world, especially in Europe, were arrested. American capital in large amounts was readily obtainable by foreign businessmen. These loans, as already noted, were the foundation of the whole system of reparations and war debts, and they also enabled Germany to expand and modernize her industrial production facilities.

The prosperity of the United States, however, was more apparent than real. A large volume of unemployment persisted throughout the 1920's, and an acute condition in agriculture made it increasingly difficult for many farmers to remain on the land when their commodities brought lower and lower prices. The buying power of consumers had been kept up in part by installment buying, much of the wealth was unevenly distributed, foreign trade was decreasing, and stock speculation had become a mania. The crash came in

October 1929, and in a few weeks stocks declined 40 per cent in value, fortunes were wiped out, business confidence was blasted, and the demand for goods was seriously curtailed.

The stock crash had repercussions in Europe. Many short-term American loans in Austria were called in, and this demand threatened the famous Austrian Credit Anstalt Bank with failure. In June 1931 this was averted only by grant of a large credit by the Bank of England. Meanwhile Germany was confronted with a serious economic crisis as foreign investors, disturbed at the trend of events, began to call in their loans. Between July 1930 and July 1931 the German government was forced to issue dozens of emergency decrees, but the economic situation became more and more desperate. By June 1931, the Reichsbank had lost 40 per cent of its gold reserve. In the face of impending disaster President Hoover in June 1931, succeeded in obtaining a moratorium of one year on all intergovernmental debts. In July 1932, at the Lausanne Conference, German reparations payments were practically canceled, the creditors agreeing that future reparations should be reduced to $714,-000,000. This drastic step was taken with the hope that the American government would also make a substantial concession in reducing war debts. But our government refused to concede that there was any logical connection between reparations and war debts. And as the depression deepened, our debtors refused to continue their war debt installments. France and other debtors refused outright in 1932, Great Britain and four other nations made "token payments" for a time, then stopped entirely in 1934, and only Finland continued to meet her schedule of payments. Meanwhile Germany had stopped her payment of reparations.

Budget deficits, unemployment, bank failures, decline in industrial production, collapse in commodity prices, and stagnation in trade characterized the world economic picture from 1930 to 1933. The people of many countries suffered from a lowered standard of living and frequently from dire want. This economic collapse was largely the result of conditions created by the First World War—more specifically, to the disturbing effects of the reparations and war debts muddle and the growth of economic nationalism.

Experiments in international finance. During the height of the depression, from 1930 to 1933, each nation tried earnestly to reduce its imports and increase its exports in order to improve its economic position. Competitive devaluation of currency played an important role in this international economic warfare. Japan in particular felt impelled to increase her exports, and to assist in gaining this objective, she depreciated the yen. This move meant that other currencies now had relatively more gold back of them. Being more valuable than the yen, the dollar and the British pound now could command or buy more Japanese goods; or, in other words, the price of Japanese exports was lowered.

Devaluation brought only temporary advantage in most instances. Other countries could play the same game, and so most countries devaluated their currency. In 1934 the United States reduced the gold content of the dollar by about forty per cent. All nations tried to increase exports and at the same time reduce imports. Quota systems were put into operation to control the influx of goods from abroad, and tariffs were boosted to even higher levels. In 1932 Great Britain, after almost a century of free trade, enacted a high tariff. In the summer of 1933, at the World Economic Conference in London, Great Britain, the various dominions, and the colonies agreed to continue the principle of imperial preference initiated at the Ottawa Imperial Economic Conference of the previous year. Imperial preference provided for lower tariffs within the empire than were given to outside nations. The net effect was to encourage trade already in existence between members of the empire but to make it more difficult for nonimperial trade to hurdle the tariff barriers now set up around the British Empire.

The abandonment of gold. Before the First World War, the flow of goods from one country to another had meant that in the last analysis each country imported about the same value of goods and services as it exported. When this balance of international payments was disturbed, a nation would export gold to her creditors to make up the difference. The loss of gold was not serious, however, as creditor nations were eager to lend capital. If a country had an unfavorable trade balance in one area of the world it was quite likely to be more than made up in another.

The depression, by preventing the natural flow of world trade, caused nations to husband their gold reserves. This trend was also strengthened by the fact that the world's gold supply was most unequally divided: the United States had more than half, and another quarter of the gold was held by Great Britain and France. By going off gold, nations could devalue their currencies, thus encouraging foreign buying and stimulating exports. These conditions led to the abandonment of the gold standard by many nations, including Great Britain in 1931 and the United States in 1933. Without gold as the controlling medium of exchange in world trade the practice of barter became more and more prevalent in international trade. This technique was especially utilized by Germany.

Attempts at recovery. The disastrous consequences of world depression led to the calling of the International Economic Conference in London in 1932. Here a report was presented showing that thirty million persons were then unemployed in the world, that the price of raw materials had depreciated more than fifty per cent, and that wheat in particular had dropped to the lowest price in the last four centuries. Little was accomplished, however, by the delegates in London. Currencies were not stabilized, the reparations and war-debt problem was not ironed out, and nothing was done to encourage the return of economic good will among the nations.

During the next six years, 1933 to 1939, recovery was sought not through cooperation but rather by attempts on the part of each nation to fend for itself. Most of them refused to buy except what was absolutely essential, yet all of them tried to achieve the maximum of exports. Seeking economic recovery, particular nations experimented with various national programs—the British with tariffs and subsidized agriculture and the United States with the New Deal. In other countries more drastic politico-economic programs were launched. Most important, the dire economic emergency was seized upon as a justification, and perhaps an excuse, for programs of military aggression.

Capitalism on Trial

Capitalist economy questioned. The depression had serious effects not only upon the international economic structure but upon the domestic economies of the various nations as well. Confusion reigned in economic relations between countries, and within the boundaries of nations people became dismayed and embittered by their misfortunes. In particular, there was growing criticism of capitalism. In the fifty years before 1914 capitalism had been subjected to a certain amount of regulation to adjust gross inequalities of wealth, assure some measure of economic security to the workers, and protect the general public from fraud. These reforms were useful to a certain degree, but they were largely nullified by the disturbing consequences of the First World War—by unemployment, poverty, and business depression. Many critics of capitalism in the postwar period decided that tinkering with the old system would not do and that capitalism must be superseded by an entirely new system.

World depression produced radical criticism and also led many with moderate views to admit that serious weaknesses existed in capitalism. Five weaknesses were singled out.

The business cycle. The first criticism aimed at capitalism was the persistence of the business cycle. Under the capitalist system, economic activity has followed a definite rhythmic pattern in which periods of economic prosperity and collapse alternate. In America, for example, there have been fourteen important business cycles since 1875, and each follows the same course of events: (1) prosperity, (2) the crisis, (3) depression, (4) recovery, and a return to prosperity which forms the first phase of another cycle. Without warning to most people the "crash" comes with suddenness and intensity, bringing unemployment, sweeping away savings, and even reducing millions to the point of starvation. Then out of depression springs recovery, and another business cycle is born. Much study has been given to this cyclical aspect of business, and many theories have been advanced in explanation. Some economists find the cause in fluctuations of the climate; others emphasize the rather intangible psychological factor of periodic waves of business optimism and pessimism. Perhaps the most important school, however, sees the business cycle with all its attendant evils as a natural outcome of the capitalistic system. The workers produce more goods than can be consumed with their inadequate wages. Surplus stocks of goods pile up, and a depression results. This last school sees a more or less planned economy as the only means of checking the ups and downs of business.

Unemployment. Unemployment was the second serious evil in the existing economic system. In 1929 it was estimated that in the past ten years there had been an average of 2,300,000 persons unemployed in the United States. Numerous factors explain this serious condition: (1) cyclical unemployment because of periodic depressions, (2) "stop-watch unemployment" caused by the introduction of efficiency-expert controls into industry, (3) amalgamation unemployment brought about by the fusion of small business units into one great merger, and (4) above all, technological unemployment through the displacement of man-power by new machines. A United States Senate committee of investigation, in referring to technological unemployment, declared that "seven men now do the work which formerly required 60 to perform in casting pig iron; 2 men now do the work which formerly required 128 to perform in loading pig iron; 1 man replaces 42 in operating open-hearth furnaces. A brickmaking machine in Chicago makes 40,000 bricks per hour. It formerly took one man eight hours to make 4501." This explains why, in spite of the fact that American industry increased its productivity at least fifty per cent between 1919 and 1929, there was a definite decline in the number of workers employed. During the period of apparent prosperity in the United States from 1923 to 1928 there was a drop of twelve per cent in employment in the manufacturing industries.

Control by a few. A third serious evil in the economic structure was the increasing tendency for business under finance capitalism to be controlled by a few great corporations which in turn were dominated by a relatively few stockholders. It has been shown that out of 200 of the largest corporations in the United States only 0.7 per cent control half of the corporation assets, one third of the business wealth, and about one fifth of the national wealth. Further, within these great corporations power is often wielded by a small inner group. Frequently the possession of as little as five per cent of a corporation's total stock permits the holders to dictate policy and also wax fat on the profits.

The maldistribution of wealth. Closely connected with this evil was the fourth problem, the unequal distribution of the wealth. It is generally agreed that the standard of living of the people of America is higher than that in any other part of the world. Yet in 1918 the following figures show a surprising maldistribution of the national income. In this year 152 persons received a million dollars or more in income, and 5442 received incomes of one hundred thousand dollars or more. Less than 900,000 got more than five thousand dollars, and only five and one-quarter million persons obtained more than two thousand dollars. Thirty-two and one-quarter million citizens received incomes of less than two thousand dollars. Recent studies show little improvement. In 1928 more than sixty per cent of American families received less than two thousand dollars a year in income, yet the United States government has estimated that no family of five can maintain itself reasonably well on an income of less than two thousand dollars. The critics of the capitalist system especially emphasize the twin evils of unemployment and inequality of wealth and point out how illogical poverty and want are in countries such as America, where foodstuffs are abundant and where the factories could produce an output of goods sufficient for all.

Industrial warfare. The fifth great weakness of the capitalist system was adjudged to be industrial warfare. In most of the industrialized countries of the world a continuous struggle has been going on between the workers and the owners of business. To obtain wage increases the workers have organized unions. This collective action has been met by management through the formation of trade and manufacturing associations in order to present a united front. Strikes by the workers have been answered by lockouts by the employers, and the use of strikebreakers by management has led to picketing by the strikers. Often bloodshed resulted. There has been no neutral body armed with sufficient authority to say what a fair return to management and labor should be in most of the industrialized countries of the world. The only alternative was industrial warfare, which utilized the same weapons of violence and might as were employed in the international sphere in disputes between sovereign states. It is true that certain countries, especially Australia and

New Zealand, were experimenting with compulsory arbitration in labor disputes, but the progress was slow.

By the end of the first decade after the war, neither nations nor men had found lasting economic security or prosperity. The nations of the world were growing farther and farther apart economically after a half century of growing economic interdependence, and people everywhere began to question capitalism.

Summary

The most interesting as well as most promising development in the decade following the First World War was the establishment of the League of Nations. During the decade from 1920 to 1930 the League acted successfully on several occasions to remove threats to peace. When a crisis arose involving a great power, however, as in the Corfu affair with Italy, the League was less successful. On the whole the record of the League in trying to establish and maintain world peace was not spectacular, but there were sufficient achievements to justify some optimism for its ultimate success. If the political activities of the League were not all they might have been, in the realm of nonpolitical affairs a much more convincing record appeared. Work in the field of public health, the efforts of the International Labor Conference to improve the conditions of labor the world over, control of the drug traffic, and many other solid achievements all testified to the League's contributions in eliminating evils which had been obstructing man's social welfare.

Encouraging as some of the League's activities were, this new body did not bring about the elimination of power politics. France, in particular, confronted by a restless and potentially powerful Germany, put her trust in her army and in a great system of alliances. Great Britain put her main reliance in her fleet. As the first postwar decade ended, it was obvious that international good will and the prospects for a lasting peace were both on the wane. Several disarmament conferences failed, and Germany resented the refusal of the great powers to rectify some of the injustices of Versailles. Then, too, she wanted to regain her former position of prestige and power and strove by every means possible to gain that end.

In the sphere of international economics, recovery in the postwar period was considerably hindered by the problem of reparations and war debts. The strain placed upon international finance by this debt tangle had much to do with the intensification of economic nationalism and the rise of tariff walls. This in turn helped bring on the world economic depression which further increased economic rivalry between nations. International trade decreased, quotas and tariffs were used to restrict imports, and devaluation was resorted to in order to increase exports. The depression also had serious repercussions in the sphere of domestic economy. As unemployment increased and actual poverty and want became widespread, an increasing chorus of criticism was raised against the capitalist system.

If international cooperation had failed to secure a signal success in the political realm, the same failure in the early 1930's was even more evident in the collapse of international trade. The statesmen of the world had failed both to remove the factors that had brought on the First World War in 1914 and, equally disturbing, they had not succeeded in re-creating the relatively free world economy that had characterized business before 1914. This twin failure, in politics and economics, had much to do with the rise of such new national political systems as Russian Communism, Italian Fascism, and German Nazism.

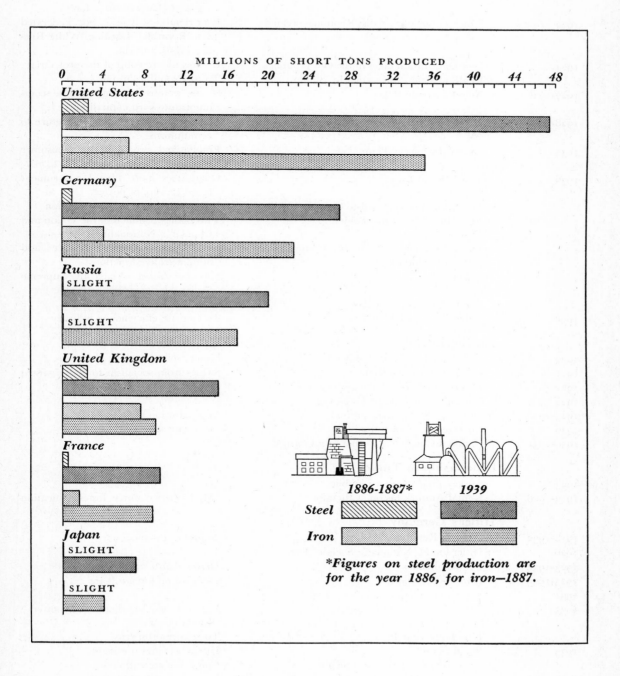

MILLIONS OF SHORT TONS PRODUCED

Figures on steel production are for the year 1886, for iron—1887.

Communism in Russia

1917	Revolution	Provisional government under Kerenski
	Lenin's coup d'état	Bloodshed, massacre of czar and family
1918-1920	War Communism period	Allies cooperate with whites, Trotsky organizes Communistic forces
1922	Union of Soviet Socialist Republics created	Four republics: Russian Soc. Federated Sov. Republic, Ukraine, White Russia, Transcaucasia
1924	New constitution takes in the new republics	Creates dictatorship of the proletariat
	Death of Lenin, succeeded by Stalin	Trotsky's ambitions fail
1927-1928	New Economic Policy	Strategic retreat from absolute communism toward capitalism
1928-1933	First Five-Year Plan	Plan for industrialization and return to communism
1933	Second Five-Year Plan	Emphasized production of consumer goods and electrification
1936	Third Constitution	Guarantees more liberal government based on rep. of powers
	Federal union increased to eleven republics	R.S.F.S.R. has dominant position
	Legislature—Supreme Soviet	Two bodies: Council of the Union and Council of Nationalities
	Executive bodies—Presidium, Council of People's Commissars	Latter has highest executive and administrative functions
	Judiciary	Supreme Court elected by Supreme Soviet
	Stalin's "purge" of leaders	
1938	Third Five-Year Plan	To increase efficiency of industry

Fascism in Italy

1920	Treaty of Rapallo with Yugoslavia	Fiume, seized earlier, given up
1921	Fascist party organized	Swings from socialism to conservatism
1922	Mussolini asked to form government	
1924	Mussolini makes himself dictator	
1925-1926	Fascist party becomes supreme	No opposition allowed
1926	Government syndicalized	Corporate state established
1930-1931	National Council of Corporations formed	

Dictatorship in Turkey

1923	Turkey proclaimed a republic	
1923-1928	Kemal Ataturk becomes dictator	Modernizes country, fosters education

Hitler's Germany

1918-1932	Weimar Republic	Attempt at democracy
1920	Hitler founds Nationalist Socialist Party	
1923-1924	Financial chaos	Dawes Plan
1925-1929	Period of prosperity	Founded on foreign loans
1931	Economic collapse	
1933	Hitler becomes chancellor	Voted four-year dictatorial power—Enabling Act
	First Four-Year Plan	To restore prosperity
1934	Blood purge	Hitler becomes president
	Persecution of Jews and religion	Control of education
1936	Second Four-Year Plan	To set up autarchic state

CHAPTER 3

New Patterns in Statecraft

ONE of the immediate results of the First
World War was the apparent triumph of democracy. In 1918 there was a firm belief that
the extension of this form of government would bring peace and prosperity to the world.
Hence out of the ruins of war in Europe there emerged a dozen or more new democratic states, including Germany, all with parliaments and other adjuncts of democracy.

The world as remade by the statesmen of 1919, however, soon proved to be unsatisfactory for the struggling new governments. The preceding chapter showed that developments from 1920 to 1930 largely added up to two failures: first, failure to reduce national
rivalries and to substitute an effective system of collective security in the hands of the
League of Nations; second, failure to remove barriers to world trade and international cooperation in the sphere of world economics.

It was partly out of this unhappy situation and partly out of the First World War
itself that new patterns of government emerged. Confronted by unemployment and
starvation and often by the ineffectiveness of their elected leaders, the people of some
countries turned to totalitarian régimes. These countries had certain basic similarities.
They were similar in that they created strong, authoritarian leaders, men who were able
to secure a following by their persuasive oratory, by their ability to organize a new party,
or by the formation of attractive programs of reform. Another common feature was the
submergence of the individual into the mass and the glorification of the state over everything else. Political liberty was reduced, and obedience to the leader and to the party
became the first charge of every citizen. The exaltation of nationalism, as we shall see
in a later chapter, led in some cases to aggression and conquest.

63

This chapter deals mainly with the development of the three most important authoritarian states in Europe, but it will also discuss briefly the achievements of dictatorship in Turkey. The advance of dictatorship in Japan will be considered in Chapter 5. We shall see how the collapse of the czar's government in 1917 paved the way for Russian Communism, how the difficulties of postwar adjustment in Italy led to Fascism, and how the German republic, after a struggle to establish itself, collapsed in 1933 during the world depression and was superseded by National Socialism.

Communism in Russia

The régime of Nicholas II. As the First World War drew to a close the triumph of democracy seemed assured. Soon after fighting ceased, however, a reaction against democratic institutions arose in Europe and elsewhere. In the Balkans, Russia, Poland, Turkey, Italy, Iran, and finally Germany, some form of strong centralized government prevailed sooner or later. The earliest and one of the most significant of these was the government of Russia, a gigantic socio-economic experiment. About one hundred seventy million people are embraced by this new state, in an area more than twice the size of the United States and having natural resources greater than all the rest of Europe (see map, page 127).

In 1914 the Russian government was still in the hands of an irresponsible clique of nobles. The czar, supposedly all-powerful, was in reality often controlled by a small circle in the imperial court. Most notorious of his advisers was Rasputin, who exercised a malignant influence over the royal family. This evil person, reputed to be a monk, was able at times to control government policy through his influence over the czarina. When an army general complained of Rasputin's influence, the czar is reported to have said that he would rather have "five Rasputins to one hysterical woman."

In any event, Nicholas II showed little capacity for guiding his country. Instead of soliciting the support of the Russian legislature, the *Duma,* he ignored and weakened it. Growing Russian industries had created a working class restless and rebellious because of low wages and intolerable working conditions. Strikes took place more and more frequently, and in July 1914 serious labor troubles broke out. The peasants were also dissatisfied. Land reform, in their opinion, was necessary to break up large estates and to distribute agricultural returns more equitably. Several political parties had developed in opposition to the existing régime. Most important of these was the Social Democratic party organized about 1890 by George Plekhanov.

Mensheviks and Bolsheviks. The Social Democratic party espoused Marxian Socialism and worked not only for the overthrow of the czar's government but also for the destruction of capitalist society in Russia. The party carried effective propaganda to the workers and organized meetings in other countries where the delegates would be safe from the Russian secret police. In 1903 an important conference was held in London. Here the organization split into two factions over the methods required to attain the Socialist state. The Mensheviks, led by Plekhanov, believed Socialism should grow gradually and peacefully, that it should "sprout under the shell of capitalism," using constitutional means. The Bolsheviks, led by Nikolay Lenin, advocated forcible methods because they believed the Socialist state could never be achieved through seeking parliamentary majorities. Lenin thought that the capitalist system, including parliamentary government as it then existed, must be overthrown by revolution. To gain this end, the Bolsheviks must bore from within, filling the workers with discontent against their employers, the bourgeoisie. Lenin's goal was rule by the working class, or, in a phrase borrowed from Karl Marx, "the dictatorship of the proletariat." When this was achieved, the capitalist class would be eliminated and all industry would be taken over by the workers' government. It was believed that the best time to accomplish a workers' revolution was during a national crisis, especially during wartime.

Although the Bolsheviks, or Communists as they were called after 1918, repudiated the democratic state and planned to establish a dictatorship, they differed fundamentally from the Fascists in Italy and the Nazis in Germany. Italy and Germany, as we shall see, would maintain a permanent dictatorship of the state and severely restrict the exercise and scope of individual freedom. The Russians, however, held that the dictatorship of the proletariat was only a temporary condition and that the final goal was a society in which the state would practically disappear. Lenin, following the ideas of Karl Marx, published his famous work, *The State and the Revolution*, in 1917. Here he made it clear that the dictatorship of the proletariat was only a transitional stage between capitalism and pure communism. Lenin asserted that "the toilers need a state merely for the suppression of the resistance of the exploiters."[1] Gradually the state would "wither away," dictatorship would disappear, and an absolutely classless society, with practically no machinery of government, would emerge. "In a classless society . . . the state, that instrument of coercion, will be both unnecessary and impossible."[2] When this stage is reached, according to Lenin, it will be possible "for society to inscribe on its banners: 'from each according to his ability: to each according to his needs.' "[3] In other words, the Fascists and Nazis looked upon dictatorship as an end in itself, while the Bolsheviks considered it as a means to an end.

The Russian revolution. The First World War pitilessly exposed the inefficiency of the czarist government. The battle of Tannenberg, in 1914, was only the first of a series of defeats for the Russian armies. Medical supplies were inadequate, and the plight of the wounded was horrible. An adequate supply of munitions was not always available. The railroads were disorganized, and the transport system was unable to carry the burdens imposed upon it by the war. As early as 1915 it became apparent that the czar's régime was nearing disaster, but a request from the *Duma* for more power in order to improve conditions in the field and at home met with a brusque refusal from the czar.

On March 3, 1917, a strike occurred in a factory in Petrograd. Within a week nearly all the workers in the city were idle, and fighting broke out in the streets. On March 11 the czar ordered the members of the *Duma* to go home and the strikers to go back to work. These orders precipitated the revolution. The *Duma* refused to disband, the strikers held great mass meetings in defiance of the government, and the army openly sided with the workers. Encouraged by the army's support, the *Duma* selected a committee to head the revolution. At the same time the radical Socialists in Petrograd formed a Soviet (Council) of workers and soldiers' deputies to oppose the czar. On March 14 a provisional government headed by the moderate liberal, Prince Lvov, was named by the *Duma*, and the following day the czar abdicated in favor of his brother, Grand Duke Nicholas, who refused to accept the throne.

Thus far the revolution had been, on the whole, peaceful. Dominated by liberal middle-class representatives, the *Duma* hoped to achieve a political but not an economic revolution. On the other hand the Bolsheviks in the Petrograd Soviet were determined that there should be a thoroughgoing change in keeping with the teachings of Marx. Nevertheless, for a few months the radical Soviet cooperated with the provisional government. In July Lvov was succeeded by A. F. Kerenski, who was more progressive than his predecessor but not radical enough for the Bolsheviks. While the government of Kerenski marked time, the Soviet in Petrograd extended its organization. All over the country local Soviets were set up. Assisted in part by funds from Germany, the Bolsheviks created effective propaganda under the slogan of: "Peace, Land, and Bread."

Lenin's coup d'état. It was fortunate for the Bolsheviks that at this time they had two great leaders. Nikolay Lenin was spirited out of Switzerland by the German government and taken in a sealed railroad car across the Russian border. Leon Trotsky, another refugee, managed to make his way to Petrograd from the United States, where he was living when the 1917 revolution occurred. In addition to these two capable leaders, the Bolshevik cause was materially strengthened by the presence of such men as Stalin, Bukharin, Kamenev, Kalinin, and Rykov.

In April 1917, Lenin declared in the Russian press that the war was an imperialist conflict between bourgeois interests, that the provisional government must go, and that its place must be taken by a republic of Soviet workers. After much maneuvering behind the scenes and several false starts, the Soviets carried out a *coup d'état* on November 6 and 7. The pro-visional government was overthrown, Keren-ski was driven from power, and a central exec-utive committee of the Soviets assumed con-trol. Lenin had accomplished an amazing feat. With a party estimated to have had only thirty thousand members, he had gained control of a country of more than one hundred fifty million people, using audacity, splendid or-ganization, and astute propaganda.

During the course of the second revolution in Petrograd, disorder and massacre were prevalent throughout Russia. Soldiers shot their officers, members of the nobility were liquidated, and peasants massacred their land-lords. The royal family had been arrested in March 1917 and later sent to Siberia. In the summer of 1918 the approach of a pro-czar White army sealed the fate of the royal pris-oners. On July 18, the royal family were herded into a cellar, so the story goes, and shot.

War Communism. The history of Russian Communism can be divided into four periods. The introductory period, lasting from October 1917 to the middle of 1918, saw the Bolshevik Revolution and Lenin's rise to power. The second period, extending from July 1918 to 1921, is known as the epoch of War Com-munism. In July 1918, the Communists estab-lished a constitution based on the following principles: (1) the dictatorship of the prole-tariat, (2) the nationalization of the land, (3) the nationalization of the banks, (4) compul-sory labor, (5) free education for all, and (6) the establishment of absolute Communism.

Having set up the new structure of govern-ment, the Communists made peace with Ger-many in the treaty of Brest Litovsk in 1918 and turned to domestic problems. Industry was chaotic, many people were starving, and hostile armies, the so-called White forces, were being formed to overthrow the Communist régime. The Allies blockaded Russia and landed troops to cooperate with the White Russians. At the height of the crisis Lenin appointed Trotsky to organize and direct the Communist forces. Allied intervention caused the patriotic Russians to forget their differ-ences, while skillful propaganda spurred the morale of the people to great heights. By 1920 the White armies had been scattered or de-stroyed. Much of this success is attributed to Trotsky who, like Carnot of the French Revo-lution, was the "organizer of victory."

The period from 1918 to 1921 was thus one of suffering and travail for all classes of Rus-sian people. The nobility lost its estates, busi-nessmen were deprived of their positions, pri-vate property was abolished, and refugees were scattered over the face of the earth. The peasant and the worker faced starvation and disease. That the Russian people as a whole were able to overcome what seemed to be in-surmountable obstacles is a tribute to the leadership of Lenin and Trotsky.

Lenin's leadership. Lenin was born in 1870 in the southeastern part of Russia. His par-ents were fairly well-to-do. In 1887 his elder brother, whom he greatly admired, was hanged for plotting to assassinate the czar, and this tragedy undoubtedly stimulated young Lenin's antipathy against the govern-ment. After being expelled from a Russian university for radical views, he went to St. Petersburg, where he passed the state bar examinations.

The profession of law had no real attraction for Lenin, who soon became engaged in polit-ical activities. After a period of banishment to Siberia from 1897 to 1900, he wandered as an exile all over Europe, plotting against the czar's government. In 1917 the German gov-ernment, hoping to weaken Russian resistance by encouraging civil war, assisted Lenin's re-turn to Russia so that he would be able per-sonally to direct the course of revolution.

When the time came, Lenin successfully undertook the immense task of governing Russia, almost without previous experience in statecraft. But for more than forty years he had been preparing for this opportunity. His success was due in part to his unswerving de-termination, his firm methods, his absolute in-tegrity, and his devotion to the Communist cause and to the principles of Karl Marx. When he died the Soviet Congress declared: "His vision was colossal, his intelligence in organizing the masses was beyond belief. He was the greatest leader of all countries, of all times, of all peoples."

Trotsky's background. Leon Trotsky was born in Russia in 1879, the son of prosperous Jewish peasants. He ran afoul of the czar's government after his graduation from high school, when he was arrested for organizing a workers' union. Attendance at a university only whetted his impulse toward Socialist agi-tation, and between 1898 and 1917 he spent four years in prison, was twice sent to Siberia, and for twelve years roamed as an exile. Trotsky was an excellent orator, but he was exceedingly vain and erratic. It is said that Lenin appreciated his gifts but never quite trusted him.

The New Economic Policy. From 1918 to 1921 the Communists attempted to apply undiluted Communist principles to the Russian economy. Banks, railroads, and shipping were nationalized, money economy was restricted, and all private property was abolished. Strong opposition to this program soon developed. The peasants wanted cash and resented having to surrender their surplus grain to the government. Many laborers grumbled at being conscripted to work in the factories, and former business managers showed little enthusiasm for administering enterprises for the benefit of the state. In the face of such opposition the Russian economic system was threatened with collapse. Mutinies became more frequent, and cries of "Down with the Soviet Government" were heard. Despite strenuous opposition from his colleagues, Lenin decided to make a strategic retreat. He felt that the Communists had been too eager to change everything at once, and he therefore inaugurated the New Economic Policy (NEP), which permitted a return to certain practices of the capitalist system.

This retreat from War Communism is the third phase in Russian Communism. The NEP was in operation from 1921 to 1928. The peasants, after paying a tax, were permitted to sell their surplus produce. Retail trading was also permitted. Small factories were returned to the management of private individuals, and a graduated wage scale was granted to the workers. This compromise proved highly beneficial. Industry revived, but there was criticism from the simon-pure Communists against the wealthy peasants, the *kulaks*, who benefited from the new order of things, and against the private businessmen, who were dubbed Nepmen.

The introduction of the New Economic Policy was Lenin's last work. For three years he worked unceasingly. In May 1922, a stroke stopped him, but he rallied and managed to carry on. In March 1923, a second stroke shattered his health, and he died in January 1924. The tomb where his body was placed became the Mecca for thousands of devout followers who came each year to pay their homage at the leader's bier.

The rivals: Trotsky and Stalin. The death of Lenin brought with it the great question of his successor. Trotsky was the best known Communist after Lenin and naturally expected to step into his shoes. But Joseph Stalin had his own views on this subject. Born in the Caucasus in 1879, the son of a lowly shoemaker, Stalin was sent as a youth to a seminary to be educated for the priesthood. Socialist propensities resulted in his expulsion. Young Stalin thereupon became a member of the Social Democratic party and between 1902 and 1913 was arrested and imprisoned at least six times. When Lenin died, disagreement over matters of policy broke out between Stalin and Trotsky. Stalin quietly placed his supporters in key posts of the government and assumed the powerful chairmanship (formerly held by Lenin) of the *Politburo*, an executive body of ten members of the Communist party.

On the surface Trotsky seemed more intelligent and brilliant than Stalin, but the stolidness of Stalin concealed great strength of will. Stalin had little trouble in removing his rival. At first he placed him and his followers in minor posts. Then they were sent to remote parts of Russia and finally in 1929 were deported to Turkey. For a time Trotsky lived in Constantinople. Then he moved to France and finally to Mexico City, where he set up a barrage of censure against Stalin and all his works. In August 1940, Trotsky was murdered in his guarded villa by a political enemy.

Russian governmental structure. During the third phase of the evolution of Soviet Russia, that of the New Economic Policy, the system of government assumed certain distinctive characteristics. The Communists started out in 1918 with a constitution establishing a state known as the Russian Socialist Federated Soviet Republic (R.S.F.S.R.). As the power of this government grew and the anti-Bolshevik forces were destroyed, the jurisdiction of the R.S.F.S.R. expanded. In 1922 the Union of Soviet Socialist Republics (U.S.S.R.) was created consisting of four constituent republics: the original R.S.F.S.R., the Ukraine, White Russia, and Transcaucasia. A new constitution was adopted in 1924.

The Soviets. The new constitution established a federal system of government, based on a succession of Soviets, that is, councils of

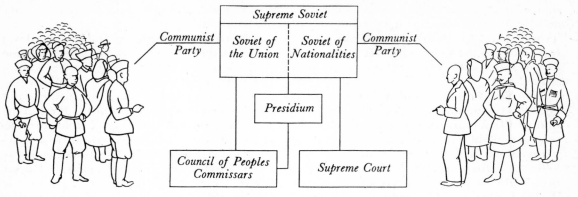

deputies, which were set up in the villages, the factories, cities, and in larger regions. This pyramid of Soviets, found in each constituent republic, was duplicated in the federal government of the Soviet Union. At the apex of the entire governmental structure was the Union Congress of Soviets. The constitution of 1924 brought about the dictatorship of the proletariat. Many persons, such as ministers, monks, members of the former royal family, and private traders, were not permitted to vote. The power of the various Soviets was negligible. They met infrequently and had little to do. There was no separation of powers among the executive, judicial, and legislative branches as exists in the United States. All these functions were exercised by the Union Congress of Soviets and the various bodies it appointed.

While the Union Congress apparently exercised sovereign political power, this body was in reality controlled by the Communist party. The *Politburo* laid down all matters of policy and was the most powerful body in the U.S.S.R. Joseph Stalin held no governmental post; it was his leadership of the party which made him virtual dictator of Russia. Practically all government posts were filled by graduates of the Communist Youth Organization: the Octobrists, the Pioneers, and the Komsomol, which enlist the youth of Russia from the age of eight to twenty-four.

The third constitution. In 1936 Soviet Russia adopted a third constitution, which brought about some notable changes in the machinery of government. This constitution defines the U.S.S.R. as "a Socialist State of Workers and Peasants" (Chapter I, Article 1). Further it declares that "All power in the U.S.S.R. belongs to the toilers of town and country as repre-

sented by the Soviets of Toilers' Deputies" (Chapter I, Article 3).

The constitution of 1936 contained provisions guaranteeing a more liberal form of government than had hitherto existed. Articles 118 and 133 constituted a kind of Bill of Rights in which the people were granted and guaranteed such political rights as freedom of speech, of the press, and of assembly. The provisions regulating elections provide for "universal, equal, and direct suffrage by secret ballot," and that all citizens, men and women, who have reached the age of eighteen "irrespective of race or nationality, religion, standard of education, domicile, social origin, property status or past activities, have the right to vote in the election of deputies and to be elected." Many people hailed these guarantees as proof that Soviet Russia was introducing the principles of democratic government as understood in the United States.

The role of the R.S.F.S.R. In structure Soviet Russia is a federal system. By 1936 the original four constituent republics had grown to eleven. (In 1940 the sixteenth was admitted.) Each of these is self-governing in regard to matters of local interest, and each contains smaller administrative areas such as autonomous republics, autonomous regions, territories, provinces, counties, and so on. The government of these local areas is carried on by a hierarchy of Soviets. Because of its much greater size and because it is the center of the most important cities, in practice the R.S.F.S.R. plays a dominant role in the federal union.

How legislation is accomplished. Legislative power in the federal government is exercised by the Supreme Soviet of the U.S.S.R., consisting of a Union Council and a Council of Nationalities. The Union Council is elected

1936
Constitution

by territorial districts throughout the union, one deputy being returned for every area with 300,000 population. The Council of Nationalities is made of various political divisions. For example, each constituent republic sends twenty-five deputies to the Council of Nationalities, the autonomous republics each send eleven, five come from each autonomous region, and so on. The total membership of the Supreme Soviet with its two houses is slightly in excess of 1100.

The executive bodies. The Supreme Soviet elects a Presidium of thirty-six members which is a kind of executive committee of the larger body. The Presidium carries on the functions of the Supreme Soviet when it is not in session. In case of a deadlock in the Supreme Soviet the Presidium arranges new elections. It convenes this legislature twice a year and ratifies important treaties. The president of the Presidium is the titular head of the Soviet Union and performs some of the ceremonial functions exercised by presidents in western democracies, such as receiving ambassadors.

Similar to the British cabinet is the Council of People's Commissars, which possesses the highest executive and administrative functions. This body is responsible to the Supreme Soviet or to the Presidium when the former is not in session. The members of the Council of People's Commissars act as the heads of the various federal departments, such as defense, foreign affairs, foreign trade, railways, and so on.

The judiciary. The highest judicial tribunal is the Supreme Court of the U.S.S.R., whose members are elected by the Supreme Soviet for a term of four years. The constitution of 1936, unlike its predecessors, is based on the principles of the separation of powers. The Supreme Soviet is responsible for legislation, the Council of People's Commissars is the executive body of the federal government, and the judicial functions are in the hands of the Supreme Court.

The Communist party in Russia. Joseph Stalin has declared that "no one dares to question that our constitution is the most democratic in the world." It is still true, however, that Soviet Russia is a one-party state, with the Communist party effectively dictating the policy of government. This fact is accepted by Stalin in his statement to the Congress of Soviets in November 1936:

"I must admit that the draft of the new Constitution actually leaves in force the régime of the dictatorship of the working class as well as it preserves unchanged the present leading position of the Communist Party."[4]

Article 126 of the constitution gives citizens the right to political expression. The Communist party, however, is the only agency listed through which this expression can be made. At the present time there are about 2,500,000 members in the Communist party, only about 1.5 per cent of the total population. In practice a candidate for a government office is rarely elected unless he is approved by the Communist party. Because Soviet Russia is in essence a one-party state numerous critics maintain there is not much democracy as we know it in Russia. To judge the situation fairly, however, the following facts should be kept in mind.

The Russian ideal. In the United States and Great Britain, as well as in other western democracies, the practice has been to focus guarantees on political bills of rights. In the Soviet Union the main emphasis at this stage is upon what we may think of as an economic and social bill of rights. Citizens are guaranteed the "right to work." The right to rest and leisure is ensured (or was before the war) by a seven-hour working day, annual vacations with pay, and rest homes and clubs for workers. Russians are guaranteed the right to "maintenance in old age and also in the case of sickness or loss of capacity to work." They are granted the right to education, a right ensured "by universal, compulsory elementary education; by the fact that education, including higher education, is free of charge; by the system of state scholarships for the overwhelming majority." Many people recognize that in the western democracies political rights have often been guaranteed in advance of social and economic rights. In Soviet Russia it may perhaps be said that the process is being reversed, that economic rights are taking precedence over political rights. Of course this view assumes that the Soviet state will gradually be democratized politically.

In defending the preëminence of the Communist party, Soviet officials maintain that it would have been impossible to introduce a mature democratic system in the Russia of 1917. Illiterate and confused, the peasants had to be given a program calculated to improve

Students in the Cherepovetz Technical College of Industrial Agriculture (Russia) spend their summers on the state farms, acting as instructors in the use of farm machinery. Here they assemble a tractor.

their status. This program the leaders provided. They were quite sure their program was what Russia needed and, therefore, that its fundamental objectives and procedures could not be questioned. "Thus all discussion and debate must keep within the bounds of the program of the Revolution. There can no longer be any debate as to the possibility of building Socialism, or as to whether what is being built is Socialism. Similarly, the collectivization of agriculture must be accepted as an established policy."[5] Within the framework, however, of the Russian Soviet plan much opportunity is given for criticism and suggestion. Administration of factories can be criticized by the workers, suggestions for improving manufacturing techniques are welcomed, and inadequacies of any industry may be aired. Thus "the mechanical working of the new institutions can be criticized constructively and this discussion is in fact constantly going on. Criticism . . . is developing organically within each group, and throughout these groups on a broader scale. It leads to changes of methods of internal organization, to new emphasis, always however within the established framework. It may in this gradual way bring considerable alterations in the structure and functioning of the various institutions and organizations."[6]

The trials of 1936. Many observers were of the opinion that the constitution of 1936 marked the beginning of a mellowing process in Russia. This belief was somewhat shaken when an epidemic of treason trials began in Russia that year. Violence had never been completely absent in the internal politics of Russia, but in 1936 it suddenly became intensified. Some of the most famous Communist leaders, including several generals, were sent to prison and executed. Stalin has been charged with weeding out these men simply because they differed with him in policy. He is said to have refused them the privilege of just trials. On the other hand, it has been suggested that Stalin found definite evidence that these men were fifth-columnists working with Hitler for the overthrow of the Socialist experiment. Those who explain the purges in this manner point out that when Hitler invaded Russia in the summer of 1941 there were no "Quislings" in the Soviet ranks. Perhaps there is some truth in the French statesman's remark: "In Russia they shot their fifth columnists. In France we put them in the Cabinet."[7] At any rate, the real reason for the executions is not yet a matter of certain knowledge.

Stalin's first Five-Year Plan (1928-1933). Lenin had been forced to give up the experiment in pure socialism and to introduce the NEP, but Stalin was determined that this compromise with capitalism should be swept away as soon as possible. In 1928 he was ready to introduce a program of economic reform which would not only destroy the last vestiges of capitalism in Russia but would industrialize the country almost overnight. His Five-Year Plan envisaged the following: (1) the collectivization of 55,000,000 acres of land into huge government farms, (2) the removal of illiteracy, and (3) the increase of industrial products by 136 per cent, of agricultural output by 55 per cent, of oil and coal by 100 per cent, and of power by 300 per cent. This vast economic program was devised by a State Planning Commission, the Gosplan. Each factory and each farm was given the opportunity to criticize its share in the plan, either to increase or decrease it. For the first time in modern history an economic blueprint controlling the entire business life of a nation had been set in motion. With the initiation of the first Five-Year Plan began a new period, the fourth in Soviet history, called the period of Socialist reconstruction. It was characterized by the advent of economic planning, the collectivization of farming, and the adoption of the new constitution in 1936.[8]

Such a program was bound to impose severe hardships on the people, for they were being asked to concentrate upon industrial equipment and drastically curtail the production of consumer goods. But the leaders succeeded in arousing a militant enthusiasm that gave the Five-Year Plan the appearance of a crusade. Remarkable results were attained. The number of industrial workers doubled, and the total industrial output in 1932 was 334 per cent above that in 1914. The largest tractor factory in the world was erected at Chelyabinsk, the greatest electric power station was constructed at Dnepropetrovsk, and the largest automobile plant was set up at Gorki. All the industries of the country were organized into great government trusts, and the process of collectivizing was pushed in agriculture.

The collective farm, or *kolkhoz*, was created by doing away with the units of land owned by the *kulaks*, established peasants. In the new type of farm thus created, the members work their land as one great unit under the direction of a board of directors. Each family retains its house, its personal effects, and a small garden. Each *kolkhoz* is allowed to work out

its own system of payments to members based on what is known as the "labor day unit." At the end of the year the collective farm computes its net earnings in cash and in kind and makes payments to the members on the basis of the number of labor days with which each has been credited.

The *sovkhoz* is the state farm. Unlike the *kolkhoz*, it does not represent the collective effort of a number of peasant farmers but is an outright state farm run by paid laborers. At the present time these state and collective farms comprise nearly ninety per cent of the land under cultivation in Russia.

While the first Five-Year Plan made notable gains, it also produced a number of disturbing results. The quality of industrial products deteriorated, and in 1932 there was a serious shortage of farm products. Erecting new factories was not so difficult, but it was almost impossible to train overnight the technicians necessary to run the new machines. The process of collectivization on the farms caused disorder and opposition among the peasants. During the hectic days of the first Five-Year Plan, huge amounts of Russian grain and raw materials were dumped on foreign markets in order to secure the necessary funds to pay for the importation of industrial equipment.

Cotton farmers belonging to an agricultural union in Turkestan, Asiatic Russia, examine their supply of seed. Part of Turkestan belongs to China, part to Afghanistan, this part (in Usbekistan) to Russia.

In 1932 Russian doctors vaccinated peasants like this woman from a collective farm in Asiatic Russia as part of the Soviet program for education in modern health methods.

Much of the grain and other products could have been used at home, but the people were convinced that sacrifices had to be made in order to make Russia more wealthy and powerful in the future. In the later stages of the first Five-Year Plan measures were introduced to cope with some of its obvious weaknesses. Differential wage scales were offered the workmen to encourage individual initiative, the unwieldy state farms were reduced in number and the collective farms were increased, and in industry the principle of piecework as a basis for pay was also extended.

The second and third Five-Year Plans. In 1933 a second Five-Year Plan was introduced which had as its goal greater concentration on the production of goods that the people could use and less concentration on making industrial equipment. Special emphasis was laid upon the electrification of the country. Factories were to be expanded for the manufacture of shoes, textiles, canned goods, and candies. A third Five-Year Plan was initiated in 1938, concerned mainly with increasing the efficiency of the industrial equipment setup under the first and second Five-Year Plans.

Many books have been written in denunciation or defense of Soviet national economic planning as exemplified in the three Five-Year Plans. Despite certain failures and weaknesses, it can be said that economic productivity in Russia during the past decade and a half has increased at an amazing pace. Joseph E. Davies, United States ambassador to Russia (1936-1938), writes: "They have painted on a ten-league canvas with a brush of comet's hair."[9]

Russian accomplishments. According to Soviet figures the three Five-Year Plans have resulted in the following accomplishments: "The share of the U.S.S.R. in total world production amounted in 1926 to 4.7 per cent. In 1936 the level of the world industrial production remained at the 1923 level. But the level of production in the U.S.S.R. increased by 4.6 times, and the share of the U.S.S.R. in world total production now amounts to about 20 per cent. The U.S.S.R. has surpassed Germany in production and now occupies the second place in the world. It is interesting to note the growth in individual branches of industry: in the production of electric power, the U.S.S.R. rose from fifteenth place in the world in 1913, to third place in 1937; in machine building, the U.S.S.R. rose from fourth to second place, having surpassed England and Germany; in tractors the U.S.S.R. occupies second place; and in the production of locomotives, cars and combines, first place in the world."[10]

One of the most important aspects of Soviet Russian policy and one on which it will perhaps ultimately be judged is its national economic planning. The following evaluation of the Russian economic experiment would seem to be an unprejudiced and fair analysis: "The details of the economic organization which the Communists are evolving—the consolidation of industry into self-governing trusts and syndicates, the cooperative stores and factories, the nationalization of railways, banks, and agriculture—these deserve to be studied and watched without bias and with the closest attention. Above all, the attempt to coordinate the entire industry of a nation as vast as Russia into a unified system, under the agency of the Gosplan (the national economic planning agency), is a daring and gigantic experiment which may prove of great value to the world; for there can be very little doubt that in every nation there is going on an evolution toward greater unification of industry, whether along socialistic or capitalistic lines, and the experience of Russia in attempting to handle so tremendous an organization is sure to reveal much by which others can profit."[11]

The new social life in Russia. Communism has not only revolutionized the economic life of 170,000,000 people through breathtaking industrialization and collectivization; it has also brought about equally drastic changes in the environment of men, women, and children, and in their attitudes toward life.

In czarist Russia women in general did not enjoy equality with men. Their education was neglected and their tasks were almost exclusively homemaking and childbearing. The Soviet government encourages girls to secure an education and to go to higher institutions of learning if they wish and if they are qualified. Homemaking is now frequently subordinated to a woman's independent career in the factory or office. As part of the emancipation of women, the government at one time endeavored to diminish the importance of the family as an institution. Efforts were made to shift the center of the people's social life from the home to the Soviet club, an important educational and recreational institution. This policy has been modified in recent years.

To make women more independent of home and family many interesting methods of caring for small children have been introduced. Those with working mothers have been placed in nurseries where they are given scientific supervision, including balanced diets and medical inspection, and are taught to play in groups. Getting a divorce used to be easy in the Soviet Union. In recent years, however, Soviet leaders have felt that this course was sociologically undesirable. Hence divorces are more difficult to obtain today.

Religion in Russia. The Soviet Union has been sharply criticized in the western world for its attitude toward religion. Lenin maintained that religion is "the opiate of the people." Russian churches were stripped of political and educational privileges and deprived of state support. Many critics of Communism called it godless, an attitude which should be qualified. There is little doubt that the Soviet leaders discouraged participation in organized religion, but the churches were not closed. At the outbreak of the Russo-German

This Turkestan girl has discarded her veil to work in a factory at Samarkand. Here she spins the fine strands from the cocoon into silk thread.

war in 1941, the patriarch of Moscow prayed for victory for the Russian cause, asking that his followers support Stalin.

The Orthodox Church of pre-revolution days, thanks to Peter the Great and his successors, was subordinated to the czarist régime and had become its complete tool. In the eyes of the intellectuals the Church stood for the perpetuation of everything reactionary—including resistance to mass education and the condonement of gross superstition, especially among the peasants. Reformers therefore believed that a new social order could be successfully introduced only if all vestiges of the old system were swept away. Today, the Church has no educational or political power, and the leaders of the U.S.S.R. are apparently more tolerant of its religious teachings. The constitution of 1936 declares that "freedom of religious worship and freedom of antireligious propaganda is recognized for all citizens" (Article 124). The more recent developments of this matter are discussed in Chapter 8.

The importance of education. Lenin once said, "Give me four years to teach the children, and the seed I shall have sown will never be uprooted." The abolition of illiteracy was made one of the goals in 1927. By 1933 illiteracy had practically disappeared in a country where illiteracy had always been appallingly high. In 1918 8,000,000 children were in school. In 1938 the attendance was estimated to be 38,000,000. Where possible the educational authorities have tried to introduce the latest educational techniques of other countries. The primary purpose of the educational system, it should be kept in mind, is to inculcate Communist ideals. "The educational system frankly rests upon class purposes. . . ."[12]

Ownership in Russia. Although capitalism, that is, the private ownership of the means of production, has been abolished in Soviet Russia, citizens can still own certain forms of private property. "The Soviet leaders draw a sharp distinction between ownership of capital for private gain, and ownership of various forms of personal property—houses, books, domestic utensils, clothes, furniture, automobiles, and so on—for private use."[13] A Russian citizen cannot own property which is utilized to make profits by the hiring of people. The only employer is the state. Real estate for personal use, automobiles, and even government bonds are classed as personal property and may be willed to the owner's children. Outside the cities the average peasant is a member of a collective farm, but he too may own his own home and even have his own garden and a few animals. Eggs, vegetables, and meat produced by the peasant on his own garden plot may be sold and the revenue reserved for his use.

Other reforms. The life of the Russian people has been affected in numerous other ways. The old policy of persecuting national minorities has given way to one of tolerance for the more than two hundred different minority groups, such as Armenians, Jews, Uzbeks, Turks, and Georgians. "Complete cultural autonomy is granted each group; teaching in the schools is in the language of the particular group; newspapers are printed in the various languages; and, for those primitive tribes who had no written language, one has been worked out."[14] Other commendable features of the Soviet system have been the extension of public health programs, the development of large housing projects, and the patronage of science, music, and drama. The number of doctors has increased from about 26,000 before the First World War to over 100,000, and the death rate has decreased from 27 per thousand to 18, with child mortality reduced from 360 to 130.[15]

The effects of the Second World War on Russia are discussed in a later chapter.

Mussolini and Italian Fascism

Nineteenth-century Italy. At the end of the nineteenth century Italy faced the future with some fear and disquiet. Political unification had been achieved, and all Italians now lived under the House of Savoy; but unification had not solved the country's most pressing difficulties. Parliamentary government was often ineffectual and sometimes corrupt. The population increased rapidly, and the task of feeding the people was a considerable problem in itself. Moreover, Italy lacked the coal, oil, and iron to make her a strong industrialized nation, although industry had advanced to some extent. Italy, famous for its beautiful ruins, matchless scenery, and brilliant singers, was also the country of the Neapolitan slums—as bad as those anywhere in Europe—of mass illiteracy and grinding poverty.

Italy entered the First World War on the side of the Allies hoping that participation would improve her lot. During the conflict Italy lost 650,000 men. The wounded numbered nearly a million. War expenditures amounted to fifteen billion dollars. But the termination of the war did not bring a solution for Italian problems. On the contrary, it only aggravated them. At the peace conference Italian claims to territory along the eastern Adriatic and in the Near East and Africa were not fully realized. Italian diplomats wasted their efforts on the Adriatic question to the neglect of more important subjects. They insisted that the valuable port of Fiume on the Adriatic Sea should be Italian. While the dispute raged between the Italians on the one hand and the British, French, and Americans on the other, the famous Italian poet and nationalist, D'Annunzio, seized Fiume. In 1920, when a compromise was reached by the Treaty of Rapallo with Yugoslavia, and the Italian government ejected D'Annunzio's forces from the disputed city, ardent nationalists in Italy were infuriated at what they considered an abject surrender of their government to Great Britain and the United States. Many others felt in 1919 that the Allies had been niggardly in the distribution of the spoils. Italian gains in Africa were almost negligible, although the nation acquired nearly 9000 square miles in Europe and more than a million and a half additional subjects.

Incompetent government. Following the armistice in 1918, Italy had five prime ministers in a period of four years. Not one of these leaders demonstrated a capacity for real statesmanship. For example, A. J. Zurcher says of one of them: "Under Facta the Italian cabinet simply abdicated. It had no policy, foreign or domestic; it had not even the firmness necessary to enforce elementary respect for law."[16] In this year a swing toward radical socialism was apparent in the country. The Socialists gained 156 seats in the parliament. Communist propaganda made its appearance in Italy, and "Long live Lenin" was heard frequently in the streets. People refused to pay their rent, workers seized factories, and numerous strikes, accompanied in many cases by bloodshed, occurred.

Conditions went from bad to worse. It was difficult to find employment for the demobilized soldiers, foreign trade was at a low ebb, war profiteers called *pescicani* (sharks) had grown rich at the expense of the masses, the trade unions controlled the railways, and the internal debt advanced six hundred per cent. A desire for strong government grew steadily. The propertied classes wanted protection against radicalism, and the jobless wanted jobs.

Mussolini's background. Italy was soon to have a strong leader, Benito Mussolini. Mussolini, who was born on July 29, 1883, had by hard work and sacrifice managed to secure an education and had finally entered a normal school. He started his career by teaching school at a salary of $10.25 a month.

Mussolini was too tempestuous and ambitious to be cooped up in a country schoolhouse, however. At nineteen he went to Switzerland, partly to see more of the world and partly to escape compulsory military training, for Mussolini was an antimilitarist critic of nationalism and the self-styled friend of the proletariat. In Switzerland he attended several universities and engaged in Socialist activities. After getting into trouble with the Swiss authorities, in 1904, the young agitator returned to his native country. During the next ten years, before the outbreak of the First World War, he made his living from teaching and journalistic activities. He ran afoul of the law in the Tyrol and was ejected from this region by the Austrian authorities. He was imprisoned by the Italian police in 1908 and again in 1911, in the latter case because of his opposition to the war against Turkey in Tripoli, which he criticized as a purely imperialist venture.

By this time Mussolini had attracted considerable attention. Radicals all over the world were following his career with considerable interest. In 1912, in recognition of his accomplishments, he was made editor of the most influential Socialist newspaper in Italy, *Avanti*. When war broke out in 1914, the young editor advocated a policy of strict neutrality. But in a few months he had forgotten about international socialism and become an ardent Italian nationalist. He now demanded that Italy join the war on the side of the Allies. Angered by this about-face, the Socialists ejected Mussolini from the party and from the editorship of *Avanti*. Undaunted, Mussolini proceeded to found another paper, *Il Popolo d'Italia*, and began again to urge Italian entrance into the war. When this event took place, he joined the army, saw active service, and was wounded by the explosion of a trench mortar. After several months in the hospital Mussolini returned to civilian life. Life in the trenches had left its mark on the former idealist and radical, for now Mussolini came back more than ever the nationalist, apparently believing fiercely in his country's destiny.

Mussolini's gifts of oratory, his swagger and bombast, and his physical magnetism were of decided value in his dealings with the Italian people. He revealed himself as much more than a mere demagogue. For a decade and more he proved to be a shrewd diplomat and a capable administrator, although his lust for power and his adulation of war eventually brought misery to the Italian people and contempt for himself from much of the rest of the world.

The birth of Italian Fascism. Fascism in Italy began with organized bands of young interventionists, which appeared late in 1914. These groups were called *fasci*, a name derived from the Latin *fasces*, a bundle of rods bound about an ax, symbolizing the authority of the *lictor* in the days of ancient Rome. In March 1919 Mussolini organized the *fascio* of Milan into a group called the *fasci di combattimento* (the fighting group). A revolutionary program formulated by Mussolini stressed universal suffrage, a heavy inheritance tax, a minimum wage law, a national assembly to work out a new constitution, control of certain industries by the workers, and the annexation of Fiume and Dalmatia. It is interesting that at the outset of Mussolini's career as a Fascist he leaned in the direction of the proletariat rather than toward the bourgeoisie. In November 1921, in a national congress held at Rome, a national Fascist party was established. By this time the Fascists had borrowed from the followers of the poet D'Annunzio the distinctive uniform of the black shirt.

Communists, whose number had continued to increase, now brawled with Fascists, in the autumn of 1920 and throughout 1921. In one city on a single day, twenty-one Communists were killed by the Black Shirts. Fascist squadrons roamed all over the country. Sometimes they acted as genuine preservers of law and order, but just as often they pounced on innocent citizens, insulted them, and even rounded up the police and put them in their own jails. Although Mussolini's original program contained some elements of Socialism, the Fascists soon were posing as the instruments of law and order and the implacable foes of radicalism. According to Mussolini the Socialists had gone too far. Now "it was his *fasci* who became the sword and buckler of the middle class and capitalist counter-offensive against Socialism."[17]

Mussolini comes to power. Amid the fights between Black Shirts and Socialists the established government remained impotent. Mussolini called it "a worn-out democracy." In October 1922 he declared at Naples: "Either the government will be given to us or we shall seize it by marching on Rome."[18] Facta, the prime minister, resigned, and the king telephoned Mussolini in Milan, requesting him to form a government. On October 30 Mussolini entered Rome, where his Fascist militia already were in control, and assumed the head of the ministry.

Although the Fascists are fond of claiming that they saved the country from Communism, authorities are able to show now that there was no real likelihood of Italy's becoming Communist. By 1922 radicalism was declining, and economic conditions actually were on the upgrade. To point out these facts, however, is not to ignore the fact that the Italian people were restlessly seeking some new government. The crosscurrents of public opinion in Italy following the war have been described thus: "The landlords and property holders were much affected by the incidents of the brief reign of radicalism. They were determined that Italy should have a government strong enough to protect private property. The university people, the professionals, and many of the young men were disgusted with the whole trend of events since 1914. They wanted to see a general governmental housecleaning and the emergence of a strong and patriotic administration. The nationalists and ex-soldiers were angered by the thought that the net result of their participation in the war might be an anarchic Italy. They too wanted to see new men at the governmental helm."[19]

Mussolini actually had only six per cent of the seats in parliament to support his policies. His opponents hoped that he would soon make some blunder which would discredit the whole Black Shirt movement. But Mussolini, who had been waiting a long time for this opportunity, played his cards shrewdly and carefully. In 1923 he succeeded in getting a law passed whereby the party with the largest number of votes in a national election was entitled to two thirds of the seats in the Chamber of Deputies. Largely as a result of this law, the Fascists obtained a sizable majority in 1924. It was a year of crisis for Mussolini. The chief opponents of Fascism in parliament were the Socialists. Their leader, Matteotti, constantly denounced the dubious methods of the Fascists. In June 1924, Matteotti was murdered, presumably by Mussolini's clique. A wave of disgust swept the country. Nearly all the non-Fascists left the legislature (the so-called Aventine Secession), declaring they would not return until it was purged of Fascist members. Mussolini, however, cleverly wriggled out of the mess and proceeded to make himself a full-fledged dictator.

Mussolini organizes Fascist government. During 1925 and 1926 the cities were deprived of their right of local self-government. Parliament was stripped of its power to initiate laws. Mussolini—now premier—obtained the right to issue decrees having the force of law. He became head of all the Italian armed forces. As the power of the parliamentary system declined, that of the Fascist organization increased. At the top of the new system the Fascist Grand Council became the principal source of authority. The leading member of this body, Mussolini, now assumed the title of *Il Duce*, the leader. Members of the Council occupied the government's ministerial posts, and at one time Mussolini himself had eight cabinet posts. The Fascist party began to run the nation. Membership in the party was open only to those who had come up from, and hence were trained in, the various Fascist organizations; political offices were open only to party members in good standing. Ten thousand local *fasci* had appeared throughout the country, each with a secretary to keep in touch with the central organization.

The Senate and Chamber of Deputies became relatively unimportant, being under the thumb of the Grand Council. The Senate, while completely dominated by the Fascist régime, was permitted to retain its original form. In 1938, however, the national lower house—the Chamber of Deputies—was abolished and the Chamber of Fasces and Corporations established in its place. After this body's 800 members had been selected by the Fascist Grand Council and the Corporations, the Italian voters were given the opportunity of registering their "popular approval in a plebiscite."

Italian Fascism defined. In brief, Fascism was (1) antidemocratic, (2) an example of what we call the corporate state, (3) ultranationalist, and (4) pledged to imperialism. Fascism has been defined as "the cult of state worship." In the Italian totalitarian state the individual had no existence, no significance, and no rights, except as a member of the state. Blind devotion and unquestioning obedience were exacted from all. In the words of Mussolini, "All in the state, nothing without the state, nothing against the state."

Fascist political theory held that mere members must not be allowed to rule the state, as in a democracy, but must instead be guided by capable rulers. This élite group of rulers was furnished by the Fascist party. It follows, also, that Fascists could not tolerate any opposition to their policies. All parties not Fascist were ruthlessly suppressed, and critics of the

At Camp Dux, Rome, Il Duce's monumental bust stands many times the height of a man. The obelisk-like structure is reminiscent of the massive portrait sculpture of the Egyptians.

new régime were banished to penal settlements on islands off the southern Italian coast. Censorship of the press was of course established, and a tribunal for defense of the state set up to punish any individuals not conforming with Fascist practices.

In the Fascist state all the units of local and provincial government were welded into a unified structure dominated from Rome. Fascism, therefore, meant the ultra-centralization of government. A new Fascist penal code was drawn up to insure the security of the Fascist system.

The corporate state. In economic matters Fascism borrowed from Syndicalism. The Syndicalists, whose main authority was Sorel in France, advocated an economic basis for a nation's political structure. Industrial unions were to be the "cells" of society, and a confederation of these unions, or syndicates, would become the governing body of the state. In such a confederation there was to be no

In pre-World War II days Mussolini's government did all possible to increase the birth rate in Italy, offering bonuses to newly married couples and establishing gifts of money for babies. Interestingly enough, this is a German cartoon.

place for the capitalist because the workers would run the government. In 1926 the Fascists passed a law in which Syndicalism was adapted to their own needs. The economic structure of the country was divided into thirteen syndicates, each representing a major economic activity. Six of these syndicates were formed from the ranks of labor, and an equal number represented capital or management. A thirteenth syndicate was set up for professional men. All syndicates, whether they represented capital or labor, came under the control of the government. Strikes and lockouts became illegal. In the event of an industrial dispute the matter was to be taken to a Labor Court, whose decision was binding.

In 1930 and 1931 a National Council of Corporations was set up, consisting of seven corporations, or divisions, whose members were obtained from the thirteen syndicates mentioned above. In 1934 the nation was reorganized into twenty-two corporations, each of which consisted of syndicates of workers and employers. Every corporation was controlled by the government. Its activities were subject to the approval of the Fascist Grand Council of which Mussolini was the chief official. In addition to the twenty-two corporations there was also created a Central Corporative Committee to harmonize the activities of all corporations. At the head of this economic pyramid sat the Minister of Corporations, a position also controlled by Mussolini.

There is a marked difference in economic theory between the Communist and Fascist states. The Communist state is determined to destroy private capital and liquidate the capitalist-managerial class. The Fascist state, sometimes defined as state capitalism, aims to abolish the class war through cooperation between capital and labor, by the compulsion of the state if need be. In Communist theory labor is the state itself; in Fascism labor and capital are both instruments of the state.

Some of the primary economic objectives of Fascism were to make Italy more self-sufficient, especially in the matter of food; to increase the power resources of the nation; and to expand Italy's foreign trade. A campaign called the "battle of the wheat" increased the home yield of this cereal seventy per cent. Extensive marsh land was reclaimed and hydro-electric power resources were increased. To some extent the intention to increase Italy's natural resources was commendable, but the drive was carried on to an extreme and uneconomic degree. Mussolini's desire to attain national self-sufficiency, a policy known in international economics as autarchy, was primarily motivated not by the exigencies of economics but rather by those of war. Many projects were launched to provide for a home supply of materials which could be obtained much more cheaply abroad. But as Mussolini saw the situation:

"Political independence—that is, the possibility of pursuing an independent foreign policy—cannot be conceived without a corresponding capacity for economic self-sufficiency. . . . We must secure in the shortest possible time the maximum degree of economic independence for the nation. . . . This plan is dominated by one premise—the inevitability of war. When? How? No one can say, but the wheel of destiny turns quickly."[20]

Fascism's extreme nationalism. The Fascist state is not only antidemocratic in politics and corporative in economics but ultra-nationalist as well. Passionate faith in and blind devotion to the great destiny of Italy were expected of the Fascist citizen. These requirements were best illustrated by the educational system, which was a medium of national propaganda. The first sentence read by the little children in school was, "Let us salute the flag in the Roman fashion; hail to Italy; hail to Mussolini." All the Italian textbooks were rewritten to conform with Fascist ideology. These texts taught the greatness of Italy, the nobility of the vocation of a soldier, the virtue of having many children, the necessity of obedience to the state, and the idea that Il Duce was always right.

Italian imperialism. Another important aspect of Italian Fascism was the stress on imperial destiny. Italy must expand or explode, as Mussolini once tersely expressed it. A high birth rate, together with a rather limited territory and meager natural resources, did give a logical cast to Italian imperialism. But it was not so much economic necessity that drove the Fascist state to expand as the belief that such expansion was a manifestation of Italy's vitality and a glorification of Italian nationalism. In the words of Il Duce: "If Italy wants to count for something, she must appear on the threshold of the second half of the century with a population of not less than 60,000,000 inhabitants. If we fall off, gentlemen, we cannot make an empire, we shall become a colony."[21]

Fascism necessitates militarism. The exaggerated nationalism of modern Italy and the determination of its leaders to expand necessitated a strong army and navy, by which Fascism hoped to attain its objectives. War was glorified. Peace became the manifestation of national decadence. In Mussolini's own words: "Only war carries human energies to the highest level and puts the seal of nobility upon people who have the courage to undertake it."[22] The cult of militarism demanded that the youth of the nation be trained and disciplined. Three organizations accordingly were established for this purpose. The *Wolf Balilla* enrolled boys from the age of six to eight, the *Balilla* enrolled those between eight and fourteen, and the Advance Guard in-

The reclamation of the Pontine marshes, malaria-infested since Roman times, is on the credit side of Fascist Italy. Farm crops, vegetables, poultry, and livestock are now raised in this region, within easy reach of Rome. This is a drainage canal.

cluded youths between the ages of fourteen and eighteen. What effect the militaristic-imperialistic policy had on modern Italian history will be told as part of a larger story in a later chapter.

Fascism has been described thus:

"Signor Mussolini's . . . dictatorship, like others in history has destroyed respect for political morality and constitutional restraint. It has been responsible for the corrosion of civic initiative and the decay of all forms of local self-government. . . . To the dictatorship, too, must be charged the moral or physical exile of Italy's leading intellectuals and the reduction of the people as a whole to a condition of political tutelage which is more characteristic of a medieval despotism than of a twentieth-century commonwealth."[23]

Efficient Turkish Dictatorship

Mustafa Kemal. Simultaneous with Italian Fascism, another authoritarian system developed in a Mediterranean land. This was the dictatorship in Turkey established by Mustafa Kemal, one of the most remarkable persons of twentieth-century Europe. Born in

Sacred to the memory of Kemal Ataturk is this small square with its statue of the great man of Turkey.   It stands in the center of a boulevard in Ankara, the modern capital his efforts produced.

1880, Kemal was educated in a military academy and in the staff college in Constantinople. As a young army officer he participated in the revolution of 1908 and distinguished himself as a military expert of the first rank in the war against Italy in 1911 and in the Balkan wars of 1912-1913. In the Gallipoli campaign his leadership had much to do with the successful defense of the Straits against British troops. After the defeat of Turkey the Allies forced the Treaty of Sèvres on the sultan, who sent Mustafa Kemal to demobilize the Turkish troops in Asia Minor. Disregarding his instructions, Kemal reorganized the troops and prepared to defy the Allies. A new government was set up at Ankara. Kemal was selected as president and commander-in-chief. In 1922 a Greek army, invited by the Allies to take over a part of Asia Minor, was forced to withdraw. In the same year the sultan was deposed, and in 1923 Turkey was proclaimed a republic.

Kemal's reforms. The new constitution was democratic in form, but in reality Mustafa Kemal was a dictator who brooked no interference with his plans. His main objective was to modernize Turkey, and under his rule the old institutions and customs of a backward oriental state were transformed or replaced within a few short years. The caliphate, the sultan's spiritual leadership of the Mohammedan world, was abolished. Education was taken out of the hands of the Church and the courts of the Church were discontinued. New law codes were promulgated. Use of the fez and of the veil for women was forbidden. Polygamy was prohibited. In addition the western Gregorian calendar, European numerals, and Latin script were introduced.

A frontal attack was made on illiteracy. Attendance at school was made compulsory until the student had reached the age of sixteen. No field of activity was overlooked by the indefatigable leader, who erected a new capital at Ankara. Turkey was rejuvenated and made more progress in the two decades after the close of the First World War than she had done during the entire nineteenth century. Because of his achievements Mustafa Kemal was called Ataturk, meaning the Father of the Turks.

In modern times such a wholesale adoption of new culture traits is nowhere duplicated except perhaps in Japan. The dictatorship Ataturk established was more palatable than most to those who believe in democratic government, because there is much to show that Ataturk did not think of his dictatorship as an end in itself but as a necessary means to raise his people to that level of education and social well-being which democratic government required. The beloved maker of modern Turkey died in 1938, admired all over the world for his constructive statesmanship.

The Rise of Hitler's Third Reich

The republic of Germany. On November 9, 1918, when the German kaiser abdicated and fled to neutral Holland, the British and French people received the news with deep satisfaction. It was their belief that, if a liberal democratic government could be substituted in Germany for the old imperial autocratic régime, the cause of peace and international good will in Europe would be greatly strengthened. The revolution that caused the kaiser to pack his bags began in the fleet on November 4. The news spread like lightning throughout Germany, and everywhere the authority of the old government crumpled. Five days after the revolt Prince Max, the chancellor, turned his authority over to Friedrich Ebert, the leader of the majority Socialists and a self-taught man of the people. The same day the republic was officially proclaimed.

Germany at this time was in a state of bewilderment. The collapse of the old imperial government, symbolized in the abdication of the kaiser, provoked much disagreement as to what should be substituted in its place. The Communists wanted a complete social as well as a political revolution. The followers of Ebert favored the path of moderation in order to establish a democratic system in which the rights of private property and individual economic initiative would be safeguarded. In December clashes occurred between the Communists, known as the Spartacists, and the followers of Ebert. Early in January desperate fighting took place in Berlin, ending in the annihilation of the Spartacists and the death of their two leaders, Karl Liebknecht and Rosa Luxemburg.

The following week, in a national election to select the members of a constitutional convention, the moderate Liberals, the Catholic Center Party, and the Socialists gained the most votes. The representatives selected by the people then convened to draw up the so-called Weimar constitution. By midsummer of 1919 their work was complete. The new constitution was a remarkable document, the work of men who believed in social and political democracy. It provided for a president, a chancellor who was responsible to the Reichstag, and national referendums. The rights of labor were guaranteed, personal liberties safeguarded, and compulsory education planned for everyone up to the age of eighteen.

Troubles of the new republic. It soon became apparent that it was easier to write a constitution than to make it work. Even while the document was being drafted, in the spring of 1919, counter-revolutions broke out in many parts of the country. These uprisings, mostly the work of Communists, were put down, but not before ten thousand persons had lost their lives. In March 1920 a reactionary leader named Wolfgang Kapp seized Berlin. This revolt, or *Putsch* as it is called in Germany, was a failure. In 1923 Munich became the scene for what appeared to be a comic-opera revolt engineered by a comparatively unknown Austrian named Adolf Hitler. The revolt was promptly subdued and its instigator sent to prison.

No sooner had internal political stability been secured than the new republic found itself confronted with financial problems. In accordance with the Treaty of Versailles, Germany had already made considerable reparation payments to the Allied governments, but these payments were stopped in 1922. During the dreadful days of 1923 when French and Belgian troops occupied the Ruhr, much that was wholesome and substantial in German society was wiped out. Middle-class savings declined because of the inflation of the mark, the moderates in political circles lost their influence to ultra-nationalists and reactionaries, and the republic began to falter. But

Not so long ago Berlin open-air cafes held gaiety and unconcern.   Table overflowed table, and greetings were called across the flagstone courtyards.   The Kroll Garden was not unlike the restaurant in the plaza at Rockefeller Center, New York City.

the republic was saved and Germany rescued from economic disruption through the French evacuation of the Ruhr in 1924, and by the Dawes Plan, which made it easier for Germany to meet her schedule of payments and enabled her to obtain large loans from abroad.

Foreign affairs. There were, too, certain encouraging developments in the field of foreign affairs. From 1923 to 1929 the German foreign minister, Gustav Stresemann, earnestly sought a reconciliation with Germany's former enemies. We have already noted how this statesman cooperated with Briand and Sir Austen Chamberlain in bringing about the Locarno agreements in 1925. In 1926 Germany entered the League of Nations, peace in Europe seemed assured, and the happy prospect was emphasized by the grant of the Nobel peace prize to Briand, Sir Austen Chamberlain, and Stresemann.

The fading of German liberalism. The stability of the new German republic was more apparent than real. Almost from the beginning of the republic the Socialist parties began to lose ground, while the conservatives advanced slowly but steadily. In 1925 the loyal President Ebert died. Into his place stepped no republican. The election of 1925

resulted in the selection of Paul von Hindenburg, a war hero, as Ebert's successor. Many people believed that the new president, a member of the proud Prussian aristocracy, would undermine the republic. But to the surprise of the whole world Hindenburg supported the constitution. The fact remained, however, that the conservative element in Germany had been able to place one of its representatives in the presidential chair.

German democratic inexperience. One of the most important reasons for the failure of the German republic was lack of experience in handling democratic institutions. The principle of proportional representation was carried so far that innumerable separate parties were formed. Only by coalition could government majorities be formed. The liberal elements in Germany were too diverse to remain united and to follow a consistent policy. Moreover, the republic dealt too gently with its enemies, who utilized democratic privileges to get into power and, once in, destroyed the institutions that had allowed them to grow.

Prosperity and depression. During the years from 1925 to 1929, in spite of the political fumbling of the republic, Germany was nevertheless quite prosperous. Tremendous sums borrowed mainly from the United States exceeded the amounts paid by Germany in reparations and enabled the country to go on a spending spree. Extensive housing activity took place, public works projects including city halls, post offices, stadiums, and roads were undertaken, and industry was expanded and modernized. Germany, next to the United States, became the second most powerful industrial nation in the world.

But the collapse of world economy in 1931 brought on an acute financial crisis in Germany as many investors tried to liquidate their German holdings. In July 1931 all the banks were forced to close and disorders took place in many cities. Unemployment rapidly increased until it reached almost 6,000,000 working families. In order to balance the national budget, emergency decrees slashed unemployment benefits and cut wages in some trades as much as 40 per cent. Desperate, jobless workers roamed the streets shouting, "Give us bread." Night after night in Berlin and Munich shootings and fighting took place on the streets as the police and military forces battled hungry mobs.

Ingredients of dictatorship in Germany. It has been customary to ascribe the triumph of Hitler to the economic misery which accompanied the depression. But other nations had depressions as bad as Germany's and did not invariably turn to dictatorship as the way out. The truth is that Nazi Germany was a compound of numerous ingredients, many of which have been in existence in Germany for centuries. Such men as Hegel the philosopher and Treitschke the historian had exalted the state at the expense of the individual. The weakness of the tradition of political liberalism in German history made the success of the Weimar republic doubtful from the outset.

Furthermore, of decisive importance in discrediting the German republic was the legend fostered by the Prussian military clique to the effect that the German army had not really been defeated on the field of battle in 1918. It had, so went the view, been stabbed in the back by pacifist liberals and decadent democrats on the home front. According to one student of German post-war affairs:

"In spite of the elaborate precautions of the constitution to forestall resurrection of a super-government of the army, the militaristic machine remained in fact unaffected by political change. Nothing could please the army leaders more than the 'stabbing-in-the-back' legend invented by nationalistic propaganda, making the Socialists and pacifists alike a convenient scapegoat for the failures of the General Staff. The German people were incapable of accepting defeat and making the best of it. Had Marshal Foch dictated the peace in Berlin, thus driving home the collapse of the army to the masses, perhaps the Germans would have learned their lesson for once."[24] For centuries the German people have been conditioned to accept and even enjoy regimentation. In many Germans, also, there has been evident a strong current of morbidity and mysticism, which was fertile soil for Nazi philosophy with its cult of the Leader, its racial dogmas, and its emphasis upon the injustices of Versailles.

Versailles in particular produced a persecution complex in the minds of many embittered Germans. The mistaken policy of France, as illustrated by Poincaré's invasion of the Ruhr, sowed seeds of hate. The reparations and the war guilt clause in the peace treaty caused further resentment. Some of the vexations and unjust features of Versailles had of course been eliminated by the time Hitler came to power—such problems as reparations, Germany's exclusion from the League of Nations, and the Allied occupation of the Rhineland. But the war guilt clause, Germany's enforced disarmament, the lost colonies, and other grievances still remained. Behind scenes worked the German industrialists, convinced that the republic was not competent to discourage, and if need be stifle, the strong trend toward Communism in certain quarters of the country.

Adolf Hitler's rise to prominence. The historian must take cognizance of all these factors as he mulls over the rise of National Socialism. Perhaps, however, the factor that explains its rise more than any other is Adolf Hitler, its creator and high priest. While it is perhaps magnifying the importance of Hitler, some authorities go so far as to assert that "The National Socialist party and the Third Reich would never have arisen without Hitler."[25]

The future creator of Nazism was born in Austria in 1889. His father was a minor customs official. An orphan at seventeen, Adolf Hitler went to Vienna with ambitions of becoming an architect or artist. Rejected as a pupil by the Academy of Art, he was forced to make his living by painting postcards and doing odd jobs. In 1911 he went to Munich where he earned a scanty living by selling small paintings. When war broke out he joined a German regiment and was sent to France where he served during the entire period of hostilities.

The armistice of 1918 found him in a hospital. When the news of Germany's defeat came he says that he turned his face to the wall and wept bitterly. The authorities in Munich were worried about Communist and other radical plots and hired Hitler after his release from the army as a special investigating agent. In the line of duty he was asked to check on a small organization called the German Workers' party.

After attending several of its meetings, Hitler joined this group. It was not long before he became the leader. In speaking before their meetings, held in various beer halls, he discovered that he possessed remarkable oratorical powers. Hitler's speeches were always compounded of the same elements: hatred of the Jews and Communists, the injustice of Versailles, and the contention that the German army had not been defeated in 1918 but had been betrayed by pacifists and Jews behind the lines.

Birth of the National Socialist party. At a mass meeting in a large Munich beer house, in 1920, Hitler announced to 2000 followers the 25-point program of the National Socialist party, the successor to the small and ineffectual German Workers' party. Among other things the program promised land reform, the nationalization of trusts, and the abolition of all income that was not actually earned. The economic proposals were clothed in generalities, but the demands for a greater Germany which should include all the German-speaking peoples of Europe, the abrogation of Versailles, and the acquisition of land and colonies for the needs of the German people were clearly stated. Thus by the end of 1922 Hitler had become a fairly important political figure. Sometimes he would hire a dozen beer halls and dash from one to the other in an automobile, delivering fiery and eloquent harangues before the various audiences. The swastika, an ancient symbol used by many primitive people throughout the world, was adopted as the emblem of the National Socialist party, now known as the Nazi party. (Nazi is a con-

traction of *National-sozialistische Partei,* meaning National Socialist party.)

Hitler's Mein Kampf. Meanwhile the Nazi organization grew, and a newspaper, the *Volkische Beobachter* (Racial Observer), was obtained as a party mouthpiece. The brown-shirted Storm Troops were recruited. In November 1923, after the failure of Hitler's Munich *Putsch,* he was sentenced to prison for a term of five years. His quarters were quite pleasant, and, assisted by some of his followers, among them his close friend and confidant, Rudolf Hess, he began to write *Mein Kampf* (My Battle). Before his work was finished his sentence was cut short, and he became a free man in December 1924.

Mein Kampf is an autobiography, a long and involved treatment of the principles and philosophy of Nazism, a statement of the objectives of Hitler's party, and a discussion of the techniques which must be utilized to achieve the desired ends. The book contains a number of observations of interest to us here. (1) History is made by great races. The greatest of these is the Aryan and its most perfect and noble exemplification is the German people whose destiny it is to be the world's foremost people. (2) Mixed nations always deteriorate and come into existence through contact with inferior peoples such as the Poles, Slavs, and, above all, the Jews. In the mind of Hitler the Jew was the arch-criminal of all time. (3) *Mein Kampf* breathes contempt for what it calls decadent democracy and challenges the menace of Communism. The first is the agency of fools, the second the weapon of nefarious criminals. (4) Hitler has little faith in the common people. Only through a great leader can they realize whatever destiny may be theirs. Writes Hitler: "The German has not the faintest idea of how a nation must be swindled if one wants to have masses of supporters." (5) In the realm of foreign policy, expansion is upheld as the rightful outlet of German energy until Greater Germany becomes a state of 250 million souls. (6) Before this aim is attained France, the arch-enemy of Germany, must be destroyed. (7) The main area of German expansion must be to the east, in the Russian Ukraine, and the two main allies utilized by Germany should be Great Britain and Italy. (8) Again and again, *Mein Kampf* heaps scorn on pacifism. War and force are held up as the only method to be used by the

In March 1936 Hitler ordered German troops, here passing in review, to march into the demilitarized Rhineland. The Fuehrer's move disregarded the last repressive clauses of the Versailles Treaty and the Locarno Pact.

strong. (9) Recourse to war had not been proved a mistaken policy by the defeat suffered in 1918, for it was not the collapse of the kaiser's armed forces that led to German defeat but the cowardice and treachery of weak souls within Germany itself.

Nazism grows in power. After his release from prison, Hitler and a devoted group of followers began the huge task of converting Germany to Nazism. His success at first was negligible. In 1925 the Nazi party had no more than 27,000 followers. In the national election of 1928 Hitler won only twelve seats in the Reichstag. So trivial did the Nazi movement seem at the time that when Lord D'Abernon, former British ambassador to Berlin, published his important memoirs entitled *An Ambassador of Peace* he made the following reference to Hitler in a footnote: "He was finally released after six months and bound over for the rest of his sentence, thereafter fading into oblivion."[26] In 1929 a distinguished German scholar, Arnold Wolfers, delivered an address in London on "Germany and Europe" without mentioning Nazism. There was hardly any need to, since Hitler's deputies in the Reichstag at this time numbered twelve. Yet in September of 1930 this number rose to 107!

Once the Nazi movement began to take hold, Hitler and his master propagandist, Joseph Goebbels, utilized every art of persuasion to convert the mass of the people to Nazism. Seldom, if ever, has there been such a propaganda campaign. All over Germany huge meetings were organized. Over each stadium a Nazi aviator thrilled the crowd with his aerobatics. Then thousands of Storm Troops marched in to form a great swastika. Martial music, the roll of drums, the trumpeting of bugles—all these sounds impregnated the air with a stirring martial appeal. No speaker was at first seen on the platform. Suspense grew as a huge spotlight was turned upon the rostrum. Into this beam of light stepped the slight Goebbels. For two hours he poured forth a torrent of eloquence: "Germany is in ruins"—"This is the result of reparations"—"The Jews are behind all our woes" —"It is only the Nazi party that can make Germany strong and prosperous, that will repudiate the reparations, obtain lost colonies, and make Germany's army and navy the fear of all Europe."

Hitler created chancellor. In 1932 when the Austrian-born Hitler became a German citizen, he ran against von Hindenburg for the

Chancellor Hitler greets the aged President von Hindenburg as Germany honors her war dead on National Heroes' Memorial Day, 1934. That is Goering at the left; Admiral Raeder is standing behind Hitler.

presidency of the German republic. Hitler was defeated, but the Nazi party continued to grow. The other political parties refused to join ranks, and it became increasingly difficult for the German ministries based on weak coalition to carry on the government. On two occasions von Hindenburg asked Hitler to join a coalition, but Hitler refused, demanding instead what was equivalent to dictatorial power. At this point a clique of aristocratic nationalists and powerful industrialists of the Ruhr conspired to place Hitler in power as the chancellor. This act they prevailed upon the aged Hindenburg to carry out, and a mixed cabinet of nationalists was created in January 1933 with Hitler at the head. The industrialists and nationalists mistakenly hoped by this maneuver to use Hitler as a means of blocking the growth of radicalism.

Dictator Hitler. Hitler, because he could not control the Reichstag, called a general election for March 5, 1933. During the campaign broadcasting stations were monopolized by Nazi propaganda. Storm Troops bullied and coerced the voters. Just before the election was held, fire gutted the Reichstag building. The mysterious conflagration was blamed upon the Communists, although it was almost certainly caused by the Nazis themselves. After the votes were counted, Hitler controlled 44 per cent of the deputies. To this large bloc was added the support of the Nationalists, another 8 per cent, giving the Nazis a bare majority.

Quickly the Nazi majority passed a law giving Hitler dictatorial power for the next four years. During the debate one of the opponents to the bill cried: "Take our liberty, take our lives, but leave us our honor. If you Nazis really want social reconstruction you would need no law such as this." The world at large, shocked at the creation of the Nazi dictatorship, was nevertheless happy to note that Adolf Hitler in addressing the Reichstag had said: "In the field of foreign relations we desire to live at peace with all nations, but only on a basis of equality. Our hand is stretched out to every people willing to forget the sad past."

Nazi terrorism. Assisted by such lieutenants as Goering, Goebbels, Himmler (head of the dread Gestapo, or secret police), Hess, and Von Ribbentrop, Hitler now ruthlessly smashed and uprooted the democratic institutions by which he was brought to power. All rival po-

litical parties were disbanded by force, and individuals who had spoken out against Nazism mysteriously disappeared. It has been estimated that 19,000 persons committed suicide in 1933 and that 16,000 died from unexplained causes. Concentration camps were built to house thousands of prisoners, and tales of horrible persecution leaked out of Germany.

In June 1934 the world was horrified at the news of a terrible blood purge in Germany. Disagreement had apparently broken out between Hitler and his old friend and supporter, Captain Ernst Roehm, Chief of the Storm Troops. Without warning Hitler and Goering struck. Roehm, Gregor Strasser, General von Schleicher and his wife, and other leaders were wiped out without trial or ceremony. In the same year President von Hindenburg died, and Hitler became both chancellor and president. It now became common to use the title Führer (leader) in referring to Hitler, and the new régime was described as the Third Reich. Its two predecessors were the ones created by Otto the Great in 962 and by Bismarck in 1871.

It is interesting to note that the old Weimar constitution of the republic has never been formally abolished. The basic constitutional document of the Nazi régime is the so-called Enabling Act, passed by the Reichstag in March 1933. This act gave the executive branch of government the right to legislate by decree. Such decrees could deviate from the Weimar constitution. The Reichstag continued as a phantom legislature, called on rare occasions to pass on acts or policies already in existence. As in Fascist Italy, practically all political power in practice was lodged in and exercised by one political organization, the National Socialist party. "The actual power of the party lies in the fact that it controls the state, while it is itself immune from supervision or interference by the state."27

Nazi persecution. In domestic affairs Hitler ruthlessly put into practice his ideas of racial superiority. A national boycott against the Jews was proclaimed in April 1933, and they were barred from public service. Discrimination of all sorts followed. Many noted scholars either were sent to concentration camps or fled the country. Among those fortunate enough to escape were such Nobel prize winners as Albert Einstein and James Franck, physicists, and Fritz Haber, the chemist.

Hitler was not contented with racial dis-

In 1933 fire burst out in twenty different places in the Reichstag, German parliament house, inscribed "The German People." The Nazis are generally credited with starting the fire, although police blamed Communists. Communist or not, a hundred members of the Reichstag were arrested.

crimination alone. All labor unions were disbanded. A new organization, the Labor Front, was set up under Robert Ley, to enroll both workers and employers. The right to strike or to call a lockout was made illegal. Both capital and labor were now subordinated to the state.

Since Nazi doctrine elevated the state above all else, a movement was instigated to subordinate religion to the Hitler régime. Revolting against such pressure, German Protestants, led by the Reverend Martin Niemoeller, naval officer in the First World War, repudiated the attempts of Hitler to interfere with religious freedom. The movement was crushed, and Niemoeller was placed in a concentration camp in the spring of 1938. Perhaps most disturbing to German Christians was the intention of some Nazi extremists to paganize the church. Speaking in 1938 Karl Barth, the noted Swiss theologian, declared: "It is impossible to understand National Socialism, unless we see it in fact as a new Islam, its myth as a new Allah, and Hitler as this new Allah's prophet."

Nazi youth organizations did not train their members in hurling the discus or throwing javelins, but specialized in hand-grenade throwing. It was peacetime, so shovels took the place of guns.

German propaganda and education. Education and public opinion were coordinated for Nazi needs. A Reich culture cabinet was set up to control literature, the press, broadcasting, drama, music, art, and the cinema. All of these agencies were to reflect only one attitude, one pattern of thought, and one stream of esthetic appreciation. Goebbels was given the task of controlling the minds and hearts of the German people with his department of propaganda. From this department, broadcasting stations sent programs abroad, jamming the air lanes to disrupt the broadcasts of other nations. Goebbels also provided radio fare for the German listener and spied on the people to see whether they listened to forbidden foreign broadcasts.

Education especially felt the heavy hand of the Nazis. The German universities, once famous throughout the world for their academic freedom and objectivity of thought, became agencies for propagating such ideas as the racial myths of Nazism. Enrollment in the universities was limited to good Nazi material, and professors were dismissed from their chairs

by the score. The school system was integrated with the German Youth Movement, which drilled and regimented boys and girls between the ages of ten and fourteen. The boys were taught above all else to be ready to fight and die for their Führer, the girls, that it was their place to mother the many babies needed by the Third Reich. Care was taken to foster the cult of athleticism. Everywhere physical culture was stressed, many of those physically unfit were sterilized so they could not reproduce their kind, and a race of super-Aryans was supposed to be in the process of creation.

The economy of Nazism. In theory and in outward form Nazism has retained capitalism and perpetuated the institution of private property. Businessmen may still take risks and be rewarded by profits, but both business and labor are rigidly controlled by and subordinated to the state. In the beginning the Nazi program was strongly socialist in tone, but the 25-point program of 1920 was so ambiguous that it enticed the support of the big industrialists, the small businessmen, and a large number of workers. It soon became evident, however, that Hitler had no intention of carrying out all the points of his program. Somewhat as Mussolini had done, he placed the state above both the laborer and the capitalist.

Between 1933 and 1939 unemployment was reduced, but the means to this end are questionable. The middle class was bowed down under a huge tax load, and the national debt was increased one third in order to give employment to the masses, who were put to work in armament factories or drafted for the army. This was, naturally, only a temporary solution of the economic problem. It led logically to the utilization of these vast armaments in aggression against other states, in order to solve other economic difficulties which continued to grow under the Third Reich.

Nazi Germany, in the field of economics, introduced a program in 1933 whose purpose was to try to restore prosperity to the nation. In 1936 the famous Four-Year plan, overlapping the first program, was initiated. The objective of this last plan was more sinister. Briefly, it was to set up an autarchic state in which Germany would be practically self-sufficient. In 1936 Hitler stated: "Within four years Germany must be independent of foreign countries with regard to all those materials that can be produced in any way by

Giant swastikas bordered the closely-packed May Day (1937) crowd as Hitler told 50,000 chosen Nazi party members that he would not tolerate church interference in German politics. He is speaking in front of the Kaiser Wilhelm Art Gallery in Berlin.

German ability, by our chemistry and our machines and mining industries themselves."[28] In many cases the chemically-created commodities cost much more and were inferior in quality to those purchasable on the world market. "The Nazi leaders, however, insisted that economic independence and military preparedness more than outweighed the resulting lower standard of living."[29] The climax of the Nazi story is covered in later chapters.

Summary

In reviewing the rise of Communism in Russia it is important to remember that the ideology of Communism is derived from the teachings of Karl Marx and has been subsequently modified by other leaders and writers. The Russian system is based on governmental control and ownership of all economic enterprise and the utilization of national economic planning. Although it advocates the dictatorship of the proletariat as a preliminary phase, Communist theory does not exalt the state as against the individual but looks to the time when the absolutism of the state and the restraints of government can be removed. The Communists, unlike Hitler's Nazis, have not resorted to a racial philosophy which seeks to exalt Russian Slavs as a super-race. The Communist state visualizes all its citizens as belonging to one class, that of the workers.

In industrialization, education, and social welfare tremendous innovations have been brought about. The schools have been expanded to a remarkable degree. Divorces, at one time easy to obtain, are being made more difficult. Home and family life are being strengthened rather than deprecated. The new constitution of 1936 registers in theory at least many gains in political freedom. Russia still remains a one-party state, where the trend so far has been to emphasize a social and economic, rather than a political, Bill of Rights. The most important aspect of Communism and the one on which it probably will ultimately be judged is its system of national economic planning.

Italian Fascism was less complex in theory and practice than Communism and is therefore somewhat easier to describe. Some of its most significant features were: (1) its ultra-nationalist character, (2) its emphasis on imperialist expansion, (3) the military nature of Mussolini's new state, (4) the national regimentation of economic life by and for the state, and (5) its antidemocratic character, which taught that the individual had no rights except as a cog in the Fascist machine.

The followers of Mussolini were wont to maintain in the early 1930's that his régime had restored order to a distraught country, that governmental administration had been improved, educational facilities expanded, and the country made more self-sufficient. They maintained, in a word, that Fascism had restored national self-respect. Many Italians, it has been said, supported Fascism because it was apparently "a means of recovering their sense of human importance." There was some truth in these assertions, but the changes brought about by Mussolini were achieved only at the cost of considerable sacrifice from the people. The price of Fascism has been too high for the advantages it supposedly bought. Education was the mere tool of Fascist propaganda. A more malignant result was the glorification of war. This, as we shall see in a later chapter, involved Italy in a conflict which not only loaded grievous losses upon the people but completely shattered whatever constructive achievement the Fascist régime could claim for Italy.

Superficially, German Nazism seemed the result of world depression, of Versailles, of an outraged nationalism, and of a lack of confidence in the weak Weimar Republic. These causes supplied the opportunity and the justification for Nazism, but did not necessarily create Nazism itself. One must look farther back in history than the First World War. Rulers like Frederick the Great had made the ideal of benevolent despotism acceptable to those who lived under it. Men like Hegel and Treitschke exalted the position of the state at the expense of the individual. Beginning in Brandenburg and Prussia, pride in a military tradition and the accomplishment of arms eventually fixed itself in the German mind. None of these sentiments were necessarily peculiar to Germany, but in other countries they were eventually discarded or became relatively unimportant.

Nazism was built on a fanatical racial ideology. It placed the German people on the pedestal of a super-race. Like Fascism it glorifies war and welcomes the opportunity to expand its power by the force of arms. A later chapter will describe the part played by the Nazis in plunging the world into a Second World War. While Communism sees the dictatorship of the proletariat as a temporary measure preparing the way to ultimate democracy and freedom for the individual, both Nazism and Fascism repudiate completely and finally all democratic practices.

In its early phases Nazism succeeded in removing some of the features of Versailles regarded by many Germans as humiliating and unfair. Some of the strong measures taken by Hitler to meet the depression in Germany might have been justified. But what started out allegedly as a means to an end, as an instrument to serve the needs of the

German people, soon became an end in itself, and one may reasonably question whether this was not the original intention. What began as a means to correct the few remaining inequalities of Versailles quickly changed to an attempt to impose on others inequalities that made those of the 1918 peace conference pale into insignificance.

COUNTRIES OF THE ESTABLISHED ORDER: 1919-1939

France

1919-1924	National Bloc government	Reconstruction of country
1924-1926	Left Cartel government	Dangerous monetary policy
1926-1932	National Union under Poincaré	Strengthened finances
1932-1936	Constant shift of French ministries	Paris riots, Stavisky scandal
1936-1937	Popular Front under Léon Blum	Leftist government
1937-1939	Conservative government	Growing cleavage between classes

The Succession States

1919-1939	Czechoslovakian republic prospers	Political liberalism under Masaryk
1926-1935	Poland, a dictatorship under Pilsudski	Problem of minorities
1918-1921	Republic in Hungary	Communist régime of Bela Kun
1921-1931	Regent Horthy dictator in Hungary	Monarchy without a monarch
1919-1939	Yugoslavia wrestles with Serb-Croat rivalry	King assassinated by Croat

Elsewhere in Europe

1919-1934	Socialist government in Austria	Civil war and defeat of Socialists
1934	Dollfuss becomes dictator	
1919-1938	Rumania struggles with minorities	
1938	King Carol becomes dictator	Growth of pro-Fascist Iron Guard
1919-1923	Radical peasant party forms Bulgarian dictatorship	
1934	Dictatorship under King Boris	Moderate régime swept away
1932	Salazar becomes Portuguese dictator	
1936	Metaxas dictatorship in Greece	
1919	Finland a republic	
	Socialized democracy in Scandinavia	
	Democracy holds its own in Switzerland, Belgium, Holland	
1923-1930	Spanish dictator Rivera bolsters corrupt system	Alfonso abdicates
1930-1936	Republic in Spain	Overthrown by Fascist revolt

Great Britain

1921-1924	Postwar economic depression	
1924-1929	Conservative government under Baldwin	Economic crisis
1929-1931	Labor government under MacDonald	
1931	Statute of Westminster establishes British Commonwealth of Nations	Gives dominions autonomy
1931-1935	MacDonald heads coalition	Accused of treason to Labor party
1935	Conservative government under Baldwin	An "old-man" government

United States

1919	Withdrawal from world affairs	Refusal to join League
1920-1923	Return to normalcy under Harding	High tariff, graft
1923-1928	Coolidge and the era of big business	Immigration restrictions
1928-1933	Hoover and the great depression	High tariff, isolationism
1933-1935	Roosevelt and the New Deal	Relief, recovery, reform

Latin America

1919-1939	Postwar period; industrialization	Rise of middle class, especially in Mexico
1919-1929	Attempt at diversification instead of specialization in economics	
	Trade rivalry: German tactics	
	Race fusion and distinctive culture	Art—Orozco, Rivera; Music—Chavez
	Pan-Americanism: Good Neighbor Policy	Hull's influence, reciprocity treaties

CHAPTER 4

Democracy on Trial

THE states surveyed in the previous chapter—
Russia, Italy, Germany—were sure of themselves, assertive, and dynamic. They were the
countries of a new order as contrasted with those which one may regard as belonging to
an established order, an order pledging allegiance to certain traditions and concepts in
the process of development since the Renaissance and Religious Revolt. The countries
of the established order placed their faith in democracy and capitalism, which in turn
rested upon the principles of individual liberty, representative government, religious
freedom, and *laissez-faire* economics. These countries were in a majority in continental
western Europe, in the British Commonwealth of Nations, and in the Western Hemisphere. Certain nations, such as the United States, Great Britain, the British Dominions,
the Scandinavian countries, and Czechoslovakia, were clearly democracies. Several other
states, including certain Latin-American republics, only imperfectly realized the democracy guaranteed in their constitutions. On the fringe of the established order were such
countries as Poland, Yugoslavia, and Bulgaria, where dictatorships loomed.

The record of the nations of the established order makes melancholy reading in the
decade and a half following the peace conference. In this chapter we shall see how nearly
all the new states created in 1919 scrapped their liberal constitutions in favor of some
form of dictatorship. We shall observe how, even in Great Britain and France, traditional champions of democracy, there was a growing lack of confidence in representative
government. Here and there European democracy seemed to flourish, as in the Scandinavian countries and Switzerland. The overthrow of the Spanish monarchy, too, was
for a time a hopeful sign that the liberal political tradition was not dying in Europe.

93

The United States in 1919 seemed in a logical position to assume leadership among the nations of the established order. She was now the most powerful and wealthy of them all. But after participating in the defeat of Germany and her allies and after her leader had proposed a League of Nations to enforce peace, the United States chose to withdraw from international affairs. During the next two decades America went through an era of industrial boom and stock speculation, a depression, and a period of partial recovery and reform.

South of the Rio Grande were the Latin-American republics. After the First World War their ample natural resources became more and more important to the rest of the world. The history of Latin America from 1919 to 1939 reflects some social and economic reform, some advance of trade and industry. The republics drew a little closer to the United States, whom they had formerly feared, when their northern neighbor chose to exchange the policy of Dollar Diplomacy for that of the Good Neighbor. Presidents Hoover and Roosevelt made a determined effort to woo the esteem and friendship of Latin America and succeeded to an encouraging degree.

The Period of French Reconstruction

The National Bloc. As November 1918 brought victory to France and her allies, the republic set about binding up its wounds and repairing the ravages of war. More than one million Frenchmen had been killed; 13,000 square miles of French land had been devastated. During the war with Germany, France had been governed by a coalition known as the Sacred Union. After the elections of 1919 the country was ruled by the National Bloc, a political group made up of conservatives, in which money interests were strongly represented. The most important leaders of the National Bloc were Clemenceau, Poincaré, and Millerand. These men, ultra-nationalists, believed in the rigid enforcement of the provisions of the Versailles Treaty. They hated Germany and feared Russia. The main task of the National Bloc, the restoration of the devastated regions of France, was accomplished in record time. It had been expected by the French government that the huge costs of rebuilding the destroyed towns in the north of France would be covered by the reparation payments from Germany. But these payments ceased in 1923, and accordingly French troops marched into the Ruhr. From January 1922 to May 1924 Raymond Poincaré was premier of France and leader of the National Bloc. More than any other man he symbolized the policy of making Germany pay for the war and keeping her disarmed.

Leadership of the Left Cartel. Poincaré's policy did not gain the approval of the British, who favored a more moderate and conciliatory attitude toward Germany. Many Frenchmen also began to see that as long as Germany was held down and her economic life throttled it would be impossible for her to pay reparations. The National Bloc therefore fell from power in 1924 and was succeeded by the Left Cartel. This coalition under the leadership of Edouard Herriot advocated the extension of government control of industry, an increase in income taxes, and a liberal foreign policy. The Left Cartel guided the destinies of France until 1926. Herriot had an enviable record in foreign affairs, for the Dawes Plan had now apparently solved the reparations tangle, French troops had evacuated the Ruhr, and Germany had signed the Locarno agreements. In the field of domestic affairs the Left Cartel was not so successful. This was especially true in the case of public finance. Although France had practically no unemployment after the war and her foreign trade by 1922 surpassed that before 1913, her monetary policy threatened to plunge the franc into the same abyss that engulfed the German mark in 1923.

To meet this emergency Poincaré was called back to power to head a National Union government and save the franc. Drastic measures were taken by the new government. Taxes were increased and expenditures curtailed.

In 1936 various groups in France succeeded in organizing the first Popular Front ministry, headed by Léon Blum (center, seated).   The Popular Front championed a forty-hour week, collective bargaining, pay raises, and paid vacations for French workers.   But the ministry was not strong enough to survive the attack of vested interests, and the reforms were not achieved.

Poincaré's policies gave French finances a new lease on life, and progress in other fields brought the enactment of workmen's insurance and the completion of the task of rebuilding the devastated areas. In 1929 Poincaré retired from public life. His passing from the political scene coincided with the appearance of a world depression and a period of storm and stress that menaced the republic.

French parliamentary government. Unlike the British system of parliamentary government, which usually operates through two major political parties, the French system has worked with a dozen or more political parties. When a premier desired to form a new government he could not depend upon the support of one dominant and cohesive party as in England but must build a cabinet of several diverse political elements. Such a bloc, as it is called, may possess unanimity of policy when it is formed. But on the slightest provocation disagreement may develop, the unity of the bloc disappears, and the premier is usually forced to resign. French cabinets were thus highly unstable political compounds. From 1917 to 1937 thirty-four separate governments held office in France.

Constant shift of French ministries. The Coalition government was faced with serious problems shortly after the retirement of Poincaré. For three years it tried to cope with rising unemployment, budget deficits, and heavy military expenditures. In 1932 France repudiated the conservative Coalition and placed a more liberal group in power. The Left Cartel, again under Herriot, now sought to solve its country's ills. But the question of paying the war debt to the United States brought about the collapse of the Herriot ministry. In the following thirteen months (December 1932 to January 1934) a period of parliamentary demoralization ensued in which five governments were placed in office. Public impatience with politicians was heightened by a railroad disaster in December 1933, when two hundred were killed. There was evidence of negligence on the railroad's part, but the government's investigation was half-hearted.

Disgust with the government was increased even more by the affair of Stavisky, who cheated French investors out of some 600,-000,000 francs. Many politicians were involved in the scandal, but the ministry in power refused to authorize an investigation. The wrath of the people smoldered, then flared forth in Paris on the evening of February 6, 1933. Thousands of angry citizens thronged the streets and tried to storm the Chamber of Deputies. In the fighting the police killed a score of rioters and injured a hundred others. The riot was quelled, and a National Union was formed under Gaston Doumergue. He demanded that the position of the prime minister be strengthened and that other constitutional changes be made so that the constant coming and going of ministries be ended. But Doumergue's suggestions were not heeded, and he resigned in November 1934.

Sentiment against the government. Pierre Laval and Pierre Etienne Flandin tried to carry on the National Union, which by now had become ultra-conservative and the agent of the wealthy and privileged classes, but the deterioration of parliamentary institutions continued. By this time the mass of French people believed their politicians to be thoroughly corrupt. The Third French Republic was assailed by enemies from all sides. The Fascist organization, the Croix de Feu, demanded: "Take France away from the politicians and give it back to the French people." Communists worked for a revolution to sweep away the bourgeoisie. Monarchists agitated for the restoration of a king. In the winter of 1934-1935, the *Petit Journal* of Paris conducted a contest to increase circulation. The paper asked its readers to answer the question "If France were to have a dictator, whom would you choose?" There was no dearth of choices—forty persons were named.

From June 1935 to January 1936 Pierre Laval was premier of France. The fall of this wily politician came when the French people repudiated the Hoare-Laval agreement in which France and Great Britain agreed to partition Abyssinia to suit Mussolini. A stop-gap ministry followed Laval but it too was forced out of office in May 1936.

The Popular Front. At this point emerged the Popular Front, a coalition composed of parties of the Left—Radical Socialists, Socialists, and Communists—united to oppose the conservative elements in the government. In June the Popular Front won a national election securing 381 of the 615 seats in the Chamber of Deputies. Léon Blum, a noted lawyer and writer, became premier. For the first time the Socialist party became the largest single party in France.

Under Blum the Popular Front endeavored to stem the influence of Fascism, to improve the country's finances, to better the condition of the workers, and to bring about certain fundamental economic reforms. In particular, Léon Blum promised to "break the power of the two hundred families who control the economic life of the nation."[1] In foreign policy the Popular Front was friendly to Great Britain and supported the League of Nations.

An epidemic of sit-down strikes at first embarrassed the new government, but gradually labor was conciliated by the passage of laws introducing a forty-hour week, higher wages, collective bargaining, and vacations with pay. Furthermore, the government extended its control over the Bank of France and initiated a public-works program. "The Blum government, in short, was for the laborer and against monopoly and Big Business. But it was equally against collectivism."[2]

Growing rift between classes. Socialists and Communists had not got along too well in the coalition, and in June 1937 Blum was forced to resign. Unfavorable trade balances, an enormous public debt, and an unbalanced budget proved too much for the Popular Front government. France swung in the direction of conservatism. The forty-hour week was ended, and strikes were energetically suppressed. A deplorable feature of French society in the late 1930's was the growing chasm between the upper and lower classes. Businessmen and financiers were horrified at the prospects of Communism and were inclined to flirt with Fascism. The working classes believed that the reforms of the Popular Front had been sabotaged and that a France dominated by a wealthy clique was hardly worth fighting for. This cleavage between classes was secretly encouraged by subtle propaganda from the totalitarian countries. And while Frenchmen quarreled, while France's economic strength and productivity were being sapped, Hitler's Germany, regimented and feverishly productive, was rapidly outstripping France in the production of armaments. The tragic ingredients explaining the fall of France in the spring of 1940 had now been supplied.

Czechoslovakia, Poland, Hungary, and Yugoslavia

The new Czech republic. The nations which arose in 1919 out of the débris of the once great Austro-Hungarian empire were called the Succession States (see map, page 35). The most important of these new countries was Czechoslovakia. Four hundred years of Austrian rule had not diminished the patriotic zeal of the Czechs, who during the First

World War were planning the emergence of a new Czech state should Austria-Hungary be defeated. The most important of these Czech patriots was Thomas G. Masaryk, who was instrumental in the creation of the new Czech and Slovak state. With the approval and support of President Wilson he published the Czechoslovakian declaration of independence in Washington. In November 1918, after the collapse of Austria, the Slovaks and Czechs joined in establishing a republic; by 1920 a constitution was adopted. Masaryk became president and Dr. Eduard Benes foreign minister of the new state.

Within an area of about 50,000 square miles Czechoslovakia had a population of fifteen million. These people were of many different racial stocks and nationalities. In addition to Czechs and Slovaks, there were such minority groups as Germans in the Sudeten area, Russians (Ruthenians), and Hungarians (see map, page 39). Altogether these minorities constituted one third of the total population. Despite the problem of the minorities Czechoslovakia prospered. She inherited most of the industries of the old Austrian empire, her soil was rich, her timber resources ample, and her minerals valuable. From the Czechoslovakian factories poured a stream of goods: glass, armaments, shoes, toys, and textiles. A large foreign trade was built up, and the government assisted small farmers by breaking up large estates. The people of the new state demonstrated that they were industrious, conscientious citizens and sincere lovers of political liberalism. Now free, the Czechs and Slovaks eagerly turned to enrich their own culture.

Difficulties of Polish independence. To the north of Czechoslovakia lay Poland. With Germany on the west and Russia on the east, Poland extended from Rumania to the Baltic Sea. She had, in the eighteenth century, been partitioned three times; in 1795 she disappeared as a national political entity. But Polish nationalism persisted despite the alien rule of the Germans, Austrians, and Russians. During the First World War there was much confusion among the Poles. Some wished to fight for Russia, others for Austria. Some saw no reason for fighting on either side. But all were agreed on the necessity for obtaining independence. With the collapse of Russia, Austria-Hungary, and Germany it became possible in 1918 to declare a Polish republic. The

Ignace Jan Paderewski, Polish pianist-patriot, was one of the organizers of the Polish republic (1918-1919). When he died in 1941, the United States placed his body with those of her war heroes in Arlington Cemetery.

two men most instrumental in its creation were Ignace Paderewski, the famous pianist, and Marshal Jozef Pilsudski, a strong-willed and capable army officer. A democratic government was set up in 1921, but it soon became evident that the Poles were not too successfully running their democracy. Corruption, deadlock, and economic instability characterized the early twenties. In 1926 Pilsudski came out of retirement to engineer a *coup d'état*. The government was overthrown, and the old warrior became dictator and remained so until his death in 1935. A new constitution was adopted in 1935 which legalized a form of dictatorial government.

Poland also had large minorities (German, Lithuanian, and Ruthenian Russian—see map, page 39). She was primarily an agricultural nation, in which the wealth was controlled by a small landed and capitalist minority. The poverty of Poland was accentuated by the high birth rate. In 1919 the population was estimated to be 20 million; in 1939 it was 34 million.

Dictatorship in Hungary. The creation of new states after the First World War resulted in grievous losses to Hungary, whose territory was reduced seventy-five per cent. More than half her population was given to her neighbors. Immediately after the armistice in 1918 a short-lived republic was set up. The peace terms imposed by the Allies and subsequent unfavorable economic conditions discredited the new government, which was followed by a Soviet republic established by the Communist Bela Kun. After only a few months this régime was overthrown by a Rumanian army, which helped itself to any plunder that could be carried away by train or truck. After the Rumanians left the country, Admiral Horthy, head of a Hungarian army, established law and order. During 1921 several unsuccessful attempts were made by Charles, the former emperor of Austria-Hungary, to regain the throne. Constitutionally, however, Hungary remained a monarchy although the throne was vacated. Admiral Horthy ruled merely as the regent of the kingdom. To all intents a dictator, the regent relied from 1921 to 1931 upon a shrewd statesman, Count Stephen Bethlen, to run the government in the capacity of premier.

Dominating all thought in Hungary was the question of revision of the Treaty of Trianon. Everywhere maps of old Hungary surrounded by a crown of thorns were displayed showing the areas lost to other countries. Like Poland, Hungary was essentially a land of peasants, but the poverty and debasement of the peasantry was even worse than that in Poland. A feudal aristocracy owned most of the land on which tenants eked out a miserable existence.

Racial rivalries in Yugoslavia. Along the eastern shores of the Adriatic Sea emerged a new state called the Kingdom of Yugoslavia, a nation slightly less than 100,000 square miles in area, with a population of thirteen million. The Croats and Slovenes of the former Hapsburg empire joined with their brother Slavs in Serbia and Montenegro, mainly Serbs, to form the state of Yugoslavia. From the outset King Alexander had difficulty in reconciling the rivalries between Serbs, Croats, and Slovenes. Political differences reached a climax in 1928 when a riot broke out in the parliament in which Radich, the Croatian leader, was mortally wounded. In 1929 the king was forced to establish a dictatorship. Five years later he was assassinated in France by one of a group of Croatian terrorists. Prince Paul, a cousin of the murdered king, now became regent until young Peter, Alexander's son, should become old enough to take over the affairs of state. In addition to the rivalry between Croat and Serb there was an acute agrarian problem in Yugoslavia, because the country had too many large estates.

Austria, Rumania, Bulgaria, and Spain

Austria tries Socialism. The Treaty of St. Germain reduced Austria's population and territory three fourths, leaving a feeble little nation about the size of Maine, with less than seven million inhabitants (see map, page 35). Vienna, once the prosperous capital of a large empire, was now a great city without an adequate hinterland to nourish it. The area of the new Austria was but 32,000 square miles, and more than one quarter of the country's population lived in Vienna. In place of the old Hapsburg monarchy a republic was established somewhat after the federal system of Switzerland. For ten years afterward Austria was faced with the specter of financial bankruptcy and widespread unemployment. There was some talk of an economic union (*Anschluss*) with Germany as a way out of these difficulties, but this was forbidden by the Allies. In 1919 nearly fifty thousand children were sent from Austria to other countries to be saved from starvation, and in 1920 many additional thousands were also sent abroad. Through the efforts of the League of Nations in 1922 extensive loans were secured for Austria which did much to ease her economic distress.

During the days of unemployment and starvation the people of Vienna turned to Socialist leadership as a way out. The Socialist administration in Vienna introduced many remarkable reforms. Slums were torn down, and nearly 100,000 dwellings were built for the working class. Clinics and kindergartens were established. It was said that the city government now watched over the interests of a citizen from his birth in a municipal hospital to his death and subsequent burial by a municipal funeral. But the Socialist experiment in Vienna aroused the fears of the conservative elements in Austria, and in 1934 class antagonism flared into civil war. The Socialists were

Karl Marx Hof in Vienna cost $4,000,000.   The apartment building housed 2000 Socialist families before revolt swept Austria in February 1934.   While Socialists fought back with machine guns, government artillery killed hundreds and pounded down the middle arch of the building.

defeated in savage fighting, mainly in Vienna. Austria was further rent by the rapid development of a Nazi movement, which looked toward union with Germany. Another group, called the *Heimwehr*, inclined to be pro-Fascist, looked to Italy for support and worked for the restoration of the Hapsburg monarchy. With resentment in the hearts of the cowed proletariat, with a program of union with Germany held out by the rising Nazi party, and with the Heimwehr demanding a monarchy, Austria was threatened with dissolution. To stave off civil war and because he was thought sympathetic to Fascist ideas, Engelbert Dollfuss, the chancellor, became dictator in April 1934. Parliament was forced out of existence.

Rumania takes a dictator. Rumania, between Russia on the north and Yugoslavia and Bulgaria on the south, was a kingdom of a little more than 100,000 square miles, with a population of nearly twenty million. This country profited nearly as much by the war as Hungary had lost, for her population and area were doubled (see page 35). But only seventy per cent of the people in the enlarged state were Rumanian (see map, page 39). Like most of the Succession States, Rumania enjoyed little tranquillity after 1919. Despite a liberal constitution granted in 1923, her peasants were restless, and large minority groups, especially the Hungarians, were a troublesome element. The domestic difficulties of Rumania were complicated by Crown Prince Carol, who had married Princess Helen of Greece. Carol fell under the influence of the now notorious Magda Lupescu. Public disapproval of this affair caused Carol to give up his rights to the throne and go, with Lupescu of course, to Paris as an exile. In 1927 Carol's father, King Ferdinand, died, and the crown went to Prince Michael. In 1930 young Michael stepped aside when his father returned to Rumania to assume the kingship.

In the next few years internal harmony was threatened by the growth of anti-Semitism and the rise of the Iron Guard, a Fascist organization. In 1938 King Carol himself became dictator of Rumania, and a new constitution was drawn up giving him the sole power to introduce legislation into parliament and the power to veto any of the parliament's actions.

Boris of Bulgaria becomes dictator. Bulgaria lost relatively little land or population as a result of the peace treaty of 1919. But the cumulative effect of being on the losing side in the second Balkan War (1913) and the First World War had whittled Bulgaria down to only forty thousand square miles, with a population of less than six million people. King Ferdinand was forced by Alexander Stambuliski to abdicate in favor of his son Boris shortly after the conclusion of peace in 1919. Stambuliski, the leader of a radical peasant party, was the head of a dictatorial government from 1919 to 1923. Important land reforms were carried out which antagonized the upper classes, who succeeded in overturning the Stambuliski government in 1923.

Repression of the peasants and lower classes followed. Stambuliski was subsequently shot, and an era of disorder ensued. This period culminated in a bomb outrage in the cathedral in Sofia in 1925, in which 150 persons were killed and more than 300 wounded.

For a brief period, from 1926 to 1931, a moderate government sought to restore civil liberties, to free political prisoners, and to balance the budget. Whatever chances of success this régime might have had were swept away by the shock of the world depression. Conservative elements, fearful of the spread of Communism, forced King Boris to head a dictatorship in 1934.

Dictators in other countries. In other small European states, the story was much the same—the waning of democracy and the rise of dictatorship. Greece ended the war as a monarchy, changed to a republic in 1924, had a king once more in 1935, and the following year got a dictator in the person of General John Metaxas. The three Baltic republics of Latvia, Lithuania, and Estonia underwent similar changes. Each of these states, formerly part of the old Russian empire, had established a republican form of government after achieving independence. But the existence of universal suffrage and one-house legislatures in each of these Baltic republics did not prevent the growth of dictatorship. Portugal was still another failure. In 1910 Portugal became a republic. Since that time she has had twenty-four revolutions. In 1932 Dr. Antonio de Oliveira Salazar became dictator, a new constitution was introduced, and the republic was superseded by a government suggestive of Italian Fascism.

Finland and the Scandinavian countries. The record of political instability and the rise of dictatorship in much of central and southern Europe disappointed the hopes of many who had fought from 1914 to 1918 for a better world. But the picture was not entirely black. In some sections of Europe representative government and political liberalism were enjoying a prosperous existence. In Finland a republic had been declared when independence was secured from Russia in 1919. The government immediately set about passing laws which provided for the compulsory purchase of large estates to be divided into small acreages for little farmers. Child labor was banned, the eight-hour day legalized, and education, from the elementary school through the university, was made free. The ideal of the Finnish leaders seemed to be to create a sturdy race of small independent farmers constituting an educated citizenry.

The Scandinavian countries enjoyed a particularly happy existence. In Denmark and Sweden the standard of living was said to be the highest in the world. In these countries as well as in Norway important social and economic reforms strengthened and vitalized the democratic way of life. Much was done for the small farmer, cooperative movements were encouraged for the benefit of both producer and consumer, and legislation was enacted to provide social insurance for the people. In Scandinavia democratic government exhibited a lustiness and an efficiency which stood out in sharp contrast to the muddle in many of the countries of central Europe. In Sweden an interesting experiment of controlled capitalism under democracy was being carried out. This experiment, called the "Middle Way," meant government control of many forms of economic activity and government operation of

Stockholm is probably the only city in the world which has wholeheartedly accepted modern architecture for her municipal buildings. These apartment houses are located on one of the numerous waterways. There are no slums in Stockholm.

mines, electric power plants, communications, and many other activities. "Disparity between rich and poor was reduced to a minimum and Sweden seemingly became a kind of Middle-class paradise."[3]

Other democratic successes. Democracy also held its own in Switzerland, Holland, and Belgium. In Switzerland some four million people living in an area about the size of the state of Maryland enjoyed reasonable prosperity and stable government following the First World War. While the parliamentary régimes in many states in Europe toppled or were discredited, government by the people prospered; so much so that it could be well said in the 1930's "the probability is that Switzerland will remain a promontory of democracy and free government projecting into a portion of Europe which seems to have forgotten all about such institutions, and that she will continue to afford a practical example of the way in which man may redeem himself from the curse of war, social strife, and racial bigotry."[4]

Holland and Belgium, while not so democratic as the Scandinavian countries or Switzerland, nevertheless possessed stable parliamentary institutions. In Belgium a disturbing factor was the growth of a form of Fascism known as the Rexist movement. Here the language question was also a complicating feature. Some two million Belgians speak only French, about the same number speak only Flemish,

and nearly one million are bilingual. Both linguistic groups were determined to perpetuate their "national culture," a fact which endangered the unity of the country.

Monarchy and dictatorship in Spain. Perhaps the most encouraging incident in postwar Europe was the elimination of the backward and corrupt Spanish government that had exploited an impoverished Spain. Throughout Spanish history there had been three privileged classes—the landowners, the clerics, and the army officers. These classes represented the bulk of the wealth and political power. The landless workers and the small farmers were left to fend for themselves. The illiteracy rate was at least forty-five per cent. One per cent of the population possessed more than half of the land. And this land supported 21,000 officers, one for every six ordinary soldiers, more than the entire German army had in 1914.

From 1914 to 1918 Spain enjoyed a temporary prosperity by supplying food and other materials to the warring nations. After the war, industry and trade lagged; industrial unrest and political instability ensued. To make matters worse, severe fighting broke out in Spanish Morocco, where the Spaniards endeavored to suppress a revolt led by a capable Berber chief named Abd-el-Krim. Graft and inefficiency characterized the conduct of the campaign. In 1921 the Spanish people were

The popular front in Spain exhibited such posters as these in the troubled days of November 1933. The city is Barcelona; the language is Catalan.

horrified to learn that an entire army of 10,000 men had been wiped out by the Moors. An investigation of this military disaster threatened to expose many in high positions in the government, and it was rumored that even the deposition of the king would be demanded. To ward off this exposé and to save the position of the privileged classes and the monarchy, Primo de Rivera set up a dictatorship in 1923 which operated until 1930. For seven years he tried to bolster up the old system by removing its most flagrant abuses and making a few concessions to the people. After the dictator's downfall, King Alfonso tried to continue the traditional arbitrary rule, but popular opposition proved too much for him. Municipal elections held in April 1931 resulted in a clearcut victory for the Republicans. Alfonso, realizing that the time had come to step down, fled the country and made his way to Paris.

The republic of Spain. The leader of the Republicans, Alcalá Zamora, became the head of a provisional government and called an election for the selection of representatives to attend a constituent assembly. Again the Liberals won a sweeping victory. The Monarchists and Conservatives held only a few scattered regions. The constituent assembly then drafted a new constitution which provided for a one-house *Cortes* elected for four years by universal suffrage. The chief executive was to be a president elected for a term of six years. The prime minister was to be responsible to the legislature.

Armed with the new constitution the Spanish Liberals turned to the task of reorganization. The Jesuit order was dissolved, and its property, worth thirty million dollars, was taken over by the state. The Church was prohibited from engaging in education, and all its schools were closed. The Republican *Cortes* next authorized the construction of nearly 10,000 school buildings, then turned to the land problem. It passed a bill giving the government authority to take 52,000,000 acres from the large landowners in order to redistribute it in small parcels. The next major effort of the new government was the reform of the army. Officers were asked to take an oath of allegiance to the republic, their number was drastically reduced, and the size of the army itself was decreased one third. The driving force behind the new republic was President Zamora and the prime minister, Manuel Azaña, a noted writer.

To many liberals in Europe the Spanish revolt was an encouraging sign that perhaps the democratic tradition would win out after all and that dictatorship, now rampant in central Europe, was only a temporary condition. That they were mistaken was demonstrated between 1930 and 1940, when the republics in Spain and Germany were overthrown and two dictatorial régimes, Fascist Italy and Nazi Germany, began a campaign of conquest to undermine democracy in Europe and elsewhere.

Great Britain and the British Empire

Great Britain after the war. After the First World War the English parliamentary system appeared listless, even worn out. It lacked dynamic leadership. A Liberal ministry had been at the helm since 1905, but in 1915 the critical state of the war brought about a coalition composed of representatives of Labor, Liberals, and Conservatives. Asquith, who had taken the country into the war, was superseded in 1916 by Lloyd George. The new prime minister, heading a coalition government, promised his people that after the war "England would be made a land fit for heroes" fresh from the trenches in France. A brief period of prosperity followed the armistice. Then England's foreign trade collapsed; unemployment reached huge proportions. In July 1921 there were two million persons unemployed, and Great Britain faced an uncertain future. Sixty per cent of her food had to be imported, and its cost could be met only by the sale of manufactured articles abroad. The war debt was forty billion dollars. Seven hundred thousand young men had not returned from the battlefield.

In spite of many serious problems Great Britain's parliamentary system somehow muddled along. Following the decision of the Conservative party to withdraw, in 1922, Lloyd George lost his majority in the Commons. He was succeeded by Andrew Bonar Law, the leader of the Conservatives, who presently retired because of ill health. Bonar Law was in turn followed by another Conservative, Stanley Baldwin, who remained in office as prime minister until the end of 1923. In the general election of this year the Conservatives gained the largest number of representatives in the House of Commons. By swinging their support to the Labor party, however, the Liberals gave James Ramsay MacDonald a majority and in January 1924 made him Great Britain's first Laborite prime minister.

MacDonald's Labor government. The British Labor party espoused the policy of gradualism; that is, it wished to see Socialism introduced slowly. Declared MacDonald: "Our labor movement has never had the least intention to try short cuts to the millennium."[5] Dependent upon the support of the Liberal party, the Labor government had to move cautiously. Hence its record in domestic affairs was not outstanding. In foreign affairs its accomplishments were more substantial. MacDonald believed in helping Germany get back on her feet. Accordingly he favored the Dawes Plan, urged the entry of Germany into the League of Nations, and supported disarmament. By working with Herriot he managed to improve relations with France. But failure to cure the country's economic ills, together with the accusation that the Labor govern-

Prime Minister Ramsay MacDonald bids farewell to Aristide Briand, French foreign minister, as the seven-power German debt holiday plan is completed in London (July 1931).

ment was pro-Communist, brought about the fall of MacDonald's ministry in October 1924.

The Conservative Baldwin government. From 1924 to 1929 a Conservative government led again by Stanley Baldwin was in power. During this period the economic crisis continued unabated; in 1926 a general strike threatened to disrupt the economy of the nation.

Although the Baldwin government extended the system of social insurance and enfranchised all women between twenty-one and thirty who had not received the right to vote by the electoral act of 1918, its general tone was conservative and at times even reactionary. In 1927 the Baldwin government passed the Trade Disputes Act, making it difficult for unions to obtain funds from their members for political campaigns. Meanwhile economic difficulties continued. In the summer of 1928, twenty-nine per cent of the mine workers in Great Britain, twenty-eight per cent of the ship workers, twenty-one per cent of the men in steel industries, and fifteen per cent of those in textile industries were unemployed.

The second Labor ministry. This failure to solve unemployment brought MacDonald back to Number 10 Downing Street in May 1929. Again the Labor party had little to show for its two years in power (1929-1931) as far as internal problems were concerned, although in foreign affairs its record was again praise-

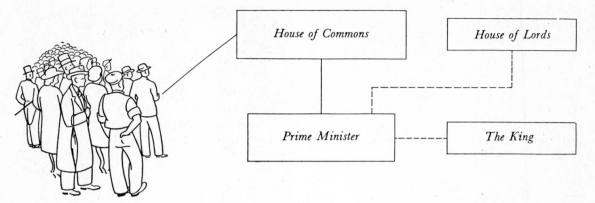

worthy. MacDonald journeyed to the United States to talk with President Hoover about peace and disarmament. The Labor government also signed the "optional clause" (Article 36 of the Statute of the World Court), which bound Great Britain to place before the Court any dispute which involved the interpretation of a treaty or international law.

The National government. The world economic crisis, forcing Great Britain off the gold standard and further increasing her unemployment, brought the second Labor ministry to an end in 1931. But instead of giving up the prime ministership, MacDonald became the leader of a National Coalition government composed of practically all the Conservatives, a goodly number of the Liberals, and a few Laborites. The rank and file of the Labor party accused MacDonald of being a traitor and renegade. The formation of the National government under MacDonald's leadership complicated party divisions, for there were now National Laborites, National Liberals, and National Conservatives (all in the Coalition) opposed by a small number of Laborites and Liberals. During the next four years the National government became in reality more and more the agent of the Conservative party, and in 1935 MacDonald resigned. His place as prime minister was taken by Baldwin. The fiction of the National government was, however, continued. By 1935 the enactment of tariff legislation, the encouragement of home agriculture, and a policy of economic cooperation with the self-governing elements in the British Empire improved England's economic condition.

Great Britain's "old-man" government. Considering the multiplicity of Great Britain's

problems and the adverse conditions which confronted her statesmen in the disillusioning post-war years, perhaps her government did as well as could be expected. But in examining the two decades which ended one war and brought in another (1919-1939) it is evident that democratic government in Great Britain lacked vitality. The leadership was, in the main, uninspiring and mediocre. Stanley Baldwin is a perfect symbol of British leadership after the war. He entered Parliament in 1908 at the age of forty-one and in almost ten years in the House of Commons made only five speeches. In 1921 he became a member of the cabinet and was made chancellor of the exchequer in 1923. When he was made prime minister later in the same year, Baldwin was fifty-nine. In 1928 the average age of Baldwin's cabinet members was sixty years; that of MacDonald's colleagues in 1931 was sixty-three and one half. No wonder that many Englishmen complained about the "tired-old-man" atmosphere in the British government. In the fateful years from 1935 to 1939, when Great Britain was suffering defeat after defeat in the arena of international affairs at the hands of the totalitarian states, the men leading the government were old and lethargic, seemingly unaware of the changing world around them.

A more serious menace to British democracy than the well-intentioned ineptness of its leaders was the alarming fact that an influential group of citizens had apparently lost their faith in the efficacy of democratic government to solve British problems. Faced with the possible breakdown of the capitalist system, fearful of Russian Communism, and disgusted with conditions in France, they began during the middle 1930's to admire more and more the strength, resoluteness, and superficial efficiency of the new régime in Germany.

The British Commonwealth.

During the period from 1914 to 1939 many important changes had been taking place in the British Empire. The development of self-government, which had been a feature of nineteenth-century British imperial history, in such colonies as Canada and Australia reached its logical conclusion as a result of the First World War. During this conflict Canada, Australia, New Zealand, and South Africa rendered valuable service to the mother country. The war effort not only obligated Great Britain to reward these people but also stimulated nationalism in these areas, by this time known as dominions.

In 1926 a British Imperial Conference declared that the mother country and the dominions were "autonomous Communities within the British Empire, equal in status, in no way subordinate one to another. . . ."[6] In 1931 the Statute of Westminster was passed by the British Parliament which, in effect, was a constitution for the British Commonwealth of Nations. From now on the dominions and Great Britain were held together by economic interests, by loyalty to the crown, and by similar ideals of language, law, and tradition.

The Dominion of Canada.

The oldest and most important dominion was Canada. After 1918 this country experienced an uneasy and difficult period of national reconstruction.

But by 1927 prosperity had again returned to the Canadians. In that year they celebrated the Diamond Jubilee of Confederation. The future seemed promising. Stocks boomed, exports increased, and the railroads profited.

In 1939 Canada had a population of about 11,000,000, of which fifty-two per cent were of British origin (including the Irish), twenty-eight per cent were French, and about five per cent were of German descent. Less than half of the population of Canada considered England as their mother country. Canada is almost embarrassingly large, larger than continental United States. W. L. Mackenzie King, Canadian prime minister, once said: "If some countries have too much history, we have too much geography." Overshadowed by the immensity of the country, the small Canadian population mainly stretches in a narrow band less than three hundred miles wide along the border of the United States from the Atlantic to the Pacific. This narrow band consists of four main economic regions: the Maritime Provinces (Nova Scotia, New Brunswick, and Prince Edward Island), Quebec, Ontario, the Prairie Provinces (Alberta, Saskatchewan, and Manitoba), and British Columbia on the western side of the Rocky Mountains. Each of these regions has its peculiar economic characteristics, which frequently conflict with those of the others.

Canada is one of the richest countries in the world in natural resources. Although she

In Quebec harbor on the St. Lawrence stands this immense grain elevator. With its loading galleries at either end, it is nearly a half mile long. Here Canada's magnificent wheat crops are stored prior to exporting.

lacks much oil, and her coal deposits are situated at the extreme ends of the country, she produces tremendous quantities of wheat, is the third nation in the production of gold, and has almost a world monopoly on asbestos. Pulpwood, silver, and nickel are also important Canadian products. Just before the depression of 1929 Canada ranked fifth among the nations of the world in value of exports. Canadian per capita exports were about three and a half times as large as those of the United States.

In 1929 the depression struck Canada with a paralyzing shock, and the government tried with little success to cope with rising unemployment, the plight of the farmers, and an alarming number of business failures. In 1934 it is estimated that 1,200,000 Canadians were either on relief or in labor camps. In this emergency the prime minister, Richard B. Bennett, advocated a far-reaching program of reform. Bennett declared, "If we cannot abolish the dole, we should abolish the system. . . . This is the end of an economic era. Capitalism will never work again."[7]

In 1935 Bennett secured the passage of eight acts in the Canadian Parliament. Their purpose was to secure a more equitable division of the nation's income and provide a greater share of social justice for the average Canadian. In 1937, after being taken to the court of the Privy Council in London, the majority of these acts were declared unconstitutional. Meanwhile depression and drought were attacking the Canadian western provinces, labor unrest troubled the east, and there was much criticism directed against the Canadian constitution, described by some as suitable only "for the horse and buggy period." After 1937 the weight of depression in Canada was somewhat lifted, but it was commonly agreed that fundamental problems relating to economic justice, the plight of the western farmers, and the improvement of the federal system of government still remained to be solved. The easy optimism of the late 1920's had now been superseded by a spirit of national stocktaking.

British South Africa. The Union of South Africa, a settlement of Dutch and British people, proved loyal to Great Britain during the First World War. However, after the conflict friction occurred on several occasions between the British and Dutch communities. The latter pressed for complete recognition of South Africa's independent status, while the former was determined that the Union, while independent, must remain a member of the British Commonwealth.

Basic to South African economy are the great gold and diamond mines which furnish a large share of the government's revenues. Without this mineral wealth the country would be helpless. The arid soil and the distance from the world's markets complicate South Africa's economic development, but perhaps the fundamental problem of the country is that of its native policy.

There are more than six and a half million natives in the Union and barely two million whites. The native question is really a series of questions: What educational facilities should be offered? What political opportunities should be given? Should the native be kept on his tribal lands, or should contact between European and black be encouraged? But underlying all these is the element of fear. The Europeans wonder whether political and economic dominance will one day pass from the white minority to the black majority. No one can prophesy what will be the outcome. Much has been done in South Africa to study the native question scientifically; and recent legislation, while not removing by any means certain disabilities suffered by the natives, has undoubtedly improved their lot, especially in the direction of providing them with land.

Australia and New Zealand. Following the war Australia and New Zealand went through the usual throes of postwar adjustment, but from 1923 to 1929 both countries were prosperous. The effects of the ensuing depression were especially severe in these dominions, for both were agricultural countries with large debts held by outside investors. Only by stringent measures did the two governments avoid default on their obligations.

In the early thirties Australia and New Zealand became more and more concerned with foreign affairs. The next chapter will discuss these at greater length. Here it is sufficient to note that both countries were apprehensive of Japanese expansion. The Australians in particular had adopted a "White Australia" policy by which they were resolved to keep their population exclusively European, preferably British. The great fear of the Australians came from a realization that they might be hard put to maintain the

"White Australia" policy in a continent so underpopulated as their own, in the face of an overpopulated Japan. This circumstance explains why Australia and New Zealand, unlike South Africa, worried very little about their exact constitutional status. Dependence upon the British fleet and the fortress of Singapore bound these South Pacific dominions closely to their mother country.

Elsewhere in the Empire. In the post-war years the tropical dependencies of the British Empire also posed many problems. India demanded self-government, as did Ceylon and Burma. The Egyptians were irked by British control of the Suez Canal, and in other African colonies the British government found difficulty in reconciling the conflicting interests of European settlers and natives.

The end of the First World War brought no peace to Palestine, which had been turned over to Great Britain as a mandate in 1920. The Arab inhabitants were resolved that the Jewish immigrants should not obtain control, while the latter were equally determined that what had once been their ancient kingdom should become a modern homeland for Jewry.

Like France, Czechoslovakia, Austria, and other European states, Great Britain and the dominions enjoyed little tranquillity after 1919. Great Britain's problems, however, were more numerous and complex, scattered as they were in many lands populated by diverse peoples.

The United States

America after the war. The First World War left its mark on the Western Hemisphere as well as on the European countries and the British Empire. Although the Latin-American republics, for example, experienced important economic developments, it was the United States whose position was most radically altered by the conflict.

While the European nations were destroying and depleting the sources of their wealth from 1914 to 1917, the United States was expanding its factories and pouring goods into Europe and South America. By 1919 it had attained first place in industrial equipment, wealth, and prestige, and it had also become the world's greatest creditor nation. The United States, so suddenly grown great and rich, had been the most conspicuous defender of democratic ideals. The country was therefore looked upon by many as the leader, both at home and abroad.

There was much to be done. The new League needed American support, and the tangle of war debts, reparations, and trade disruption demanded sympathetic attention. But the expected leadership was not forthcoming. Almost overnight the American people seemed to have forgotten the Wilsonian ideal. They quite definitely turned away from the international scene to concentrate upon domestic affairs. An industrial boom completely absorbed the nation. While many parts of the world were struggling with serious economic problems, the United States enjoyed almost unbelievable prosperity. The League of Nations was a vague memory, nationalism triumphed over internationalism, conservatism over liberalism.

The period of readjustment. While the basic result of the war upon the United States had been to increase the nation's wealth enormously, Americans nevertheless experienced several years of confused economic and social readjustment. Industrial warfare between capital and labor characterized the years 1919-1922. The managers of industry endeavored to recover some of the ground lost to labor during the war through collective bargaining and better wages; the ranks of labor were equally determined to hold these gains. In 1919, 3000 strikes involved four million workers.

Industrial strife was further stimulated by the business depression of 1920 and 1921. The prosperous war years had been made possible largely by huge exports to Europe. By 1919 the warring nations had used up their funds and credit. In consequence American foreign trade declined. At home, too, there was a revolt of the consumer against "the high cost of living." A buyers' strike curtailed American production. The result was a depression in 1920 and 1921 in which manufacturers tried to cut down costs, especially by lowering wages. The repercussion was the strike of 600,000 coal miners and 300,000 railway shopmen in 1922. But now the post-war boom had commenced, at first slowly, then with breathtaking momentum.

In addition to economic troubles in the im-

In 1922 the eighteenth "prohibition" amendment had become law and New York drys dumped 50,000 barrels of whiskey into the street.

mediate post-war years, there was an unfortunate upsurge of exaggerated nationalism, manifesting itself in a hunt against persons or groups accused of radicalism. In particular the attorney-general made numerous arrests and carried out deportations of anyone suspected of "red" sympathies. Five members were expelled from the New York legislature because they were Socialists, an action vigorously denounced by Charles E. Hughes, one of the country's most eminent statesmen. The most exaggerated form of intolerance was the activity of a new Ku Klux Klan which singled out for its attention immigrants, Catholics, Jews, the League of Nations, and pacifism. Its membership in 1924 was over four million, but it declined after this date.

In politics the two most important events were the ratification of the eighteenth amendment in January 1919 and the passing of the nineteenth amendment in the summer of 1920. The eighteenth amendment prohibited the sale of intoxicating liquor; the nineteenth gave women the right to vote. Both of these measures had been brought about largely by the war. In order to conserve grain during the war, the production of beer and other alcoholic beverages had been restricted or entirely forbidden. The nineteenth amendment came into being because women in America had played an important part in the war effort. They made increasing demands for the right to vote. Woman's suffrage was the nation's answer.

The "return to normalcy." In 1920 Warren G. Harding, the Republican candidate, was elected to the presidency on the platform of a "return to normalcy." The inauguration of Harding as president in 1921 ushered in twelve years of Republican dominance in American politics. It soon became apparent that by "normalcy" President Harding meant conservatism in domestic affairs and resistance to the liberal progressivism embodied before the war in such measures as the Clayton Anti-Trust Act and the Underwood Tariff Act. In foreign affairs the new president was bent on isolation and repudiation of the League of Nations. Speaking confidently of America's ability to take care of itself, Harding declared in his inaugural address, "We seek no part in directing the destinies of the world." Other Republican leaders announced that the League issue was "as dead as slavery." In accordance with this policy the American ambassador in London was "instructed to inform the League's authorities that as the United States had not joined the League she was not in a position to answer letters from it."[8]

In 1922 Congress enacted the Fordney-McCumber Tariff Act, establishing the highest rates in American history. A similar high tariff had been passed in 1921 by Congress but vetoed by President Wilson, who maintained, "If there ever was a time when America had anything to fear from foreign competition that time has passed. If we wish Europe to settle her debts, governmental or commercial, we must be prepared to buy from her."[9] In 1922 a bill calling for payment of a bonus to soldiers of the First World War (fifty dollars for each month in service), was passed by Congress. Vetoed by Harding, the bonus issue appeared again before Congress and became a political football.

Less than a year after its inauguration, Harding's administration became the storm center of an exposé of graft and corruption. While the ugly truth was being uncovered, the president, in ill health, had taken a trip to Alaska. On his return his condition became grave, and he died in San Francisco. The knowledge that those whom he had placed in high office had betrayed his confidence probably aggravated his illness. Congressional investigating committees at length

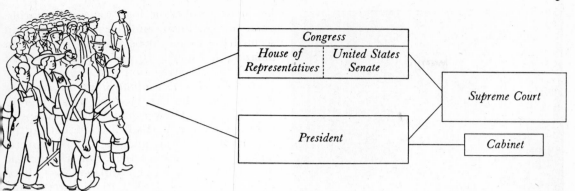

uncovered the whole sordid affair. The most infamous scandal had to do with government oil reserves at Teapot Dome. The Secretary of the Interior obtained at least $400,000 for himself from the oil companies in this shady deal.

It hardly seems likely that Harding had any direct hand in the scandals. The truth apparently is that his friends and political cronies used him as an innocent dupe. Harding was beyond his depth in the White House.

The era of Big Business. In 1923, after the death of Harding, the then Vice-President Calvin Coolidge became the chief executive. As governor of Massachusetts he had gained the reputation of being both safe and sound. He assured the people that the scandals were now over.

Even more than Harding, Coolidge stood for a return to conservatism. The progressive movement of the first decade of the twentieth century had little appeal for him. He favored high tariffs, the reduction of taxes, and governmental assistance to industry. The philosophy of President Coolidge was best summed up in his own dictum: "The business of the United States is business!"

In 1924 a Soldiers' Bonus Bill, providing insurance to war veterans, was introduced into Congress and passed over Coolidge's veto. The Johnson Immigration Act became law in 1924. Immigration had been restricted in 1921 by a law which introduced the so-called quota system. The number of aliens admitted from any country was to equal three per cent of the total number of persons of that nationality living in the United States in 1910. About 350,000 immigrants could thus come into the country each year by the terms

of the act. The law of 1924 reduced the quota to two per cent and in addition provided that as soon as possible the so-called national-origins principle should control future immigration. By this scheme, finally adopted in 1929, immigration was limited to 150,000 each year; and the number of emigrants from each nation was to be so fixed that the national origin of the American people in 1920 would not be changed. One vexing feature of the Johnson Act was the express exclusion of the Japanese. This end had been practically secured by the Gentlemen's Agreement of 1907, and the new arrangement was keenly resented by Japan. It did much to poison Japanese-American amity.

The American people were satisfied with Coolidge's record as the presidential election neared in 1924. The Democrats tried vainly to raise the issue of corruption so rampant during Harding's régime. But under the warm glow of rising prosperity all was forgiven, and with such slogans as "Keep cool with Cal" and "Coolidge or Chaos," the Republicans won easily, gaining 54 per cent more votes than the combined votes of Robert LaFollette, the leader of a Progressive party, and John W. Davis, the Democratic aspirant.

During the second Coolidge administration there were few outstanding pieces of legislation. The national debt was lowered, and efforts were made at farm relief. Like the bonus, the problem of what to do for the farmer confronted Congress throughout the postwar decade. Agriculture failed to revive after the depression of 1920-1921. During the war, motivated by high prices for agricultural products, American farmers had bought thousands of tractors and land at boom prices. In

New Yorkers put out flags, cheered, waved, and threw tons of paper and ticker tape into the jammed streets when Admiral Richard Byrd returned from his flight over the South Pole in November 1929.

1919 the total farm debt was four billion dollars. With the depression, prices tumbled; wheat that brought $2.14 a bushel in 1919 was down to $.93 in 1923. Farm income declined from fifteen and one half to five and one half billion dollars. Yet fixed payments on debts had to be continued. After several unsuccessful attempts to aid the farmer, Congress finally passed the McNary-Haugen Bill in 1927 and again in 1928. Each time it was vetoed by President Coolidge.

Notwithstanding the depression in agriculture, the United States continued to enjoy what seemed to be dazzling prosperity in 1927 and 1928. Trade with the outside world kept factories at the peak of production. Radios, automobiles, rayon, cloth, moving pictures, and electric refrigerators were produced in great quantities, and the people had plenty of money to spend for them. Business optimism was reflected in an era of stock speculation that became a virtual mania. The stock mar-

ket, mass production, high wages, high tariffs, great foreign loans, and the installment plan seemed for a time to be working together in amazing harmony. It was the high tide of American self-satisfaction and content.

Herbert Hoover's administration. Another Republican, Herbert Hoover, became president in 1929. Hoover had been a successful mining engineer, he had directed Belgian relief during the war, and he had been secretary of commerce since 1921. His Democratic opponent in the bitter campaign was Alfred E. Smith, the first Irish Catholic ever to obtain the presidential nomination. A liberal in politics, Smith was a product of the "sidewalks of New York." While governor of New York state he had made a name for himself as a progressive sponsor of social legislation. He came out boldly for repeal of prohibition. However laudable the aims of prohibition, it was true that the amendment had given rise to a new set of problems which seemed to many people more dangerous to the public than the evil which prohibition aimed at abolishing. Police forces were corrupted, and otherwise respectable citizens became lawbreakers. The taint of the "pay off" was found among government officials, while the bootlegger grew rich in defiance of law and order.

Hoover won the day on what one historian termed "Prosperity, prohibition, and prejudice." When the new president assumed office in 1929, he had behind him a Republican Congress and a country enjoying unbounded prosperity. The president indicated to Congress the necessity of action in three fields: tariff revision, farm relief, and law enforcement.

Hoover desired downward revision of the tariff, but after what one newspaper termed "the unrestrained play of selfishness and of petty politics," the Smoot-Hawley Tariff Act was passed in 1930. Tariff rates were raised on an average of 20 per cent over those already created by the act of 1922. More than one thousand economists from nearly two hundred colleges and universities joined in sending a protest to Hoover urging him to veto the bill. The bill was not vetoed.

In June 1929, an agricultural-marketing act was passed to bring relief to the farmer. This established a Federal Farm Loan Board controlling a fund of half a billion dollars to stabilize prices. The hoped-for results did not follow, and farm prices continued their downward trend. A special commission was created to study the problem of prohibition enforcement. But the commission's answer, couched in the Wickersham Report (1931), was disappointingly vague and divided, implying merely that some change in the machinery of prohibition was essential.

Foreign policy. From the beginning of Coolidge's term in 1923 to the end of the Hoover administration in 1933, the general trend of American foreign policy was isolationist. But some broadening of American interest and activity in international affairs took place. The United States, which had originally ignored messages from the League, began early in the 1920's to send unofficial observers to League meetings. In 1923 and again in 1927 American financial experts had taken a leading part in arranging for reparation payments. As early as 1921 Harding had called an international conference at Washington to study the problems of the Pacific. The famous Nine-Power Treaty grew out of this conference.

Presidents Harding, Coolidge, and Hoover all tried to get the United States to join the World Court, but none was successful. Other instances of American activity in the international scene were attendance at the Disarmament Conference at Geneva in 1927, the signing of the Kellogg-Briand Pact in 1928, and representation at the London Naval Conference in 1930. In 1932 an American representative sat on the Lytton Commission of the League of Nations which denounced Japanese aggression in Manchuria.

The great depression. In shocking contrast to the golden days of prosperity was the heavy fog of depression which settled on the United States in October 1929, when a catastrophic stock-market crash paralyzed American business. Farm foreclosures came by the thousands. By 1932 business failures numbered at least 30,000; the number of unemployed was somewhere between 12 and 15 million; foreign trade had fallen from 9 to 3 billion dollars. Five thousand banks closed their doors in the years 1929-1932.

The depression was a plain warning that the easy-going ways of a young and carefree nation were outdated. It was realized now that natural resources had to be safeguarded, that the banking system and security exchanges should

This is one of the twelve large dams built by the Tennessee Valley Authority for the development of electrical power in the Tennessee River basin.

be controlled in the public interest, and that purchasing power had to be given to all the people to keep industry moving. It was apparent also that citizens in a democracy had to pay at least as much attention to their duties in a democratic state as they had been paying to their rights and privileges.

The New Deal. In the midst of this stock-taking Franklin D. Roosevelt, the Democratic standardbearer, became President of the United States. Under his leadership a program to cope with the national emergency was put forth in 1933. Called the New Deal, it had three objectives: relief, recovery, and reform. Many millions of dollars were appropriated for the relief of the unemployed, and vast sums were expended for the construction of public works in the hope that such activity would stimulate economic recovery. The Civilian Conservation Corps offered employment and educational opportunities to thousands of young men. Federal Housing Administration encouraged building activity and gave, especially to lower-income groups, an opportunity to finance home building under liberal terms. Some plainly significant, as well as controversial, measures were taken to reform the economic structure. Measures were instituted to guarantee the bank deposits of small investors. The sale of stocks and bonds was regulated by a Securities Exchange Commission. The Tennessee Valley Authority was created by the government to produce power at reasonable rates that would constitute a "yardstick" for public utilities. The National Labor Relations Board was designed to protect labor and give it the right to collective bargaining. Most important of all was the Social Security Act, passed in 1935. For the first time in the history of the United States a comprehensive scheme for unemployment insurance and a plan for old-age retirement were introduced.

The full significance of the New Deal cannot be estimated at this early date. Its opponents contend that it has given too much power to the labor unions, that it has created a vast and irresponsible bureaucracy at Washington, that it has spent public funds in a profligate fashion, and that it seeks to destroy the capitalist system. Its supporters, on the other hand, maintain that the New Deal represents a reasonable compromise between the old and discredited system of *laissez faire* with its unbridled opportunities for exploitation and, at the other extreme, the tyranny of an all-powerful state under a totalitarian régime. They say that its aim is not to destroy capitalism but rather to preserve it by adapting it to new circumstances.

Latin America (1919-1939)

L*atin America and the war.* Latin America itself did not figure very prominently in the First World War, but the epochal struggle nevertheless quietly inaugurated a new era of trade in the Western Hemisphere. The fighting nations had made huge demands for Latin-American products, such as her cereals, meats, wool, hides, nitrates, copper, manganese, and oil. But export restrictions, high prices, and lack of ships made it difficult to get goods into Latin America from abroad. This unequal situation tended to encourage home-made products. The consequent development of industry and the increased buying power of Latin America resulted in a considerable increase in her foreign trade, which grew from less than three to more than five billion dollars. The mileage of railways was doubled, new highways were constructed, and public utilities were installed.

Fundamentally, however, Latin-American economy was not firmly established. There still remained several inescapable weaknesses. One was the lack of resources for an industrial economy, mainly iron and coal. A second was the predominantly agricultural basis of economic life. A third was the dangerous specialization of Latin-American economy.

Economic specialization. Although a vast storehouse of natural riches, Latin America compromised her economic future by drawing political boundaries which forced many of her countries to depend for their sustenance upon one product alone. Hence no distribution of

economic risk has been possible. The welfare of most of the Latin-American countries has been so bound up with the export of particular agricultural or mineral resources that these countries have become enslaved by world market prices. Brazil is dependent upon a world market for its coffee, which accounts for one half of Brazil's annual exports. To check production and keep up the price of coffee, Brazil has been forced to burn nearly a sixth of the coffee crop each year. Costa Rica also is mainly a coffee-exporting country. The other Central American states are so bound up with the world's demand for one particular commodity that they have been popularly dubbed "the banana republics." In Chile the national economy has been dependent upon the export of nitrates and copper. In Argentina and Uruguay it has been meat and wheat. Cuban prosperity has been dependent upon sugar exports, and Mexico relies upon foreign sales of oil and silver. Economically far off balance, Latin America has been less equipped against loss of foreign markets through wars or depressions than almost any other region. (For effects of present war, see pp. 40-42.)

Prosperity and depression. During the decade 1919 to 1929 Latin America carried forward economic diversification and industrialization. Local industries grew, and comparative prosperity prevailed. Seven nations adopted new constitutions of a liberal nature, and political stability seemed to be more prevalent, for six out of the twenty-one republics were tranquil from 1913 to 1929. The Indian was given greater attention, laws were passed for his protection, and land was made available for his use. This hopeful period of progress, however, was abruptly ended by the onset of the depression in 1929. Depending upon the export of one or more raw materials, such as oil or copper, for their prosperity, the Latin-American countries suffered critical economic conditions when world prices collapsed. These difficulties in turn increased political instability.

The depression took its usual fatal course in most of the states, leading to bankruptcies, unemployment, business stagnation, decline in public revenues, excessive governmental borrowing, government debt defaults, and even political revolutions. Within a year after February 1930, seven of the twenty Latin-American republics had revolutions. Recuperation was slow and painful, but the economic disasters had at least served to accelerate the vast socio-economic revolution which had been stirring since the First World War.

The economic outlook. Recent observers look to the growing industries of Latin America for a more promising future. In Argentina, the leading manufacturing nation in Latin America, industry had so progressed by 1939 that factory products almost equaled in value the agricultural products that had hitherto founded Argentine economy. Cities like Buenos Aires in Argentina, São Paulo and Rio de Janeiro in Brazil, Santiago in Chile, Mexico City, and Havana are rapidly developing into important manufacturing centers in Latin America's drive toward industrialization. Yet the relative scarcity of iron and coal, as well as a notable lack of local available capital, does not encourage the development of extensive manufacturing. The greatest progress has been made in the manufacture of consumer goods, and while all of the leading Latin-American states visualize the development of heavy industry, only Chile and Mexico seem sufficiently endowed with the necessary natural resources. Over $10,000,000,000 of foreign capital have been invested already in Latin America, but it appears unlikely that our southern neighbors will be able to realize their plans for industrialization without obtaining even more foreign capital and encouraging the further backing of enterprise by European and United States investors.

When former President Calles returned to Mexico in 1935, some voters, loyal to a subsequent administration, pinned a caricature of Calles on a mule's face and paraded through the streets of Mexico City. "This mule is for sale," the rider announced.

The fact has not been substantially altered, despite recent industrialization, that the prosperity of Latin America depends largely upon its ability to sell agricultural and mineral products abroad, mainly to Europe and the United States. The desire of the Latin Americans to trade abroad has always been met by an equivalent eagerness on the part of Europe and the United States to exchange manufactured goods for Latin-American raw materials. Trade rivalry among the great powers in Latin America has been, consequently, intense.

Although for thirty years the United States has been the largest single trader with Latin America, in normal times Europe as a whole represents Latin America's most important market. Of the total Latin-American trade in 1938, Europe took approximately fifty-four per cent of the exports and supplied forty-four per cent of the imports. The United States took thirty-one per cent of Latin America's exports and provided thirty-four per cent of its imports in the same year. The importance of a European market for Latin America has been even greater than the figures show, for the United States has done most of its Latin-American trading with the Caribbean states, leaving the great states of South America proper far more dependent upon Europe than

By 1936 Brazil had begun to modernize her methods of coffee production. Here a youth spreads coffee berries to commence drying on prepared soil. When they are half dried, they will be removed to ventilators for completion of the process.

the over-all view would indicate. Unfortunately, the dangers, both to the United States and to South America, which are inherent in the reliance of South America upon European trade cannot be solved by any great diversion of South American trade to the United States, for with the exception of such items as Brazilian coffee, Bolivian tin, and a few others, the United States produces most of the materials prominent in South America's exports. As we shall see, however, war has brought changes.

Trade rivalry. The United States has always been greatly concerned over the political ramifications of Latin America's economic reliance upon Europe. Until recently, keen trade and investment competition between the United States and Great Britain has dominated the Latin-American economic scene. At the turn of the century, Germany began to loom in importance as a trade rival, and after a temporary eclipse because of the First World War and postwar economic debility, Germany again surged forward, dangerously challenging the Anglo-American trade ascendency in Latin America. Most of Germany's trade gains were made at the expense of the British; since 1910, in fact, only the United States and Germany have made any substantial gains in the Latin-American market. While on the eve of the Second World War the United States still had a greater annual market in Latin America

than both Germany and England combined, it was highly significant that by then Germany had dethroned England as the nearest competitor of the United States.

Concern over the ascending prominence of German trade was necessarily intensified by the realization that Nazi-German rivalry was neither friendly, honorable, nor purely economic. Thanks to governmental sponsorship, Germany long before the Nazi régime was able to grant longer terms and better and easier conditions in its business transactions with Latin America. The Nazi system was even more effective. By resorting to barter, Nazi Germany had competitors at her mercy. Barter deals based upon the notorious *Aski* mark proved the most formidable weapon. Germany would offer to take great quantities of the staple export of some short-sighted Latin-American state and then pay for it with *Aski* marks, good only to buy German exports. The system at first appeared highly attractive to Latin America, but in the long run its advantages were typically one way. Prevented by the *Aski* mark from gaining foreign exchange, committed to buy German goods and only those goods—at artificial prices chosen by the Nazis—the disillusioned Latin Americans were being undersold with their own goods in the world market. Moreover, the Nazi methods became exceedingly dangerous when the Germans began capitalizing upon their ability to draw Latin America into a foreign-trade slavery. The threat of being able to create an accompanying political subservience became so great that by 1936 the Americas had already begun to unite in an effort to counteract it.

Social reform. There is a close correlation between the economic revolution which began at the close of the First World War and an accompanying social revolution. It had been hoped that the increase of factories, with their higher wages, would eventually raise social as well as economic standards and create a middle class that would act as a stabilizer for Latin-American governments. That hope is at present being realized in the more advanced republics. Modern Mexico has perhaps outstripped all the others in the process of social change. While certain other Latin-American states have gone further in some aspects, Mexico may justly claim to have epitomized the social revolution which has affected all of

Latin America in one way or another. As one authority has pointed out:

"In Mexico may be observed in process the rise of the *mestizo* and middle class into control of the state and toward ampler economic boundaries; the rise of the Indian, the revalidation of his culture and his participation in political life; the development of a conscious proletarian movement; the defeat of its landholding class and the partial solution of the agrarian problem; the growing freedom of women; the smashing of the political and economic power of the Church; the increasing strength of organized civilian life against militarism, still very dominant; the winning of unabridged national sovereignty and increasing economic independence from foreign imperialism; the rapid expansion of popular education; the painful advance toward greater political stability."[10]

Social reform in all of Latin America has grown out of socio-economic problems which have existed for centuries. Most prominent among these problems have been those of the land, illiteracy, sanitation, and clerical influence. The land problem has been especially acute. Vast feudal estates have re-created a medieval serfdom in most of Latin America. Statistics show that Brazil has 45,000,000 people and fewer than 800,000 landowners; four fifths of the arable land is owned by 3000 people. In Argentina, nearly thirty per cent of the total area under cultivation is in estates of 25,000 acres or over. The arable soil of Chile is owned by seven per cent of the population. In 1934 thousands of Colombian peasants, driven to desperation under the age-old system of absentee landlordism, rose up to demand titles to the holdings on which they and their forefathers had toiled under virtual feudal bondage. Only in Mexico, where before the First World War it took an entire day on a railroad train to cross some farms, has there been any extensive land reform.

Some of the oldest and finest universities in the world are located in Latin America. Generally, however, educational opportunities have been lacking for the poor. Illiteracy is prevalent throughout Latin America, varying from twenty-five per cent in countries like Argentina or Costa Rica, to seventy-five per cent in Brazil, and to even a higher proportion in some of the countries of the Caribbean area.

With the recent democratic movements, however, more attention has been given to education, especially in Argentina, Chile, Uruguay, Paraguay, Mexico, Cuba, and Costa Rica. Latin America is beginning to believe that its promises for the future must be won largely in the schools.

Health and sanitation problems have been particularly challenging to Latin America, where ignorance, poverty, and often debilitating climate have combined to create deplorable conditions. It has been said that as many as two thirds of the people of Spanish America suffer from one or another of the many tropical scourges of the hemisphere. The mass of the people know little about sanitation and personal hygiene, and the death rate, especially among children, is extremely high. In the past ten years, however, the Latin-American countries, particularly Bolivia, Chile, Mexico, and Venezuela, have spent increasing sums for public health.

The problem of the Church has been politico-economic. In Latin America certain officials of the Church have combined with the landed interests to oppose the liberals. The clerical-liberal struggle became a government-clerical struggle wherever the liberals won power, for the liberal government officials found they could make few moves without encroaching upon some prerogative claimed by the Church as its special field. In the majority of the countries, Church and state have now been separated, but the problem is yet far from solved.

Social trends summarized. In summary, the socio-economic revolution has opened new horizons to Latin America. The gradual development of a middle class, where before there had been only a few extremely rich and the extremely poor, is the accompaniment of industrialization and land reform. The realization of practical democracy and stable government is the accompaniment of the more equal distribution of wealth. Rising political, economic, and social standards will bring greater health and sanitation. Latin America is perhaps just now passing over the threshold to the realization of its greater potentialities. Before this is accomplished, however, Latin America will have many problems to deal with, and their solution will in no small measure depend upon the moral and even material support of the United States,

Netherlands investors built up great oil refineries like this one at Curacao in the Dutch West Indies, guarded in the Second World War against sabotage by Allied troops.

Race fusion and distinctive culture. If Latin America's economic and political problems are solved there is every reason to believe that a rich and distinctive culture will be created, able to play an even more notable role in world civilization. Important racial factors are now working in this direction. Latin America is the outstanding example of the fusion of European stock with non-Europeans.

Latin-American culture has always been much more European in nature than that of the United States because the whites, looking toward Latin Europe for cultural inspiration, were the dominant group. During the past three hundred years, the European culture transplanted to Latin America has made important contributions in literature and thought. The most promising aspect of Latin-American culture, however, is not that modeled in the past, very largely upon European forms, but a distinctively new culture which utilizes native patterns, especially in art and music. Unlike the situation in the United States, where the North American Indian contributed little toward the new national culture, in Latin America after a long period of European domination the great mass of pure Indian and half-breed blood is beginning to assert itself. Thus after many generations of neglect the Indian's folk music, dances, art, and handicrafts are coming into prominence.

Latin America is now creating a new musical idiom, independent of European tradition. The themes and rhythmic patterns of aboriginal music joined often to Negro forms are giving rise to much musical creativeness. Latin America has two world-famous musicians who are active in its musical Renaissance. Carlos Chavez has done much research in native music and has been in charge of the Mexican National Conservatory of Music. Heitor Vila-Lobos is a prolific composer, a native of Brazil, whose main aim has been to make his countrymen a nation of music lovers. One of the ways by which he hopes to achieve this is the arrangement of masterpieces for choral singing.

The modern art of Latin America is especially noteworthy, showing many signs of multiple race-culture contributions from such sources as the Negro, the Spanish, and above all the Indian. Many Latin-American painters are finding inspiration in native types and scenery. Portinari is one well-known Brazilian artist who paints the life around him instead of copying European models. Cesáreo Bernaldo de Quirós, long a painter in Europe, returned to Argentina to paint a series of canvases depicting the life of the *gaucho* and country scenes. José Clemente Orozco became known for his interpretation of political struggles in Mexico. Diego Rivera, another famous Latin-American painter, has used the Indian as a symbol of Mexico's culture.

Literature is also finding it need not go abroad for its models. Of late, Latin-American writing has become more realistic and more rooted in the life of the country. Since 1920 prose writing has shown much interest in the exploitation of the Indian, has utilized native folklore, and has evidenced much concern for the oppressed.

Pan American policies. The profound revolution in Latin-American political, economic, and social life has fortunately been paralleled by an equally profound revolution in the relations of the United States to Latin America. The First World War and the subsequent era of prosperity, however, did not bring any modification of the policies of Dollar Diplomacy and Theodore Roosevelt's Big Stick. Actually, the postwar Washington administration avidly capitalized upon investment opportunities in Latin America to strengthen the political and economic hegemony of the United States. At an inter-American conference held in Havana in 1928, the Latin-American delegates took the opportunity to display their resentment of what appeared to be the increasing "interventionism" of the United States. Certainly, the era of good will and inter-American solidarity seemed as far from realization at Havana as it ever had been.

A change began to take place in the Latin-American policy of the United States under Secretary of State Stimson in the Hoover administration. The formerly vigorous protection of the lives, property, and investments of United States citizens was appreciably modified; the Marines were withdrawn from Nicaragua, and preparations were made for their withdrawal from Haiti; the depression revolutions of Latin America were given a free hand, thus marking the general repudiation of the Wilson policy of supporting only constitutionally established régimes in Latin America. As one authority has stated, however:

"Such modifications in our Latin-American policy were in many ways a forecast of the good-neighbor policy later proclaimed by Franklin D. Roosevelt. But they were piecemeal and almost surreptitious. They seemed to be made unenthusiastically and reluctantly under the pressure of strong opposition to former aggressiveness."[11]

The Good Neighbor policy. Despite praiseworthy beginnings under President Hoover, it was the Roosevelt-Hull administration that secured the program known as the Good Neighbor policy. In his 1933 inaugural speech President Roosevelt committed the United States to "the policy of the good neighbor— the neighbor who resolutely respects himself, and because he does so, respects the rights of others—the neighbor who respects his obligations and respects the sanctity of his agreements in and with a world of neighbors."

Avenue 18th of July is "Main Street" in Montevideo, Uruguay. Contrast the nineteenth-century "eclectic," domed skyscraper in the rear with the modern office building in the foreground.

The new policy was given further definition by Sumner Welles of the state department when he said later:

"Our new policy of the Good Neighbor has been predicated upon the belief of this government that there should exist an inter-American political relationship based on a recognition of actual and not theoretical equality between the American republics; on a complete forbearance from interference by any one republic in the domestic concerns of any other; on economic cooperation; and finally on the common realization that, in the world at large, all of the American republics confront the same international problems, and that, in their relations with non-American powers, the welfare and security of any one of them cannot be a matter of indifference to the others."[12]

Adding significantly that acts and not words were required, Welles was soon able to prove the good intentions of the Roosevelt administration. Late in 1933 Secretary of State Hull signed at Montevideo an agreement by which he committed the United States to uphold the principle that "no state has the right to intervene in the internal or external affairs of another." In February 1934 an Export-Import Bank was established in Washington to help finance and facilitate foreign trade, especially with Latin America. In May 1934 a treaty was signed with Cuba expressly abrogating the Platt Amendment and the right of the United States thereunder to intervene in that country. In August 1934 the Marines were withdrawn from Haiti. In September 1934 the United States signed with Cuba its first reciprocal trade agreement; six more were signed in the next two years with Latin-American countries. Only little over a year had passed since Franklin D. Roosevelt first proclaimed the Good Neighbor policy, but by the end of 1934 his sincerity had been amply proved by deeds.

Consistency has been the keynote of the Roosevelt Good Neighbor policy ever since its inception. The changes in the policy of the United States were welcomed by the Latin Americans, who soon began to view the United States with an unprecedented confidence and esteem. In the words of one authority: "The stern policeman and the imperialistic colossus had become the Good Neighbor. At the end of 1938 the economic position of the United States in Latin America was stronger than ever and it possessed the friendship of most of its neighbors."[13] Dividends were to come soon.

Summary

Confidence in democratic institutions seemed unbounded at the conclusion of the First World War. Nearly all the states emerging from the débris of the vanquished German and Austrian empires started their national existence with liberal constitutions. In practically all of them—Rumania, Poland, Austria, and others—self-governing institutions soon gave way to dictatorial régimes.

In 1919 France apparently had everything a nation could desire. The old enemy across the Rhine had been crushed, and Alsace-Lorraine had been returned to the fold. France was certainly the undisputed master of Europe and after the war enjoyed a measure of economic prosperity. But the heavy burden of rebuilding her devastated war regions, the cessation of German reparations payments, and the onerous financial burden of subsidizing many allies in eastern and central Europe gradually undermined economic stability. National budgets were not balanced; chronic political instability and corruption among politicians gradually weakened the French position as the leader of Europe.

Great Britain soon began to realize that her victory in 1918 was largely illusory. Successive prime ministers tried in vain to solve the ensuing problems. In 1924 the people turned from the Conservative party under Baldwin and placed MacDonald in power. This leader of the British Labor party shared with his rival, Baldwin, the political spotlight in England's troubled decade after the war. Neither of them made much headway in overcoming England's difficulties. The depression in 1931 gave Great Britain a National government, which did manage to make some progress in economic recovery. While it would be incorrect to assert that democratic institutions were waning in Great Britain, there were numerous disturbing indications that British leadership was not sufficiently dynamic to adapt itself to the conditions of a new age.

In the Western Hemisphere the Latin-American republics had democratic institutions which were often a façade for dictatorial régimes. In these states much remained also to be done—to divide the land more equally, to offer more adequate educational opportunities, and to raise the standard of living of the people. Progress was made in this direction in several of the republics, but here too the onslaught of the depression in 1930 retarded and even undid some of the achievements.

The United States in 1919 had two more years of leadership by Woodrow Wilson. No constructive governmental measures were enacted during this period, for the Congress and the American people were merely marking time until they could have a chief executive who would lead the way back to "normalcy." Such a man was Warren G. Harding, whose short term, however, was blighted by corruption among his highest officials. His successors at the White House, Calvin Coolidge and Herbert Hoover, were better qualified to give the nation what it wanted: prosperity, isolation, and national confidence. For six years, from 1923 to 1929, the American scene was tranquil. The country seemed to be securing what it wanted without recourse to the wishes or needs of the rest of the world. In 1929 depression came to shatter the illusion of glittering prosperity and to reënforce the fact that in the long run the world is economically interdependent. Twelve years of Republican dominance closed in 1933 when Franklin D. Roosevelt, a Democrat, became President of the United States. With decision and speed the new President inaugurated a scheme of relief, reform, and recovery—the New Deal—which took the United States far from the conservative policies of the early twenties.

India

1919	New constitution	Did not satisfy nationalists
	Rowlatt Acts give police power	
1920	Gandhi's civil disobedience campaign	Bloodshed and noncooperation
1930-1932	Round Table Conferences accomplish little	Non-participation of Congress
1935	Government of India Act	Federal government with many restrictions
1941	National Congress demands independence	Leadership of Nehru
1942	Failure of Cripps Mission	

Eastern Asia and Western Powers

Great Britain: Hong Kong, Singapore	Largest Chinese investor
France: Indo-China, Kwangchow	Small investment
Holland: Netherlands East Indies	Economic exploitation
United States: Philippines	Not heavy investments in China, Japan
Russia: geographical consideration	Political, not economic stake
Oceania: strategic value	Wake, Guam, Fiji, mandates

China

1898-1918	Reactionary government of Tzu Hsi	Last of Manchu rulers
1900	Boxer rebellion against foreigners	Harsh treaty imposed by west
1912-1915	Sun Yat-sen forms Chinese republic	Yuan Shih-Kai and reaction
1916-1926	Disorder and disunity	Rival governments
1926-1930	Chiang Kai-Shek unites country	Economic and educational advance

Japan

1894-1895	Victory in war with China	Treaty of Shimonoseki
1902	Alliance with Great Britain	
1904-1905	War with Russia nets gains in Korea, Manchuria	Treaty of Portsmouth
1910	Annexation of Korea, or Chosen	
1915	Twenty-one Demands on China	To reduce China to protectorate
1922	Nine Power Treaty to protect China	
1922-1931	Economic and Industrial advance	
1931	Attack on Chinese	Nonintervention by powers
1932	Puppet régime set up in Manchuria	Called Manchukuo
1936	Japan joins Axis	
1937	Invasion of China	
1938	"New Order" proclaimed	Economic self-sufficiency

The Line-Up

1939	Allies: Australia, New Zealand, India, Burma, Malaya, Indo-China, Chinese concessions, Oceania	India protests inclusion in war without independence
	Axis: Japan, Thailand	
	Neutral: Russia, Netherlands East Indies	

CHAPTER 5

The Orient Astir

ON Sunday morning, December 7, 1941, Japa-
nese airplanes suddenly appeared over the American naval base at Pearl Harbor in
Hawaii. This action was a tragic surprise to the naval and military forces of the United
States and to the American people as well. For many months they had been looking
apprehensively at Europe, the main theater of the Second World War. In that direction,
as always in the past, seemed to lie the chief threat to American security and peace.
The great problems which precipitated the war had their center in Europe, and the
Atlantic had become increasingly smaller with the development of air power. Yet it
was from Japan, with whom America had never fought a battle, and in the vast expanse
of the Pacific, that war came once more to a shocked American people.

Wars are seldom the result of sudden whims on the part of nations, and when the
Japanese government decided to strike at Pearl Harbor, it had reasons it deemed important. This chapter shows in part what these reasons were and traces the sequence of
events in the Pacific area during the twentieth century up to 1939. The tragedy which
occurred at Pearl Harbor was the outcome of historical forces which for the past fifty
years had been revolutionizing the entire structure of oriental civilization.

The pages to follow have significance in another way. From early times the orient
and occident, despite numerous contacts, tended to evolve along paths of mutual exclusiveness. Then, in the eighteenth and nineteenth centuries especially, the barrier of
isolation was broken down under the impact of western culture upon such countries as
India, China, and Japan. The eventual triumph of westernization set in motion new
historical forces which today are creating sweeping changes in the world pattern.

121

But we should bear in mind that the westernizing process did not affect all Asiatic countries equally. Whereas western machines and education only partially modified life in China and India, they brought about a vast economic and social revolution in Japan. Therefore, while India and China did not learn the means of attaining power to command international respect, Japan made herself powerful enough to embark upon a program of imperialistic aggression, the full effects of which were felt only in the Second World War.

India Seeks to Rule Herself

The Morley-Minto reforms. In 1857, it should be noted, the British government had to cope with a rebellion in India known as the Sepoy mutiny. While the British put down this threat to their dominance and introduced numerous reforms to improve the political situation, Indian nationalism did not wither. On the contrary, by 1880 it was apparent that nationalism was growing rapidly. During the next quarter of a century it grew even more self-assertive. Confronted by the spread of violence, the British government between the years 1907 and 1909 carried out the Morley-Minto reforms. Up to this time the government had been almost completely bureaucratic. Now the various provincial legislatures in India were given elected Indian majorities, and an Indian was permitted to sit in the executive council of the governor-general. The legislature of the central government remained under British control. Moderate nationalists were satisfied for the time being, but they were presently repudiated by many more aggressive nationalists who regarded the others as old-fashioned and who were determined to obtain complete independence for India. Violence continued until 1914, the year of the outbreak of the First World War.

Indian loyalty to Great Britain. Many observers had predicted that when such a conflict came Great Britain would find India a serious liability. But when hostilities commenced in the summer of 1914, nearly all unfriendly acts against Great Britain ceased. The native princes sent large sums of money to London for the purchase of war equipment, and at the moment when the German army was threatening to break through to British lines in Belgium, an Indian expeditionary force of some fifty thousand men arrived in France and was hurried to the battlefield, where it soon proved its worth. As the war continued, Indian regiments were sent to east Africa, and other contingents participated in the campaigns fought in the Near East.

Moves for self-government. For the first three years of the war there was little unrest in India, but by the spring of 1917 it was obvious that the Indian people expected compensation from Great Britain in the way of more self-government. In the summer of 1917 it was announced in the British Parliament that the goal to be attained in India was the gradual development of self-government as part of the British Empire. India expected that as soon as the war ended steps would be taken to put this policy into effect. When victory came in 1918 to Great Britain and her allies, India eagerly awaited the reforms which had been promised. A commission had already been sent to India to frame a new constitution, and its proposals were made public in 1919. These did not provide for full self-government, as Indian nationalists had hoped, but represented only a step in that direction.

No one can say whether the proposed governmental reforms might have proved satisfactory in a tranquil atmosphere, but any chance of their acceptance in India was swept away by the outbreak of a struggle between the British and the Indian nationalists. Unrest developed, and in an ill-advised moment the British decided to pass the Rowlatt Acts, giving the police and other officials extraordinary powers to ferret out subversive activity. Disappointment with the political situation, epidemics, the high cost of living, and the Rowlatt Acts made many nationalists demand sweeping changes.

Gandhi. The chief nationalist was Mohandas K. Gandhi. Born in 1869 of middle-class parents, Gandhi had been sent to London to study law. Upon his return home he found the practice of law disappointing, and thereupon went to South Africa, where he built up a lucrative practice. So far he had been a normal businessman, but suddenly his outlook on life and his standard of values were completely revolutionized. The new Gandhi repudiated wealth, condemned violence, practiced ascetic self-denial, and above all believed that true happiness can be achieved only by service.

Gandhi began his career as reformer and champion of his people in South Africa. The Indians in this British dominion were victimized by numerous laws which restricted their freedom of movement, prevented them from buying property, and imposed special taxation. Gandhi forced the government to remove some of these restrictions. His method was not force but rather passive resistance or noncooperation. With Gandhi as their leader the Indians in South Africa carried on various strikes—including hunger strikes; they refused work, held mass demonstrations, and marched into areas where their presence was forbidden by law. Some of his followers were beaten, and many were thrown into prison, but Gandhi persisted in noncooperation and continued to secure concessions for his countrymen.

When he returned to his native land shortly after the First World War broke out in 1914, Gandhi was welcomed as a hero. Something in his character appealed strongly to the Indian people, who for centuries past had revered the mystic and the ascetic. During the war Gandhi cooperated with the British government, but the Rowlatt Acts and the disappointing concessions of the new constitution led him to announce his determination to force the British to give India self-rule.

The civil-disobedience campaign. In the spring of 1919 Gandhi actively introduced his campaign. A mass *hartal*, or strike, was announced in which all work was to cease and the population was to pray and fast. Contrary to Gandhi's plan, riots took place, Europeans were killed, and a body of soldiers was sent to try to restore order. By command of General Dyer a large body of unarmed Indians, assembled contrary to the general's orders, was dispersed by gunfire, several hundred being killed. All hope of cooperation between Indian and Briton was temporarily at an end. During these tragic days the new governmental system was set up, but members of the powerful National Congress who were behind Gandhi refused to take office under the new constitution. Gandhi, although at the peak of his popularity in 1921, suffered a temporary

A crowd of admirers surrounded Mohandas Gandhi as he arrived by ricksha at the viceroy's palace in September 1940. His visit followed the British offer to give India dominion status if she would aid the British war effort.

eclipse when his program failed to obtain *Swaraj* (independence) from the British. For his civil-disobedience campaign Gandhi was sentenced in 1922 to six years' imprisonment. However, he was released in 1924 when Ramsay MacDonald became prime minister.

Round Table Conferences. There was little peace in India in the 1920's, and during 1928 and 1929 a group of experts from Great Britain, the Simon Commission, toured the country preparatory to making recommendations for changes in the structure of government. In June 1930 the Simon Commission issued a survey of the Indian situation which suggested only a cautious advance in the direction of self-government. Meanwhile Gandhi had initiated another campaign demanding self-government. A new and promising road opened in 1930 when a series of Round Table Conferences was arranged in London. At the first of these conferences the world was electrified by the news that the Indian princes had agreed in principle to the idea of creating a great federal union in India. Up to this time India had consisted of two great political divisions: British India, ruled directly by the British, and the native India of the princes, composed of a number of distinct political units each ruled by a rajah or other Indian ruler under the final protection and authority of the British government. Unfortunately, the safeguards needed to protect the Mohammedan minority under the new government were not settled to the satisfaction of either Hindus or Moslems, and in the second conference (1931) the native princes and the delegates from British India could not agree as to the best type of federation. Vigorous anti-British demonstrations broke out in India, becoming very serious in 1932. Neither the second conference nor a third one (in November 1932) achieved tangible results.

The Government of India Act. In March 1933 a proposed constitution was made public. For two years this was heatedly discussed by members of the British Parliament and by Indian leaders. After prolonged debate the Government of India Act became a law in August 1935. Although the new constitution provided for a substantial degree of self-government, it did not give India complete independence but created a federal government consisting of the viceroy and a legislature composed of a council of state and a legislative assembly. To these houses both the Indian princes and the eleven provinces of British India were to send representatives. In the provinces the government was under the con-

trol of the Indian lawmakers, subject to certain safeguards in the hands of a British governor. In the central government all the departments of government were transferred to the Indian legislators except those of defense, religious affairs, and foreign relations. These remained in British hands. In addition a supreme court was established. The Government of India Act expanded the franchise, thereby giving the vote to about thirty-five million persons in provincial elections. By 1941 that part of the act dealing with the provinces of British India was in force, but the federal system had not been launched, owing to the hesitancy of many of the native states to come under the central government.

Nationalist policies and the war. That a vast number of Indians were dissatisfied with existing political conditions was indicated by the insistent demands of the Indian National Congress during 1941 for Indian self-rule. These nationalists, led by the dynamic Pandit Jawaharlal Nehru, were convinced that Great Britain's record in the past did not justify Indian participation in the Second World War, that the paramount issue for India was freedom.

The success of Japan in the South Pacific in the opening months of 1942 demonstrated that not only British interests in Asia but the political future of India itself were menaced.

The sacred cattle of India leisurely roam the principal bazaar street in Delhi. It is a poor country, and the animals are underfed. They are literally not worth their salt, but Hindu law forbids the natives to kill them.

On March 23, 1942, Sir Stafford Cripps arrived in India. For many years a champion of Indian home rule, Cripps brought with him a proposal from the British cabinet for full dominion status for India after the war. Cripps held numerous conferences with Hindu and Moslem leaders, but unfortunately no agreement was reached among the interested parties. The British government maintained that it must have the final decision regarding the defense of India at such a critical time; the nationalist leaders wanted more active Indian participation. The Moslems demanded assurances that under the proposed scheme they as a minority would be protected, while the Hindu leaders would not accede to a plan calling for virtual Moslem autonomy.

When Cripps finally departed for London, his mission had achieved no immediate success. A short time later, as the Japanese armies overran Burma and struck dangerously toward India proper, Gandhi announced that the Indian people should meet the invaders with a policy of noncooperation. He also demanded that the British grant India freedom at once.

The social aspect of India. India, it must be remembered, is not a country in the ordinarily accepted sense of that term, nor is it a nation. Rather, it is a vast subcontinent, as large as all of Europe excluding Russia, and a congeries of nations. Mere size is not necessarily a bar to progress, but India has a complexity of religions and a social stratification not found elsewhere in the world. In 1500 the population was estimated at 100 million; today it is over 400 million, and in 1950 it may exceed 450 million. As most of the people are engaged in tilling the soil, the tremendous increase in population has caused the farms to be fragmented into uneconomical holdings. A high birth rate is accompanied by a high death rate. In New Zealand the expectation of life is 62 years; in India it is 28.

India's millions do not form one homogeneous unit. It is estimated that there are at least 225 different languages in use, to say nothing of minor dialects. Arbitrary divisions in Indian social and economic life exist because of the deep-seated antagonism between the Hindu community (about 280 million) and the Moslems (some 90 million). Within Hinduism itself there are about 2000 castes and sub-castes. Politically there exist the dualism of the provinces of British India (the terri-

Although India is predominantly agricultural, she has turned over most of her factories to war production and is making nearly all her own war materials. These workmen are shaping a piece of white-hot metal.

tory of which was annexed to the Crown) and the 600 native states in the India of the rajahs. Some of these states are as large as the entire British Isles and have a population of several million. Each of these states, small or large, follows its own customs and form of government. It was the aim of the Government of India Act of 1935 to merge these states with the provinces in a national political structure, but, as has been stated, the rajahs have not yet come under the proposed federal government.

Economic life in India. Ninety per cent of India's population lives a rural life in the 700,000 villages which dot the countryside. For thousands of years rulers and régimes have come and gone in India, but the peasant, the *ryot*, has paid little attention to politics. His mind is concerned with the state of his crops, a current religious ceremony, or payments to the moneylender. The Indian peasant typically celebrates certain important occasions, such as the marriage of a son, with lavishness which he can ill afford. This custom plays into the hands of unscrupulous moneylenders who charge as high as thirty-seven per cent interest for their loans.

Hundreds of thousands of peasant families barely manage to survive on their diminutive farms. An average peasant's budget shows an annual income of about one hundred dollars. Farm produce valued at sixty-one dollars provides the food budget of the peasant and his family. The left-over crops (when sold) bring in about thirty-nine dollars in actual cash. Out of this sum six dollars is paid out for land tax, leaving thirty-three dollars to be spent on education, clothing, medicine, and the like. But interest often amounting to as much as twenty dollars is due yearly to the moneylender. It is evident that such a budget does not provide a decent standard of living.

A basic feature of Hindu religion—in contrast to some other religions in India—is its belief in the sacredness and unity of all animal life and its refusal to kill animals or eat meat. This aspect of Hinduism has important economic consequences. The refusal to take any form of animal life results in the accumulation of immense numbers of unproductive cattle. India maintains 215 million out of the total 690 million cattle in the entire world. The barren, maimed, and aged cattle are kept, and they eat much of the all-too-scarce fodder which might be used to feed better stock. Although there are about sixty cattle for every one hundred persons in India, the milk consumption per person is very low.

The conflict of forces. Indian leaders see in parliamentary self-government the answer to India's problems. Gandhi has succeeded in arousing his countrymen from their lethargy and in kindling for the first time in the long history of India a dynamic feeling of national unity in a large part of the population. India must sooner or later be its own master. But when? What kind of social, political, and economic structure should be created? Gandhi would apparently return India to the handicraft days of the family spinning wheel and shun the factories that are becoming more and more common in the larger Indian cities.

But economists believe that industrialization is necessary for India in order to raise the standard of living of its teeming masses. Pandit Jawaharlal Nehru, realizing that much of Indian poverty springs from evils in the native social and economic structure, is attacking not only British rule but also the exploitation of the peasant by the moneylender and landowner. Nehru advocates the doctrine of socialism. If India's poverty is to be ameliorated, there must be an improvement of village life. Already the government has worked out certain regulations and plans: (1) each village must have a school, (2) villagers are discouraged from spending large sums on marriage ceremonies, (3) vaccination is required, (4) small model houses are being built and village drains and supplies improved, and (5) the milk and egg supplies have been increased.

India is on the march. It is probable that sweeping changes, peaceful and violent, will occur. India today is a disturbing complex of forces ancient and modern, religious and secular, capitalistic and socialistic, eastern and western. But since even more complex problems have been solved throughout history, it is reasonable to hope that India will be able to work out her own unique pattern of life. Meanwhile, as we shall see in Chapter 7, the Indian problem continued to be one of the most difficult of the war.

The Great Powers in Eastern Asia

Western interests in eastern Asia. No Asiatic country has been left unaffected by the impact of western, that is European and American, interests. In India, Burma, the Netherlands East Indies, the Philippines, and Indo-China the control has been more or less direct. In China, Persia (Iran), and Siam (Thailand), the control has been less obvious, perhaps because the economic domination has not been accompanied by out-and-out direct rule or political suzerainty. Japan is unique in that it adopted the techniques of the west without accepting domination. In fact, militant Japan set out to oust western power from eastern Asia and convert the area to her "New Order." It is therefore necessary to review the political and economic interests of the major powers in this part of the world.

Great Britain's stake in the Far East. Exclusive of its control of India, Great Britain was still probably the greatest investor in Asia during the period at hand and therefore had

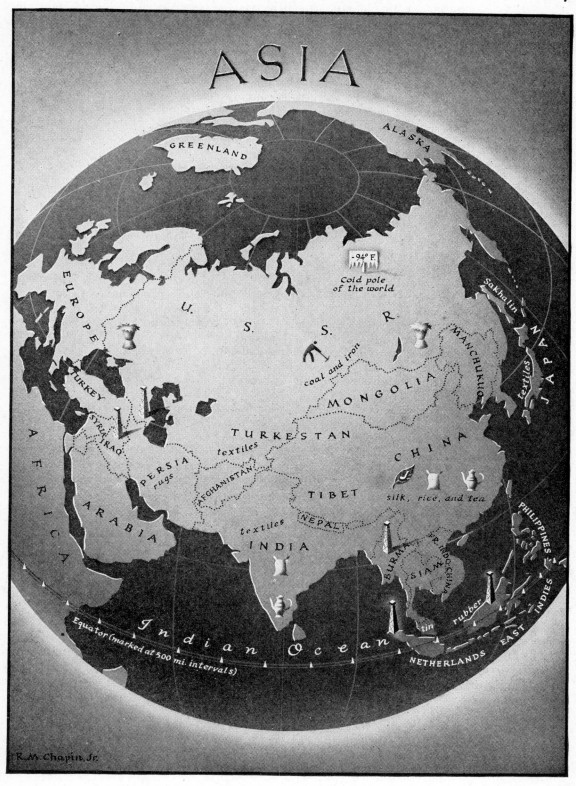

ASIA

GREENLAND

ALASKA

-94° F.
Cold pole
of the world

Sakhalin

EUROPE

U.   S.   S.   R.

coal and iron

MONGOLIA

MANCHUKUO

JAPAN

textiles

TURKEY

SYRIA IRAQ

TURKESTAN

CHINA

AFRICA

PERSIA
rugs

textiles

AFGHANISTAN

TIBET

silk, rice, and tea

PHILIPPINES

ARABIA

textiles

NEPAL

INDIA

BURMA   FR. INDOCHINA

SIAM

tin   rubber

EAST   INDIES

Equator (marked at 500 mi. intervals)

Indian Ocean

NETHERLANDS

R. M. Chapin, Jr.

the most at stake. That helps explain why the British taxpayer was called on to construct huge naval strongholds at Hong Kong and Singapore at a cost of hundreds of millions of dollars. The British flag waved over Burma, the Malay Peninsula, British North Borneo, British New Guinea, and numerous smaller sites of strategic importance, such as various islands in the Pacific. Nine million Britishers had established permanent homes in Australia and New Zealand. Hundreds of millions of English pounds were invested in tea and rubber plantations, gold and tin mines, oil wells, rice fields, and spices. It is estimated that the British had invested half a billion dollars in southeastern Asia (including $150,000,-000 in the Netherlands East Indies). From British Malaya came forty per cent of the world's rubber and tin, eleven per cent of its copra, and nine per cent of its tungsten. And southeastern Asia paid British and other western shareholders large dividends.

Great Britain and China. British economic interests were even more strongly involved in China. It is estimated that in 1900 the total British investments in China amounted to about $260,300,000. In 1914 this figure had jumped to $607,500,000, while in 1930 British investments stood at $1,189,200,000.[1] Twenty-five per cent of this amount was involved in import, export, and general trade, 21 per cent in real estate, 18 per cent in manufacturing, 14 per cent in transportation, 12 per cent in banking and finance, and the rest in public utilities, mining, and miscellaneous items. In 1902, British money represented 33 per cent of the total foreign investment in China; in 1930 it stood at 36.7 per cent.[2] British investments centered principally in the prosperous Shanghai area and the Yangtze valley.

Great Britain has been interested in protecting these investments as much as possible and has favored on the whole comparatively little change in the status quo. During the thirties the British government was conciliatory to the point of appeasement. It made no effort to slow down Japanese expansion so long as these were confined to Manchuria and northern China. The defensive attitude of the British in eastern Asia prior to 1939, and to some extent later, was due to their fear that they were not strong enough in the Far East to cope with a Japan which could threaten British interests in China and British Malaya and perhaps even in Australia and New Zealand.

French activity. France has not played so dramatic a role in eastern Asia as other occidental powers. Its possessions centered about French Indo-China, an area which contained about twenty-one million people in 1931. Indo-China is immensely rich in mineral and agricultural resources. France also used Indo-China as a springboard to advance its interests in southern China, such as building a railroad into that area. The French secured a leasehold at Kwangchow and concessions at certain treaty ports. To protect their investments in eastern Asia as well as possessions in the Pacific, the French established a naval base on the east coast. French investments in China in 1902 were worth $91,000,000; in 1914, $171,-400,000; and in 1930, $192,400,000. Compared with some other countries, French investments were small, representing but 5.9 per cent of the total foreign investment.[3]

With Great Britain, France played an important part in the internal affairs of Siam (Thailand), lying between French Indo-China and Burma (see map, page 127). France and Great Britain attempted to prevent the domination of Thai affairs by the Japanese, a domination which would critically affect French and British interests in the adjoining territories.

The Netherlands East Indies. In 1941 the Netherlands East Indies had an estimated population of 70,000,000 distributed over some 3000 islands possessing an area of 735,267 square miles. The Netherlands East Indies extend east and west for a distance longer than continental United States and are sixty times the size of Holland itself. Java is the most densely populated area in the world. In 1941 it was estimated that Europeans numbered only 250,000 out of this huge population. The Chinese numbered well over 1,200,000, and other foreign Asiatics, more than 110,000. The rest were natives, of the ethnological group known as Indonesians, a highly industrious people of the Mohammedan faith. The spread of education has fostered in these natives an increasing desire for self-government. And Dutch administrators have had to face the problem of a growing trade unionism.

The Netherlands East Indies play a strategic role in the world economy, whether in times of peace or war. Besides producing great quantities of copper, manganese, petroleum, and phosphates, the islands supply 90 per cent of the world's quinine requirements, 85 per cent of its pepper, 33 per cent of its rubber, 18 per cent of its tin, 17 per cent of its tea, and 12 per cent of its sugar.[4] The Indies have been a lucrative field for many foreign investors, although the Dutch have had by far the greatest stake in these islands.

"Western capital is invested in banking, shipping, mining, and agriculture, with agriculture taking the lion's share. The amount of outside capital invested in the East Indies is estimated at from four to six billion florins. Three fourths of this capital is estimated as Dutch. The Dutch East Indies Government bonds, now aggregating about a billion and a half florins, are held abroad, practically all by the Dutch. Before 1930 the profits on these investments ran as high as 400,000,000 florins yearly. During the worst of the depression years these profits practically disappeared and today are only a fraction of what they were in 1930."[5]

Dutch policy in the Indies. The possession of the Indies has had a striking effect upon Holland and her economy. Millions in profits have gone to the governing country. As a result, the Dutch have ruled the Indies from an economic rather than from a political or social standpoint. This does not mean that they have not been concerned with such colonial problems as hygiene, education, and the general well-being of the natives. But their principal aim has been to govern the islands so as to exploit their economic resources as efficiently as possible.

Holland maintained a small but efficient navy and army in the Netherlands East Indies, although the Dutch realized always that their strength would avail them nothing against such powerful neighbors as the British or the Japanese. Great Britain has had rich adjoining territory in the Malay Peninsula and Burma and so could supply herself with the vital products of southeastern Asia. From the British, the Dutch have had little or nothing to fear. But with the Japanese, the situation has been different. Modern and semi-industrialized Japan is lacking in those mineral and agricultural resources which bring so much wealth to the investors in the Netherlands East Indies. Furthermore, Japan showed herself during the

In Tarakan, Borneo, Dutch oil wells were built native style, with thatched roofs. These fields fell to Japan in 1942.

thirties as more than willing to use her powerful navy and army to obtain hegemony over an area extending from Manchuria to Java. The Dutch were powerless to resist conquest alone and depended on the British as allies in such an emergency. As the Second World War drew near, an apprehensive Dutch gaze was constantly turned toward the northern horizon, where war clouds were gathering.

United States interests. The United States, too, has had an important role in eastern Asia during the present century. An American, John Hay, was intimately associated with the famous Open Door policy at the turn of the century to insure China's territorial integrity and make possible equal privileges for all nations trading with the Chinese. President Theodore Roosevelt aided in the negotiating of the Treaty of Portsmouth, which concluded the Russo-Japanese War. American business interests created a link across the Pacific which could be broken only at a painful price. Furthermore, as a result of the Spanish-American War, the United States found herself in pos-

A native worker taps a rubber tree on a Sumatra plantation in the Netherlands East Indies. Rubber sap flows at the rate of two drops a second.

session of the rich and coveted Philippines.

The United States, however, has never been so heavy an investor in the orient as Great Britain. In 1931 American investments in China amounted to only $196,800,000, or 6.1 per cent of the total foreign investment, as compared with Japan's 35.1 per cent and Great Britain's 36.7 per cent.[6] "Consequently, if it is investment interest that determines the strength or weakness, from the power standpoint, of national policy, it is clear that there had been relatively little incentive to the United States to utilize effectively its power to establish its China policies."[7] On the other hand, American investments were greater in Japan than in China.

The question of Philippine independence.
The Tydings-McDuffie Act of March 24, 1934, provided that the Philippines were to get complete independence on July 4, 1946. This act, while striving to please the Nationalists, stipulated that the United States was to retain power over such matters as foreign relations

and military affairs until 1946 arrived and was therefore committed to maintaining order in the Philippines up to that time. Economic ties were as strong as political ties. Whereas in 1899 American goods being shipped to the islands were valued at only $1,150,000, in 1929 these products were worth $92,592,959. By 1934, eighty-four per cent of Philippine exports was going to the United States.

Other factors entered into the question of what to do with the islands. Certain American economic interests in competition with Philippine interests favored the severing of political ties. American naval and military strategists argued the value of the Philippines as a protection of those trade routes whereby America got its much-needed supplies of rubber, tin, and other products. Still another question was the threat of the Japanese, who coveted the islands for their resources and as an outlet for surplus population at home.

U. S. policy in the orient. When the entire far-eastern picture is taken into account, a truer view of the position of the United States during the period up to 1939 results. The United States asked no territorial acquisitions and did not seek war. It did not have enough economic stake in China to feel that there was vital need to take drastic action against Japanese aggression. Nevertheless the United States was committed to oppose any power which threatened to dominate by force all of Asia and the western Pacific. An embargo against Japan might provoke war and would certainly result in a loss of profitable commerce. It is true that the United States government refused to recognize Japan's puppet state of Manchukuo in 1932, which had been created at the expense of China, but it did not prevent American materials of war from being sold to Japan. It thus helped Japan to humiliate China, kill innumerable Chinese, injure Americans and American properties—and blast Pearl Harbor.

Other European powers. Other occidental powers have long been involved in eastern Asia, but their influence has not been so great as those already mentioned. Prior to the First World War Germany won important concessions in the Shantung peninsula and elsewhere in China, besides gaining control of the Caroline and Marshall Islands in the South Seas. Germany's defeat destroyed its imperialist position in eastern Asia, but the post-

Terraced rice paddies covered with water lace the countryside in Java, part of the rich Netherlands East Indies. Thrifty natives also raise fish in the shallow ponds between their fields.

war years saw German-Chinese relations become friendly. German officers were sent to train China's national army. This political friendship was reflected in the growth of German trade in China. In return for tungsten, antimony, cotton, wool, hog casings, and so on, Germany exported to China dyes, munitions, iron manufactures, and machinery. Before the reopening of the Sino-Japanese struggle on July 7, 1937, Germany had taken the place of Great Britain as the third most important nation in China's trade.

Italy has never had territorial acquisitions in the Far East. Most Italians living in China have done missionary work, and Italian investments there have been insignificant. During the late thirties Italy's attitude toward eastern Asia was conditioned by its growing ideological solidarity with Japan. Belgium became a larger investor in China, especially in railways. Portugal kept as a colony only the small port of Macao on the south China coast.

Russia. The Soviet Union has occupied a unique position in eastern Asia because its territory stretches continuously from the Baltic Sea in Europe to the Pacific Ocean (see map, page 127). Russia adjoins China and Japan's puppet state of Manchukuo. Because of its economic system, the Soviet Union stresses self-sufficiency. Foreign investments are condemned as capitalistic and imperialistic. Therefore the stake of the Soviet Union in eastern Asia has primarily depended upon its geographical position and is political

rather than economic. Russians have bought and sold on a basis of mutual advantage with all the countries of eastern Asia. On the political front, however, the Soviet Union witnessed periods of crisis during the years leading up to 1939. Early in the twenties China and Russia entered into favorable relations, and Russian advisers came to China. After 1927, however, Chiang Kai-shek became increasingly anti-Communist. In the decade that followed, his armies tried to destroy Chinese forces designated as Communist which opposed him. Thereafter, the Soviet Union took a less friendly attitude toward the Chinese, although it allowed war materials to proceed to China in her fight against Japan.

With Japan the Soviet Union has had many altercations. Russia looks on the island kingdom as a great potential enemy in the east, and during the thirties the two nations attempted to jockey into favorable positions. The Soviet Union viewed the establishment of Manchukuo with apprehension, fearing that it might become a springboard for activities in eastern Siberia. There have been numerous clashes along the border, owing in part to lack of definite boundary lines. Problems relating to fishing rights have also been a sore spot between the two powers for a long time.

The Pacific islands. Spread throughout the vast expanse of the Pacific is Oceania—innumerable small or large island possessions of the great powers. These outposts, war was to show, are important principally for strategic reasons:

On Luzon island in the Philippines a native farmer plows his small muddy plot with a water buffalo. This plantation had belonged to one family for several generations before the Japanese came.

they can be used as naval and air bases. New Caledonia, one of France's most prized oceanic possessions, is an area of considerable economic importance because of its rich nickel deposits. The German-owned Caroline and Marshall islands were turned over to Japan at the end of the First World War as mandates. These and other islands in the Pacific were fortified by the Japanese. The British controlled such centers as Fiji, and the Australians controlled groups of small islands south of the equator which used to belong to Germany but were later given as mandates to Australia. The

United States has made use of her oceanic possessions for purposes of strategy and commercial air travel. The Hawaiian Islands were fortified to serve as an outlying defense for continental America, although this group of islands is also economically desirable for its sugar and pineapple production. Wake Island and Guam lie advantageously on the route to Manila and for this reason were used as key centers in the air service which was inaugurated between the Philippines and the United States.

Western contributions in the orient. To this point the treatment of the role of the great powers in eastern Asia has stressed the importance of their financial stakes in that area and has shown how these investments have helped shape national policies. That the actions of Europe and America in China and neighboring lands have been motivated by economic interests of sometimes the most selfish and ruthless nature cannot be gainsaid. But the picture would be incomplete without a mention of other aspects of occidental activity in eastern Asia. Many colleges and schools have been established by various western organizations for the increase of education among the peoples of eastern Asia. This work has been done largely by missionaries, many of whom have given unceasingly of their energy for the betterment of the people of Asia. Western powers have also cooperated in sending to the Far East engineering experts to construct needed public works. Doctors have proved invaluable in establishing hospitals and clinics, in helping to check epidemics, and in educating the populace to the necessity of public health measures. And, as we shall see later, the western powers pledged themselves in the 1920's to respect the territorial integrity of China. Many occidental leaders tried to strengthen the political status of India by encouraging home rule.

China Tries to Change

Chinese losses to Japan. From the period of the first Anglo-Chinese War (1839-1842) to the end of the nineteenth century, China was forced to kowtow to the demands of foreign powers. European nations exploited her mercilessly, stripping her of strategic ports, wresting important economic concessions, and imposing upon her such humiliations as extraterritoriality, customs regulations, and the sta-

tioning of foreign warships in Chinese waters. A weak central government and lack of national unity made it impossible for China to resist these encroachments upon her rights.

But the real blow came not from occidental nations but from that small land which China had always regarded with amused contempt. What China had to learn was that a nation as small as Japan could defeat her easily because, in an industrial and military sense, her aggressive neighbor was thoroughly westernized. Trouble brewed for some time between the two nations, especially over the control of Formosa and Korea. Finally a dispute arose over China's claim to suzerainty in Korea, war broke out in 1894, and the brief Sino-Japanese struggle resulted in a humiliating defeat for China. By the Treaty of Shimonoseki in 1895, China was forced to relinquish claim to Korea (which Japan later annexed in 1910), hand over the rich Liaotung peninsula and Formosa, pay an indemnity of $150,000,000 to Nippon for a war which the latter had brought on, and grant the Japanese further commercial and extraterritorial privileges.

Europe exploits China. China's defeat was the signal for the renewal of aggressive actions by western powers, which robbed Japan of the advantages of her recent victory by forcing her to give back the Liaotung peninsula in return for an extra indemnity from China. These nations were afraid to let Japan take the strategic peninsula, and Russia in particular was at that time trying to obtain control of all Manchuria for herself. That their motive was utterly selfish is proved by their subsequent actions. In 1895 France confirmed her mining and railroad concessions in Indo-China, and Great Britain obtained an extension of the boundaries of Burma and additional trading privileges. Germany in the meanwhile had been trying to get the fine harbor of Kiaochow and mining rights in Shantung peninsula. The murder by brigands of two Roman Catholic missionaries of German nationality in 1897 gave the kaiser's government an excuse to seize territory, including a ninety-nine year lease to Kiaochow Bay plus some two hundred square miles of adjacent territory. Germany was also given exclusive mining and railroad rights throughout all of Shantung province.

Russia, Great Britain, and France now made their demands. Russia obtained a twenty-five-year lease to Dairen and Port Arthur on the tip of the Liaotung peninsula with the right to build a railroad across Manchuria, known as the Chinese Eastern Railway, allowing Russia to dominate Manchuria completely. In 1898 Great Britain obtained the lease of Weihaiwei, a naval base, to protect her interests in northern China against growing Russian control. In

the same year France leased Kwangchow in southern China for ninety-nine years.

The Open Door policy. China was now in imminent danger of disintegrating completely. Manchuria and Mongolia were under Russian domination; the Shantung peninsula was virtually a possession of Germany; much of southern China was controlled by France. Hong Kong, Weihaiwei, and the rich Yangtze valley, created as a special "sphere of influence" to be exploited economically, belonged to Great Britain. A halt, or at least a hesitation in the disintegrating process, was provided by the United States, not solely because of high-minded desires but largely out of the aim of Washington to safeguard its own interests in the orient. It is probably true that American imperialism had been less obnoxious in China than that of any of the large European powers, but the United States had taken little or no action in China at this time, in part because its energies had been devoted to acquiring the Philippine Islands. However, in 1899 Secretary of State John Hay asked the major powers to agree (1) not to interfere with any "sphere of interest" or any leased territory, (2) to have the Chinese tariff apply to all merchandise in such regions and to allow the Chinese government to collect this tariff, and

(3) to permit all nations to enjoy the same harbor dues and railroad charges. In 1900 several powers had agreed to Hay's request. The famous Open Door policy was born.

The "hundred days of reform." At this time China was rousing herself to cope with these foreign dangers. The humiliation of her defeat by Japan had particularly incensed the younger Chinese thinkers, who now agitated for reform. The young Kuang Hsu emperor showed himself to be sympathetic to their cause when in 1898 he instituted what came to be known as the "hundred days of reform." The reforms included an attempt to modernize the civil service examinations, the establishment of a school system along western lines (including the founding of an imperial university for the study of both ancient and modern knowledge), and the encouragement of railway and industrial expansion. Unhappily for China, however, the reactionaries at court protested bitterly against these innovations and formed a powerful faction about the Empress Dowager, Tzu Hsi. In September 1898, she seized and imprisoned the emperor, executed some of the leading reformers, and took over the government. With Tzu Hsi in control, an attempt was soon made to lead China to salvation by reaction.

The Boxer Rebellion. China has for centuries had many secret societies of a religious or political purpose. After the suppression of the reform movement a group of secret societies united in an organization known as the "Righteous Harmony Fists"—called by westerners "Boxers." At first the Boxers were strongly anti-Manchu because of the reactionary measures of "Old Buddha" (Tzu Hsi), but by 1899 their chief object of hatred had become the foreign nations who were stripping China of her possessions and power. With the addition of rowdy elements to their ranks, the Boxers started a campaign to rid China of all Christians and "foreign devils." Many Europeans were killed, including the German minister, and the legations at Peking were besieged. For months foreign residents there and elsewhere were in constant peril, and not until August 1900 did an international army force its way to Peking and effect the release of the foreigners besieged there. After Peking was captured, many Europeans, Japanese, and Americans who composed the force committed grievous acts of vandalism, plundering the palaces of their priceless art objects, burning private dwelling places, and putting numerous Chinese to death. In the protocol of 1901, which concluded the Boxer Rebellion, China had to agree to apologize for the murder of the German minister and other foreign officials, allow the outside nations to police a larger area around Peking, fulfill many other irritating obligations, and pay to the foreign powers an indemnity of about $333,000,000. The United States returned most of the indemnity which China owed her, and the Chinese government set this sum aside for sending students to American universities.

Cultural revolution in China. China had failed to save herself by conservatism. Now a growing number of Chinese thinkers were becoming convinced that China's only salvation lay in adopting some of those western techniques by which smaller enemies had been able to humiliate her. The old cultural structure underwent profound changes. This period of transition is by no means over; in fact, the mammoth cultural revolution in which the most dynamic elements of the occident are being integrated with the permanent values of the orient is perhaps only now getting into full swing. At any rate, the young Chinese intellectuals at the beginning of the century saw the necessity for radical change. Moreover they believed that so long as the reactionary officials, Chinese and Manchu, of the Manchu dynasty headed the government, China could never hope for real progress. Not only were the military and civil leaders incompetent and inefficient in the main, but they and their subordinates were corrupt.

Hostility concentrated upon the Manchus persisted despite their attempts to institute various reform measures. In 1905 the Manchus discontinued the old civil-service examinations and introduced tests designed to include economics and political science as well as the traditional questions. The army was partially reorganized, and a constitution was promised to the people. Provincial assemblies were convoked in 1909 and a national assembly in 1910. Unfortunately for the Manchus, their last relatively able but unenlightened leader passed away in November 1908. With the death of Tzu Hsi, the dynasty soon crumbled. The heir apparent was but a child.

In the meantime the young rebellious elements had much to complain about. In 1904

Before the Japanese occupation Morrison Street in the Tatar city section of Peiping, China, had become one of its modern thoroughfares. The wide sidewalks bordered with Chinese signs and the spacious boulevards with their cyclists were a far cry from the dark and twisted streets of older China.

the government of British India was threatening China's shadowy suzerainty over Tibet. At this time also China was unable to prevent the Russians and Japanese from making use of her territory as a private battlefield. The ranks of the reformers increased, and the revolutionary fervor of the Young China party was heightened by youthful intellectuals who had studied western subjects in China and abroad.

Reformer Sun Yat-sen. Ultimately the most important leader of the movement was Sun Yat-sen (1867-1925). This outstanding revolutionist was born in a village about forty miles from Canton, the son of a tenant farmer. When about thirteen he went to Hawaii, where an older brother lived. There Sun Yat-sen received a western education. In 1879 he was put in an Anglican school, where he became a Christian convert. His shocked brother had him recalled to China, but the youthful Sun began to disfigure and destroy the images in the village temple. As a result of these sacrilegious acts, Sun had to flee to Canton, where an American Protestant missionary doctor helped him. Once more he resumed his studies with Protestant missionaries in Hong Kong.

In 1892, Sun Yat-sen received a diploma in medicine. Taking up practice in Macao, he set about organizing a reform society. The Portuguese government ordered him to leave, not because of his political actions, it is said, but because he was competing with Portuguese physicians. Going to Canton, Sun sent a petition to Peking asking that agricultural schools be founded. When this request was refused, he helped organize a revolt against the Manchus. The discovery of the plot forced him to flee in 1895 to Hong Kong and then to Japan, the United States, and Great Britain. Wherever he went, he sought aid in his now almost fanatical desire to create a new China. He came near being executed in 1896 when the Chinese legation captured him in London. But the British government ordered his release, and Sun Yat-sen was free to continue agitating against his Manchu enemies.

The Republic of China is born. Sun's great opportunity arrived in 1912 when the 268-year-old Manchu dynasty abdicated, and China for the first time in its long history became, in name, a republic. The revolution which brought about this dramatic turn of events was won with relatively little bloodshed. A revolt had broken out in September 1911, over a foreign loan to finance certain railways. The outbreak spread unexpectedly when some imperial troops mutinied in the Yangtze valley and joined the new movement. Soon a republic was declared in the region, and several cities fell to these forces. General Yuan Shih-kai, whom the Manchus summoned to quell the revolt, was dissatisfied with the government, and he procrastinated sufficiently long to allow the revolution to spread like wildfire through the provinces. The revolutionists assembled at Nanking where, on December 28, 1911, they elected Sun Yat-sen president of the republic. He had been out of the country when the revolt began but had now returned triumphantly to China.

Before Sun Yat-sen arrived home, however, the revolutionists had been negotiating with Yuan Shih-kai, the most powerful military figure in the country. He soon persuaded the imperial clan and others surrounding the young emperor that the Manchu dynasty was doomed. On February 12, 1912, edicts were promulgated by which the emperor abdicated, and Yuan Shih-kai was asked to form a republic. It was agreed on both sides that the emperor was to live at peace in his palace in the northern part of the Forbidden City of Peking in possession of his title and a large annuity. To prevent internal dissension, Sun Yat-sen declined the presidency, and the republican group at Nanking elected Yuan Shih-kai. China now faced the future as a republic.

Dissension in the government. Yuan possessed the largest army and the blessing of foreign powers and republicans alike, but he had not the idealism of Sun Yat-sen and shortly began scheming to restore the monarchy with himself as emperor. The provisional constitution adopted in March 1912 had put the office of president under the jurisdiction of parliament. The first parliament was controlled by the radicals who had engineered the revolution and organized themselves into the Kuomintang (Nationalist party). In 1913 trouble broke out when Yuan concluded a large loan with banking groups of Great Britain, France, Germany, and Russia, thus placing the government under their influence. Furthermore, he replaced certain military commanders in the south with his own henchmen. The outcome was a new rebellion, endorsed by Sun Yat-sen. With the suppression of the revolt by Yuan, Sun had to flee to Japan. Yuan, now firmly entrenching himself as president, dismissed the Kuomin-

tang members from parliament in November 1913, dismissed parliament itself in January 1914, and in 1915 announced the imminent restoration of the monarchy with himself as emperor. Rebellion spread in the last month of 1915, Yuan's prestige evaporated, and in June 1916, the discredited dictator died.

A decade of disorder. Dissension in the government continued for the next decade (1916-1926). Squabbles at home and incidents abroad brought added misery to the struggling republic. It is impossible here to trace the confusion that existed in Chinese political circles during these years. In 1917 one military chieftain actually declared to a surprised world that the Manchu dynasty had been restored, but the "restoration" did not last. For a time the country was divided between two would-be governments, one at Peking, the other at Canton. The one in the south was composed largely of the radicals who had engineered the Revolution of 1911-1912 and who had adhered to the constitution of 1912. The Canton government, not nearly so powerful as the conservative Peking administration, elected Sun Yat-sen as president in 1921. Meanwhile the Peking government was enfeebled as rivalries developed between cliques and warlords fought for control.

Sun Yat-sen's philosophy. A social philosopher who was abler as a propagandist and revolutionist than as a political administrator, Sun Yat-sen and his Kuomintang government did little to reunite the country. However, the social ideology which he formulated during this period had important results for the future. In 1923, unable to obtain aid from the foreign powers in his attempt to overcome the Peking government, he called in certain Soviet advisers. The chief of these Russian helpers was the influential and brilliant thinker, Michael Borodin. Owing to the confidence placed in Borodin and his associates, the Kuomintang soon adopted many of the planks of the program subscribed to by the Communist party in the Soviet Union.

After his death on March 12, 1925, Sun Yat-sen became a national hero. Weekly memorial services were held before his picture. To the present day Sun Yat-sen maintains his exalted position in the minds of many Chinese republicans of various shades of thought. Sun left a will and certain books which were adopted as infallible guides for the country. One of these volumes, *San Min Chu I,* or the *Three People's Principles,* became the manual of the Kuomintang. The three Principles are (1) nationalism—the liberation of China from foreign domination; (2) democracy—"government by the people and for the people"; and (3) livelihood—economic security for all the people.

China united under Chiang Kai-shek. In 1926 the armies of the Kuomintang began to drive northward. Their chief Chinese leader, a young man of military ability, was Chiang Kai-shek. The armies encountered little real opposition, and by early spring, 1927, the Yangtze valley was reached, and important cities such as Shanghai were occupied. But dissension broke out in the Kuomintang itself between radical and conservative elements. Because the Communists frankly opposed organized religion and Confucian morality to the shocked antagonism of much of the nation and because of Chiang Kai-shek's own leanings toward conservatism, a split became inevitable. The murder of several foreigners at Nanking and attacks upon others by certain radicals in March 1927 brought about the cleavage. The moderates under Chiang created a government at Nanking, and before the end of 1927 public opinion had crystallized behind this régime. Back to the Soviet Union went the Communist advisers; many radicals were driven into exile (including the widow of Sun Yat-sen), and the Nanking government came to depend for financial support upon the foreign bankers at Shanghai. Meanwhile, in 1927, Chiang Kai-shek married Mei-ling Soong, a sister of Madame Sun Yat-sen, and so further cemented his position among his countrymen. The next summer, the Nationalist armies moved northward again and by June had entered Peking. With peace between the northern war leaders and the Kuomintang, China appeared once more to be united.

The world at large now looked forward to a time of internal harmony and growing stabilization in China. There was little doubt that China's chances for success were the brightest since the Revolution of 1911-1912. The country was being administered by men trained in, or influenced by, the west. The Nationalist government was enacting measures designed to unite all China and integrate the techniques of the occident with the ideals of the orient. The new capital, Nanking, was alive with bustle and plans for the future, and

The historic meeting of Jawaharlal Nehru, Madame Chiang Kai-shek, and General Chiang Kai-shek took place in India in February 1942. Here leaders of the two greatest Asiatic countries met to discuss problems of Indian independence.

the foreign situation had improved. China was protected by the Nine-Power Treaty of 1922; she was a member of the League of Nations; many of those in America and Europe who wished China well advocated the abolition of extraterritoriality and other concessions against which the Chinese were protesting effectively by employing an ancient weapon, the boycott; and Japan appeared, on occasion, relatively conciliatory in her attitude to China.

Anti-Nanking groups. But the sympathizers of the young republic were overlooking several aspects of national life which caused endless friction. In many places the people were being tyrannized by bandits, especially where the strength of the Nanking government was least effective. Famine in the northwest cost the lives of millions. In 1929 certain military leaders who were dissatisfied with the policies of the Kuomintang broke away. By the following year, however, they had been defeated, and the government of Chiang Kai-shek was secure from attack from this source.

But trouble was arising now between the Nanking régime and the Chinese so-called Communists. During 1930-1933 extensive areas were in the hands of these anti-Nanking

In February 1936 the stand of a wealthy (by Chinese standards) tea vendor in Canton looked like this. The best of its kind in the city, the stand was patronized by well-to-do merchants.

groups. While many of the Chinese Communists were active believers in the principles of Marx and had attended a university at Moscow which the Soviet Union had started in 1925 for Chinese students, other groups involved in the revolt were in reality local military forces or even bandits. The Communist banner attracted many landless peasants who did not understand the dialectics of Marx but who had suffered greatly from personal privation and who now understandably wanted to wrest land from the rich proprietors. Chiang Kai-shek turned with great severity upon these elements, and untold numbers of so-called Communists were put to death. In fact the criticism has been levied against Chiang that he was more interested in 1931 in fighting his countrymen than in warring against the aggressors from Japan. However serious this internal trouble might have become for the Nanking government, it was overshadowed by developments in Manchuria in 1931 which will be discussed later in this chapter.

The economic evolution of China. In the early twentieth-century commerce increased rapidly, for the Chinese represented the largest potential market in the world, and the foreign powers were interested in taking whatever advantage they could of this fact. China's total foreign trade was seven times as great in 1929 as it had been in 1894. Nevertheless, China still is almost entirely self-contained, and her civil warfare, currency insecurity, inefficient transportation system, and national poverty have all combined to keep her virtually undeveloped in the economic world. Some progress has been made with the building of factories and the adoption of western machinery. The manufacturing of cotton goods, for example, has reached impressive proportions. Unfortunately, however, these cotton mills and other factories are largely owned or controlled by foreign entrepreneurs to whom go the sizable profits. Exports which have also added to China's growing economic life include silk, tea, vegetable oils, and products from the mines. China has colossal economic potentialities, but until they are exploited for the advantage of the Chinese people, the inhabitants of the republic will continue to suffer.

The progress of Chinese education. The intellectual changes that have taken place in modern China are phenomenal. In the words of Kenneth S. Latourette, "In some respects, between 1895 and 1933 the mental life of China moved farther from its old moorings than that of the west had done between the thirteenth and the twentieth centuries. It was in greater turmoil than at any time since the Chou."[8] Whereas at the beginning of the century the educated class was extremely small and concerned almost exclusively with classical subject matter, by 1931 China had 34 universities and colleges with 17,285 students, some 1300 secondary schools with 234,811 pupils, and innumerable primary schools affording the basic elements of education to about 9,000,000 persons. When the total population of China is considered, this figure may not appear impressive until one remembers the remarkable advances made in only a very few years. The Chinese people venerate learning. Even during the present conflict, in which whole university centers have been destroyed, their students have trekked sometimes hundreds of miles inland to reorganize their college life. New institutions, in fact, have been created during the past few years.

Other cultural changes. The intellectual pattern of the land has been modified in other ways. The printing of books has increased manyfold, and hundreds of important western treatises have been translated and disseminated. Scholarly journals have made their appearance, contributed to by some of China's most energetic minds. One of her outstanding scholars is the brilliant and far-seeing intellectual, Dr. Hu Shih. Hu Shih is American-educated and when in China lectures and writes continually. He is associated with the renaissance of modern Chinese thought, emphasizing the value of the physical and social sciences rather than the precepts of Confucius, and championing the use of a new and simplified written language, *pai hua,* or "plain speech." Scholars such as Hu Shih have also labored for the adoption of Mandarin as a national speech so that scholars and laymen from all parts of China can converse intelligently.

Modern China's social changes. The social life, morals, and customs of modern China have been considerably altered. The movies have both helped and hindered the Chinese to visualize western life. The larger cities have installed telephones, electric lights, and modern water systems. Newspapers, factories, railways, movie houses, and neon signs are also to be seen. Occidental dress has made its way among the people. Chinese fashions such as long fingernails (to indicate that the aristocratic bearer did not soil his hands with work), the queue which the Manchus made the Chinese wear as a mark of national inferiority, and the bound feet of women, a cruel self-imposed fashion which was supposed to add to the appeal of the ladies, are disappearing. Folk ways are changing at the same time, as are ancient family traditions, the deference (and even submission) of youth to age, the acceptance of concubinage, and the former social stratification. China is in the process of a social revolution—propelled further, as we shall see (Chapter 8), by the war. However, it will take many decades to create the new China with its blending of the orient and occident, for in the rural districts especially the people are slow to change ancient customs.

Japan Expands

Japan's imperialism. The island kingdom of Nippon made phenomenal advances in the decades following the visit of Commodore Perry in 1853. There was a complete reorganization in the government, army, and navy which created a westernized nation.

The next big event in the nation's history took place in 1894 with the outbreak of hostilities against China. The issue concerned Korea, and although the outside world looked for a Chinese victory because of overwhelmingly superior numbers, the well-trained Japanese army and navy inflicted upon the forces of China a swift and utter defeat. By the terms of the Treaty of Shimonoseki, signed on April 14, 1895, China had to recognize the independence of Korea, cede the Liaotung peninsula to Japan (which, as we saw previously, three of the great powers made her return), cede also the island of Formosa, open various cities in China to Japanese trade, and pay a huge war indemnity. That victory marked the beginning in modern times of Japanese imperialist expansion on the Asiatic continent and the rise of the military clique in Japan.

Japan was by now on the way to recognition as a first-class power, a reputation accentuated in 1900 during the Boxer Rebellion, when Japanese soldiers, in conjunction with western military forces, performed heroic feats at the relief of the Peking legations. In January 1902, Japan scored a diplomatic triumph by an alliance with Great Britain. Both parties looked upon such an alliance as a threat to Russian expansion, while the prestige it gave the Japanese in European eyes was considerable. If either party became involved in a war, the other would use its influence to prevent other nations from attacking its ally. If a third power entered the fray, Japan or Great Britain, as the case might be, would come to the assistance of its ally.

The Russo-Japanese war. With the diplomatic horizon cleared and the army and navy growing in size and efficiency, Nippon entered into its next conflict with quiet confidence. This time the war was directed against Russia. Soon after Russia, Germany, and France had forced Japan to hand back the Liaotung peninsula to China, the Russians had negotiated with the imperial government of China for the lease of Dairen and Port Arthur on the tip of the peninsula, as well as the right to build a railroad across Manchuria to connect with the Trans-Siberian line. Japan had not let this incident go unnoticed and was only biding her time to challenge the strength of czarist Russia. This rivalry of imperialistic ambitions brought on a war early in 1904. Japan was conceded only the slimmest chance to de-

Women were fighting to obtain civic rights in the Japan of February 1931.   Here a Buddhist woman's organization is engaged in lettering signs to be used in the campaign.

feat a nation which appeared to be almost impregnable. But to the world's surprise, Russia proved herself almost unbelievably corrupt and incompetent at this time. Russia's poor showing was in part the result of the universal unpopularity of the struggle among the Russian people, who staged an unsuccessful rebellion at home shortly afterward. A disastrous naval defeat sealed Russia's hopes. When President Theodore Roosevelt at the request of Tokyo offered to negotiate peace terms on June 9, 1905, both combatants agreed.

By the Treaty of Portsmouth, signed September 5, 1905, Japan acquired the southern half of the island of Sakhalin (instead of an indemnity of $580,000,000 as had been demanded), the leaseholds to the Liaotung peninsula and Port Arthur, and various Russian railway and mining rights in southern Manchuria. Japan's paramount position in Korea was also conceded, paving the way to annexation of that peninsula in 1910. Nippon was fully accepted as a first-class power, a position attested by the renewal of the Anglo-Japanese alliance on August 12, 1905.

Further acquisitions on the mainland. Holding an important position in far-eastern affairs, Japan merely had to bide her time once more before embarking upon further imperialism. Korea was next in line with Japanese aims and, as earlier stated, was annexed to the empire on August 29, 1910. Korea's old name of Chosen, "Land of the Morning Freshness," was officially adopted. When the First World War broke out in 1914, Japan told Germany on August 15 to take all warships out of the Far East and to turn over the Kiaochow territory to Japan "with a view to the eventual restoration of the same to China." When Germany did not reply to this request, the Japanese government declared war on August 23 and seized the territory.

The Twenty-One Demands. Then, on January 18, 1915, the president of China was presented with terms which startled the world by disclosing the aim of Japanese imperialists on the Asiatic continent. These were the notorious Twenty-One Demands, which would have made of China little more than a Japanese protectorate. The other powers did little to hinder the success of Japanese ambitions, preoccupied as they were with the gigantic struggle in Europe. China was swept with indignation but had not the physical means to protest effectively. On May 25, 1915, the Chinese government under threats of coercion had to accede to the first sixteen demands, while the rest were reserved for later consideration. "Among other things these treaties confirmed Japan's newly won position in Shantung province and extended her railway and territorial rights in south Manchuria to the end of the century. American protests helped block the most sweeping of the demands, which would have made China a Japanese protectorate."[9]

The European powers secretly agreed in 1917 to support Japanese claims in the peace conference that would follow the First World War. The United States, while not agreeing to support these claims, admitted, by the Lansing-Ishii agreement of November 2, 1917, that Japan deserved "special interests in China" owing to her "territorial propinquity." The Allies had evidently chosen to forget that China had also entered the war on their side and was entitled to respect and consideration.

Postwar Japan. Japan's role in the Far East was secure after the war; she controlled in one way or another Shantung, Manchuria, southern Mongolia, and the German islands north of the equator, besides those territories and concessions she had wrested from China and Russia prior to the war. By this time the power of Japan had increased to such proportions that the United States and the British Dominions in the Pacific area were frankly alarmed. Various acts were passed discriminating against Japanese ownership of land in several of the American states. In 1921 Great Britain allowed her treaty with Japan to terminate without renewal.

The table[10] at the bottom of this page shows the phenomenal increase of Japan's economic power invested in China since 1902 and why the other powers were alarmed at this development.

The Washington Conference. Great Britain and the United States drew together to restrain Japan's expansionist program, especially in naval matters, and the United States called the Washington Conference in 1921. The conference was attended by delegates from Great Britain, France, Italy, Holland, Portugal, China, Belgium, Japan, and the United States. The purpose of the conference was to decide not only upon naval matters but also upon problems affecting the entire Pacific area. The three leading naval powers, Great Britain, the United States, and Japan, consented to reduce the tonnage of their capital ships so as to achieve a respective ratio of 5-5-3. While this agreement made official the inferiority of the Japanese fleet to those of the other two powers, it recognized the position of the Japanese navy as the third most powerful in the world. By the Four-Power Treaty the United States, Great Britain, Japan, and France agreed "to respect their rights in relation to their insular possessions and insular dominions in the region of the Pacific Ocean."

In 1922 the well-known Nine-Power Treaty was signed at Washington. All the signatories agreed to respect the independence, sovereignty, territoriality, and administrative integrity of China. Furthermore, they were to use their influence to preserve the Open Door Policy and "to refrain from taking advantage of conditions in China in order to seek special rights or privileges which would abridge the rights of subjects or citizens of friendly states, and from countenancing action inimical to the security of such states." It is impossible to square Japan's acts in China today with the pact which she signed in 1922, just as it is difficult for the other signatories to excuse their remaining apathetic toward China until they were themselves drawn into war against Japan in December 1941.

Earthquakes and politics. From 1922 to 1931 the spotlight switched largely from foreign to domestic issues. In September 1923, Japan was devastated by a terrible earthquake which destroyed large areas of Tokyo, Yokohama, and other densely populated centers. Hundreds of thousands were killed or injured, while billions of dollars of property damage

	1902		1914		1931	
	Millions of dollars	Per cent of total	Millions of dollars	Per cent of total	Millions of dollars	Per cent of total
Great Britain..........	260.3	33.0	607.5	37.7	1,189.2	36.7
Russia...............	246.5	31.3	269.3	16.7	273.2	8.4
Germany............	164.3	20.9	263.6	16.4	87.0	2.7
France..............	91.9	11.6	171.4	10.7	192.4	5.9
United States........	19.7	2.5	49.3	3.1	196.8	6.1
Japan...............	1.0	0.1	219.6	13.6	1,136.9	35.1

resulted from the national catastrophe. Universal sympathy was aroused, and millions of dollars were subscribed by Americans and others to relieve the distressed areas. The ingenuity and courage of the Japanese people came to the fore at once, and reconstruction of Tokyo and other cities along the most modern lines was soon set in operation.

In March 1925 the Manhood Suffrage Bill was passed, granting the franchise with few exceptions to every male above twenty-five. By this bill the number enfranchised jumped from 3,000,000 to 12,000,000. "This change forced Diet members to spend large sums in electioneering, and made them more dependent on capitalist support. Consequently, it strengthened the capitalists' control over the Minseito and the Seiyukai (political parties). At the same time it made possible the rise of labor and left-wing parties, which began to win Diet seats."[11]

The increase in suffrage did relatively little to democratize the nation. The cabinets in power were not subject to the same control by the lower house as they were, say, in British parliamentary procedure. In Japan the cabinets continued to be made and broken largely by the House of Peers, or the Privy Council, or the military clique. We must not forget that the army and navy authorities were virtually independent of civil control, and they could—and frequently did—force the country to do their bidding.

Economic progress in Japan. In the economic sphere, Japan forged ahead rapidly. Thousands of factories were built, and the manufacturers of the country undersold foreign competitors in the world market, owing in part to the low standard of wages prevailing in Japan and to the modern machine techniques which the Japanese industrialists were swift to adopt. In the field of textiles especially, Japan captured one market after another. Commerce and industry were controlled by a few great concerns in whose hands the greater part of the country's wealth was concentrated. The two greatest financial powers were the houses of Mitsui and Mitsubishi. The Mitsui interests, for example, controlled banks, trust companies, industrial plants, department stores, shipping lines, mines, power companies, paper plants, and so on.

Japanese economic prosperity, however, was scarcely on a firm basis. It depended upon the maintenance of a large volume of exports, the sale of which gave funds to buy raw materials and foodstuffs abroad. For Japan now had a population of 65 million living on an area smaller than the state of California, of which only one fifth could be cultivated.

Japan Prepares for a "New Order"

Japanese designs on China. The problems which Japan faced in 1931 could not easily be solved. The population was growing rapidly, and it would take increased industrialization at home and increased commerce abroad to take care of unemployment. But Japan was lacking in resources, and her home market was limited. The solution appeared to rest with China, rich in resources and possessing an unlimited market. Perhaps both nations might have profited mutually through cooperation, whereby China would have been encouraged to sell raw products to Japan, getting manufactured goods in return. But the situation in both countries seemed to make cooperation impossible. China had not forgotten the Sino-Japanese war of 1894, the annexation of Korea, or the Twenty-One Demands. Meanwhile Japanese leaders were alarmed at the progress China was making toward unification, modernization, and utilization of economic resources.

By 1930, because of social and economic conditions, the Japanese army had gained control of governmental leadership. Japan was in the throes of a critical depression. Whereas in 1929 her export and import trade had been worth 4,365,000,000 yen, in 1931 it had fallen almost by half to 2,383,000,000. Unemployment, wage-cuts, strikes, rural misery, and a growing acceptance of Marxist beliefs characterized the crisis. The militarists chose a policy not of internal reform and reconstruction but of foreign conquest. By this means they hoped to allay unrest at home, unite the country, and somehow rectify Japan's economic problems through the forcible acquisition of new territory and markets. Furthermore, a successful military campaign would enhance the prestige of the army. The venture stood a better chance of succeeding if it occurred before China had become unified.

The Manchurian campaign. Without warn-

This is the Japanese colony of Bokuryo in Manchukuo, looking not unlike Alaskan towns on our own continent. Manchukuo was a "wild west" to the Japanese, and they planned to devote twenty years to its development.

ing, in September 1931, the Japanese army attacked Chinese forces in Manchuria. It is possible that this action was taken by army leaders without the authorization of the Tokyo government. Unable to cope with the invader, the Chinese government appealed to the League of Nations. This body appointed a committee of inquiry, known as the Lytton Commission, which later made a report condemning aggression in Manchuria while trying not to affront Japan. Beyond expressing regret at the invasion of Manchuria, no action was taken by the League. The government of the United States declared in the so-called Stimson Doctrine that it would not recognize conquests made in violation of existing treaties. But this action failed to elicit positive response from other great powers, which were in the throes of the world-wide economic depression.

Without allies and apparently with only fair-weather friends the Chinese resorted to a nation-wide boycott of Japanese goods. This led to armed reprisal by Japan. An expedition was sent to Shanghai, in January 1932, to teach the Chinese a lesson. Much to the surprise of the Japanese militarists it took more than a month to capture the great city. On February 18, 1932, Manchuria was renamed Manchukuo and recognized in September 1932 by Japan. The abdicated Manchu emperor of China became its first ruler.

As 1933 opened, the Japanese began to push farther to the south into Chinese territory. A portion of north China was occupied, and armies were sent into districts south of the Great Wall. Helpless in the face of this aggression, the Chinese leaders decided to make a temporary truce with Japan to slow down the invasion and give China a chance to prepare for the critical struggle for national existence which was bound to come. In May 1933, therefore, the T'ang-ku Truce was signed, whereby the Nanking government reluctantly recognized Japanese conquests in Manchuria and north China.

Meanwhile, Japan found its position in the League of Nations untenable in the face of the Lytton Report. On February 17, 1933, Japan gave formal notice of its intention to withdraw. How fateful the Manchurian campaign was can now be recognized. It showed that a great power could embark with impunity upon a course of aggression; it marked the beginning of the collapse of the League of Nations' prestige. From then on, it seemed, the world was to be governed by considerations of national interests and power politics exclusively.

Problems in Manchukuo. The Japanese hoped that the new puppet state of Manchukuo would prove economically profitable, and they poured vast sums of money into their new investment. The results were disappointing. The hoped-for immigration by Japanese settlers did not come up to expectations. New industries in Manchukuo competed with industries in Japan. The problem of maintaining law and order remained acute; so-called "bandits" (often Chinese patriots) made life so miserable for the authorities that the Japanese army had to create "protected villages"—villages surrounded by high walls into which the population of the countryside was herded. Less than half as much money was expended on education as the Chinese had spent, and the Chinese colleges were disbanded. Furthermore, the new educational philosophy placed emphasis on Confucian doctrines of right conduct and submission to one's superior.

But an even graver charge has been leveled at the Japanese attempts to break the spirit of their Chinese subjects in Manchuria. In Manchukuo and north China in 1933 an opium monopoly was established, and the use of narcotics was actually encouraged in those areas where the Japanese army had control. In the words of an American representative to the League's Opium Advisory Committee: "[Manchukuo and north China] constitute the one region in the world where the governing authority not only makes no effort to prevent the use of narcotic drugs but actually profits by the rapid increase of narcotic addiction."[12] Meanwhile the Japanese peasant at home had to work longer to help pay for the economic fiasco in Manchukuo.

A united front in China. Between 1933 and 1936 there was comparative peace between Japan and China. The Japanese were trying to consolidate their position in the north, while the Chinese national government under the leadership of Generalissimo Chiang Kai-shek was attempting to cope with internal problems. Unhappily for China, virtual civil war raged between Chiang Kai-shek's forces and those of the Chinese Communists. Chiang tried to subjugate the Red armies but only succeeded in driving them away from the Nanking area to the northwest, where they were now in closer contact with the Soviet Union. Chiang opposed the Chinese Communists' economic doctrines, while they in turn charged that Chiang was more willing to fight his own countrymen than he was to fight the Japanese invaders. This last view was in some measure held by regional leaders in Canton also. In 1935 the heads of the Chinese Communists demanded a united front against the Japanese, stating that the first objective of all China should be wholehearted resistance against foreign imperialism and aggression. On December 12, 1936, Chiang was actually kidnapped by rebels for two weeks. Instead of killing him as they might easily have done, they asked him to lead a united China against the common

Terrified Chinese flee the invading Japanese on the outskirts of Peiping, China, in June 1933, just before the signing of the Sino-Japanese truce. Hundreds of Japanese troops reënforced the Peiping Japanese legation guard.

enemy. The rebels were also influenced by the obvious national feeling of solidarity behind Chiang that showed itself during his period of abduction. The result was that Chiang returned safely to Nanking, and the basis was laid for a common working agreement between the national government and the Communists. China was unified in time to meet the next Japanese thrust.

Background of the "incident." The next Sino-Japanese military "incident," as the Japanese have preferred to term an affair which has caused millions of casualties and lasted for several years, broke out on July 7, 1937. Mr. Y. Suma of the Japanese Foreign Office described the renewal of hostilities in this manner: "You see there is China, a very beautiful girl. And here is Japan, a very strong young man. . . . And the young man is determined to marry that girl. You understand . . . determined . . . to . . . marry her."[13]

Back of that plot lay many factors. Japan's costly venture in 1931 had not paid the expected dividends. Militarists and industrialists in Japan hoped that the control of China's richer areas in the south would bring the prosperity they had expected from Manchukuo. The situation at home was unhealthy. Agricultural rents were rising while living costs among the industrial workers were also mounting. The workers were agitating against their landlords and employers, but the patriotic, patient Japanese mind is such that it would not protest against a national war sanctioned by the emperor. Japanese capitalists were alarmed by the foreign trade situation. In 1937 Japan faced the prospect of having to export gold to pay for a billion yen adverse balance, brought about by the heavy increase in imports from abroad and a loss of exports resulting from mounting costs of production and an increasing world hostility toward Japanese policies. All these elements, and the desire of Japanese military and naval leaders to increase their power, underlay the "incident" of July 7, 1937.

The outbreak of hostilities. Fighting broke out in the north. Meanwhile in August, 1937, the Japanese attacked Shanghai by land, sea, and air. Despite a heroic resistance for which the Japanese had not bargained, the Chinese finally lost the city and had to begin retreating inland. The Japanese advance up the Yangtze valley went rapidly, and Nanking, the capital, was captured December 15, 1937. The horror of the story of Nanking's destruction, looting, and raping by Japanese soldiers shocked the world and served to steel Chinese resistance. In the north the Chinese armies were also forced to retreat, and the Japanese set up a provisional government at Peiping (formerly Peking). The Chinese, instead of capitulating after the fall of Nanking, established a new capital farther up the Yangtze. In October 1938, this city in turn fell to Japanese forces. In the same month the Nipponese captured Canton, whence military supplies had been shipped to the Chinese armies. Canton fell easily because the Chinese thought that the enemy would not attack so close to Hong Kong. However, British prestige had hit a new low a month before with the Munich appeasement settlement, and so the Japanese boldly set foot in Canton. The Chinese, despite their forced withdrawal from the coast, moved their capital still further inland to Chungking on the upper Yangtze and continued the war against the extended Japanese lines.

The incident became a war, and the weeks which were expected to end it have lengthened into years. It is estimated that the war in China has cost Japan at least $5,000,000 a day besides hundreds of thousands, if not millions, of casualties. As a result of the crisis, the military forces in Japan became virtual masters of the country's political and economic structure. But it would have been folly to expect the Japanese people to rebel soon under such war conditions. Their whole history and conditioning had bred in them a reverence for authority and an almost unbelievable indifference to hardship and even death in any cause designed to enhance the glory of the Sun Goddess' empire.

The "New Order" proclaimed. On November 3, 1938, the "New Order in eastern Asia" was proclaimed. Its objectives were stated to be the destruction of the Chiang Kai-shek régime in China, the expulsion of western interests in eastern Asia, and the establishment of "a self-sufficient economy through the formation of a close Japan-Manchukuo-China closed-door bloc."[14] When the democracies found themselves embroiled in a second great international war in September 1939, Japan still had as its principal objective the creation of its cherished "New Order in eastern Asia."

The Pacific Situation: 1939

Alignment of the Pacific powers. When Europe plunged into war in September 1939, the effect upon the Pacific area was to differentiate more clearly the alignments which had been developing there during the preceding years. The presence of war in Europe made its spread to eastern Asia highly probable, if not almost certain, because of the strong economic and colonial ties between the European powers and the Asiatic countries.

In terms of alignment there were the following categories: on the Allied side were the possessions and interests of the British Empire and France, including Australia, New Zealand, India, Burma, British Malaya, Indo-China, numerous concessions in China, and British and French Oceania. These areas were actively at war with Germany and Italy. The situation in India was obscured by growing demands on the part of the Indian Nationalists for independence. In a second category were the economic interests of Germany and Italy in the Far East, which were relatively unimportant. In the third category were numerous neutral nations, divided on ideological grounds at least. Japan was bound by common interests to the Axis alignment in Europe and was engaged actively in an expansionist program against China. Thus Japan would favor German and Italian interests in eastern Asia and work against the Allies and their sympathizers. Thailand was likewise pro-Japanese and anti-Ally in sympathy. Sympathetic to Great Britain and France in their war (and possible future allies) were the Netherlands East Indies, China, and the United States. Holland was trying desperately to remain neutral as war broke out in Europe in 1939, but in eastern Asia the Dutch knew that only by collaboration with the British could they withstand Japanese aggression against the Netherlands East Indies. The United States was openly sympathetic to the Allies and China, and anti-Axis and anti-Japanese feeling mounted steadily.

The situation of the Soviet Union was by no means so clear-cut. Russia and Japan had for generations regarded each other as dangerous enemies, and the Soviet Union had sent war supplies to China to aid her against the Japanese. But the signing of a non-aggression pact with Germany prior to the outbreak of war in 1939 altered matters considerably.

Japan was linked by an anti-Communist pact with Germany and Italy, and now that Hitler and Stalin apparently had settled their differences, the Japanese were forced to retreat in bewilderment from their former strong anti-Russian attitude. It looked in 1939, however, as though the Soviet Union would adopt a policy of wait-and-see in eastern Asia.

In view of the history of the various powers in far-eastern affairs it was only logical to suppose that the large powers in the Pacific would adopt the course of action they did. Obviously, the course of events in the Pacific area rested primarily with Japan, for since 1931 (in fact since the Sino-Japanese war of 1894) Japan had been the prime disturber of the status quo.

Similarities in Nazi and Japanese policy. The Japanese and Nazi militarists had much in common. Economically they looked upon themselves as "have-not" nations which could gain resources only at the expense of such "have" powers as Great Britain, France, and the United States. Both had strong views of racial superiority; Hitler rhapsodized about the Aryan type, while the Japanese maintained that they were the descendants of the Sun Goddess and had a divine mission to perform in bringing their superior culture to the rest of Asia—in fact to the entire world, according to certain chauvinists. After Japan had successfully defied the League of Nations in its Manchurian conquest and had served as an example to Hitler, the two nations spent the next decade in cajoling and threatening smaller nations with remarkable success. German and Japanese techniques were often similar. A typical approach was the establishment of puppet régimes, with the army as the real master. Both nations took advantage of the apathy of the larger powers or appealed to them on the grounds that they were fighting Communism and were the enemies of the Soviet Union.

Axis "squeeze play." The Germans, Japanese, and to a lesser degree the Italians were executing a gigantic "squeeze play." Unqualified revisionists and expansionists, they were, on the surface at least, ideologically in strong agreement. The weakness of the League in connection with the Manchuria affair showed Hitler that he could ignore the Treaty of Ver-

Occasion for this "huddle in Berlin" was Adolf Hitler's reception of the Japanese ambassador, Saburo Kurusu, on the occasion of the 2600th anniversary of the founding of the Japanese empire. Foreign Minister von Ribbentrop is at the ambassador's right, and Hitler is flanked by his interpreter, a man named Schmidt. It happened in December 1940.

sailles with impunity. Like Japan, Germany left the League of Nations in 1933. As will be seen in the next chapter, the Abyssinian conquest of 1935-1936, the reoccupation of the Rhineland by Germany in 1936, and the Spanish Civil War all dragged the system of collective security into the dust in Europe.

In 1936 the Rome-Berlin Axis was formed, as was the Japanese-German Anti-Comintern Pact. This latter agreement was directed against Communism and served to link the co-signers closer together. The "incident" of 1937, which began in July, was followed in November by Italy's adherence to the Anti-Comintern Pact and Mussolini's notice of withdrawal from the League of Nations, given in December 1937. In 1938 the annexation of Austria by Hitler took place, and in September came the Munich appeasement, by which the prestige of the democracies fell to hitherto unplumbed depths. One month later the Japanese ignored the danger of a possible clash with the British at Hong Kong and captured nearby Canton. Hitler and Mussolini had the democracies "on the run" in the west; the Japanese press was now insisting that Asia should be for the Asiatics and that it was high time that the western powers cleared out of China.

In March 1939, Hitler took over Czechoslovakia, and within a few months the Japanese had blockaded British and French concessions at Tientsin and were subjecting British subjects to gross insults. The "squeeze play" re-

sulted ultimately in war in Europe in 1939. What would happen in eastern Asia?

Reactions of the democracies. Certainly the democracies were not completely blind to the dangerous position of their interests in the Far East. The British people seethed with rage at the humiliation to which they were subjected by the Japanese, and more and more Americans began to protest the selling of high-octane gasoline and war materials to Japan. The Netherlands East Indies, Australia, New Zealand, Indo-China, and the Philippines studied each new aggressive act with apprehension. The British government spent millions of pounds on the naval base at Singapore so as to create in southeastern Asia a key defense center for its rich possessions. The Dutch augmented their naval forces and reduced the length of army service in order to build up reserves of manpower having military training. The Soviet Union was realistic enough to station a large well-trained army in Siberia as well as great numbers of airplanes and submarines at Vladivostok.

The reaction of the United States to the Pacific situation was especially based on its complex relations with Japan. The American people had long been sympathetic toward the Chinese. As a whole they resented the Twenty-One Demands which the Japanese foisted upon a hapless China in 1915. The growth of Nippon's power as a result of the war was disturbing to the United States, and in the Washington Conference (1921-1922) the United States and Great Britain fixed the naval ratio of the three naval powers at 5-5-3, with Japan on the short end. The Nine-Power Treaty guaranteeing China's territorial integrity was more acceptable to America than to Japan.

Relations between the two countries were considerably improved by the generous help given by Americans after the disastrous earthquake of 1923. But this was offset by the passage in 1924 of an act which excluded Japanese immigrants from the United States. The Chinese had been excluded since 1882 except under certain conditions. The Japanese people took the exclusion act as a deep affront. In 1931 Secretary Stimson led the way in proposing nonrecognition of Japan's conquest of Manchuria. Relations deteriorated even further during the thirties because of increased hostility of Americans toward Japan's expansion and the open friendship and aid given by our government to China.

On the economic front, also, relations were strained. Japan's lower standard of living enabled it to produce and sell many goods more cheaply than the United States, with the result that Japanese businessmen captured more than one market that used to bring profits to American manufacturers. And the danger which Japan's expansion in southeastern Asia might prove to their supply of rubber, tin, and tea stimulated many interests in America to devise strong strategic policies and plans of action.

Summary

This chapter has briefly traced the development of the major areas of eastern Asia during this century up to the year 1939. We have seen how India attempted to gain self-government but had not succeeded in solving its religious, social, or economic problems at home, or in persuading Great Britain to go far toward granting it home rule. China tried to extricate herself from exploitation by creating a republican form of government, unifying her various social and political groups, and resisting Japanese aggression. The evolution of Japan into one of the foremost world powers culminated in a dynamic expansionist program during the years 1931-1939. Attention has also been given to the numerous colonial possessions and interests held in eastern Asia by the major western powers and how they have been affected by events in the orient.

The most eventful decade in the recent history of eastern Asia was that from September 18, 1931, to December 7, 1941, and the motivating power was Japan. The actions which developed in that part of the world prove beyond any doubt that an inseparable tie-up now exists—and will continue to exist—between east and west. During the period we have studied, Japan allied herself with the Axis powers in a campaign which had a sweeping revisionist and expansionist program for its purpose. Concomitantly in Europe and Asia they were trying to forge "New Orders." On the other hand, China found herself linked to the cause of the western democracies, and everywhere it was the same struggle to resist aggression and ruin.

These developments were clearly a climax in the world's history. The civilizations that sprang up along the Indus and Ganges, the Wei and Hwang Ho, and in the archipelago off eastern Asia seemed for centuries so remote from those of Egypt, Greece, Rome, and Europe that the world appeared to be split for all time into "East" and "West." But while these two great cultural segments evolved largely in mutual exclusiveness (though not nearly so exclusively as has been believed in the past), it was inevitable that men would in some age smash the cultural barriers. Improved transportation gradually drew the areas together, and the Industrial Revolution enormously hastened the process.

THE
PRESENT

PART TWO

Ordeal of Our Time

CHAPTER 6

A World Divided

CHAPTER 7

Since Stalingrad

CHAPTER 8

On the Home Fronts

CHAPTER 9

Preparing for Tomorrow

O N SEPTEMBER 1, 1939, Hitler's legions marched into Poland, and the Second World War began. On that fateful day an era in world history closed. It had been an era which tried to find a solution for war by creating an ill-supported League of Nations—and failed. The era had witnessed the rise of dynamic new ideologies and the apathy of the static nations toward what was to menace their very existence. It had watched a resurgent, aggressive nationalism bluff and bludgeon an appeasing democratic system into a position no longer tolerable. There was a feeling almost of relief when the clouds of total war, which had hung so menacingly and so long over the nations of Europe, finally broke. People everywhere knew that the old era of blundering, groping, and nerve-breaking tension was at last over. For good or for ill, it was to be replaced by something new.

What that "something" will be cannot yet be known. It may be, as George Bernard Shaw pointed out, that the really important things which will develop out of the war will be those which we could never have foreseen. Certainly history has taught us to expect the unexpected.

But in the course of the war, certain developments were taking place which deserved notice. One was its global nature, far more apparent than was true of the First World War. Battlefronts existed in the Soviet Union, in western Europe, in China, Africa, the Aleutians, and the South Sea Islands. Journalists wrote about the Battle of the Atlantic, of the Pacific, of the Caribbean, of the Mediterranean. Virtually no segment of the earth's surface escaped the holocaust which started in the Polish Corridor.

Another development to be considered was the totality of the Second World War. Civilians had to face air bombardments and starvation blockades as though they, too, were soldiers. Women participated on a scale hitherto unknown. Belligerents converted their industrial systems into "all-out" war machines. The dangers which entire populations had to face in common started to bring about undreamed-of social change. Duties which rich and poor performed alike—air-raid work, fire fighting, and airplane spotting—brought about a new sense of common purpose and solidarity.

A third important development was the ideological nature of the Second World War. People everywhere felt that this was not just a war of rival imperialisms. They saw the rise of a foe who based his actions upon a carefully thought-out political and social philosophy. It was a war between the "Four Freedoms" of democracy and the New Order of Germany, Italy, and Japan. Fascism openly avowed that war is beneficial, that nationalism and not internationalism is desirable, and that democracy is inherently decadent. In this war also was highlighted the struggle between the opposing viewpoints of equality of races and a superior or ruling race—a *Herrenvolk*. A dynamic reaffirmation of their belief in democracy began to find voice in the peoples of the United States and the British Commonwealth of Nations. This new-found enthusiasm for an old and cherished ideal expressed itself in many groping plans for the creation of a truly democratic world in the postwar era.

D URING the first phases of the Second World War the opponents of totalitarianism again and again were forced to suffer the tragedy of too little and too late. The Third Reich and its allies possessed a preponderance of arms and trained men and swept on from victory to victory in all theaters of the conflict. But in the summer of 1942 the fortunes of war turned in favor of the Allies. Along the home fronts, over the worldwide battlefields, they achieved virtually full consecration to the tasks of total war, and finally upset the heretofore inexorable march of the Axis toward world domination. By the autumn of 1943 it was clear that the totalitarian states had not only been stopped; they faced inevitable defeat.

As the men and women of the United Nations passed from the nightmare of improvised defense to the satisfactions of successful offense, the question of what kind of world should be reconstructed after victory received increasing attention. While the leaders of the United Nations met at Moscow, Cairo, and Teheran to survey conditions on home and fighting fronts and to formulate military strategy and postwar policy, numerous unofficial groups back home explored the same problems.

The issues raised by the postwar period were both numerous and complex. They related to switching industry from war to peace production, the caring for millions of uprooted peoples in the devastated areas, the punishment of Axis leaders guilty of criminal acts, and the administration of conquered territory. They related to the prevention of further wars. Shall the League of Nations be revived? Can a world federation be formed? Should an ambitious blueprint for an international order be shelved for the less ambitious but perhaps more realistic scheme of a benevolent Grand Alliance of the main world powers? Such were some of the questions asked by men all over the globe as the menace of totalitarianism began to recede and the prospects for victory welled forth.

Abyssinia and Spain

1935-1936	Italy invades, conquers Abyssinia	Failure of League sanctions
1936	Hitler remilitarizes Rhineland	Violation of Versailles Treaty
1936-1939	Civil war in Spain. Fascist victory with Axis aid	Nonintervention of Great Britain, France

Road to Munich

1936	Mussolini announces Rome-Berlin Axis	
1936-1937	Anti-Comintern Pact against Russia	Germany, Italy, Japan
1938	Nazi purge	Removes restraining influences
	Hitler takes over Austria, demands Sudetenland	Chamberlain's appeasement efforts
1939	Munich conference	
	Complete capitulation of Czechoslovakia	

Blitzkrieg over Europe

March 1939	Hitler demands Danzig and part of Corridor	
August	Russo-German Pact	Complete reversal of alignment
September	Poland invaded, conquered	Germany and Russia divide country
	England, France declare war	
1939-1940	Standstill in the west	Maginot vs. Siegfried Line
	Russo-Finnish war	
1940	Fall of the western nations: Norway, Low Countries, France	Dunkirk, occupied and unoccupied France
1940-1941	The battle of Britain	All-out bombing fails of purpose
	Italian invasion of Africa, Greece stopped	British raid on Italian navy
	German drive to the Near East	
	Dismemberment of Rumania	
	Annihilation of Yugoslavia	Greece overwhelmed
	Invasion of Crete	British retreat
	Blitzkrieg against Russia slowed	
1942	War in the Pacific	Fall of Hong Kong, Singapore, Java, Burma, Australia threatened
	All-out Axis drive	Battle for Russia

United States and the Spreading War

1939	New neutrality legislation revised	
1940	The draft: Selective Service Act	First peacetime conscription
Jan. 1941	Lend-Lease Bill	Cash and carry favored Allies
March	Occupation of Iceland	
November	Repeal of neutrality law	
December	Japs attack Pearl Harbor	
Jan. 1942	Pan American Conference at Rio	
Jan.-May	Fall of Philippines	Heroic battle of Bataan
May-June	Battles of Coral Sea, Midway	
July	Increasing American participation	

CHAPTER 6

A World Divided

By the postwar settlement of 1919, in the activities of the League of Nations, and in the Locarno agreements of 1925, Germany, Great Britain, and France appeared to have settled their differences. The League seemed to be achieving encouraging if not brilliant success in promoting international harmony, and the signing of the Kellogg-Briand Pact renouncing war as an instrument of national policy in 1928 seemed to promise a new era of peaceful cooperation among nations.

Never have hopes been more thoroughly dashed than in the decade from 1930 to 1940. The restraints and guarantees embodied in collective security, the Nine-Power Treaty, the Locarno agreements, and the Kellogg-Briand Pact all disappeared before the onslaught of undeclared wars, unprovoked aggression, and irresistible blitzkriegs. The period of international disorder was inaugurated by Japanese aggression in Manchuria in 1931, when the League of Nations received its first serious setback. War between China and Japan raged intermittently throughout the next decade. While China was fighting for her national existence, western Europe experienced the Italian conquest of Abyssinia, the Fascist revolt in Spain, and a succession of diplomatic crises. All this foreshadowed the Second World War that came in September 1939.

In 1934, "the year of blood," the world was given a preview of the shape of things to come. In February the Stavisky scandal caused rioting in Paris, and in the same month the Socialist experiment in Vienna was brought to a bloody conclusion when Chancellor Dollfuss turned the Austrian army on the workers. In June Hitler carried out his blood purge, murdering Ernst Roehm and other prominent Nazi leaders.

In July the world was given another example of frightfulness when, in an attempted plot to seize Austria, the Nazis killed Dollfuss. The trail of blood next led to the streets of Marseilles, in France, where King Alexander of Yugoslavia was murdered by a Croatian terrorist from the king's own country. As the year 1934 drew to a close, a news dispatch disclosed that Abyssinian and Italian troops had fought a battle on the Abyssinian border. Europe, and indeed the world, was to have little tranquillity from then on.

In tracing the background for the war which came in September 1939, particular emphasis will be placed upon the following: (1) the Italian conquest of Abyssinia (known also as Ethiopia), (2) the Spanish Civil War, (3) the annexation of Austria, (4) the Munich Agreement, and (5) the dismemberment of Czechoslovakia. These events led to the Polish crisis that precipitated war in September 1939. What may be termed the Second World War will then be discussed in terms of eight fundamental phases, to the summer of 1942. Developments from that turning-point are covered in later chapters.

Fascism Triumphant in Abyssinia and Spain

The conquest of Abyssinia. Italy was the first European nation to follow Japan's lead in aggression. As Mussolini became increasingly convinced of the imperial destiny of his régime, his speeches grew more and more bellicose, bristling with such statements as: "War is to man what maternity is to woman." "Perpetual peace negates the fundamental virtues of mankind, which are revealed only on the bloodstained battlefield in the full light of the sun." The logical spot for Mussolini to strike was Abyssinia, the only important independent native state left in Africa. Furthermore, the Italians had suffered a humiliating defeat at the hands of Abyssinia in 1896.

On December 5, 1934, fighting broke out between Abyssinians and Italians over a sec-

In July 1936, before going into exile, Haile Selassie arrived at Geneva to plead before the League of Nations the hopeless cause of his conquered country.

tion of land on the frontier. On the fourteenth of the same month Emperor Haile Selassie sent an urgent message to the League of Nations, expressing his fears. In May 1935 the League gave the affair serious consideration and tried to arrange for arbitration of the dispute. In the meantime large forces of Italian troops were passing through the Suez Canal on their way to eastern Africa.

In July 1935 Abyssinia appealed vainly for support from the United States. Outside the framework of the League, France and Great Britain were trying desperately to dissuade Italy from carrying out her plans. Fear of Germany made France want to keep Italy as a friend, and if France had to honor her League pledges against aggression, the invasion of Abyssinia would undoubtedly terminate Italian friendship. Great Britain also was anxious to settle the dispute without invoking pressure by the League in order to present a unified front against Germany. But in Great Britain the Conservative government was faced with the fact that in a recent poll several million votes had been cast in favor of supporting the League at all cost, even war, in order to maintain international law and order. The government of Great Britain was thus forced to agree to certain measures against Italy instituted by the action of the League. France tried to retain the friendship of Great Britain by supporting the League but attempted also to make this support as ineffectual as possible so that Italy would not be offended. Under such circumstances the League action was doomed to failure.

On October 2, 1935, Italian troops invaded Abyssinia. Despite the audacious argument of the Italian delegates to the League that Abyssinia, not Italy, was the aggressor, the League voted to impose sanctions against Italy. This action meant prohibiting shipment of certain goods to Italy and denying her credits. Sanctions were put in force on November 18, but oil, the all-important commodity without which no modern army and navy can fight, was not included in the list of prohibited articles.

While the League was endeavoring to apply pressure against Italy, Italian troops were advancing with little difficulty into Abyssinia. Their progress was facilitated by the use of bombing planes, mustard gas, and tanks. Fighting valiantly, Haile Selassie's warriors were driven back, crushed, and scattered. In May 1936 the Italians entered Addis Ababa, the Abyssinian capital, and the conquest was practically completed. The whole sorry story ended in July 1936, when sanctions were removed, and the League of Nations admitted another catastrophic setback. Collective security had failed against Japan and now had fared no better with Italy. Haile Selassie, an emperor without a country, became an exile in England, the first of several royal exiles.

Military occupation of the Rhineland. The Treaty of Versailles provided that the German Rhineland should be permanently unfortified, and in the Locarno agreements of 1925 Germany pledged herself to abide by this arrangement. When Hitler came to power in 1933, an ambitious disarmament conference was in session at Geneva. Little progress was made, however, and in October 1933 Germany not only withdrew from this conference with the plain intention of rearming herself but withdrew from the League as well. In March 1935, in defiance of the Treaty of Versailles, Hitler introduced conscription. But the conflict over Abyssinia gave him his first big opportunity. His opponents were divided. While the sanction wrangle was in progress, German troops marched into the Rhineland on March 7, 1936.

France mobilized 150,000 troops and considered using force to compel the German troops to evacuate the Rhineland, but Great Britain refused to support such a measure. Many Englishmen thought it hardly worth while to risk war over the demand of a country to fortify its own territory. There were others, however, who recognized the danger in allowing Hitler to break an agreement with little or no protest. As one speaker put it, "What we all wanted to know was 'What is Germany's limit?' You might take the view that Hitler's system required him to have about two stunts a year, and if he were to govern Germany for another twenty-five years, this would mean about fifty more stunts. But if you took the other view—that Germany might stabilize and settle down—then there might come a point . . . when she might say that she had now got restitution and would therefore now stop."

Spanish unrest and revolution. Germany's repudiation of Locarno was followed shortly by the Civil War in Spain, which not only shattered that country but threatened to involve all of Europe. The Spanish constitution of 1931, established after the downfall of the monarchy, had not brought prosperity and stability to Spain. On the contrary it caused serious clashes between the forces of the right and the left. During 1934 and 1935 there was danger that reactionary groups would gain control of the government and nullify most of the progressive legislation enacted in the early days of the republic. In 1936 a coalition of liberal and leftist elements obtained control of the government. Fascist sympathizers were imprisoned, and many military officers who had been engaging in political activities were pensioned. The government tried to steer a middle course, but it satisfied neither the leftists, who were anxious to have revolutionary social changes immediately, nor the ultraconservatives, who were against all reforms. The government was powerless to maintain order. Conservatives and radicals fought and murdered each other early in July, and on July 17 regiments in Spanish Morocco revolted against the government.

Dress rehearsal in Spain. From the outset it was apparent that the totalitarian powers, Italy and Germany, were behind the uprising. Large numbers of Italian planes were made available at once to the Fascist insurgents, whose leader was General Francisco Franco. The Franco Rebels planned a quick campaign. Most of the regular troops were faithful to Franco, and little trouble was anticipated. But the Spanish people in many sections rose *en*

Soldiers of the Spanish Loyalist Army relax during a lull in the fighting before Madrid. Though ill-equipped, they were tough and resourceful fighters.

masse. The Loyalists, representing the people, quickly formed a militia, and volunteers from Austria, Poland, Germany, the United States, and Great Britain flocked to Spain to fight against Fascism. The Rebels got to the outskirts of Madrid, but there they were held. During 1937 the Rebels captured several important strongholds, but the Loyalists dealt a serious blow to a large Italian contingent at Guadalajara.

More and more the struggle in Spain became a proving ground for the coming clash between the totalitarian and democratic powers. Franco claimed he was fighting for Christian civilization against Bolshevism. Both Germany and Italy sent thousands of troops and tons of war equipment to the Rebels. Russia sent large amounts of material and some personnel to the Loyalist government at Madrid. On the Spanish battlefields Germany, Italy, and Russia tried out their new cannon and combat planes. It was a dress rehearsal for the real drama of war even then in the making.

Instead of permitting arms to be sent to the recognized Loyalist government which had the right to purchase them in self-defense under international law, Great Britain and France tried to avoid unpleasantness with the dictators by creating a nonintervention sys-

tem for Spain. The nations of Europe agreed not to send weapons to either side. But while France and Great Britain held scrupulously to this bargain, Italy and Germany flagrantly sent assistance to Franco. Russia also sent assistance to the Loyalists at Madrid but not on a scale to offset German and Italian aid. All through 1938 the struggle raged, and in December Franco's army of 300,000 men struck at the Loyalist stronghold of Barcelona. The city was captured, and thousands of refugees escaped to France, where those who were not turned back were interned. In March 1939 Madrid fell, and the Spanish republic was no more.

The outcome. Peace brought only famine to distracted Spain. Cities were wrecked, the countryside pillaged, and the farms neglected. Some 500,000 political prisoners were placed in custody, and many were subsequently executed. Most of the reforms instituted by the republic under the constitution of 1931 were repealed, labor unions were abolished, and a Fascist system similar to that in Italy was estab-

Even women rallied as full warriors to the Spanish Loyalist cause. Ernest Hemingway has immortalized fighters like these in "For Whom the Bell Tolls."

lished. The head of the state was Francisco Franco, the *caudillo* (leader), endowed with absolute power.

The affair in Abyssinia represented a setback for Great Britain and France, but the triumph of Franco was even more damaging to their prestige and security. Athwart the frontiers of France and at one end of Great Britain's Mediterranean lifeline the totalitarian powers had established their own creature who might, if need be, arise to do their bidding.

Milestones to Munich

The Rome-Berlin Axis proclaimed. In announcing the military reoccupation of the Rhineland in the spring of 1936, Hitler had stated, "We have no territorial demands to make in Europe." But the course of events during the next two years in Europe increased Hitler's strength enormously. The period of revisionism against the Treaty of Versailles gave way to Nazi determination to undermine and destroy all opposition in Europe.

Italy was a decisive factor in the new course of events. Up to the end of 1934 Mussolini had posed as the guardian of Austrian independence, and in January 1935 a French-Italian colonial agreement had been signed although it was never ratified. France gave Italy certain areas in Africa, and both nations pledged support to each other in European affairs. In July 1935 General Gamelin of the French army went to Rome to map a common plan of action in the event of war with Germany.

Up to this point Germany was diplomatically isolated in Europe, an avowed enemy of Russia and confronted by Great Britain, Italy, and France. But the Abyssinian incident and the imposition of sanctions changed all this, and Italy became the friend of Germany. In November 1936 a Rome-Berlin Axis was announced by Mussolini, and both Axis countries, as we have seen, pursued a common policy in supporting Franco in Spain. Axis solidarity steadily grew throughout the next year, 1937, and in September Mussolini made a visit to Berlin.

British appeasement and Axis strength. By 1937 it was evident that Europe was entering a new and very dangerous phase in international relations. The united front against Germany had been broken. Great Britain, which had allowed its armaments to drop, was alarmed by this development and announced in February 1937 an arms program which would require the expenditure of seven and a half billion dollars in the next five years.

In May 1937 Stanley Baldwin gave up his post as British prime minister and was succeeded by Neville Chamberlain. Great Britain's new leader had a horror of war and was determined to explore every possibility for reaching some equitable understanding with the dictators. Despite criticism at home and snubs from those he wished to placate, Chamberlain persisted throughout 1937 in trying to ease international tension.

Late in 1936 Germany had made an Anti-Comintern Pact with Japan against Russia, and in 1937 Italy subscribed to this pact. Chamberlain was confronted with a Rome-Berlin-Tokyo Axis, the three members of which were increasingly strenuous in their demands for more living space for their people. Germany began to insist upon her right to colonies and *Lebensraum* (living space) in Europe, Italy declared that the Mediterranean should be under Italian control, and Japan began to talk about a New Order which would allow her to dominate China and southern Asia. The words of Mussolini boded no good for Chamberlain's appeasement policy: "The struggle between two worlds can permit no compromise. Either we or they."

The year 1938 marked the termination of the first phase in Hitler's foreign policy and inauguration of a new and much more daring program. By this time the German army had amazing strength. In the air the *Luftwaffe* far exceeded the air fleets of Great Britain and France.

Hitler's Austrian coup. One of the cardinal principles in Hitler's *Mein Kampf* was the union within the Reich of all German-speaking peoples in Europe. In 1934 Hitler attempted to annex Austria, which had more than six million German-speaking people. An uprising was organized for July 25. Nazi agents took over the Vienna broadcasting station, and another group occupied the governmental offices, where they murdered the Austrian chancellor, Engelbert Dollfuss. Mussolini be-

Signs of the times. Not long after the Austrian Anschluss, a photographer found this workman changing the name of the former City Hall Square in Vienna.

gan to mobilize troops at the Austrian frontier, however, and resistance within Austria against the Nazi *Putsch* strengthened. The conspiracy collapsed, and in 1936 Hitler signed a pact with Austria recognizing "the full sovereignty of the Austrian Federal State."

On February 4, 1938, a Nazi purge took place. The minister of war and several other high officers were removed because they refused to countenance some of Hitler's proposed actions. The restraining influence of these officers was superseded by the leadership of Joachim von Ribbentrop, who became one of Hitler's right-hand men. Early in February the Austrian chancellor, Kurt Schuschnigg, received an invitation, or a command, from Berlin to visit Hitler in his mountain retreat. The stories about this interview seem to agree that Hitler suddenly broke into a rage, accusing the chancellor of mistreating Nazis in Austria.

Hitler demanded the inclusion of several prominent Nazi sympathizers in the Austrian cabinet and the release of Austrian Nazis who had been imprisoned, especially Dr. Seyss-Inquart. Schuschnigg steadfastly refused to adhere to this view. On his return to Vienna, the chancellor made Seyss-Inquart minister of the interior but declined to go any further. By the end of February the world became aware that a crisis was brewing in Austria.

The blow fell on Friday, March 11. American radio listeners were told at 2:15 p.m. that Schuschnigg had resigned, at 2:45 that German troops were crossing the frontier, and at 3:43 that the swastika had been hoisted over the Austrian chancellery. Meanwhile Nazi agents in Austria took over the government, and on Saturday, March 12, German troops occupied most of the country.

Germany aspires to the Sudetenland. Austria disappeared from the international pond with scarcely a ripple. Maxim Litvinov, the Russian foreign minister, suggested a conference among the United States, Great Britain, France, and Russia to discuss preventing further aggression, but nothing came of it.

After the Austrian coup, Hitler moved on to his next objective, the annexation of the Sudetenland. (This was the name given to the area around the edges of Czechoslovakia peopled mainly by Germans; see map, page 39.) In 1919 the Sudeten area had been turned over to the new republic of Czechoslovakia for three reasons: (1) although German-speaking, Germans in the Sudeten area had never been part of Germany but part of the Austro-Hungarian empire; (2) the area formed a strategic eastern frontier for Czechoslovakia; (3) it was economically integrated with the rest of Czechoslovakia. Suspecting the Nazis' next move, France promised protection to the Czechs, and Great Britain said that war in this area could not be localized.

In a speech before the Nuremberg Congress on September 12, 1938, Hitler attacked President Benes of Czechoslovakia as a liar and labeled his government criminal. The Sudetens, he declared, "are being oppressed in an inhuman and intolerable manner." Continuing, Hitler screamed into the microphone, "And I say that if these tortured creatures cannot obtain rights and assistance by themselves, they can obtain both from us." Immediately after this speech Chamberlain arranged for a conference with the Führer, and on September 15 sped from England in an airplane to

On his arrival at the Munich airport on September 29, 1938, Prime Minister Chamberlain (center) was invited to review a picked group of Hitler's Storm Troops. He is flanked by Foreign Minister von Ribbentrop and Sir Nevile Henderson and accompanied by Nazi army bigwigs.

Germany. Hitler bluntly informed him that he was determined to secure self-determination for the Sudeten Germans. This was not an easy task, for not less than 400,000 Czechs lived in the districts which were mainly German and not less than 750,000 Germans in the predominantly Czech areas. Returning to London, Chamberlain met with Daladier, the French premier, and both agreed to accept Hitler's demand. A note was sent to the Czech government by France and Great Britain. The plan agreed upon required Czechoslovakia to cede all areas in which the Germans numbered more than fifty per cent. Plebiscites were to be held in other areas where Germans lived, Czechoslovakia was to become a neutral country, and France and Great Britain were to guarantee its new borders. After heated discussion the Czech cabinet acquiesced.

On September 22 Chamberlain again met Hitler in Germany. To Chamberlain's surprise and consternation Hitler presented new demands that the Czechs evacuate within one week all areas marked on a prepared map and that all military material, goods, and livestock in these areas be turned over to the Germans immediately. Chamberlain returned to London without obtaining a settlement. The Czechs were advised that Great Britain and

France would help them if they resisted Hitler's newest demands. Tuesday evening, September 27, Chamberlain gave a radio message to the world in which he expressed his desire for peace but warned that Great Britain would fight if "any nation had made up its mind to dominate the world by fear of its force."

The Munich Conference. On Wednesday, September 28, the British House of Commons assembled to hear a report by the prime minister. As he neared the end of his address, a messenger delivered a note from Hitler inviting him to attend a conference at Munich. The following day four men met at the Nazi headquarters in Munich, and for thirteen hours these men—Hitler, Mussolini, Daladier, and Chamberlain—worked out the details of the surrender of the Sudetenland. No Czech representative was present. The terms of the Munich Agreement provided that the Czechs were to withdraw from the disputed area in four stages between October 1 and October 8 and that in the remaining areas where large German groups lived an international commission should conduct a plebiscite. The four powers agreed to guarantee the new frontier.

An interval of uneasiness. The Munich Agreement brought relief to millions of Europeans half-crazed with fear of war, but it

PRELUDE TO WAR

2 Germany takes Rhineland

8 Russo-German pact

7 Danzig and the Polish Corridor

3 Spanish Civil War

4 Rome-Berlin Axis

6 Czechoslovakia subjugated

5 Austrian Anschluss

Madrid ★ ★ Guadalajara   • Barcelona

Dodecanese Is.

1 Italy takes Abyssinia

R. M. Chapin Jr.

was still a question whether this settlement was to be followed by another crisis. Many hoped for the best but feared the worst. Anthony Eden declared, "Foreign affairs cannot indefinitely be continued on the basis of stand and deliver. Successive surrenders only bring successive humiliations." Alfred Duff Cooper, the first lord of the admiralty, resigned his post and declared, "The premier believes he can come to a reasonable settlement with Herr Hitler on all outstanding questions. He may be right. I hope he is. But I cannot believe it." Winston Churchill in a denunciation of the Munich Agreement said, "The utmost the prime minister was able to gain for Czechoslovakia has been that the German dictator, instead of snatching his victuals from the table, has been content to have them served to him course by course."

Not long afterward it became manifest that

the surrender at Munich by Great Britain and France had purchased only a brief respite from additional Nazi demands. With callous disregard for the rights of the Czechs, the German government took over the Sudetenland and the border areas. Only ten days after the Munich conference, Hitler gave a speech which showed little trace of conciliation. He boasted of the military power of Germany, told France and Great Britain not to meddle with Germany's affairs, and warned the British in particular that trouble would follow if a "war-monger" like Churchill was given a post in the British cabinet.

In November a terrible wave of Jewish persecution swept over Germany. For a whole day Storm Troops and ruffians burned and looted Jewish shops and synagogues. Thousands were sent to concentration camps.

Expansionism announced. Meanwhile the success of Franco in Spain had made Mussolini and Hitler more contemptuous than ever of France and Great Britain. Mussolini openly demanded the cession of French territory in Africa and the Mediterranean. On November 30, 1938, there were shouts in the Italian Chamber of Deputies for Tunisia, Corsica, Savoy, and Nice. In January 1939, in a speech before the Reichstag, Hitler warned the world that Germany would not be content to remain deprived of some of the great land areas controlled by nations such as Great Britain and France. The plain truth, he said, was that Germany was overpopulated and must have room to expand.

Czechoslovakia's total capitulation. The mounting fears of French and British statesmen were confirmed in March 1939. After the Munich Agreement, President Benes had resigned in order that his anti-Nazi views would not embarrass the Czech government. In November the Czech government had given a large measure of self-government to the Slovaks and Ruthenians. The country was then really a loose federation of three peoples.

But the new arrangement was not allowed to work. Disorder and treachery among the Slovaks and Ruthenians were fostered by Nazi agents. The Czech president, Emil Hacha, took energetic measures to maintain order and dismissed the Slovakian premier, who went at once to Berlin.

Early in March a bitter attack against the Czech government was inaugurated by the German press. Another coup was in the making. On March 14 Hitler summoned President Hacha and his foreign minister to Berlin. Arriving late in the evening, Hacha and his aid were taken to the German chancellery to be interviewed by Hitler. The conference lasted until 4:15 a.m. For several hours the Czech officials were subjected to all kinds of threats in order to make them sign a document placing their country under the so-called protection of Germany. Finally Hacha capitulated. His signature was a mere formality, however, for German troops were already crossing the Czech frontier. The Nazis entered Prague, capital of Czechoslovakia, on the evening of March 15.

Emergency measures in England and France. The shock of the final conquest of Czechoslovakia and Hitler's callous violation of pledges made at Munich ended the appeasement policy of France and Great Britain. Chamberlain, the chief advocate of appeasement, was embittered by Hitler's latest action. In April, for the first time in Great Britain's long history, the government authorized the conscription of young men for military training in time of peace.

Meanwhile a tremendous arms program was launched for which Great Britain began to spend five million dollars a day. Plans were made to expand the fleet, air-raid shelters were built, a barrage balloon system for the chief cities was introduced, and the Royal Air Force was increased. In Paris Daladier obtained special emergency powers to push forward national defense.

Hitler Looks toward Poland

The Polish Corridor. Nazi Germany under the leadership of Hitler had thus far enjoyed amazing success. In the last coup of March 1939, the Nazis without firing a shot had obtained three hundred million dollars in gold and in foreign credits from the Czechs, the Skoda munitions works, valuable timber resources, and large stocks of arms. Apparently certain of his ability to annex territory and conquer nations without resorting to actual fighting, Hitler turned to the next item on his list: the Polish Corridor. It will be recalled

During the battle for Britain the Germans were obliged to keep constant patrol against retaliating British bombers. Here a Nazi night fighter's crew readies his plane for his part in defending the Heinkel aircraft works.

that in the eighteenth century Poland had been partitioned among three states: Prussia, Russia, and Austria. In 1919 the Treaty of Versailles had turned over West Prussia to Poland in order to give the new Polish state an outlet to the sea (see map, page 35). This Polish Corridor was ninety per cent Polish, but Danzig, at the mouth of the Vistula and the Corridor's chief seaport, had a population of 400,000, nearly all German. In spite of Germany's dislike of the corridor between Germany proper and East Prussia, Hitler had made a ten-year nonaggression pact with Poland in 1934.

Hitler demands and the "Stop Hitler Front."
Late in March 1939 it became known that Hitler had proposed to Poland that she cede Danzig to Germany and that permission be given the Nazi government to occupy a narrow strip of land connecting Germany with East Prussia—a corridor across the corridor. On March 31, Chamberlain warned the Nazi government in a speech to the House of Commons that "in the event of any action which clearly threatened Polish independence" and in case the Poles resisted, the British would "at once lend the Polish government all support in their power." France concurred in this declaration.

The Polish question which precipitated the Second World War went through three sepa-

rate stages—the first lasting several months. From March through April, Hitler made known his demands, and there was much diplomatic maneuvering as Great Britain and France attempted to organize a "Stop Hitler Front." In April the French and British gave guarantees against aggression to Rumania and Greece, and in May the British succeeded in winning Turkey as a quasi-ally. Hitler abrogated his nonaggression pact with Poland.

The courtship of Russia. The second phase in the Polish question was an interim period from May to August in which the main activity was a duel between Germany on the one hand and Great Britain and France on the other for a Russian alliance. When Great Britain made her guarantee to Poland, it was thought in London that this would be sufficient to restrain Hitler, but as the summer of 1939 wore on, it became evident that war was likely. In such an event it was imperative that Great Britain secure a strong ally in eastern Europe to join her in aiding Poland. In April negotiations with Russia were started by France and Great Britain, and in July a Franco-British military mission was sent to consult with the Russian staff. Since 1934, when she joined the League of Nations, Russia had condemned German aggression and supported the League principle of collective security. But Great Britain in particular up to this time had not been anxious to cooperate closely with Russia because British leaders were suspicious of Russian policy, had a dread of Communism, and were not greatly impressed with the Russian army.

At Munich Russia was completely disregarded in the partition of Czechoslovakia. As the power of Hitler grew and that of France and Great Britain waned, Stalin, the Russian leader, evidently decided to change his policy. The first indication of this decision was the replacement of Foreign Minister Litvinov in May. In August the world was amazed, and Great Britain and France in particular were stunned, at the news that Russia and Germany had signed a nonaggression pact on August 24. With the pact in his pocket Hitler believed that Great Britain and France would not dare to oppose his Polish ambitions. For their part France and Great Britain realized that if they wished to stop Germany from dominating all of Europe they must fight.

Last-minute peace moves. A third stage in the Polish dispute began. Prime Minister Chamberlain wrote a personal letter to Hitler, saying that Great Britain would not countenance the solution of the Danzig question by the use of force. From several quarters appeals were made for peace—from the Pope, the king of Belgium, and President Roosevelt. During the last two weeks of August the British government also made strenuous efforts to bring about a peaceful solution of the Polish question.

The German ultimatum. On August 29 the German government demanded that the Poles send an emissary with full power to make an agreement with Hitler. The Polish government hesitated in complying, for it knew all too well the treatment meted out to Schuschnigg and Hacha. Near midnight of August 30, the British ambassador, Sir Nevile Henderson, saw Von Ribbentrop, the German foreign minister, who rapidly read aloud a list of sixteen terms which were to have been presented to Poland. But since no emissary had arrived, "it was now too late," in Von Ribbentrop's own words. Poland meanwhile was ready to undertake negotiations but not to accept demands at a moment's notice, and her ambassador went to see Von Ribbentrop the night of August 31. The Polish ambassador was thereupon given the demands, which he tried to communicate to Warsaw, only to find that the wires had already been cut and the war had already begun. The German government then read its terms over the radio and declared that they had been rejected.

The invasion of Poland. Before either the British or the Polish governments had had a chance to examine the German demands, Nazi troops had crossed the Polish frontier early in the morning of September 1. Fighting began without a declaration of war, and the German air force began its blast of Polish cities. In the afternoon Nevile Henderson notified the Nazi government that unless fighting ceased Great Britain would fulfill her treaty obligations to Poland.

On the morning of September 3 Chamberlain with the full consent of his cabinet sent an ultimatum to Germany, demanding that the invasion of Poland be halted. The time limit was given as 11 a.m. of the same day. At 11:15 the British prime minister broadcast a message to his people stating that the country was at war. France took similar action.

After an interval of only twenty-five years since the First World War Europe was again at war. In 1914 there was enthusiasm on both sides when the conflict commenced, and few sacrifices or concessions had been made by the various countries in order to arrest war. On the other hand, 1939 saw the vast majority of people in Europe, and indeed the world, dreading war and seeking to preserve peace. Many efforts had been made to satisfy what Nazi Germany called her "legitimate aspirations."

Concessions gained at Munich had been ruthlessly exploited to dismember Czechoslovakia. Despite the warnings of British and French statesmen and the anxiety of people all over the world the Nazi régime next applied its coercive techniques against Poland. The causes of war are usually complex and the conflict of 1939 is no exception. But there can be little doubt that the immediate and most important cause was the Nazi government's determination to get what it wanted regardless of consequences. Brusquely sweeping aside all suggestions of conciliation and arbitration, Hitler attacked Poland. This country naturally fought back to maintain its existence; Great Britain and France took up arms because the very existence of a free Europe was at stake.

Blitzkrieg over Europe

Stages of the war. The conflict that followed can truly be thought of as the Second World War, so widespread was its action. It may be helpful to think of the first three years of the war (September 1939 to July 1942) as involving eight phases of development:

(1) Blitzkrieg in Poland: September 1939.
(2) Standstill in the west: October 1939 to April 1940.
(3) The battle for Europe and the fall of the western nations: April to June 1940.
(4) Great Britain under fire: July 1940 to May 1941.
(5) The Italian campaigns: October 1940 to April 1941.
(6) The German drive to the Near East: beginning in April 1941.
(7) Blitzkrieg versus Russia: beginning June 1941.
(8) The war enters the Pacific: December 7, 1941.

Blitzkrieg in Poland. On September 1, 1939, as has been indicated, without any declaration of war German columns crossed the Polish frontier from four angles, while squadrons of bombing planes dropped their deadly missiles upon hangars and landing fields. The Poles fought with great courage, but from the outset they were overwhelmed. The Polish army numbered over a million men, but it was built upon nineteenth-century conceptions of warfare. It had the best cavalry regiments in Europe but little mechanized or motorized equipment and an inadequate air force. In a few days the world witnessed the drama of a new military technique in operation. This was the blitzkrieg, or lightning war, which unleashed tanks, motorized artillery, parachutists on Polish soil, and blackened Polish skies with bomber squadrons. In a few days the Polish air force was destroyed, communications were disrupted, and the Polish army was demoralized.

In view of later developments when Nazi Germany attacked the Soviet Union, it is probable that Russian leaders suspected Hitler's aggressive designs early in 1939. Russian troops, therefore, were sent into eastern Poland to secure a protective strip of territory between German-conquered Poland and the Soviet Union.

For several weeks Warsaw held out even though its inhabitants were subjected to an almost constant bombardment from German artillery and German planes. But resistance was hopeless, and the city capitulated on September 27, signalizing the end of all fighting in the country except by a few patriotic "bitter-enders" here and there. At the end of hostilities a Russo-German treaty partitioned Poland for the fourth time, giving each nation approximately half the country.

Standstill in the west. An unreal and perplexing period of inaction now began along the Franco-German frontier, where two gigantic fortress systems faced each other—the Maginot and Siegfried lines. The Poles had expected assistance from their allies, but France and Great Britain could do nothing. Planes might have been sent, but the destruction of Polish airdromes and landing fields by the Nazi *Luftwaffe* rendered this impossible. General Gamelin tried an offensive feint here and there against the Siegfried Line and in a fortnight captured about 100 square miles of German territory, which was lost as soon as Nazi reinforcements arrived from their triumphs in Poland. Until the spring of the next year, 1940, action along the western front was practically limited to night patrols in the no-man's-land between the two lines.

Great Britain and France had nestled their armies snugly behind the Maginot Line. There was to be no repetition of the slaughter of the First World War. British and French generals believed that it would be suicidal for any army to try to storm either the Maginot or the Siegfried Line. According to many experts modern warfare was to be one of position, not of movement, in which the nations with the greatest economic resources would eventually emerge triumphant. British and French leaders expected to blockade Germany with the superior Allied navy and gradually starve her out. For more than six months the war followed this pattern, and many people both in Europe and America were suspicious of the genuineness of the struggle.

The Russo-Finnish war. In this phase of the war the only real fighting, ironically enough, was not between the major contestants but between Finland and Russia. Late in September 1939 Russia demanded and obtained mutual assistance pacts with the three Baltic republics of Latvia, Lithuania, and Estonia. Soviet troops were given the right to occupy certain strategic areas in the three countries. The three republics were joined to the Soviet Union (in August 1940). Russia then made similar demands of Finland, but the Finns refused to turn over the required territory. Soviet troops thereupon crossed the Finnish frontier.

Again the world was astonished—the Finns put up stiff resistance. A strongly fortified system called the Mannerheim Line barred the path of the Russians across the Karelian isthmus. In the open country of northeastern Finland, bands of Finnish ski troops harassed and broke up numerically superior enemy forces. But no nation of four million could be expected to hold out against a foe the size of Russia, and in January 1940 sheer weight of numbers began to tell. The League denounced Russian aggression, many volunteers from the non-totalitarian countries flocked into Finland, and there was talk of an Anglo-French expeditionary force. Norway and Sweden, however, refused to grant transit rights to any such force.

On March 12, 1940, Russian terms of peace were accepted. Finland promised to make no alliance contrary to Russian interests, guaranteed Russia the use of the railroad across Finland to Norway and Sweden, leased important naval sites to Russia, and ceded a large area of her territory. .

At the time of Russia's invasion of Finland condemnation of this action was widespread in many countries, especially in Great Britain, France, and the United States. As in the case of eastern Poland, however, the trend of opinion in many quarters following Hitler's later attack on the Soviet Union was to regard Russian policy toward Finland as having been a drastic but understandable measure taken to create a zone of defense against probable Nazi aggression.

The battle for Europe. Great Britain and France might have planned to carry on a long war of attrition against Germany, but the Nazi leaders had a different plan, daring, ruthless, and drawn up with consummate skill. The tremendous power of the greatest military machine in history again struck like lightning. Early on the morning of April 9, German troops occupied Denmark. At the same time small Norwegian defense units were over-

whelmed by swarms of Nazi troops who came ashore from innocent-looking merchant vessels or who had been on Norwegian soil for some time in the guise of tourists.

The Germans were assisted by a Norwegian Nazi sympathizer, Vidkun Quisling, who had been Norwegian minister of defense. With clocklike precision the German invasion of Norway was carried out as the Nazi forces took over the main strategic points: Narvik, Bergen, and Oslo. Units of the British fleet attempted to intercept German transports carrying troops, and some of these vessels and their escorting warships were sunk. But this effort failed, and in three weeks some eighty thousand German troops had been landed by plane or naval transport.

On April 15 a British force arrived at the Norwegian port of Narvik, and in the next few days other Allied troops were disembarked at other harbors. The expeditionary force lacked equipment, especially anti-aircraft guns, and after two weeks was forced to evacuate under heavy bombardment from Nazi aircraft. The justification for German invasion of Norway and Denmark was, according to the Reich government, the fact that both these countries were in imminent danger of attack by Great Britain and France and hence needed German "protection." Hitler's move had given him a valuable larder of food, timber resources, easy access to the valuable iron mines of northern Sweden, and important air bases from which to menace the British Isles. The Nazi success also demonstrated to certain neutral European powers the alleged invincibility of German arms.

Invasion of the Low Countries. On the evening of May 9, 1940, Hitler and his leading Nazi aids attended various musicals and movies in Berlin. There was nothing to indicate that one of the greatest battles in world history was to commence at dawn the next morning. As 4 a.m. approached, German armies received orders to attack Belgium, Luxemburg, and Holland. As the troops moved forward, swarms of Nazi bombers attacked forts, railroad junctions, airfields, and cities in these three countries and in northern France as well.

Holland was the scene of the heaviest fighting, and her great cities were pounded by German bombing planes. Two hours after the invasion had begun, the German minister to the Dutch government presented an ulti-

Overlooking nothing, the Nazi blitzkrieg army uses a convenient canal barge as a pontoon bridge to invade Holland. Bicycle and motorcycle troops are crossing by it, prepared to infiltrate the Low Countries.

matum demanding the surrender of the country. As in the case of Norway and Denmark, the Reich claimed to possess "irrefutable evidence of an immediately threatening invasion by British and French forces . . . prepared a long time beforehand with the knowledge of the Netherlands and Belgian Governments." The demand to surrender was summarily rejected, and the Dutch armed forces braced themselves for the struggle against the invader. Again, resistance was hopeless. On May 13 the Dutch royal family headed by Queen Wilhelmina fled to England. On May 14 the Dutch military authorities surrendered to the Germans.

On the same day that had brought war to Holland, the conflict burst upon Belgium. Again the attack came without warning. On the morning of May 10 British and French were already on their way to support the Belgian defense line. The following day, however, the Germans captured a supposedly impregnable fortress, the pivot in Belgian defense. A week after the fighting began, German forces captured Brussels.

Invasion of France: Dunkirk. After French forces had been hurried north to assist the hard-pressed Belgians, the German high command struck at a weak spot in the French line, and by May 19 a gap of sixty miles had been made in the northern part of the Maginot Line. Large numbers of heavy tanks supported by dive bombers rapidly cut a swath to the west. German panzer divisions next reached a

point on the English Channel, and the Allied troops in Belgium were cut off from the main French army.

In this hour of national peril the French premier, Paul Reynaud, replaced General Gamelin with General Weygand. The new supreme commander tried to rally his troops with the message, "The future of France depends upon your tenacity. Hold tight the soil of France. . . . Look only forward." But bad news came from Belgium on May 28 when King Leopold announced the surrender of his army. In danger of encirclement, the Allied forces in Belgium retreated to Dunkirk on the seacoast. While picked suicide squads slowed up the German advance, thousands of Allied troops waded into the surf and were picked up by boats of every description. Out of an original force of 400,000, 335,000 men were successfully evacuated.

The fall of France. With the conquest of Luxemburg, Holland, and Belgium completed, the German forces directed a final blow at France. The assault commenced June 5. In five days the invader was within thirty-five miles of Paris, and the French government fled. Anxious to get in at the kill and satisfied that both Great Britain and France would be out of the war in a few weeks, Mussolini declared war against France on June 10. In explaining this action, Il Duce declared:

"This gigantic conflict is only a phase of the logical development of our revolution. It is the conflict of poor, numerous peoples who labor against starvers who ferociously cling to a monopoly of all riches and all gold on earth.

"It is a conflict of fruitful, useful peoples against peoples who are in a decline. It is a conflict between two ages, two ideas."

In vain did General Weygand improvise new tactics to stop the German forces. The French were outnumbered in men, in motorized equipment, and above all, in airplanes. On June 14 Paris fell, and Weygand informed the French government at Bordeaux that the situation was hopeless. Premier Reynaud wished to continue the struggle, but the majority of his cabinet believed further resistance was impossible. Reynaud thereupon resigned, and Marshal Pétain, 84-year-old hero of Verdun in the First World War, became premier.

While the French leaders initiated negotiations with the Germans, the Maginot Line was captured, and southern France was threatened. Actual negotiations began on June 21. In the same old dining car in which Marshal Foch had imposed armistice terms on the Germans in 1918, the French representatives received the Nazi terms. On June 22 the French delegation signed the armistice agreement. Nearby stood a granite block on which now ironically was inscribed:

"Here on the Eleventh of November, Succumbed the Criminal Pride of the German Empire, Vanquished by the Free Peoples Which It Tried to Enslave."

France was split into two zones, occupied and unoccupied. All the French coast was controlled by Germany. The cost of occupation was to be paid by France. All French forces were to be demilitarized, and the French fleet was to be turned over to the Axis powers with the understanding that the surrendered naval units would not be employed against Great Britain. More than two million French prisoners were to be held until the end of the war. An armistice agreement was also made with Italy, and a small strip of France on the Italian border was occupied by the forces of Il Duce. In unoccupied France the French government was to manage its own affairs, supposedly free from any interference. In reality France became the puppet of the Nazi government.

The Vichy government. The Third French Republic, born in 1871 as the result of a defeat suffered in the Franco-Prussian War, now perished in another defeat administered by the

Symbol of German military exactness, the seated soldier seems to be, as for all practical purposes he is, part of the gun on which he rides.

same enemy. Meeting in the city of Vichy on July 9 the French parliament signed the death warrant of the republic. It was a stormy and tragic meeting. As the names of some of the French leaders who had only recently guided the destinies of France were read during the roll call, jeers and hisses filled the room. The parliament voted to give power to Marshal Pétain to draw up a new constitution. On July 11 the Marshal was made chief of the French state with dictatorial powers. The new government soon showed that it had buried the old democratic principles of Liberty, Equality, and Fraternity. In their place the people were to be guided by Labor, Family, Fatherland. Outright Fascism had come to France.

The naval battle of Oran. The impact of the German blitzkrieg left France demoralized, impotent, her republican institutions discredited, but across the Channel the British people seemed suddenly to discover a new reservoir of power and confidence. The genesis of this new spirit came with the resignation of Neville Chamberlain as prime minister and the appearance of Winston Churchill in his stead. Chamberlain resigned his office just as

Under bombing with such results as are shown here, the people of London never relaxed in their dogged insistence that Germany be defeated. This view was taken from the top of St. Paul's Cathedral.

Nazi troops poured into the Low Countries.

The major part of the French fleet, cooped up in the harbor of Oran in Morocco, was sought out early in July by a British squadron from Gibraltar. Fearing that the Nazi government might obtain the French vessels and use them in the fight against Great Britain, British naval chiefs demanded that the French fleet either continue the struggle against Germany or agree to demobilization. Upon the refusal of this ultimatum, the British squadron opened fire and destroyed four French battleships and several destroyers.

Great Britain under fire. From July to October the war entered its fourth phase. Great Britain was at bay, faced by invasion. With most of the tanks and guns of the British army lost at Dunkirk, only the British navy and a numerically weak air force barred the way across the narrow English Channel. In June heavy daily air raids were commenced by the Germans. Increasing in intensity, the raids assumed vast proportions early in August. Waves of German planes crossing the Channel from convenient bases in France tried to blast British airdromes and disrupt communications. Apparently failing in this purpose the German *Luftwaffe* then concentrated upon the bombing of London. During the first two weeks of September thousands of bombs were dropped on the city. Hundreds of buildings were destroyed, with a heavy loss of life.

The main objective of Nazi tactics was to secure air superiority over Great Britain, to drive the Royal Air Force from the sky as a prelude to German invasion. But the R.A.F. showed unexpected strength. On August 15 alone, 180 German airplanes were shot down by British fighter planes, and between September 6 and October 5 Germany lost almost 900 planes. Meanwhile heavy bombers from Great Britain ranged over Germany and particularly over French channel ports where barge concentrations, assembled for invasion, were destroyed. By the end of October it became evident that German hopes for an early invasion of Great Britain had been frustrated. Nevertheless the bombings continued, as we shall see.

The Italian campaigns. The failure of the summer bombings of England was followed by the fifth phase of the war, the Italian period. By autumn of 1940 it was apparent that Mussolini was determined to secure a few victories of his own. They would not only add to the glory and prestige of Fascism but would also provide more bargaining power when the final peace terms were imposed on Great Britain and France.

The grand plan of Fascist strategy was to inclose the British possessions, the Sudan, and British Somaliland, as well as Egypt, in a vast encircling movement. Italian troops under Marshal Graziani were to proceed east from Libya, cross the Egyptian border, and then capture Cairo and the Suez Canal. Once the canal was captured, the British lifeline via the Mediterranean to India and the Far East would be cut. From Italian east Africa other Italian armies were to strike in the north and west making their way to southern Egypt and the British Sudan. If this plan succeeded, Mussolini would gain a great African empire.

Italian troops assisted by native soldiers seized British Somaliland during August. This placed Italy in a position to threaten the entrance to the Red Sea. Early in September

Marshal Graziani headed an army of 300,000 men against Egypt and captured a point a few miles within Egyptian territory. But here the invading army stalled. In the meantime Mussolini made plans to obtain a virtual protectorate over Greece. This would have given the Italian fleet valuable bases, such as Crete and Corfu, enabling them to challenge the British naval squadron in the eastern Mediterranean. But on October 28 the Greek government refused to accede to a three-hour ultimatum from Italy. To the further amazement of the world, Greece stopped the invading Italians and pushed them back into Albania. Harried by British aircraft, the Italians were forced to retreat across Albania, and by November more than 1000 square miles of Albanian soil had been conquered by the Greek army.

The British retake Africa. The next setback Italy received was the raid on the naval base at Taranto by British torpedo-carrying planes. When the smoke cleared, half of the battleships in the Italian navy had been put out of action. Meanwhile the British army of the Nile, under General Archibald Wavell, had been quietly preparing a counterstroke against Graziani in Egypt. On December 9 a large number of British tank units attacked, and in a few days the Italians had been forced back into Libya. Thousands of prisoners were taken as Wavell's men pushed deeper into Libya. At the same time fresh imperial troops from India and the Union of South Africa attacked Italian forces in eastern Africa. Italian Somaliland was overrun, British Somaliland was recaptured, Eritrea was conquered in April, and the British entered Addis Ababa, the capital of Abyssinia. As a crowning discomfiture to the Italian command, the British fleet managed to entice the Italians into the Aegean Sea in April and to inflict serious losses on their fleet — at least three heavy cruisers and several destroyers.

Germany meanwhile. The fifth phase of the war saw little major activity on the part of Germany. It was Italy's affair, although Hitler's partner had nothing to show but defeats and setbacks. But Hitler was far from unoccupied. The submarine war was carried on against British shipping, especially in the North Atlantic. The British were at a disadvantage because the Irish Free State refused to allow the British fleet to use its ports. The convoy system did much to reduce the submarine hazard, but in the spring of 1941 it was plain that the Battle of the North Atlantic was now the most serious threat to Great Britain.

The failure of German mass raids in the summer of 1940 and the surprising strength of the British air force caused Air Marshal Goering to alter his tactics. Daylight raids had been too costly. In the autumn months of 1940, therefore, increasing use was made of indiscriminate night bombing. Neither Germany nor Great Britain was able to counter this attack effectively. On the night of November 15, the English city of Coventry was almost completely gutted by high explosive and incendiary bombs. The important ports of Bristol, Plymouth, and Southampton were bombed again and again, and on the night of December 29, the German air force tried to destroy London by fire. Some 10,000 two-pound incendiary bombs were dropped. The damage was severe. The old Guildhall, a dozen famous historic churches, many large office buildings, and most of Bookseller's Row containing 6,000,000 books were destroyed. Throughout the spring of 1941 night bombing on Great Britain continued. In May it was announced that since the start of the raids 35,000 civilians had been killed and many more severely wounded. Throughout the ordeal the British people, inspired in part by the dogged leadership of Winston Churchill, remained steadfast in their determination to oppose Hitlerian Germany.

The German drive to the Near East. The first three rounds of the war went to the Germans and the fourth and fifth to the British, who held off the *Luftwaffe* and with the aid of Greece inflicted numerous defeats upon Italy. In April 1941 Hitler initiated another great offensive, the sixth phase of the war. This was designed to succor his hard-pressed Italian ally in Albania, to get control of the Balkans, and to use the Balkan peninsula as a stepping stone to mastery of the Near East with its Suez Canal and the rich oil fields of northern Iraq.

Rumania dismembered. While Italy was trying to invade Greece, the Nazi high command was laying the groundwork for its projected drive toward the Near East. As long as France remained strong, Rumania tried to evade any commitments until it became more

As Britain began to challenge with good results the vaunted invincibility of the German Luftwaffe, such planes as these were put into the skies. In the foreground is a Wellington bomber, in the background a Spitfire fighter.

evident which side would win in Europe. When France collapsed, Rumania decided that she must cooperate with the Nazi régime. King Carol II of Rumania, in June 1940, made his country a totalitarian state by decree, and British oil properties were seized. While Germany was preoccupied in the west, Russia demanded, on June 26, that Rumania cede to her a large slice of territory, most of which had been taken from Russia in 1918. King Carol appealed to Germany and Italy for assistance, but these powers, anxious to prevent a major war in the Balkans at this time, advised capitulation.

After the cession of the territory, two other neighbors of Rumania decided to present their claims. Bulgaria demanded territory which she had lost to Rumania in 1913, and Hungary asked for the area taken from her in 1920. Again a Balkan war appeared imminent, and during the summer months of 1940 Berlin and Rome, acting as arbiters, forced Rumania to cede most of the disputed territory. One of the results of the dismemberment of Rumania was the abdication of King Carol II, who fled the country. Another, and much more important, consequence was that Rumania became a puppet state of Germany.

Between November 20 and 24 both Hungary and Rumania came into the Axis camp by accepting the terms of the alliance signed by Germany, Italy, and Japan in September 1940. In March 1941 the Nazi diplomats also brought Bulgaria into the Axis.

The invasion of Yugoslavia. Two Balkan nations still remained to be taken care of, Greece and Yugoslavia. Although Greece was inflicting heavy losses on Italian forces in Albania, it was desirable to secure control over Yugoslavia before sending aid to the hard-pressed Italians. In preparation for the advance into Greece large quantities of material and thousands of men were sent into Bulgaria and massed on the Greek frontier. When Berlin presented its demands to Yugoslavia late in March 1941, Prince Paul and his two co-regents decided there was no recourse but acceptance. On March 25 Yugoslavian delegates at Vienna agreed to permit the passage of German supplies through the country and to undertake certain measures of economic cooperation. Two days after the pact was signed, the government of Prince Paul was overthrown, and King Peter, just seventeen, was placed on the throne by an anti-Axis government. This startling development was welcomed in Greece, and Great Britain pledged her aid in the event of German aggression.

On April 6 German armies attacked Greece and Yugoslavia simultaneously. The motorized equipment, Stuka bombers, and fighter planes of the blitzkrieg were again in action. The Yugoslavs had waited too long before deciding to defy Hitler. Their army was not fully mobilized, and staff talks for cooperation had not been carried on with the Greek command.

In what was evidently meant as an object lesson to the people of Europe who might have ideas of defying German policies, the *Luftwaffe* carried out a terrible bombing attack against the open and unfortified capital of Yugoslavia, Belgrade. At the same time German tank divisions, moving with unexpected rapidity over mountain passes, destroyed the Yugoslavian forces. It had been thought that the rugged terrain might slow down German operations, but the panzer divisions seemed as much at home on the mountainous mule tracks of Yugoslavia as on the plains of France.

Greece overwhelmed. The collapse of the Yugoslavian armies allowed a strong German force to push in the direction of the great Greek port of Salonika. Another Nazi army punched its way across Thrace and reached the Aegean Sea, thus trapping a Greek army at the Turkish border. Assisted by British troops the Greeks put up a magnificent fight. But the Allied troops were hopelessly outnumbered in tanks, in planes, and in men. During the last week in April the position of the Greeks and British became desperate. On April 23, the Greek army that had kept the Italians on the run in Albania but was now caught between both the Italian army and a German force was compelled to surrender. The British managed "another Dunkirk." The navy evacuated some 48,000 British soldiers to Crete and Alexandria.

By May 1, after a campaign of just three weeks, Hitler had conquered two more countries, and King George of Greece had set up his government on the island of Crete. Great Britain had been forced to weaken the army of the Nile in order to send troops and equipment to Greece. This weakness became apparent during April when German and Italian forces in Libya suddenly assumed the offensive

while the battle for Greece was going on. In the space of a few days Libyan posts were recaptured, and the enemy had again reached the Egyptian frontier.

Revolt engineered in Iraq. With perfect timing the Nazi high command also presented Great Britain with another military problem. On April 4 the pro-British government in Iraq was overthrown by an Arab leader with pro-Axis leanings. From Iraq's rich oil fields a pipe line more than one thousand miles long carried this essential fuel to Palestine, where it was available for the British fleet operating in the Mediterranean and for the British army of the Nile. Shortly after the new leader came to power, a British contingent was landed at Basra to protect the oil fields in accordance with treaty arrangements between Iraq and Great Britain, arrangements which gave the latter the right to maintain troops and air fields in Iraq.

On May 2, the day after the termination of the Greek campaign, severe fighting broke out in Iraq between British and Iraqi forces. The pattern of Nazi strategy was evident. German troops would arrive by air from Greek airdromes. But before this could be carried out with good chance of success, the island of Crete had to come into German hands, and arrangements had to be made with the French government to permit German transport planes en route to Iraq to use facilities in French Syria.

The invasion of Crete. On May 19 thousands of German parachutists dropped from transport planes on Crete. Desperate fighting took place as British troops tried to prevent the few air fields on the island from falling into the hands of the aerial invaders. At the same time units of the British fleet sought to prevent the ferrying of troops from Greece. After two weeks of fighting, superior power in the air crushed British resistance, and during the first weeks of June the small British force had to be evacuated by a British fleet under constant attack from German dive bombers.

By June 1941 it appeared that Hitler had won the battle for the Mediterranean and that his armies were in a position to launch an offensive against the Near East and the Suez Canal. Axis troops were menacing the western frontier of Egypt. With Crete in their hands the Germans seemed ready for an assault against both Turkey and French Syria, if they resisted the powerful Nazi war machine. In this way Palestine and Egypt could be attacked from the north by way of Greece and Crete and from the west by way of Libya.

The United States and the Spreading War

American isolation. Before examining the seventh phase of the war, it is necessary to consider the effect of the conflict upon the United States. As the battle for the Near East and the Mediterranean reached a climax and Japan, as will be shown later in this chapter, attempted to establish her New Order in Asia, the eyes of all the remaining neutrals—especially those in the New World—anxiously followed the tide of conflict. This was especially true in the United States. After the First World War the United States had lapsed into her traditional isolation, critical of the Treaty of Versailles, which she refused to sign, and indifferent to the League of Nations, which she refused to join.

Between 1920 and 1930 the desire of the American people to avoid international complications grew rather than diminished. The repudiation of the war debts by her former allies strengthened the belief that participation in the war in 1917 and 1918 had been a mistake. From 1934 to 1936 a Senate investigating committee under Senator Nye studied the role played by armament makers in the First World War and exposed huge profits. This in itself fell far short of explaining the United States' entrance into the conflict in 1917, but many Americans believed, more than ever, that the nation had been stimulated by the desire for profits on the part of a few financiers. In April 1937 the American Institute of Public Opinion revealed in one of its polls that seventy per cent of people canvassed believed that it had been a mistake for the United States to go to war in 1917. In 1934 Congress passed the Johnson Act prohibiting debt-defaulting governments from marketing their securities in the United States, and in January 1935 the Senate refused to sanction American entry into the World Court.

Neutrality legislation. As war clouds appeared on the horizon in 1935 in the shape of the Italo-Abyssinian dispute, Congress enacted neutrality legislation designed to keep the country out of war. Various amendments were made in 1935, 1936, and 1937, and in them isolationist sentiment reached an all-time high. The traditional policy of freedom of the seas, of the right of a neutral to carry on legitimate trade with belligerents, was scrapped. It became unlawful for any nation at war to obtain munitions from the United States, American citizens could not travel on the ships of belligerents, and the "cash and carry" provision permitted any nation to purchase certain raw materials and goods, provided that nation took them away in its own ships. Congress hoped the legislation would keep war at a distance. The State Department, however, pointed out that this legislation did not make any discrimination between aggressor and nonaggressor nations. In the event of war no nation could buy arms in this country.

As the menace of the totalitarian nations became greater in both Europe and the Far East after 1935, there was a strong minority group in the United States that believed the neutrality legislation was a mistake, that it encouraged aggression in other parts of the world, and that such aggression in the long run would become so serious as to demand American participation for purposes of national security. With the hope of arousing the American people to the dangers in the world situation, President Roosevelt in October 1937 gave his famous "quarantine speech" in Chicago. In it he declared:

"The peace, the freedom, and the security of 90 per cent of the population of the world is being jeopardized by the remaining 10 per cent, who are threatening a break-down of all international order and law. Surely the ninety per cent who want to live in peace under law and in accordance with moral standards . . . can and must find some way to make their will prevail. . . . There must be positive endeavors to preserve peace."

After this speech was delivered, however, it was obvious that American public opinion would not countenance any action involving the United States in the "quarrels of other nations."

United States attempts at arbitration. The Sudeten crisis in September 1938 confronted the American government with the alarming prospect of a war which might spread to the Far East, in view of the fact that Japan had been an ally of Germany since 1936. On September 26 President Roosevelt sent a cable to Hitler, urging that he utilize peaceful negotiation, rather than war, in the Sudeten crisis. The following day another appeal was cabled to both Hitler and Mussolini by President Roosevelt.

After the Munich Agreement American public opinion was profoundly shocked by the anti-Jewish riots which broke out in November 1938. In an unusually blunt statement the American Chief Executive declared, "I myself could scarcely believe that such things could occur in a twentieth-century civilization." Then came the final partition of Czechoslovakia in March 1939. With the approval of the President, Sumner Welles, Undersecretary of State, issued an official statement declaring that "acts of wanton lawlessness and of arbitrary force are threatening world peace and the very structure of modern civilization." Again President Roosevelt sent messages to the leading nations of the world asking if they would give a pledge not to attack any one of thirty specified states for a period of ten years. Other nations eagerly gave this pledge, but none was forthcoming from Germany or Italy.

The neutrality policy questioned. In the spring of 1939 revision of the neutrality legislation became an important issue in Congress. Secretary of State Cordell Hull wanted the law amended to permit this country to sell munitions to any belligerent that could pay cash and carry them on its own ships. The shipping of the United States would still be denied access to war zones. Since Great Britain and France controlled the seas with their superior navies, in practice this would mean that Germany and Italy would be denied the purchase of American munitions. Amendment of the neutrality law along these lines, according to Mr. Hull, would serve as a warning to Germany and Italy that in the event of war American arms would be made available to Great Britain and France. Amendment of our neutrality legislation, however, was blocked by the isolationist faction in the Senate, which threatened to hold up action by resorting to a filibuster. In the opinion of many members of Congress there was no prospect of war in Europe, and hence no need to change the American neutrality policy.

United States reaction to the war. The Polish crisis of August 1939 saw President Roosevelt again trying to serve the interests of peace. Appeals were sent to Hitler, to the king of Italy, and to the president of Poland. As we have already seen, these efforts availed nothing, and war came on September 1. In a situation which differed from that of 1914, the

As war clouds gathered on the American horizon, this earnest audience sought a formula to keep the United States at peace. Within three or four months the Japanese would bomb Pearl Harbor, ending such efforts.

American people—that is, the great majority—took sides from the very day that war broke out. It was the general opinion that war had been brought about by Germany and Italy, and sympathy lay with Great Britain and France. The American people detested Nazi ideology and methods and hoped for an Allied victory. But the overwhelming opinion was that America should not interfere in the struggle. This attitude was taken with few qualms, as most Americans believed that Great Britain and France alone would defeat Germany.

It was acknowledged, however, that certain changes should be made in existing neutrality legislation. In November 1939, therefore, a new act was passed providing for the exclusion of American citizens, planes, and vessels from combat zones and for the sale of munitions to any belligerent able to carry such goods away and pay cash. Having made this concession to the Allied cause, America waited for the expected defeat of the Nazi régime.

But defeat was not forthcoming, and in April 1940, there came instead the conquest of Norway and Denmark and then in May the blitzkrieg in the Low Countries and France. The Nazi victories made a profound impression on America. For the first time the full implications of a totalitarian victory began to be seen by American public opinion. With a hostile Japan in the Pacific and the French fleet conceivably in the hands of Germany, the whole strategic outlook for America had been revolutionized. Isolation was coming with a vengeance, but it was the kind of isolation which meant being alone in a troubled world, devoid of allies and surrounded by warlike and expansionist powers.

Rearmament and aid to Great Britain. While Great Britain battled for existence as the *Luftwaffe* tried to establish control of the English sky, steps were taken by the United States in answer to what had become in reality a national crisis. Arms were sent immediately to Great Britain to take the place of those lost at Dunkirk. A rearmament program was introduced contemplating the expenditure of more than seventeen billion dollars. In particular a gigantic naval building program was initiated, providing for the construction of two navies—one for the Pacific, the other for the Atlantic. In May 1940 a National Defense Advisory Board was entrusted with the or-

ganization of the rearmament effort. Later in the year a special office for production management for defense was set up. In June President Roosevelt moved to broaden the base of his cabinet by adding two outstanding Republicans: Colonel Frank Knox, a newspaper publisher, who accepted the post of Secretary of the Navy, and Henry L. Stimson, a former Secretary of State, who assumed the post of Secretary of War.

On August 18, 1940, it was announced that the President and Premier Mackenzie King had agreed to establish a permanent joint board on defense to coordinate the defense measures of Canada and the United States. In September much discussion was aroused by President Roosevelt's revelation that he had authorized the exchange of 50 over-age destroyers to Great Britain for the right to construct naval bases in Newfoundland, the British West Indies, and British Guiana. In the event of the defeat of Great Britain these bases would constitute an invaluable protective screen, especially in the Caribbean area, where the protection of the Panama Canal was of crucial concern to American strategy.

During the summer of 1940 the main issue was that of conscription during peace time. Although it was foreign to historical tradition, the gravity of the international situation convinced most of the people that compulsory military training was vital in developing a trained army. On September 16 the Selective Service Act became law, and the following month more than 16,000,000 men between the ages of twenty-one and thirty-six registered for the draft.

As the autumn months of 1940 unfolded, there was much discussion and controversy on the problem of how far to go in assisting Great Britain. The presidential campaign of November made little political capital of this issue. Both President Roosevelt and the Republican aspirant for the presidency, Wendell L. Willkie, were in favor of all aid "short of war." Both before and after the election, however, radios and countless auditoriums throughout the land echoed the arguments of the America First Committee, which branded aid to Great Britain as the open door to war, and the Committee to Defend America by Aiding the Allies, which urged all possible support of Great Britain. On December 29, 1940, the United States took

THE ATLANTIC CHARTER

THE PRESIDENT of the United States of America and the Prime Minister, Mr. Churchill, representing His Majesty's Government in the United Kingdom, being met together, deem it right to make known certain common principles in the national policies of their respective countries on which they base their hopes for a better future for the world.

First, Their countries seek no aggrandizement, territorial or other;

Second, They desire to see no territorial changes that do not accord with the freely expressed wishes of the peoples concerned;

Third, They respect the right of all peoples to choose the form of government under which they will live; and they wish to see sovereign rights and self-government restored to those who have been forcibly deprived of them;

Fourth, They will endeavor, with due respect for their existing obligations, to further the enjoyment by all States, great or small, victor or vanquished, of access, on equal terms, to the trade and to the raw materials of the world which are needed for their economic prosperity;

Fifth, They desire to bring about the fullest collaboration between all nations in the economic field with the object of securing, for all, improved labor standards, economic adjustment and social security;

Sixth, After the final destruction of the Nazi tyranny, they hope to see established a peace which will afford to all nations the means of dwelling in safety within their own boundaries, and which will afford assurance that all the men in all the lands may live out their lives in freedom from fear and want;

Seventh, Such a peace should enable all men to traverse the high seas and oceans without hindrance;

Eighth, They believe that all of the nations of the world, for realistic as well as spiritual reasons, must come to the abandonment of the use of force. Since no future peace can be maintained if land, sea or air armaments continue to be employed by nations which threaten, or may threaten, aggression outside of their frontiers, they believe, pending the establishment of a wider and permanent system of general security, that the disarmament of such nations is essential. They will likewise aid and encourage all other practicable measures which will lighten for peace-loving peoples the crushing burden of armaments.

another step in the direction of aiding Great Britain. In a fireside chat to the nation President Roosevelt declared:

"We must be the great arsenal of democracy. For us this is an emergency as serious as war itself. We must apply ourselves to our task with the same resolution, the same sense of urgency, the same spirit of patriotism and sacrifice as we would show were we at war."

Two weeks later the Lend-Lease Bill was introduced into Congress, giving the President power to manufacture, sell, lease, lend, or exchange any arms to any country "whose defense the President deems vital to the defense of the United States." The bill became law on March 11, 1941, after much debate in and out of the halls of Congress, and the country now prepared to make available to Great Britain and others billions of dollars of war material. In April the United States assumed the defense of the Danish possession of Greenland.

Pan-American cooperation. The United States was now pursuing three definite policies: rearmament at home on a truly colossal scale, all-out aid to Great Britain, and cooperation with the Latin American republics. In conferences called for the purpose of mapping common action, the twenty-one American republics set up a neutral zone extending 300 to 1000 miles from the shores of the Western Hemisphere into the North and South Atlantic. They warned belligerent warships not to come into this neutral zone. Further, an agreement was drawn up for the provisional administration of European colonies in the Western Hemisphere, in the event that such a step became necessary, to prevent Germany from securing French and Dutch colonies in the Caribbean area. After 1940 the realization of the common danger faced by all the peoples of the Western Hemisphere tended to draw the twenty-one republics closer and closer together.

Sharpening of U. S. policy. Early in the spring of 1941, alarming British shipping losses presented the administration at Washington with the prospect that supplies made available to the British under the terms of the Lend-Lease Bill might find their way to the bottom of the sea rather than to England. This emergency precipitated the convoy issue. Wendell L. Willkie and members of the President's cabinet gave strong support to the idea of convoying merchant vessels to Great Britain with American warships.

While the majority of citizens did not support the isolationist point of view, there was much confusion of thought, and the time had come for a clear and unequivocal statement of the government's policy. There could be little doubt where the American government stood and what it proposed to do when the President's fireside chat of May 28 ended. President Roosevelt accused the totalitarian states of aiming at world domination. He stressed the suicidal folly of waiting idly until the totalitarian attack actually began to rain bombs on American cities. The President said: "When your enemy comes at you in a tank or a bombing plane, if you hold your fire until you see the whites of his eyes, you will never know what hit you. Our Bunker Hill of tomorrow may be several thousand miles from Boston." Coming to the convoy issue, President Roosevelt stated: "Our patrols are helping now to insure delivery of the needed supplies to Britain. All additional measures necessary to deliver the goods will be taken."

As a means of speeding up production and uniting public opinion behind the great task of making America an arsenal of democracy the President announced the existence of an unlimited national emergency. No one could deny that America had now made her choice. The United States had committed herself and dedicated vast resources to the task of defeating Hitler and his totalitarian allies.

During the summer and fall of 1941 the United States accelerated and expanded her support to all nations fighting aggression. A military mission was sent to China to facilitate more aid to that country, and American military observers also assisted the British in the Near East. During July troops occupied Iceland, where the United States established a military base. In August President Roosevelt and Prime Minister Churchill, with their chief advisers, met secretly "somewhere in the Atlantic" and drafted the Atlantic Charter (see page 175).

The war draws closer. While the intensification of American aid to Great Britain and China was taking place, several American ships had been sunk by Nazi submarines. In May 1941, the *Robin Moor* was sunk in the South Atlantic, outside of any war zone.

Other merchantmen were sunk during August and September. On September 11 the President announced a policy of "shooting at sight" any Axis vessels found in the Atlantic defense zones. After an attack on an American destroyer early in October (the ship remained able to make port safely), another destroyer, the *Reuben James,* was sunk by a submarine in the North Atlantic, with heavy loss of life. This event led Congress, upon the recommendation of President Roosevelt, to repeal the major provisions of the neutrality law prohibiting American ships from entering belligerent waters and from being armed. The American public did not realize how close the war had come to them. But by November 1941, if the country was not yet a belligerent, it certainly was not a neutral.

The War Encircles the Globe

Blitzkrieg versus Russia. Following the successful invasion of Crete in May 1941, a widespread German offensive against Palestine and Egypt appeared logical. Instead, on June 22, a gigantic panzer attack was launched by Hitler's armies against Russia, despite the nonaggression pact signed between the German Reich and Russia in August 1939. Thus began the seventh major phase of the war. In a proclamation to the German people, Hitler charged that the Russians were plotting to conquer Europe. He said that one hundred sixty Russian army divisions had been stationed along the German frontier, menacing the security of the Reich. In Hitler's words, "to safeguard Europe from the Jewish rulers of the Bolshevik center in Moscow" Germany was forced to attack Russia.

Hitler's decision was probably influenced by several factors. To carry on a long war, Germany had to secure new stocks of raw materials. All of Hitler's needs could be served by two areas in Russia. The Ukraine, a district somewhat larger than California, called the Soviet breadbasket, produced tremendous crops of wheat, corn, and rye. In the eastern Ukraine the industrialized Donets Basin produced more than seventy per cent of Russian coal and large amounts of iron. The Donets Basin was also important for its automobile factories, chemical plants, and steel mills.

The second Russian area of value to Hitler was the Caucasus, a wide neck of land between the Black and Caspian seas, one of the world's richest oil regions. The oil wells here, producing 90 per cent of Russia's oil, were naturally a great attraction to the Nazi army, whose stocks of the vital fuel were being depleted rapidly.

In addition to needing raw materials, Hitler probably feared Russia. She was getting too strong for his comfort. Before United States' aid in war supplies to Great Britain challenged the resources of the Reich, all possibility of Russian "danger" had to be removed. The Nazi leaders also hoped to sell their attack on Russia as a crusade against Communism. Since many people in the subjugated European countries feared and disliked Communism, it was thought that the attack might rally these groups behind Hitler.

The Germans accordingly launched a major offensive against Russia from the Baltic to the Black seas. Assisted by Rumanian and Finnish forces, the panzer divisions had little difficulty in pushing Soviet forces out of the

These German prisoners, taken when the Russians struck back on the Kalinin front, do not appear to like the Russian cold. Unprepared, Hitler appealed to the German people for clothes for the troops.

THE WORLD

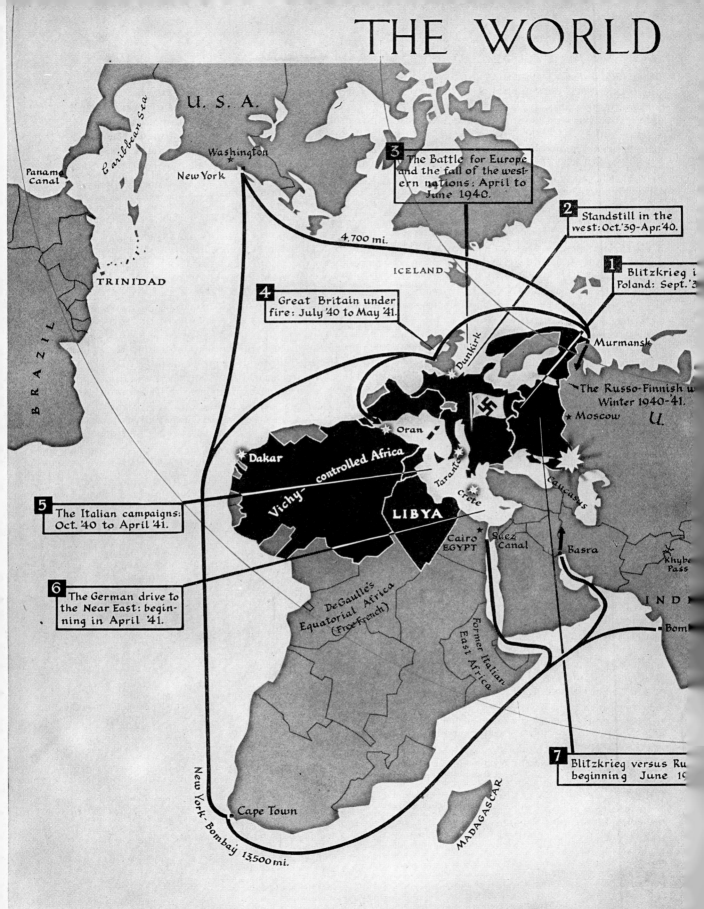

3 The Battle for Europe and the fall of the western nations: April to June 1940.

2 Standstill in the west: Oct.'39-Apr.'40.

1 Blitzkrieg i Poland: Sept. '3

4,700 mi.

ICELAND

Murmansk

4 Great Britain under fire: July '40 to May '41.

The Russo-Finnish w Winter 1940-'41.

Dunkirk

★ Moscow   U.

Oran

★ Dakar

Vichy- controlled Africa

Taranto

Crete

Caucasus

LIBYA

5 The Italian campaigns: Oct. '40 to April '41.

Cairo EGYPT   Suez Canal

Basra

Khybe Pass

6 The German drive to the Near East: beginning in April '41.

DeGaulle's Equatorial Africa (Free-French)

Former Italian East Africa

IND

Bom

Panam Canal

U. S. A.

Washington ★

New York

Caribbean Sea

TRINIDAD

B R A Z I L

Cape Town

New York-Bombay 13,500 mi.

MADAGASCAR

7 Blitzkrieg versus Ru beginning June 19

R. M. Chapin, Jr.
September, 1942

AT WAR

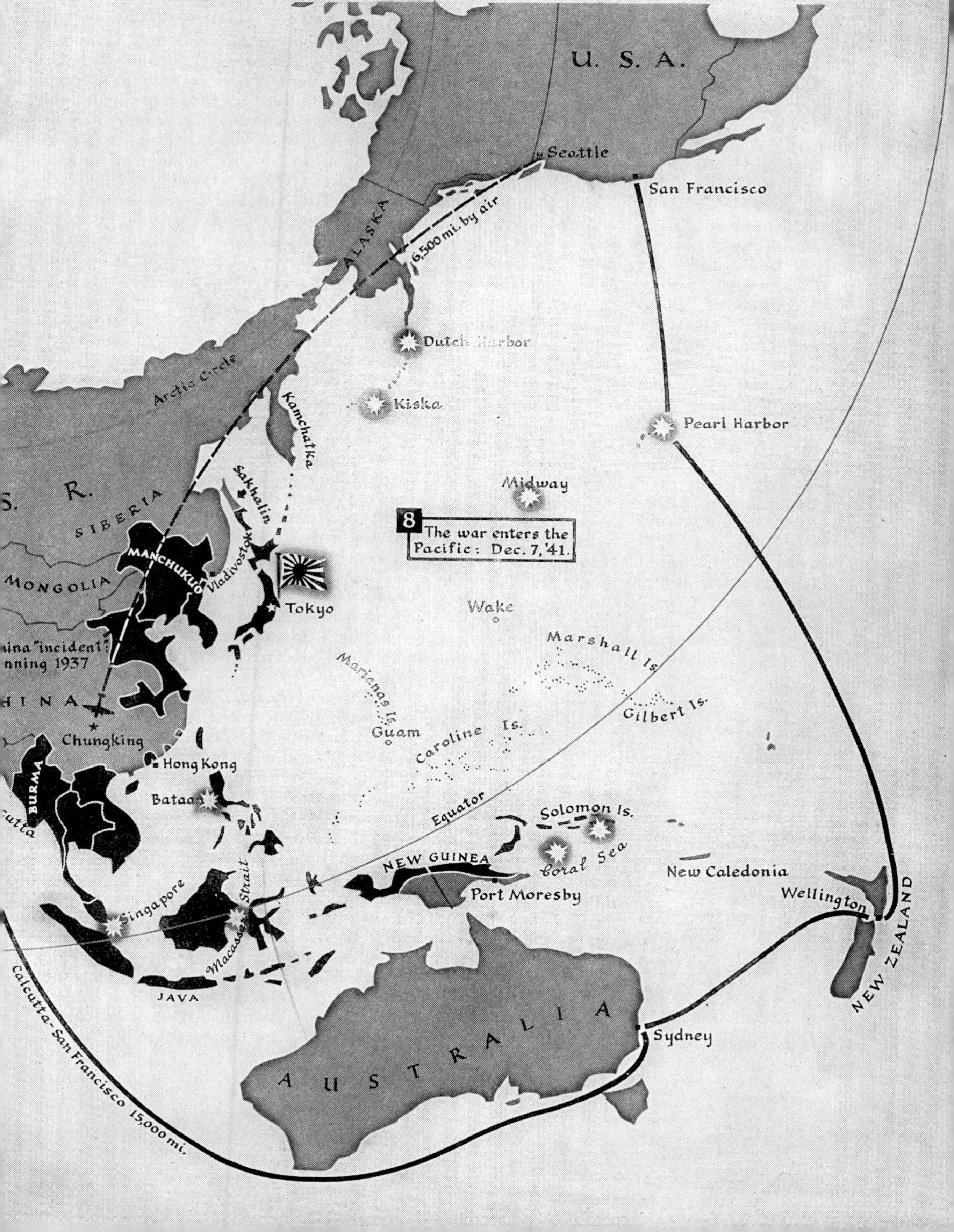

U.S.A.

Seattle

San Francisco

6,500 mi. by air

ALASKA

Arctic Circle

Dutch Harbor

Kiska

Pearl Harbor

Kamchatka

Midway

S. R.

SIBERIA

Sakhalin

Vladivostok

MANCHUKUO

8 The war enters the Pacific: Dec. 7, '41.

MONGOLIA

Tokyo

Wake

Marshall Is.

"incident"
nning 1937

Marianas Is.

Gilbert Is.

CHINA

Guam

Caroline Is.

Chungking

BURMA

Hong Kong

Bataan

Equator

Solomon Is.

cutta

New Caledonia

NEW GUINEA

Coral Sea

Singapore

Wellington

Macassar Strait

Port Moresby

NEW ZEALAND

JAVA

Calcutta - San Francisco 15,000 mi.

AUSTRALIA

Sydney

border area acquired by Russia from 1939 to 1941. Estonia, Lithuania, Latvia, and other regions were conquered by the German forces.

On the borders of Russia proper, a second German offensive struck in the direction of Leningrad in the north, Moscow at the center, and Kiev to the south. The summer saw a titanic battle in progress, both sides claiming to have inflicted hundreds of thousands of casualties on their foes. The Russians had to give ground. Yet to the astonishment of the world, the blitzkrieg at times seemed to falter and prove ineffective. Russian morale was high, and a scorched-earth policy destroyed everything of value left behind by the Russian army. Hitler had a difficult problem in maintaining his long lines of communication.

New allegiances. Since 1939 British statesmen, and indeed the world in general, had regarded Russia as virtually the ally of Nazi Germany. Following the German attack, however, Churchill declared that any nation fighting against Hitler was the ally of Great Britain. In July 1941 a mutual assistance pact was signed in Moscow between Russia and Great Britain. At the same time the government of the United States declared that Lend-Lease material would be provided to Russia. Late in September an Anglo-American war mission arrived in Moscow to work out a program of war aid for the Soviet Union.

Continued Nazi advance. During the summer, Soviet forces had been compelled to

Mud as well as snow slowed up the Nazi blitzkrieg in Russia. This German soldier, wearing a camouflaged raincoat, plans to tow one tank with another.

surrender the key city of Smolensk guarding the approaches to Moscow, and Leningrad was almost encircled. Kiev, in the south, the gateway to the Ukraine, had fallen. German pressure continued during September, and early in October a smashing attack designed to knock out and destroy Russian resistance was begun. In his proclamation to the German armies, Hitler claimed that already 2,400,000 Russians had been captured and that victory was at hand.

In October and November victory for the Nazi armies appeared imminent. Leningrad was surrounded, and fighting was carried on in the suburbs. The Nazi forces penetrated to within forty miles of Moscow, and the Russian government was moved to the temporary capital of Kuibyshev, far to the east. In the south the Ukraine had been overrun, the Dnieper River crossed, and Kharkov captured. The strategic Crimean peninsula had also fallen with the exception of the naval base at Sevastopol. Late in November the gateway to the Caucasus and its oil fields, Rostov on the Don River, was captured. Stalin appealed to Great Britain to ease German pressure by opening a new front in western Europe, but the only aid forthcoming from Great Britain was an energetic air offensive against the Channel ports and western Germany, which perhaps diverted some Nazi air squadrons from the Russian front. The British, however, did dispatch tanks and other supplies to Russia.

The turn of the tide. The Russian situation improved suddenly late in November 1941, when the Russian winter with its blinding snowstorms and subzero temperatures began to derange Nazi communications and slow down the drive. During the first week of December the Russian armies counterattacked along the entire 1500-mile front. Rostov was recaptured, and the Russians advanced into the Ukraine. Before Moscow the Germans were forced to give ground, and the pressure on Leningrad was relieved. On December 21 Hitler removed his supreme commander and himself assumed command. The Nazi chief announced that the Russian war had "exceeded all past notions" and that his soldiers must hold on till spring. The "ever victorious" German army appeared to be on the defensive.

By mid-January 1942, the Russians had recaptured more than 100,000 square miles and were less than 100 miles from the Latvian frontier between Leningrad and Moscow. This brilliant counterstroke of the Soviet armies raised hopes in all countries fighting Nazi Germany that perhaps the debacle of Napoleon's invasion of Russia in 1812 was to be repeated.

Great Britain in the Near East. The Russian campaign had meanwhile given Great Britain an opportunity to strengthen her defenses in the Mediterranean and the Near East. Following the conquest of Crete by Nazi parachutists at the end of May, no new German advance was made. This gave British troops the chance to gain full control of Iraq. Just before the Russo-German war broke out, the British turned their attention to French Syria. The situation in this country can be understood only by reference to the position of France.

Unoccupied France. Following the armistice with Germany in June 1940, the status of France was little short of pitiable. Marshal Pétain was willing to cooperate to a limited extent with the German victor as long as this did not necessitate taking up arms actively against his former ally, Great Britain. But there were many French leaders in high places who apparently were quite willing to do anything Germany proposed. The situation was further complicated by the Free French movement under General Charles de Gaulle. After the tragic collapse of France, General de Gaulle established a Free French government in London to carry on the war by the side of Great Britain. About one quarter of the French empire sided with De Gaulle and repudiated the Vichy government of Pétain. Support for De Gaulle came from Frenchmen all over the world who deplored the renunciation of democracy at Vichy and believed that from such colonies as Morocco, and with the aid of the French fleet, Pétain should have continued the struggle against Germany.

Until April 1941 Pétain had been able to hold in check those in the Vichy government who were in favor of full collaboration with Nazi Germany. The collapse of Yugoslavia and Greece, the British reverses in north Africa, and the lack of national unity in the United States on the question of "all-out aid to Great Britain" persuaded Pétain that France now had no choice other than to do Germany's bidding. By the middle of May Vichy announced full cooperation with the Nazi régime, and German planes en route to Iraq began to use air bases in French Syria. In retaliation these fields were bombed by British air squadrons, and open conflict seemed imminent between France and Great Britain.

British successes in Syria, Iran, Egypt. The prospect of full French collaboration with Germany in turning over strategic bases in Syria caused the British government to act decisively. On June 8 British troops supported by a Free French contingent entered Syria. Only "a token resistance" was anticipated, but the Syrian forces, on orders from Vichy, resisted savagely. Only after two weeks of fighting did Syria fall to the Allied forces.

There was yet another area of great strategic value in the Near East, especially after Russia became an ally of Great Britain. This was Iran, formerly known as Persia, which constituted a vital corridor through which supplies could be sent to Russia via the Persian Gulf and then north through Iran to the Russian Caucasus. Both Great Britain and Russia became alarmed, however, at the pro-Axis sentiments of Iran's ruler and the fact that the country was filling up with German technicians. On August 25, 1941, following the refusal of authorities in Iran to expel the German agents, British and Russian forces invaded the country. Four days later all resistance ceased. The decision of the Nazi government to attack Russia had enabled Great Britain to gain control of a great block of territory stretching from the Mediterranean to the Persian Gulf and thence to India.

During September and October when Germany was fully occupied with her great offensive in Russia, the British forces in Egypt were receiving large consignments of American Lend-Lease material. By the middle of November the British commander in the Near East, General Auchinleck, was in a position to plan an offensive against the Nazi forces under General Rommel that had been menacing the Egyptian border since April. On November 21 the British, using in large measure American tanks and American pursuit planes, struck at Rommel's forces. By the end of December the British army had pushed the German army with its Italian allies more than eight hundred miles to the west, had captured the important base of Bengasi, and had taken more than 36,000 prisoners. The Near East and now Egypt had been rendered secure, for the time being, from Nazi pressure.

Japan in the Pacific. During the years of the Abyssinian and Spanish wars, Munich, the Polish crisis, and finally war in western Europe, the Far East (as we have noted in a previous chapter) followed a similar pattern of lawlessness. Japan, successful in the conquest of Manchuria, determined to press forward to additional victories while the great powers in Europe were quarreling among themselves and the United States was attempting to isolate itself.

In 1938 Japan informed the United States that she was determined to establish a régime in Asia in accordance with her own interests, implying that all the former treaties safeguarding American commercial rights were henceforth inoperative. Answering this declaration, the American government bluntly informed Japan that it refused to recognize the New Order in Asia and that it would not relinquish any of its rights.

The outbreak of war in Europe in 1939 gave Japan a golden opportunity to press her drive against China to a successful conclusion and, with this done, even perhaps to capture the colonies in the Far East controlled by the western powers. Late in 1939 several strong offensives against the Chinese forces holding the hinterland were carried out, but the lines held. Unable to smash Chinese resistance, Japan now turned to other promising fields of endeavor. In the spring of 1939 she commenced a squeeze play in the orient by seizing the Chinese island of Hainan. This island dominated French Indo-China and gave Japan valuable bases in the event of attack against British Malaya or the Dutch East Indies. It was this action that caused the United States government to move its fleet to Pacific bases in April 1939.

Japanese pressure on European powers. After the collapse of France in the spring of 1940, a Japanese diplomat candidly declared: "We should not miss the present opportunity or we shall be blamed by posterity." Raw materials such as oil and iron were becoming difficult to procure as a result of the European war, and the rise of anti-Japanese sentiment in America also made this country an uncertain source for raw materials. By controlling Indo-China, the Netherlands East Indies, and perhaps British Malaya, Japan would remove most of her fears on this score, and enriched by her booty she could deal with the obstinate Chinese at her leisure.

Throughout 1939 Japan made open threats against Great Britain in the Far East and even blockaded British and French business districts in Chinese cities. In June 1940 Japanese troops concentrated near Hong Kong, the British colony on the Chinese coast, and in July the British decided to close the Burma Road—the vital artery of supply for the Chinese armies. In the summer of 1940 pressure was also extended to the Netherlands East Indies. No action was forthcoming, however, perhaps because Secretary of State Hull warned that the United States would not tolerate any change in their status.

Defeated France also felt Japanese pressure. In June 1940 Pétain agreed to permit Japanese observers to watch traffic in Indo-China. The object of this demand, of course, was to prevent supplies from reaching the Chinese forces via French territory. In the fall of 1940 France had to allow Japan to set up air bases in Indo-China and land a limited number of soldiers. In the meantime an amateur in aggression was encouraged by Japan to distract France still further. This was Thailand, formerly Siam, which demanded the return of territory originally taken from her by France and added to the colony of Indo-China. After several months of wrangling, Japan stepped in as mediator in March 1941 and brought both Thailand and Indo-China under her control.

Growing concern of occidental powers. Contrary to Japanese expectations, Great Britain had not been conquered in the summer of 1940. The United States clearly manifested a determination to keep both China and Great Britain in the field. Thus Great Britain was able to reopen the Burma Road in the fall of 1940, and the United States made large loans to China. The totalitarian states were now plainly worried. Japan feared the intervention of the United States in the Pacific, and Germany was not at all sure that the United States would keep out of the European struggle. In September 1940 Germany, Italy, and Japan had signed a military alliance "to assist one another with all political, economic, and military means when one of the three is attacked by a power at present not involved in

As the truth of America's greatest naval defeat began to come home to the people, the Navy released this tragic picture showing the U. S. S. Arizona down and aflame after the Japanese attack on Pearl Harbor.

the European war or in the Chinese-Japanese conflict." This pact, directed at the United States, was ample evidence that the European war was becoming a world conflict.

The A.B.C.D. powers. Confronted with Japan's ambitious Asiatic intentions, America, Great Britain, China, and the Netherlands East Indies in the spring of 1941 began to consult with each other on common measures to be taken to check further Japanese aggression. These conferences created what was known as the "A.B.C.D." front against Japan. Backed by friends, the Dutch felt able to reject Japanese pressure for oil and more liberal trade concessions in June 1941. In July Japanese strategy became apparent when under a new pact with the Vichy government for "common defense" additional Japanese troops were sent into Indo-China. Domination of this French colony placed Japanese forces in a position (1) to strike at Burma through Thailand and cut off the one remaining route of supplies to China and (2) to march through Thailand south into the Malay Peninsula and launch an attack against the English naval base of Singapore.

In retaliation for Japan's action in Indo-China, America, Great Britain, and the Dutch froze all Japanese funds late in July, making it impossible for that country to obtain addi-

tional vital materials from members of the A.B.C.D. front. The freezing order was followed by parallel warnings by Great Britain and the United States against Japanese designs on Thailand.

Japan was faced with the alternative of backing down or casting the die, whatever the stakes, in favor of a great empire in southeast Asia. She made the latter choice. In October her premier was replaced by General Tojo. An avowed militarist now headed the cabinet of Japan. While additional troops were being sent to Singapore by Great Britain, and arrangements were being made to recall all American marines in China, and while the pro-Axis Tojo cabinet became more and more truculent, a special envoy was dispatched in November from Tokyo to Washington. The envoy was Saburo Kurusu, a veteran diplomat, whose task it was to convince the American State Department that Japanese policy in the Pacific was in no way prejudicial to the interests of the United States.

The attack on Pearl Harbor. On November 26 the United States, acting for the A.B.C.D. powers, presented proposals to Kurusu for a peaceful agreement in the Pacific, requiring Japanese withdrawal from China and the termination of Tokyo's collaboration with the Axis. News of Japanese

Bombers like these were assigned the task of protecting America's coastline against marauding Axis submarines, a contest that developed into major proportions. Such planes were also used to give Tokyo its first bombing.

troop movements toward Thailand (Siam) early in December caused President Roosevelt to send an urgent appeal to the Japanese emperor on December 6. The following day, Sunday, while Kurusu and the Japanese Ambassador Nomura were delivering a note to the American Secretary of State, announcing Japan's refusal to continue negotiations, word was received from the Hawaiian Islands that Japanese planes based on aircraft carriers had carried out a destructive bombardment of the naval base at Pearl Harbor. It was shortly admitted that this attack had brought about the loss of two battleships, several smaller craft, and many planes.

The issue joined. On December 8, following the President's recommendation, Congress declared war on Japan. Germany and Italy followed the Japanese attack by declaring war on the United States on December 12, and the following day Congress declared war on these two powers. Great Britain, her Dominions, the conquered and refugee governments of Europe, and the Caribbean and Central American republics also declared war on Japan. In all twenty-six nations now stood arrayed against Germany, Japan, Italy, and their satellites. The greatest global struggle in all history was now under way.

Initial Japanese successes. Any complacency that existed in America was considerably reduced after Pearl Harbor by Japan's initial successes in the Pacific. On December 8 and 9 Japanese attacks were made against the

Malay Peninsula, the Philippines, Hong Kong, and the three American naval bases of Guam, Wake, and Midway. The defense of Singapore was made much more difficult by the loss of two British battleships, destroyed by Japanese bombing planes. Almost at will, without fear of naval attack, Japanese troops could now be landed from transports along the Malayan coast.

Heavy fighting followed the landing of Japanese forces in the Philippines on December 9. For three weeks the American army of General MacArthur was able to hold the enemy before Manila. On January 2 this city fell, and further American resistance was confined to a small area in the Bataan peninsula and on the heavily fortified island of Corregidor. Throughout January the world watched with admiration the outnumbered forces under MacArthur hold their lines against heavy attack. After heroic resistance a small detachment of marines was overwhelmed on Wake Island, Guam also was lost, and on December 26 the British crown colony of Hong Kong had surrendered.

During January the Japanese arc of operations expanded, for the real prize was the Malay Peninsula and the Netherlands East Indies. Landings were made in British North Borneo. Other points of attack in the Netherlands East Indies were harbors along the eastern coast of Borneo and points on the island of Celebes. Japanese contingents landed on New Guinea and other nearby islands. From these islands the Japanese could now make plans to attack Australia. Meanwhile British imperial forces were being forced back in Malaya. By mid-January the Japanese were less than 100 miles from Singapore. At the same time a Japanese army driving west from Thailand was menacing the vital Burma Road. To offset these numerous Japanese successes the A.B.C.D. powers had, after almost two months of war, gained only one outstanding success. This was the sinking of numerous vessels of a Japanese convoy in the Macassar Strait presumably taking troops to invade Java.

The United Nations. The initial success of Japanese arms was due largely to her surprise attack and to her state of full military preparedness. The one great power capable of defeating Japan was the United States. Both Great Britain and Russia were occupied in Europe with Germany and Italy. The power of the United States, however, was largely inert and could not be immediately exerted against Japan. It was also apparent that the best way for the United States, Great Britain, China, and their associated allies to achieve victory was to work out a scheme of grand strategy in which every nation would be allotted the task best suited to its resources and capacity. Such a plan was undertaken hardly more than a fortnight after the Pacific phase of the Second World War began.

On December 22 Prime Minister Churchill arrived in Washington, accompanied by high-ranking officials, to discuss the conduct of the war with President Roosevelt and his aids. At the same time Anthony Eden was closeted with Joseph Stalin in Moscow on a similar errand. A few days after the British and American statesmen had begun their discussions, it was announced that twenty-six nations had signed an agreement which pledged each signatory to use all of its resources to defeat the Axis powers, not to sign a separate peace, and, finally, to accept the provisions of the Atlantic Charter (page 175) agreed to by Roosevelt and Churchill during the preceding summer. On January 2, 1942, a unified command in the southwestern Pacific theater of war was announced.

On January 6 President Roosevelt, in his annual message to Congress, laid down the gigantic war program considered essential for Allied victory. During 1942 the government asked for the production of 60,000 planes, 45,000 tanks, and 8,000,000 tons of merchant shipping. In 1943 production was to be even greater. The armament program called for an expenditure of fifty-six billion dollars in 1942, more than half the national income of the United States. To insure the utilization of material and munitions where they would do the most good against the enemy, Great Britain and the United States agreed to pool all their resources. A series of boards was set up in January 1942 to decide upon the allocation and priority of supplies.

The conference at Rio. Shortly after going to war with Japan the United States tested the fruits of the Good Neighbor policy inaugurated with Latin America about 1930. In January 1942 a Pan-American Conference of the twenty-one American republics met at Rio de Janeiro to discuss their attitude following an unprovoked attack upon one of their number —the United States. There had been a time, only a decade or so ago, when not one Latin American republic would have raised a finger to assist the United States. But during the past ten years the United States had spared no effort in earning the good will of her southern neighbors. The conference at Rio de Janeiro was the first real test of the new policy.

The United States wanted a unanimous rupture of diplomatic relations with the Axis powers. This objective was supported by several other nations, especially Mexico. Unanimous action was not obtained at the conference because of the opposition of Chile and Argentina. The final declaration recommended severance of relations with Japan, Germany, and Italy. By the end of January nineteen Latin American republics had either broken off relations or were at war with the enemies of the United States. Only Chile and Argentina held aloof.

While not complete, a victory for the Good Neighbor policy had been won at Rio de Janeiro. The United States made arrangements to send Lend-Lease aid to her Latin American friends, to assure them of needed industrial supplies, and to work out unified plans for combating Axis espionage in the Western Hemisphere.

The Japanese plunge ahead. The initial efforts of the United Nations to mobilize their fighting strength and attain unity of purpose

The crew of a Curtiss Commando, giant troopship, welcomes a U. S. army scout car, the familiar "jeep." The ship is designed to transport field artillery, aircraft engines, tractors, and fully equipped troops.

did little to halt the expansion of Japanese forces in the Pacific theater of war. On February 15, after a furious battle in which British troops had been unable to halt the Japanese, the Singapore fortress fell. Thousands of British troops were taken as prisoners.

In the latter part of February the Japanese were closing in on Java, the most valuable island in the Netherlands East Indies. A small naval flotilla comprised of Dutch, American, and British units tried to destroy Japanese naval concentrations, but Allied force was insufficient, and in a great battle the Japanese wiped out practically all opposition. Without fear of naval interference, the Japanese now landed large bodies of men on the beaches of Java and pressed into the interior. The Dutch, assisted by a few contingents of Australian and American soldiers, fought valiantly. But outnumbered and without adequate air power, the resistance quickly crumpled.

While the Japanese were carrying out their conquest of Java, they had also initiated a drive against the British colony of Burma, terminus of the Burma Road. A successful campaign would close this vital artery to China and interfere with supplies being sent by Great Britain and the United States to the forces of Generalissimo Chiang Kai-shek. Japanese forces converged on Burma in mid-January from Thailand and the Malay Peninsula. Rangoon, the capital, was captured early in March. The Japanese then launched an offensive toward the north in order to secure Lashio, the southern end of the Burma Road. Chinese troops under the command of an American officer, General Joseph W. Stilwell, reinforced the British army, but the Japanese could not be halted. Lashio fell on April 30, and in the first part of May the Chinese forces were pushed out of Burma. The Japanese also gained some territory in China along the Burma Road. A few thousand British troops managed to escape into India. Burma joined the long list of Japanese conquests.

In the Philippines General Douglas MacArthur had carried out brilliant defensive tactics against Japanese forces much superior to his own. Despite gallant resistance American opposition gradually was worn down.

Food and medicinal supplies were depleted. On April 9 the remnants of the army on Bataan surrendered, and some 40,000 American and Philippine troops were captured. Corregidor fortress still held out with its satellite island forts in Manila Bay, but it too was stormed, and the garrisons were forced to capitulate on May 7.

Threats to India and Australia. The fall of Singapore, the conquest of the Netherlands East Indies, and the end of American resistance in the Philippines placed India and Australia in jeopardy. By April Japan was threatening to control the Bay of Bengal. The Andaman Islands were captured; they gave Japan air bases near enough for bombing the important Indian city of Calcutta and the strategic British island of Ceylon. At this juncture the British government sent to India a special emissary, Sir Stafford Cripps, to try to obtain full support of the Indian people in the war effort. After several weeks of negotiation Sir Stafford failed to secure agreement with Indian leaders over the vexed problem of self-government. While active support of the all-important Indian National Congress in prosecuting the war was not obtained, the Indian leaders did not at this time seriously hinder Great Britain's efforts to defend India.

Battles of the Coral Sea and Midway. During the battle of Bataan the American government transferred General MacArthur to Australia to assume full command in this area. Large numbers of American troops and quantities of equipment were convoyed across the Pacific to bolster Australian defenses. The position in the Bay of Bengal and the Indian Ocean, as well as the defenses of Australia, was materially improved by two highly important victories of American naval task forces.

Early in May a savage encounter between Japanese and American fleets and aircraft took place in the Coral Sea. This engagement destroyed fifteen of the enemy's ships and damaged twenty more. The United States lost the carrier *Lexington*, a destroyer, and a tanker.

The second important naval encounter occurred in early June when United States forces, mainly aircraft, intercepted large Japanese fleet concentrations apparently sent to capture the strategic base of the Midway Islands. A severe defeat was suffered by the enemy. Four aircraft carriers were sunk, two large cruisers were disposed of, and several

of their battleships were severely damaged.

These naval victories were greatly significant. They stopped the Japanese advance toward the east and continental United States; they represented, in fact, a turning point in the Pacific war.

Encouraging also were the British capture of Madagascar, a potential naval base for the Japanese in the Indian Ocean; the bombing of Tokyo and other Japanese cities by American flyers led by Brigadier General James Doolittle; and heavy air attacks from Allied bases in Australia against Japanese bases in the Dutch East Indies, especially Timor, and on the island of New Guinea.

The Japanese attack on Midway was part of a larger engagement aimed at attaining still greater strength in the Pacific. It had been preceded by the bombing of Dutch Harbor in Alaska. Toward the end of June, the Japanese succeeded in occupying two small islands at the end of the Aleutian chain, off Alaska.

Summer 1942. In the summer of 1942 the war was being fought in all parts of the globe. In the Japanese-dominated Pacific General Douglas MacArthur's forces in Australia were harrying Jap bases. In Russia the Nazis were again on the offensive. The war in Africa, opened by the Italians in the fall of 1940 and taken over by the Germans in 1941, again became active as General Erwin Rommel's forces drove the British back in Egypt. Japanese planes bombed Dutch Harbor in the Aleutians, and Japanese troops secured a foothold on the island of Kiska, threatening Alaskan shores. The supply lines of the Allies stretched long and far over the globe (see map, pages 178-179). In contrast, Axis holdings, compact and often contiguous, made enemy problems of communication and supply relatively easy. In late spring and midsummer of 1942 a mighty Axis drive for victory began.

The battle for Russia. During the winter months the Nazi armies had been forced to assume defensive tactics in Russia. Intense cold and constant harrying by the Russians caused much loss in men and material. With the coming of spring and better weather Nazi armies started their long-awaited drive for victory against Russia. The initial effort was made in the Crimean peninsula, the eastern part of which fell to the Germans on May 23. To divert German strength Marshal Timoshenko had opened an offensive against the

As the United States went into production as the arsenal for democracy, this picture was taken in the Boeing Aircraft plant at Seattle. It shows the final assembly of the nose and center fuselage sections of the famous Flying Fortresses.

enemy in the vicinity of Kharkov, but the German drive in the Ukraine continued. The mighty fortress of Sevastopol, the last remaining Russian foothold in the Crimean peninsula, was attacked constantly by German forces during June and fell to the Nazis on July 1. German pressure then switched north, to the neighborhood of Kursk, where one of the heaviest attacks of the entire war was hurled against Russian positions. The objective was to reach the Don River and cut the vital railroad line connecting Moscow with south Russia. After bitter fighting the Germans crossed the Don and pushed east from their original positions and south toward the oil fields of the Caucasus.

If Russia suffered a major defeat, the war would be prolonged, and both the United States and Great Britain would be menaced. This fact was fully realized in both Washington and London. In the spring and early summer there had been much talk of a second front in Europe to aid Russia. American troops in considerable force reached prepared billets in Northern Ireland, and high-ranking American officers went to London to discuss the strategy of the war. A form of second front was introduced when industrial centers in Germany were raided by British air forces consisting at times of more than a thousand planes. The crucial situation of Russia also brought the Soviet Foreign Commissar V. Molotov to both London and Washington. An important treaty was negotiated with Great Britain, and the United States and Russia signed a mutual aid agreement.

The Axis drive on Egypt. As part of the Axis victory campaign for 1942, the German Afrika Corps under General Erwin Rommel launched an offensive against the British Eighth Army in Libya in May. For nearly three years the contending armies had seesawed back and forth over the desert. Rommel's latest push was the sixth campaign fought in Libya between the British on the one hand and the Germans and Italians on the other. Early in June the British army seemed to be holding its own. But after a defeat on June 18, the battered British forces began a rapid retreat. A garrison left to hold Tobruk was captured by Rommel with some twenty-five thousand British troops, according to Berlin claims, on June 21. The successful German army crossed the Egyptian border and by July 1 was only seventy miles from Alexandria. In the first week of July the British commander, General Auchinleck, reorganized his troops and commenced a heavy air offensive against Rommel's long lines of communication. The immediate threat to Alexandria, base of the British Mediterranean fleet, had been halted.

The Japanese persist in China. Checked in the mid-Pacific at Midway and unable to advance any closer to Australia, Japanese forces turned their attention to their first intended victim—China. In May Japanese troops opened an offensive in south China designed primarily to secure possession of the main railroad lines. Possession and control of these lines would give Japan an all-land network of communications extending from north China to Singapore. Troops and supplies could be moved along this route without fear of attack from American warships. By June the Japanese had captured the disputed railroad line and were pushing west into the heart of China. Denied the use of the Burma Road, the Allied nations found it increasingly difficult to send supplies to China.

The outlook for the United Nations. In July 1942 the Second World War was approaching the end of its third year. Involving at least eight distinct phases, the conflict had begun primarily as a war between Germany on the one hand and Great Britain and France on the other. By the end of the third year the war had become a global conflict involving the three Axis powers with their satellite allies and twenty-nine United Nations.

While crucial battles were being fought in Egypt and Russia, a less dramatic but equally heroic struggle was taking place in Europe. In the face of all forms of intimidation—forced labor, mass execution of hostages, extermination of villages—the conquered peoples of Europe refused to cooperate in Hitler's New Order. Sabotage, espionage, and assassinations showed that the Dutch, Norwegians, Poles, Serbs, French, and others were only waiting the day when they could rise and assist the armies of the United Nations to overthrow Nazi tyranny.

Great Britain had limited manpower but extensive productive capacity in the war; Russia had much greater manpower but inadequate industrial equipment for her vast armies; and China had virtually nothing except manpower. The United States was the heart of the opposition to the Axis, for she had manpower and immense productivity. But she was, in a sense, on the fringe of the battle areas, and so in a more limited way was Great Britain. The task of the British and even more of Americans was to transport men and supplies from the fringe to the center of the struggle (see map, pages 178-179). This war, therefore, was called "the perimeter war," in which Allied lines of communication were three to fifteen times longer than those of the Axis. In addition to the terrific assault against Egypt and Russia, the Germans also carried on a less spectacular offensive against the United States, a submarine campaign which accounted for more than 400 Allied vessels by the summer of 1942.

Indeed the situation from the standpoint of the United Nations in the summer of 1942 appeared critical. But if Russia could beat down the German onslaught without losing too much to Hitler; if the Allies could hold the Near East and Egypt, thus insuring a route of supply via the Persian Gulf and Iran to Russia and preventing Germany from reaching India and joining hands with Japan; and if Chinese resistance could stand up against increasing Japanese pressure, it was thought that the tremendous industrial potential of the United States might be able to operate toward the end of 1942 in favor of the United Nations.

United States' war effort. Granted the continuation of the heroism of Russian, Chinese, and British soldiers, plus the Free French and guerrilla bands of patriots in conquered Yugoslavia, the United States would be given a few more vital months to put her fighting forces into action fully equipped. America at war in the midsummer of 1942 gave every indication of a nation stripped for action. There were many evidences that the full power of the United States would soon be thrown into battle areas throughout the world. Naval units were in the Mediterranean; flying corps were being built up in Egypt, India, Australia, England, and China. Technicians were working in supply depots and transportation services in Iran, Egypt, and the Red Sea area. Large contingents were manning bases along the supply routes to Australia and in the Atlantic from Iceland to the Caribbean.

Defense factories, army cantonments, shipyards busy on merchant marine or warship construction rapidly increased their facilities. By the end of June President Roosevelt revealed that in the previous month 4000 planes, 2000 pieces of artillery, and more than 100,000 machine guns had been produced. This prodigious war effort was of necessity influencing the life of the people in every direction. The manufacture of private automobiles had ended, dim-outs were in operation along the Pacific and Atlantic coasts, gasoline rationing and rigid rationing of tire sales restricted the use of automobiles. Mounting taxes, shortages in many commodities heretofore abundantly available, and the requirements of civilian defense became the lot of Americans within a few months after Pearl Harbor.

Basic issues of the war. The sacrifices and derangement of normal living routines were willingly accepted by a vast majority of American people. The reason was to be found in the basic meaning of the Second World War. What were the issues? What were the United States and her allies fighting for and fighting against? The most obvious issue was self-preservation. The United Nations were fighting to prevent three powers—Germany, Japan, and Italy—from securing world domination and with it the control of the trade and raw materials of the world, for their own use. But apart from self-preservation, the United Nations were also fighting against countries which championed a philosophy repugnant to their way of life. The United States, the British Commonwealth of Nations, and other states believed in the dignity and worth of the individual. In the Axis nations the state alone was

important. Such a philosophy denied to the individual religious freedom, voluntary participation in government, and freedom in thought and speech.

That the Axis powers, particularly Nazi Germany, gave allegiance to views that struck at the very heart of the humanistic tradition of western civilization was a fundamental fact. The Axis glorified war, ridiculed pacifism, and exalted martial Spartanism. Its militarism was conveniently tied to a super-race idea which rationalized the use of force, for force was considered the instrument that elevates nature's elect to the pedestal of world mastery.

Many people in the twenty-nine nations pledged to oppose the Axis realized there was much in the world before 1939 that had been illogical and unfair. They realized that the United Nations were not fighting to maintain and perpetuate a perfect world. But these men saw in an Axis triumph only an intensification of such old evils as militarism, excessive nationalism, and intolerance. Only by the defeat of Germany, Italy, and Japan could certain human values, already in existence, be preserved, strengthened, and made the basis for a better civilization after peace had been secured.

Summary

This chapter has shown how, in the early 1930's, efforts toward collective security were halted by a series of defeats. In the face of the rapidly growing military power of Germany and Italy, Great Britain and France seemed impotent, incapable of action. After Hitler's accession to power in 1933 a span of five years followed in which Germany succeeded in scrapping most of the remaining provisions of the Treaty of Versailles. This period of Revisionism, from 1933 to 1938, was followed by German attempts to achieve continental domination in Europe. Four factors largely explain Hitler's success during the period of Revisionism. First, Great Britain and France were unable to see eye to eye. British statesmen were inclined to believe that France was endeavoring to dominate Europe and that, in the long run, her policy of keeping Germany down could not be successful. Second, pacifist sentiments were very pronounced in both France and Great Britain. The average citizen in these countries was resolved that war should be avoided at all costs. This resolution enabled Hitler to succeed, because he realized that, although the democracies might threaten to use force, in the last analysis they could be made to back down. Third, Italy threw her strength on the side of the Third Reich. This move made it increasingly difficult for the democracies to oppose Hitler. Finally, influential elements in Great Britain were inclined to regard Germany as a buffer against Russia. Both German Nazism and Russian Communism were regarded with suspicion by British statesmen, but it was preferable—so they thought—to placate Germany so that she would destroy Russia. Out of these elements the policy of "Appeasement" was born, a policy which existed with full vigor from 1933 until Munich in 1938. Appeasement was scrapped early in 1939, when both Great Britain and France realized that the true intentions of the Hitler régime were not merely to rectify the injustices of Versailles but to dominate Europe and the world as well.

During the decade from 1930 to 1940 Europe was once more the scene of two great antagonistic camps—Great Britain and France on the one side and Germany and Italy on the other. This rivalry became a world-wide conflict when Japan became a member of the Axis. Gradually the world became divided into two hostile groups: the democratic powers and the totalitarian states.

War broke out in Europe in 1939. Beginning with the conquest of Poland, the war spread throughout Europe, into Africa, Asia, and the Far East. By the spring of 1941 the swastika flew over Norway, Denmark, Holland, Belgium, and France. Great Britain had survived an all-out bombing. Italy controlled Albania. Rumania and Bulgaria were German puppets. Greece and Yugoslavia had been crushed. In north Africa the Axis and British forces seesawed in the desert for control of Egypt and Suez. In the summer of 1941 the Nazi blitzkrieg descended on Russia but was soon slowed. The global nature of the war was indeed becoming more pronounced. For the first year of the war the United States tried to maintain a policy of neutrality; during the second year she tried to remain a nonbelligerent while sending all possible aid to Great Britain. By the summer of 1941 collaboration had reached the point of a Churchill-Roosevelt meeting resulting in the Atlantic Charter, which, though couched in general terms, contained the long-awaited statement of war aims. Conflicting interests with Japan in the Pacific area would probably have drawn the United States into the war sooner or later. But the unprovoked Japanese attack on Pearl Harbor catapulted the United States into full belligerency in December 1941.

The year 1942 brought the Japanese conquest of the Philippines, Java, and Burma with the consequent threat to Australia and India. The necessity of a global strategy was recognized by the establishment of a United Nations command in the Pacific and the creation of various joint boards for shipping and supply. While Japan was sweeping through the Far East, Germany launched two all-out attacks, one on Russia to gain the coveted Caucasus oil fields, the other in Libya to secure the British fleet base at Alexandria. As for the United States, by July 1 her participation was being increasingly felt on the far-flung battlelines of the Second World War.

The Russian Front

June 1942	German drive on Voronezh	
July-Sept.	Invasion of Caucasus region	Crusade for a second front
Aug.-Sept.	Siege of Stalingrad	Heroic defense of city
December	Russian offensive at Voronezh	German ring around Leningrad broken
Jan. 1943	Russian gains in Caucasus	End of menace to oil fields
	Russian victory at Stalingrad	Destruction of complete Axis army
February	Recapture of Kursk and Rostov	Germans in N Caucasus hemmed in
July	German summer campaign begins	
Aug.-Sept.	Russians take Orel and Belgorod	Greatest tank battle in history
	Red Army frees Smolensk	
Oct.-Nov.	Germans driven from Caucasus	Moscow Conference
	Kiev goes to Red Army	Ukraine rapidly being recaptured

Fighting in the Pacific

June 1942	Japanese attack Aleutians	Attu, Kiska invaded
July	Japanese land at Buna and Gona	Threat to Australia
August	Japanese advance toward Port Moresby	Allies bomb Buna, Lae, Salamaua
	Allied offensive in Solomons	Tulagi, Gavutu taken
Oct.-Feb. 1943	Guadalcanal in hands of U. S.	Great naval victory
	Japanese ousted from SW New Guinea	
May	Attu falls to Allies	
June	Americans land in S New Georgia	
August	Fall of Kiska; Munda captured	Menace to Alaska ended
September	Salamaua and Lae fall to Allies	
	Finschhafen taken by Allies	
Nov.-Dec.	Makin and Tarawa fall to Marines	

War in the Mediterranean

June 1942	British troops surrender at Tobruk	
August	Battle at el Alamein	
October	Beginning of new British offensive	Infantry plays great role
November	Americans under Eisenhower land	
	Morocco, Algiers, Oran fall to Allies	Darlan assumes civil administration
Nov.-Dec.	British occupy Tobruk, el Agheila	Scuttling of French fleet at Toulon
January		Casablanca Conference
March	Allied bombing of Sicily and S Italy	Air supremacy won by Allies
May	Bizerte, Tunis captured	End of Nazi resistance in Africa
		Roosevelt, Churchill in Washington
June	Surrender of Pantelleria	Fortress crushed by air power alone
July	Amphibious invasion of Sicily	Fall of Mussolini; Badoglio new premier
August	Messina falls to American troops	Mediterranean virtually an Allied lake
September	Italy surrenders unconditionally	Badoglio breaks with Axis
October	Italy declares war on Germany	Mussolini head of puppet régime

War in the Far East

June-July 1942	Japanese advance in southeast China	Crisis in India
	Capture of Hangchow-Nanchang railway	
	U. S. Army air force in China	Heavy raids on Japanese bases
	Japanese drives checked by Chinese	
August	Civil disobedience in India	Gandhi, Nehru in British custody
December	Failure of limited offensive against Japanese in Akyab attack	
March-Nov. 1943	Japanese blockade	Serious threat to Chinese economy
December	Battle for Changteh	

CHAPTER 7

Since Stalingrad

By the summer of 1942 the Second World War had been raging for three years. The actions were more widespread than ever, the fighting more intense, and the issues for which men died more fateful and clearcut. In July 1942 the armies of the United Nations everywhere were on the defensive, but a truly amazing transformation in the military fortunes of the war took place during the subsequent months. Events carried the United States and her allies from defense to offense, from imminent defeat to the growing prospect of victory.

The War in Retrospect, 1939-1942

Basic features of the war. In this study of the phases of the war since Stalingrad, it will be helpful to review the outstanding features of the global conflict thus far: (1) the surprising military strength of Russia; (2) the complete military and political collapse of France, and DeGaulle's efforts to rebuild it in exile; (3) the failure of Italian Fascism; (4) the astonishing striking power of Japan; (5) the pertinacity and fighting spirit of the British; (6) the inability of the Nazis to secure the co-operation of subjugated Europeans; (7) the rapidity of total war mobilization in the United States; (8) the unity existing between Latin and North America; (9) the growing importance of air power; and (10) the tremendous distances involved in transportation and supply for the Allies (see the maps, pages 194 and 195).

The military score. In summer, 1942, the score stood heavily against the Allies: (1) The Nazis in Russia had completed their conquest of the Crimea. (2) Hitler's Africa Corps stood poised in North Africa to deliver final blows and take Alexandria. (3) The Japanese were consolidating their positions in the Solomons and New Guinea. (4) They had taken possession of several Aleutian Islands, particularly Attu and Kiska. (5) Burma was in the hands of the Japanese. The danger of Japanese invasion of India was rendered more acute by the internal crisis in India. (6) China was again feeling the brunt of Japanese attack. Supplies from abroad could only trickle in.

193

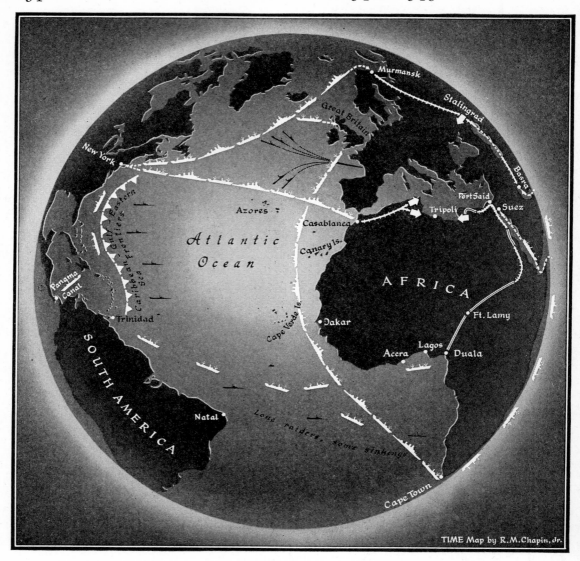

TIME Map by R.M.Chapin, Jr.

Crest of Axis Power

Russia: Hitler's objective. In 1942 there was still time for Hitler to strive for the prize which he had sought unsuccessfully in the summer of 1941—the defeat of Russia, which would leave him free to turn against Great Britain and the United States.

It seems apparent that the German objective was not to destroy the Russian armies. This had proved impossible in 1941. But the Nazi High Command did expect to cripple the Russians and, more important, cut off their vital war supplies. By striking in the south and securing the control of the Ukraine region and the Caucasus, the Germans would deprive the Russians of oil, iron, manganese, and great food-producing areas. Such a military success would also cut the Russian forces in two. At the same time such conquests, it was hoped, would rectify the acute Nazi shortage in raw materials, especially oil.

The Germans possessed almost overwhelming strength. The *Luftwaffe* was supreme in the air; the Nazi generals had at their disposal more than a million superbly equipped and

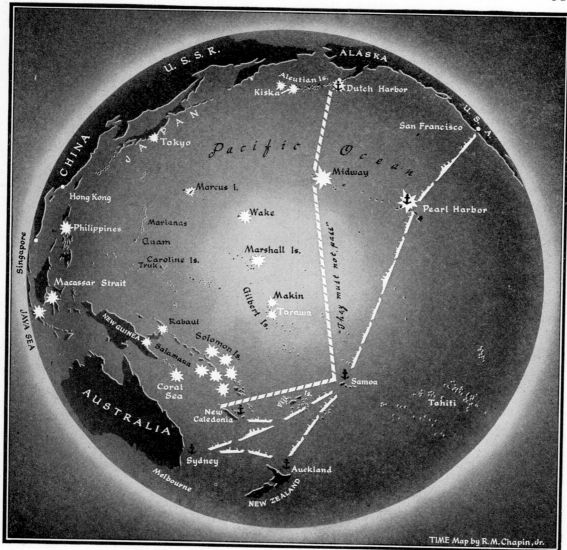

TIME Map by R.M.Chapin, Jr.

trained troops. Russia, on the other hand, began the 1942 campaign weakened by the loss of many important industrial regions and by the subjugation of one third of her population.

Drive on Voronezh. On June 28, 1942 the Germans began a heavy attack from Kursk. The main objective of Field Marshal Fedor Von Bock was the city of Voronezh on the Don River, the wheat center of the Don region and a railway center for Russian defense. The new offensive was based on what the Germans chose to call *Motpulk*, mechanized mass movement. The Nazi forces used heavier tanks, better mobile guns, and more dive bombers than they had in previous operations of their dreaded *Blitzkrieg*.

After two weeks of fighting, German forces reached the vicinity of Voronezh and managed to cross the Don River at several points. The Russian defenders of the city, under the direction of Marshal Timoshenko, kept the German pontoon bridges and rubber boats under heavy fire, and squadrons of Soviet *Stormovik* planes strafed the attacking troops. Although Von Bock's forces succeeded in breaking into the city on several occasions, their hold was precarious, and by July 16 Russian counterattacks began to push these

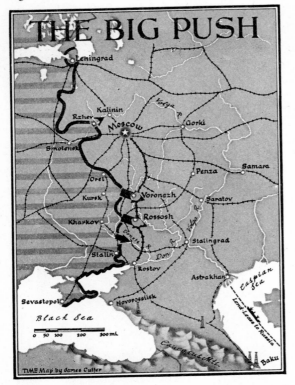

THE BIG PUSH

TIME Map by James Cutter

the Black Sea, captured Novorossiisk. This was Russia's last good naval base on the Black Sea. Pushing eastward along the fringes of the Caucasus Mountains, the victorious Germans drove the desperate Russian forces back toward the Caspian Sea and Baku. The latter part of September, however, witnessed a change in the fortunes of war. German tanks could not be used effectively in the rough terrain. October saw Von Bock's troops held just fifty miles from Grozny, and the rich prize of Baku had not been secured.

The epic of Stalingrad. While the Germans were carrying on their Caucasus campaign, which had been halted just short of its goal, other Nazi armies were striving to crush all Russian resistance in the Don River bend, to capture the important industrial city of Stalingrad, and to push east to Astrakhan on the Caspian. Stalingrad was a symbol of the first Five-Year Plan. From a mere country town it had grown into a great industrial city of 500,000. Stretching twenty miles along the Volga were its numerous factories, one of which produced more than 50,000 tractors a year. On August 22 a Nazi spearhead was established across the Don, and a week later an all-out assault was hurled against the Stalingrad defenses.

This battle was the fiercest of the war to date; more than one million men were locked in a gigantic struggle. On September 12, the Germans battered their way into the city, but the defense was carried on from street to street by both Soviet soldiers and civilians whose motto was "Ni shaya nazad" (Not one step back). Nazi *stukas* might pulverize buildings, but from cellars and crannies in the ruins Soviet troops fought on and held their own. Losses were estimated to run as high as 6000 for the Russians and 2000 for the Germans daily. On September 22 a grand assault paced by 200 tanks reached the center of the city but was finally forced to withdraw. By October, although the Germans still retained their possession of parts of the city, it was obvious that they did not have sufficient strength to effect its complete capture.

Stalingrad had become in World War II what Verdun was to the Allied cause in World War I: a symbol of indomitable courage.

The battle for Egypt. When the Nazi High Command launched its summer campaign against the Russian positions before Voronezh,

spearheads out of Voronezh, then a mass of ruins. To the south other German units had pushed eastward, reaching the Don about halfway between Voronezh and Stalingrad. It was this penetration into Russian territory enclosed within the great bend of the Don that menaced both the important city of Rostov and the entire Caucasus region to the south. (See the map above.)

Nazi push in Caucasus. Halted at Voronezh, Von Bock's soldiers opened a strong drive toward the eastern Black Sea area and the Caucasus. The rich iron and coal region of the Donets Basin was overrun first, and on July 23 the Nazi forces reached the outskirts of Rostov. Five days later the city fell to Von Bock. Pressing forward, the Nazis entered the northern Caucasus region. Baku, producing 70 per cent of all Russia's oil, was only 700 miles away. The Grozny and Maikop oil fields, contributing 18 per cent, were much nearer.

Advancing as much as eighteen miles a day the German armies captured Maikop on August 9. Most of its wells had already been destroyed by the Russian defenders. On September 6 the Nazis, edging down the east coast of

A Red Army soldier takes his stand behind a chest of drawers during fierce street fighting in Stalingrad. The soldiers are trying to dislodge Germans from houses in the background.

an equally important German drive was in progress on the borders of Egypt. Early in June the British had lost a crucial tank battle against Rommel's Africa Corps, and on June 21, 25,000 British troops were forced to surrender at Tobruk. Rommel raced ahead into Egypt, taking Matruh, while the retreating British forces under General Auchinleck prepared to make a stand at el Alamein. On this 35-mile front, with the Mediterranean guarding one flank and a marshy depression the other, Auchinleck's men halted Rommel's advance toward Alexandria, only 70 miles away.

Throughout July sporadic fighting was carried on in the desert. Neither side was strong enough to break through, and the whole outcome depended on the flow of supplies and reinforcements. The United States supplied ships to help send 50,000 British troops to Egypt, and hundreds of Sherman tanks from American armament plants were rushed around the southern tip of Africa to Egypt. Rommel contrived to get large forces from southern Italy, and Axis shipping landed much equipment in Africa.

In this battle of supply the small British island outpost of Malta was important as it menaced the Axis supply route. The Germans and Italians made every effort to destroy Malta; by the fall of 1942 it had suffered 2537 raids.

By the end of August, Rommel felt strong enough to stab again at the British troops. The British Eighth Army, meanwhile, had been strongly reinforced and placed under the direct command of Lieutenant General Bernard Montgomery. Auchinleck had been succeeded by General Harold Alexander, who assumed direction of all British forces in the Near East. On August 31 the Germans, assisted by Italian divisions, attacked the southern flank of Montgomery's men entrenched behind minefields, desert "boxes," and wire barricades. The attack penetrated twenty-five miles but was later forced back to its initial starting point. It was in this battle, at el Alamein, that United States tank crews had their first experience in desert fighting.

It is important to keep in mind that Rommel made his attack at the same moment when Von Bock was thrusting against Stalingrad. The two movements were in reality parts of gigantic pincers which, if successful, would advance toward each other from the north and south and squeeze out all United Nations resistance in the Caucasus and in the Middle East. The next Axis move could then be an advance toward India from the west, with the Japanese in a position to attack that country from conquered Burma.

Russian resistance at Voronezh and Stalingrad and the halt of Rommel at el Alamein ended for the time being the great summer drive of the Axis powers in the western theaters of war. But in this global struggle, thousands of miles away from the Nile or the Don other fighting of a decisive nature was taking place in the Pacific.

Japan halted in China. In China, Japanese armies in the late spring of 1942 attacked strongly in the southeast provinces. The aim was to secure control of important railways and to obtain the major air bases from which, otherwise, Japan might be bombed when adequate bomber forces arrived from the United States. Fear of such an attack had been active in Japanese quarters since the famous Doolittle raid on Tokyo and other cities on April 18, 1942. In June and July, the Japanese carried forward their advance. Capture of the important strip of railway between Hangchow and Nanchang brought closer the Japanese plan of establishing an all-rail communication route from Shanghai to Singapore. At the same time the Japanese secured a few important air bases.

The loss of the Burma route had practically closed China to the outside world. The most pressing need of the Chinese was for heavy artillery and airplanes, without which defeat in the long run seemed inevitable. A small American air force, the A.V.G.'s, or Flying Tigers, had rendered great assistance to China and Burma. In June 1942 it was announced that a new United States Army Air Force was to be established in China under the command of Brigadier General Claire L. Chennault. On July 6 a communiqué described the first operations of America's new air squadrons in China. Chennault's pilots frustrated a heavy bombing raid on the Chinese capital, Chungking, on July 27, and his bombers made heavy raids on the Japanese bases at Hong Kong, Hankow, Canton, and Foochow. The Japanese made determined efforts to destroy American air bases but were not successful and lost numerous planes. En-

couraged by the advent of this new air power, the Chinese struck back and checked the Japanese drives. The Japanese were driven from the vital Hangchow-Nanchang railway and from some of their recently won air bases.

The collapse of the Japanese offensive was puzzling to many military observers, as China's air power was weak and her armies lacked equipment. Some believed Japan failed because of a growing need for supplies and manpower in other war theaters, especially the South Pacific. The important thing, however, was that China after five years of war had been able to hold and then hurl back a determined Japanese offensive; and there was now prospect of more and more assistance from her allies, as the huge armament program of the United States got into high gear.

Crisis in India. Aid to China could hardly reach her unless India was held as a great base for military operations of the United Nations. From India, when Allied strength became sufficient, the reconquest of Burma could be undertaken and the lifeline to China reopened. And perhaps from India sufficient armies might be mustered not only to recapture Burma but to drive the Japanese out of Malaya and southeast Asia. In the spring of 1942, however, the Chinese cause was seriously menaced by the danger of internal collapse in India. Mohandas Gandhi pressed his demand for Indian independence from Great Britain with more vigor. Impressed by the successes of the Japanese in the Pacific, in Malaya, and in Burma, Gandhi apparently believed that before the Japanese were actually in a position to invade India from Burma the British troops and government officials should leave the country. The connection between India and Great Britain should be immediately severed. He argued, "The presence of the British in India is an invitation to Japan to invade India. Their withdrawal would remove the bait. Assume, however, that it does not, free India would be better able to cope with invasion. Unadulterated non-cooperation would then have full sway."[1] On April 27, 1942, Gandhi urged the Congress Party to adopt a resolution which demanded the evacuation of all foreign soldiers from Indian soil. India then would follow the policy of pacifism and attempt to negotiate with Japan. Gandhi argued in his resolution that "Britain is incapable of defending India. Japan's quarrel is not with India; she is warring against the British Empire." There were numerous Indians, however, who doubted whether moral force and passive resistance would have much influence upon the Japanese once they were inside India.

Gandhi's resolution of outright pacifism was rejected by the Congress, but its leaders decided to adopt his proposal for a program of civil disobedience if Britain would not withdraw immediately from the country. Further, Gandhi's ideas of negotiating with Japan were scrapped for a policy of a free India, once British control had been removed, "throwing all her great resources into the struggle against aggression of Nazism, Fascism, and Imperialism."[2] On August 8 the Congress Party endorsed a resolution demanding Britain's withdrawal from India, calling on all Indians to engage in a mass struggle on nonviolent lines. The following day Gandhi, Nehru, and about 200 other leading Indian nationalists were taken into custody by the British government. Rioting, sabotage, and strikes then followed in many parts of the country. Railway stations and lines in particular were destroyed. In general, however, the mass of people failed to respond to the call for mass civil disobedience. Several weeks elapsed before order was restored in the main centers of revolt.

The failure of Gandhi's mass movement was due in part to the belief in many circles of Indian public opinion that such a program with the Japanese ready to batter at the gates of India was suicidal. In particular Mohammed Jinnah, leader of the Indian Mohammedans, called Gandhi's demand fantastic and warned that he would cease to cooperate with the government if it gave in to the Congress. While Gandhi's Congress Party declined in influence the Moslem League, led by Jinnah, advanced. Known as Pakistan, Jinnah's plan called for the creation of a Moslem state separate from Hindu India.

Although some semblance of order had been restored, the situation remained quite unsatisfactory, and certainly pleasing to Japan. If all parties concerned—British, Hindus, and Mohammedans—had exhibited more moderation and the spirit of compromise, some solution might have been found. Even in certain British quarters there was a demand that America and China "should help to compose a quarrel which injures every one (of the United Nations)." The crisis in India posed an almost insuperable problem: how to satisfy Great Britain's determination to be responsible for defending India from Japanese invasion; how to meet the demand of the Congress Party for immediate independence; and how to reconcile the various opposing factions in India.

Japan's New Guinea campaign. Following the Japanese conquest of Burma, Malaya, and Bataan in the Philippines, and the Dutch East Indies, the number one question in the Southwest Pacific was: will Japan attack Australia? She seemed in a good position to embark on such an undertaking from bases at Rabaul in New Britain and Lae and Salamaua in New Guinea. The danger would be immediate if Japanese units succeeded in capturing Port Moresby, capital of Australian Papua in southwestern New Guinea. The Japanese were also strengthening their position in the Solomon Islands, notably on Guadalcanal, which pointed menacingly toward the United Nations' bases on New Hebrides and New Caledonia. The defense of these bases was essential to maintain the supply route from the United States to Australia.

With Port Moresby as their objective, Japanese landing parties were put ashore in July 1942 at Buna and Gona on the western side of the long tip of southern New Guinea. Their goal was only 120 miles away, but they would have to cross the mountains, follow a rough trail over a 7000-foot pass, before they reached it. Nevertheless the Japanese troops made good progress. Adept in jungle fighting and painted green for camouflage, the invaders advanced across the mountains and reached Kokoda by the first week of August. In the next month the Japanese had penetrated to within 34 miles of Port Moresby. Less success was achieved when they landed at a bay below Gona and Buna with the plan of streaking across southern New Guinea at its narrowest point. They were met by Australian troops; these would have annihilated them entirely if naval craft had not managed to evacuate a small remnant.

In view of the imminent menace to Port Moresby and later to Australia itself, General MacArthur concentrated all his available air power to disrupt the Japanese attack. Heavy bombing raids were made against Buna, Lae, and Salamaua. The lines of supply of the advancing Japanese column were heavily damaged. Without adequate supplies and reinforcements the Japanese strength diminished, and counterattacks forced a Japanese retreat as September ended. A threat to western Australia via southern New Guinea was ended.

Struggle for Guadalcanal. The first offensive of the United Nations in the Pacific was undertaken in the southern Solomons. On the night of August 7 a combined force of United States naval units and transports moved against the islands of Guadalcanal, Tulagi, and Gavutu. Japanese positions were first bombarded by the warships and bombed from the air. Then marines in steel-walled barges were landed on the beach. Tanks, tractors, light cannon, and machine guns were quickly set on shore. In Tulagi and Gavutu the fighting was fierce but brief. Small Japanese detachments fought to the last man. On the island of Guadalcanal the Japanese were more numerous. With great difficulty the marines succeeded in obtaining control of a small area seven miles wide along the beach, which included a vital air field.

During the months of August, September, and October fighting on the land, on the sea, and in the air continued with unparalleled ferocity at Guadalcanal. On the night of August 9 a Japanese naval squadron surprised an Allied force and sank four cruisers guarding the troops and supply ships unloading in the harbor. In the days that followed, Japanese planes bombed the marines' beachhead continuously, and light naval forces bombarded their positions from the sea. A fortnight later a Japanese task force was driven off by American air power with the loss to the Japanese of a small carrier and damage to other vessels. In mid-September the Japanese again made a determined attack with warships, supported by a simultaneous offensive by the Japanese troops on Guadalcanal. Marine positions were penetrated, but the attack was finally repulsed. During this action the United States lost the modern aircraft carrier *Wasp*, by submarine attack.

October saw no diminution in the struggle. The Japanese succeeded in landing reinforcements, and naval action off Guadalcanal was continuous. In one battle—the battle of Cape Esperance—a United States task force with the loss of one destroyer disposed of two heavy

THE U.S. ATTACKS

TIME Map by R.M.Chapin,jr.

cruisers, one light cruiser, and three destroyers. In another—the battle of Santa Cruz Islands— United States forces sank two destroyers and inflicted damage on two battleships, two carriers, and four cruisers. The United States' loss, however, was heavy: a destroyer and the carrier *Hornet*.

The marines on land were proving more than a match for the Japanese, although the manner of fighting was new to them; it was a return to the fighting by stealth which characterized the French and Indian War of the eighteenth century. The battle was waged in dense jungle country. Here the Japanese waited in dense grass or strapped high as snipers in coconut palms. No American soldier in previous wars had ever met such an opponent. It was kill or be killed. But the fate of Guadalcanal hinged not so much on land action as on events that might take place on the sea. The naval losses sustained by the United States, especially in aircraft carriers, had been serious, and if command of the sea was obtained by Japan, defeat on Guadalcanal was a foregone conclusion.

Crusade for a second front. During the fateful summer of 1942 the people of the United Nations staggered but somehow maintained their fortitude and belief in final victory. This period of crisis was characterized by an insistent demand in many quarters for more energetic measures against Nazi Germany. This became a veritable crusade for the Russian concept of a second front, an invasion against Nazi Europe to relieve the desperate plight of the Russians.

The only offensive, and that of a limited character, had been the spectacular British Commando raid on the French coast, at Dieppe. Resistance was unexpectedly strong, and the Commandos, mostly Canadians, withdrew after suffering heavy casualties. This was a foretaste of what hazards the invasion of Nazi Europe involved.

Controversy over a second front, however, largely subsided for a while (see p. 215) with a new turn of events late in October. In Russia, North Africa, the South Pacific, and the Aleutian Islands, the tide of victory changed rapidly in favor of the United Nations.

Emergence of Allied Strength

British offensive in North Africa. On October 23 the British Eighth Army assumed the offensive. Its commander, General Montgomery, announced: "For three years we have been trying to plug holes all over the world. Now, thank God, that period is over." On a forty-mile front at el Alamein an artillery barrage was opened up that rocked buildings in Alexandria, seventy miles away. Sappers advancing through the German mine fields cleared a corridor for the infantry, who were then followed by the tanks. By November 6 the German forces with their Italian allies were in full retreat westward across the Egyptian border.

As the defeated forces fled, they were harried from the air by continuous bombardment. Supply trucks, tanks, and columns of troops were blasted by waves of British and American bombers. Many German troops of the Africa Corps were captured, and six divisions of Italians were abandoned by Rommel. Advancing into Libya, the British Eighth Army captured Tobruk, the best port between Alexandria and Tunis. As November ended, the British had occupied and passed beyond Bengasi and were half way to their final objective of Tripoli. Fortified by American planes, Canadian trucks, and immense supplies from Great Britain, the army of Montgomery pursued the scattered remnants of the Africa Corps. The Eighth Army showed great power, organization, and mobility.

During the first half of December there was a lull in the fighting as the British army advanced on el Aghéila, a natural defense position protected by wide salt-flats. Here Rommel was expected to make a stand after retreating 700 miles from el Alamein. This strong position, however, was evacuated by the German forces, and by December 21 Rommel's decimated battalions were again in full retreat. On January 23 the Eighth Army entered Tripoli, thus capturing the last remnant of the Italian empire; Rommel's army crossed into French Tunisia and barricaded itself in the Mareth Line, a defensive position originally built by the French on the Tunisian border. Other German forces were already in Tunisia. How they came to be there will constitute part of the story of the next phase of the North African front.

Allied invasion of French North Africa.
Early in November, American troops from a
huge convoy of 850 ships were landed at various points along the French North African
coast. (Study the map above.) The troops
were under the unified command of Lieutenant General Dwight D. Eisenhower. Their
immediate objectives were Algiers, Oran, and
Casablanca. The operation was brilliantly
carried out in coordination with the British
Eighth Army's offensive against Rommel in
Egypt. Morocco and Algeria were invaded.
Tunisia, it was expected, could be quickly
overrun following the occupation of these territories. French North Africa, administered by
Vichy officials, was groaning under the heavy
demands made upon it for raw materials and
food stuffs by the Nazis. Everything, therefore,
was done to assure the French people that the
forces of the United Nations came not as con-
querors but as deliverers.

On the whole, resistance was half-hearted
and the casualties of the American expedition
were light. Algiers fell in one day, and Admiral Darlan, a high Vichy official, was captured. At Oran the fighting was more bitter,
but hostilities ceased on November 10. Casablanca also saw fierce fighting and a French
fleet put out of action. On November 11
Admiral Darlan ordered all commanders in
French North Africa to cease hostilities. He
then assumed the civil administration of the
territory in the name of Marshal Pétain, head
of the French state. The new régime was accepted by the American military authorities,

since Darlan for his part was now ready to
cooperate with the United Nations. There
were many people in Great Britain and the
United Nations who resented this "deal" with
a Vichy official who had been notoriously anti-
British and in favor of collaboration with Germany, but authorities insisted it was necessary
on the grounds of expediency. Explaining his
action, Admiral Darlan stated that in 1940 he
believed an Axis victory was possible; in 1941
he believed no victory could be achieved by
either side; but at the end of 1942 he was convinced that Germany would lose.[3] To facilitate military cooperation with General Eisenhower, Darlan appointed General Henri
Giraud as commander of the French North
African forces.

Repercussions of the invasion of Africa.
The response of Hitler to the occupation of
French North Africa was swift. On November 11 German troops took over what had
been known as Unoccupied France, and the
fiction of the Vichy government as an independent administration was, at long last, practically ended. At the same time Italian forces
took over the French island of Corsica.

There was still another repercussion of the
North African invasion. Contrary to the Armistice of 1940, Hitler decided to reach for the
French fleet, lying in the harbor of Toulon.
Just before daybreak, November 27, Nazi
armored units overpowered the French guards
and raced to the docks. From the flagship of
Vice Admiral Jean de Laborde was flashed the
command: "Carry out Order B." Immediately

This picture, smuggled out of France, shows part of the French fleet sinking to the bottom of Toulon Harbor. The scuttling of the French fleet was one of the most dramatic incidents of the war.

ship after ship exploded and settled to the bottom. Over sixty warships were destroyed, including the famous *Dunkerque, Strasbourg,* and *Algerie.* Only four submarines succeeded in escaping from Toulon. General de Gaulle, referring to the heroism of the French crews, among which loss of life was heavy, stated that in their supreme test the sailors had followed the course of true patriotism, that "in one brief moment they saw through the odious veil of lies which since June 1940 hung before their eyes."

Climax in Africa: Tunisia. Two days following the first American landings, the British First Army under Lieutenant General Kenneth A. Anderson disembarked at Algiers and started a rapid advance into Tunisia. It was expected that the Tunisian campaign would be an all-British affair. Anderson's First Army would sweep to Bizerte and Tunis from the west while Montgomery's Eighth was advancing from the east in the direction of the Tunisian border. If Anderson had been successful, the Tunisian campaign would have been over in a few weeks. As it was it took six months of savage fighting. Immediately following the American occupation of North Africa, the German High Command commandeered every type of air transport available in southern Europe and flew thousands

of soldiers to Tunisia, where the French could offer little resistance. Lines of communication from Bizerte to Sicily were only 200 miles, and over this short stretch of water tanks, artillery, and troops were ferried.

The First Army entered Tunisia on November 17 and two days later contact was made with the Germans. The British were hindered by lack of airfields and the unusually heavy rains, the heaviest in several years. By December, Anderson's troops had reached a point about a dozen miles from Tunis; but the Germans, who by this time outnumbered the British in men and had the advantage of operating from all-weather airfields and shorter supply lines, counterattacked and drove them back. For the next few months the line of battle in northern Tunisia remained fixed, with intermittent sparring for important positions in the hilly country.

Until the Eighth Army of Montgomery could break through the Mareth Line, the combined forces of von Arnim in northern Tunisia and Rommel could concentrate superior strength on the Allied armies, even though the latter had been reinforced by French and American contingents. The Germans struck first at the French and inflicted heavy losses. Early in February Rommel attacked American positions and drove through

Faid Pass. His next objective was Kasserine Pass, and he gained this. In the engagement the American forces lost 100 tanks and four times the casualties suffered by the Germans. Rommel was then in a position to outflank the First Army in the north. Instead, because all available reinforcements were sent to aid the Allies, Rommel was checked and then forced to retreat from the Kasserine Pass.

The construction of new air bases, improvement of lines of communication, a change of generals, and arrival of vast quantities of artillery and tanks began to turn the tide in March. United States forces regained most of the ground lost in February, and the British drove through the Mareth Line. Command of the air passed to the armies of General Eisenhower. While von Arnim's and Rommel's fighter planes were knocked out of the sky over Tunisia, Allied bombers destroyed Axis shipping that was bringing supplies from Sicily. Sweeps were also made over targets in Sicily and southern Italy, and harbor installations and air fields were destroyed.

The climax to the Tunisian campaign came in April. During this final phase, American, British, and French troops attacking from the east, west, and south relentlessly forced the Axis divisions back to the sea. American soldiers performed magnificently in capturing vital points in victories that helped soften the sting of their defeat at Kasserine. Unchallenged in the air, Allied fighters and bombers broke up and shattered Axis resistance. In one day Allied planes sank twenty-five Axis ships, unloaded 1,250,000 pounds of bombs, and made 2500 sorties. Bizerte and Tunis were captured simultaneously on May 8. A remnant of the Axis armies hoped to make a stand on the peninsula east of Tunis, but Allied troops broke into the promontory before lines of defense could be set up. There was no prospect of a German imitation of the British at Dunkirk. Allied naval craft patrolled the coastline of Tunis and sank or captured any boats that attempted to evacuate troops. On May 12 Allied headquarters announced the end of all organized Axis resistance.

One of the most astonishing features of the final round in the Battle of Tunisia was the sudden capitulation of the Axis forces. They surrendered by the thousands, not emulating their brethren at Stalingrad, who just four months before had fought to the end when

Everyone seems to be having a good time as these members of the R.A.F., somewhere in North Africa, relax during time off from the war. Note the bullet holes in the box on the far right.

surrounded by Russian armies. To some observers this meant the Nazi soldier was losing his early blind faith in ultimate victory; he no longer believed in useless sacrifice. But Germans in Africa had fought fiercely until it became apparent that U. S. preponderance in planes and tanks was overwhelming. The military box score in Tunis was 266,000 Axis prisoners, with casualties estimated at some 323,-000. To these figures must be added the prisoners taken in the Eighth Army's victory over Rommel in Egypt. As for the Allies their casualties were less than 70,000.

Summing up the Tunisian campaign, and the other African campaigns which preceded it, Winston Churchill, speaking before Congress on May 19, declared:

"All the vast territories from Madagascar to Morocco, from Cairo to Casablanca, from Aden to Dakar, are under British, American, or French control. One continent at least has been cleansed and purged forever from Fascist or Nazi tyranny. The African excursions of the two dictators have cost their countries in killed and captured 950,000 soldiers."

Defense to offense in Russia. While Nazi and Fascist divisions were being defeated and captured by the thousands in North Africa, momentous events were taking place along the 1500-mile Russian front. It will be recalled that in October 1942 the *Wehrmacht* of Hitler was prevented only by the slightest margin from capturing the key city of Stalingrad and from obtaining the precious oil of the Caucasus. During their great summer drive the Nazis had lost many men and used up vast quantities of equipment. Hitler's determination not to withdraw from Stalingrad, despite the warnings of his generals, placed his armies in an extended bulge which was vulnerable to Soviet flank attack. Furthermore, any successful Russian attack from Stalingrad southwestward to Rostov would menace the German forces in the Caucasus with encirclement. In the event of large-scale fighting, the Nazi High Command would find it difficult to rush in reinforcements—especially aircraft—because of the gravity of the situation in Egypt, where Rommel was retreating before the advancing Allied armies.

Such were the circumstances when the Russians began a savage offensive on November 19. Soviet divisions pressed forward northwest and southwest of Stalingrad. New reserves had come up quietly to the front and crossed the Volga at night. The prime objective of the offensive was to surround and destroy 300,000 Germans around Stalingrad. In three days the Russian troops drove fifty miles to the Don and sped westward another ninety miles. In little more than a week 66,000 prisoners were taken, together with much booty, such as heavy guns and tanks.

Another Russian attack was opened west of Moscow. At this point the Nazis held a menacing salient only 130 miles from the Russian capital. The two key fortified German points in this area were Rzhev and Vyazma. The second offensive, therefore, was directed against Rzhev. This powerful Nazi position, or hedgehog as it was termed, was by-passed, surrounded, and its 75,000 defenders threatened with extinction.

In mid-December a third Russian offensive broke on the Voronezh front. Spearheads pushed southwestward and surrounded a strong German position. The strategy of this drive was to make a junction with other Soviet divisions pushing southwest of Stalingrad. A closing of the pincers would trap large numbers of the enemy in the bend of the River Don, would doom the Nazi army before Stalingrad, and at the same time menace Rostov. While Nazi troops attempted to hold their own around Stalingrad, at Rzhev, and southwest of Voronezh, two additional offensives were initiated at the extreme ends of the eastern front. In the far north a determined effort was made to break the German ring around Leningrad. This was accomplished in January when a narrow corridor was punched through to the long-beleaguered city. At the same time Russian armies northwest of Rzhev exerted pressure in the direction of the old Latvian border. At the other end of the battle line, far to the south, a Russian offensive drove against the Nazi positions in the Caucasus. Early in January considerable progress was being made northeast of the important Grozny oil area. Russian forces also edged their way north along the Black Sea in the direction of the Sea of Azov.

January 1943 was the most disastrous month so far in the war for the Nazis. All along the eastern front the dearly won German gains of the last summer were being nullified. In the desperate engagements the Rus-

RUSSIAN SEESAW

TIME Map by R. M. Chapin, Jr.

sians were aided by their "General Winter." Skis were placed on much equipment, the troops wore long white robes and capes, and above all, the men were warmly clad. On the other hand the severe winter disrupted Nazi communications and found German troops insufficiently clad in spite of the fact that furs and blankets had been confiscated for the Russian front from conquered territories.

It was in January that the Nazi forces before Stalingrad, hemmed in between the Don and Volga rivers, were trapped. On the eighth of this month the Soviets demanded that the encircled troops surrender. They refused. Two days later the final drive began which was to hack the Nazi divisions to shreds. By the end of the month only a few isolated pockets of Nazi resistance remained in Stalingrad. On the last day of January the Nazi commander, General von Paulus, surrendered with a pitiful remnant of his men. Since November 19, when the Stalingrad battle had begun, 300,000 Nazis had been killed or captured. Stalingrad in October 1942 had become the symbol for unexcelled fortitude and heroism for the United Nations; by the following January it had also become the grave for an immense Axis army and the first real catastrophe suffered by the Nazis.

The various offensives undertaken by the

Russian High Command in addition to the mopping-up activities at Stalingrad were pushed vigorously throughout January. The Caucasus was being rid of Nazi armies, the bend of the Don where there had been such savage fighting in the summer of 1942 was completely cleared of them, and a new offensive was launched directly east of Voronezh toward Kursk and Kharkov. During February several strategic Nazi positions were taken, including Kursk, an important city midway between Voronezh and Kiev; Rostov, the city which was the only land corridor through which Nazi forces in the north Caucasus could escape; and Kharkov, the third largest city in the Soviet Union and key to the whole rich industrial Donets Basin.

These conquests proved to be the high point of the Russian winter campaign. Other gains were made. The danger to Moscow was eased by the capture of Rzhev and Vyazma, and penetrations were made south of Leningrad. The last crucial battle of the winter took place west of Kharkov. Here Russian divisions pushed toward the Dnieper River in a drive that threatened to entrap German forces strung along the Sea of Azov. Success in this region of the southern Ukraine would also deprive the Third Reich of any opportunity of utilizing its rich resources: water power of the Dnieper, the vast grainfields, and the coal of the Donets Basin. The Nazi High Command determined, therefore, to throw back this Russian offensive at any cost. About 325,000 reserve troops, presumably assembled originally for a new Nazi offensive, were now thrown into the battle by the Germans, together with a tank force estimated to be 1000 strong. An unusually early spring thaw hindered the Russians, whose lines of communications were extended in comparison with their enemy's. The result for the Russians was a serious setback; outnumbered, they fell back. Kharkov fell again to the Germans on March 16. With difficulty Russian troops were finally able to hold the German offensive along the Donets River.

If the high hopes of forcing the German armies out of the southern Ukraine were dashed by this counterstroke, it yet remains true that the Russian winter campaign of 1942-1943 was a brilliant achievement and one which cost the Axis dearly in men and materiel. There has always been much controversy concerning statistics of losses and gains on the Russian front. Even if the following Russian figures, given at the end of March, be substantially discounted, the score remains very impressive: 850,000 men killed, 343,000 captured, 183,000 square miles of land liberated, 5000 planes destroyed, 9000 tanks put out of action or captured, and 20,000 guns seized or destroyed. The Russian offensive may be credited with the following major achievements: (1) destruction of a complete Axis army at Stalingrad, (2) capture of Rzhev and Vyazma, potential bases for a German offensive against Moscow, (3) breaking of the Nazi cordon around Leningrad, and (4) removal of the serious menace to the Caucasus oil fields.

May brought little change in the positions along the Russian front from Leningrad to Rostov. While the spring thaws were taking place, both sides waited for the ground to harden and mustered their reserves. Most observers in the United Nations were of the belief that Hitler would make another supreme bid for victory in Russia in the early summer of 1943.

Japan turned back in the Solomons. In the Solomons, as we have seen, desperate fighting both on land and sea in October left the issue still largely in doubt. Another crisis came in mid-November with the most determined Japanese effort up to then to conquer the American beachhead on Guadalcanal. A large Japanese fleet of transports was assembled at the bases of Rabaul and Buin. Another fleet of fighting craft, which included 2 battleships, 4 cruisers, and 10 destroyers, sailed from the base of Truk and made for Guadalcanal. The Japanese strategy was to destroy the U. S. fleet and thus enable the transports to land their troops unopposed from the sea. The battle was joined just after midnight, November 13. The American fleet commanded by Rear Admiral Daniel Callaghan audaciously rushed between two Japanese ship columns. In this melee the U. S. cruisers and destroyers engaged Japanese battleships at close range. One battleship was so badly damaged that it sank by morning. The *U. S. S. San Francisco*, flagship and spearhead of the attack, was severely damaged, and Rear Admiral Callaghan and the captain were killed on her bridge.

The fighting continued until the morning of November 15. For the first time American battleships tried their striking power against Japanese sea power. One of America's new battleships, the *South Dakota*, proved her worth by sinking three Japanese cruisers at long range. Despite the absence of carriers, which left them with no protection from attacks by United States land-based planes, the Japanese persisted in trying to land men from their transports. The result was a field day for the American air forces and the almost complete annihilation of the Japanese convoy. In this decisive battle the Japanese losses were: 2 battleships, 8 cruisers, 6 destroyers, 8 transports, and 4 cargo ships. American losses were 2 light cruisers and 7 destroyers. This victory was an outstanding achievement not only for the American officers and men who so well turned back the Japanese threat but also for Admiral William F. Halsey, commander of the U. S. naval forces in the South Pacific. Guadalcanal was now "saved." The balance of naval power had been tipped to the American side.

Failing by frontal attack to regain Guadalcanal, the Japanese for the time being resorted to swift night convoys which landed small bodies of troops on the beaches of the island. On the last day of November the night convoy was intercepted. One United States cruiser was sunk; the Japanese loss was heavy—2 cruisers, 4 destroyers, and 2 transports. In all, 12,000 Japanese troops were killed. During the first week of February the Japanese, realizing that the game was up on Guadalcanal, switched from trying to infiltrate reinforcements to the island to evacuating some of its personnel. For a week at least a dozen air battles and motor torpedo-boat engagements took place in which an American cruiser was sunk and several Japanese destroyers were lost. The objective of evacuating the Guadalcanal force only partially succeeded. By February 10 all organized resistance on the island had ceased.

On this small patch of land, only 100 miles long, bitter fighting had raged for six months. The Japanese had fought to "save their face" and also to prevent the United States from securing what would probably become a strategic springboard for a great offensive against Japanese strongholds in the South Pacific. The losses sustained by American forces, especially the navy, were heavy, but the Japanese had suffered much more. Their losses in the entire campaign were estimated to be: 166

Battle-weary U. S. Marines plod their way through the fire-blacked remains of a captured village on Guadalcanal. Some of the bloodiest fighting of the war took place on this island.

warships and transports, 800 planes, and at least 60,000 men.

Japan checked in New Guinea. In the narrow peninsula in southwestern New Guinea the Japanese were retreating over the mountains as fast as they had advanced in their original drive on Port Moresby. A widespread air offensive under the command of Lieutenant General George C. Kenney was undertaken by the Allies. Heavy bombing attacks were carried out against such important Japanese bases as Rabaul, Lae, Salamaua. These prevented further Japanese reinforcements from reaching the New Guinea coast in the vicinity of Buna. A gigantic job of air transportation was carried out under Lieutenant General Kenney's direction. American troops from their bases in Australia were flown 600 miles to New Guinea. Eighteen thousand were then ferried by air over the mountains. As the Japanese were pressed down from the crest of the mountains, they fought stubbornly to keep from being pushed into the sea between their two strong points of Buna and Gona.

Australian and American airmen brought in artillery, jeeps, and even a field hospital accommodating 250 beds. An average of a thousand tons of supplies was carried to the jungle battlefield by air each week.

General MacArthur arrived in New Guinea in November to direct personally the operations, which were now reaching the crucial stage. In the first part of December both Buna and Gona were captured. Early the next month all Japanese resistance in southwestern New Guinea had been rooted out. The fighting there surpassed in savagery even that on Guadalcanal. Around Buna and Gona in the thick jungle the Japanese had a web of trenches and machine-gun nests which had to be taken one by one. One correspondent observed that nowhere in the world at that time were American soldiers engaged in such desperate, merciless, bitter, bloody fighting.

The naval victory in November, the mopping up of the last remnants of Japanese resistance on Guadalcanal in February, and the ousting of the Japanese from southwestern

New Guinea ended a phase of the war in the South Pacific in which the United Nations had, on the whole, the better of the fighting. But no decisive victory had been won which guaranteed the supremacy of the United Nations in the South Pacific. The Japanese might again try to recover Guadalcanal, might set in motion an offensive against southwestern New Guinea. Even if this were not done, if the offensive rested with the forces of General MacArthur, there would likely be desperate fighting as the fleets and armies of the United Nations pushed northward against Lae, Rabaul, Truk, and other Japanese strongholds.

Reversal of roles in the Aleutians. From October 1942 to May 1943 important action was taking place in the North Pacific, fully six thousand miles from the Solomon Islands. In June 1942, when Japanese aggression in the Pacific was at high crest, the American people were disturbed to learn that Japanese forces had been landed on Attu and Kiska, islands in the Aleutian group. Wake Island and the Philippines were remote, far removed from America proper, but the occupation of Kiska and Attu was a different matter. The Japanese were coming dangerously close to the North American mainland.

Meanwhile careful and secret preparations were being made by the United States High Command to stage an offensive in the Aleutians. Large quantities of equipment were sent north to Alaskan bases. To keep the general public at home and also, of course, the Japanese from knowing what was coming, this project of Alaskan supply was dubbed the "Blair Packing Company." In August American troops began round one in the Aleutian battle by landing on Adak Island some 200 miles from Kiska. A fighter base was immediately set up at Adak. Round two followed, in which American planes kept up a constant bombing of Kiska throughout the fall months. In January another round was completed when United States troops occupied Amchitka, an island in the Rat group of the Aleutians. This gave a base only sixty miles from Kiska.

The fourth round in the Aleutian campaign was started on May 11 and lasted for three weeks. During this period the island of Attu was captured and practically its entire Japanese garrison was annihilated. The Attu victory made almost inevitable the fall of

Kiska, the last Japanese base in the long island chain. This island was now outflanked; Attu is 172 miles west, and Amchitka, 63 miles east. Another significant result of the reconquest of Attu was that the role of menacing invader in the Aleutians had been reversed. Instead of the Japanese looking toward the Alaskan mainland, the Americans now looked toward Paramoshiri, the nearest Japanese naval base.

The burden on China. From the fall of 1942 to the spring of 1943 the general trend of the war in Russia, in the South and North Pacific, and in the Mediterranean was favorable to the United Nations. In two main areas of the global struggle, however, no clear-cut victories had been registered by the United Nations, and the Japanese still enjoyed an unchallenged strategic initiative. These areas were China and the India-Burma theater.

In the world conflict the United Nations between October 1942 and April 1943 had concentrated mainly upon the Axis powers in the west. Some serious setbacks had been inflicted upon Japan, but these operations had been designed only to keep open the supply lines of the United Nations and to forestall any growing menace to the safety of Australia. While such strategy brought success in general, it placed a heavy burden upon war-weary China.

China continually felt the offensive power of the Japanese invaders as they stabbed here and there trying to uncover a weak link in the

Chinese chain of resistance. The scattered Japanese drives lacked force, however, and made only limited gains. Valuable assistance to the armies of Chiang Kai-shek was given by the American air force under Chennault.

While China heroically maintained an effective resistance on the battlefield, disquieting developments in the spring of 1943 were apparent. There was natural impatience over the failure of Great Britain and the United States to send large-scale aid to the Chinese theater, and criticism of the United Nations' strategy of defeating Germany first. On the Chinese domestic front the Japanese blockade had resulted in a serious scarcity of all goods. Said Mrs. Wellington Koo, wife of the Ambassador to Britain, "China is nearer collapse on the economic front than at any other time dur-

ing the course of the war." Notwithstanding her serious internal problems China continued to resist; during her long struggle with Japan, resistance to what appeared hopeless odds had become almost a national instinct. As Madame Chiang Kai-shek put it: "From five and a half years of experience we are convinced it is the better part of wisdom not to accept failure ignominiously, but to risk it gloriously."

The fate of China was largely bound up with events in the India-Burma area. The Burma Road, artery of Chinese supplies, had not been reopened after the Japanese overran it in the spring of 1942. A Japanese invasion of India in the fall of 1942 seemed likely. But losses in the South Pacific halted such an offensive and, further, under the direction of Sir Archibald Wavell a large army had been assembled on the Burma-India border. This force was largely Indian, reinforced by British troops and American air units.

During the winter of 1942-1943 heavy and constant air raids were carried out from India on Japanese installations in Burma. In retaliation the Japanese raided the great Indian city of Calcutta and other points, but in general, air superiority was maintained by the Allies. So improved were the defenses of India by December 1942 that Wavell essayed a limited offensive against the Japanese. The objective was the important port of Akyab on the Gulf of Bengal. After a promising start this offensive bogged down and initial gains were lost to the Japanese at heavy cost to the British. As in China, the striking power of the United Nations was not sufficiently strong to challenge the Japanese.

Pattern for Victory

Conferences and action. In the latter part of May 1943 the war leaders of Britain and the United States met in Washington to survey a brightening panorama. This was the fifth meeting of President Roosevelt and Prime Minister Churchill. Four months earlier the two chief executives had met at Casablanca in North Africa for a conference which resulted in the famous "unconditional surrender" formula for the Axis nations.

Following the conference unusual Allied activity was reported in the Mediterranean area. On May 30, 300 United States planes bombed Naples and objectives at the tip of the

Italian peninsula. Early in June, air attacks and naval bombardment by units of the British fleet commenced against Pantelleria, a small fortified Italian island between Tunisia and Sicily. In all, 3500 tons of bombs were dropped on the naval base. On the eighteenth day of the siege, following three Allied ultimatums, the white flag was hoisted and the Italian commander signaled, "Beg surrender through lack of water." This was the first time in history that a major fortress had been crushed completely by the sole use of air power. In a few days three Italian islands near Pantelleria surrendered.

ROUTES
TO
BERLIN

TIME Map by R.M.Chapin, Jr.

Suspense in Europe. Throughout June 1943 the entire world of the United Nations was in suspense, while the Axis countries were on edge from "invasion jitters."

In the face of an Allied invasion that might come from England the Nazis hesitated to commit too many troops in a Russian offensive. However, the growing might of the

Reich's other foes demanded that Russia be crushed while there was yet time. The German High Command was forced, therefore, to launch a summer offensive against Russia on the fifth of July. Four days later the Allies began to invade—not Germany's Atlantic bastion, but the Italian island of Sicily.

Invasion of Sicily. The first Allied soldiers to reach Sicily were American paratroopers, whose assignment was to knock out pillboxes, seize airfields, and spread confusion back of the Axis lines. While the paratroopers were carrying out their tasks, a huge armada of 3266 ships left the coast of North Africa and began to disembark troops about 3 a.m., the morning of July 10. Battleships, cruisers, destroyers, transports, and special landing boats were used in the greatest amphibious invasion in all history. Within 48 hours, 80,000 men had landed on Sicilian beaches, together with 7000 vehicles, 300 tanks, and 700 guns.

The invasion was directed at the southern shore of Sicily, with the American Seventh Army forming the left wing, Canadians in the center, and the British Eighth Army on the right flank. The initial landings were accom-

On the lookout for enemy snipers, an American reconnaissance unit marches through smoke from burning buildings in captured Messina.

plished with little loss and beachheads were quickly consolidated. Patton's men were met by a fierce tank assault which almost succeeded in driving them into the sea. Desperate resistance and the arrival of heavy guns saved the day. Another large factor was the gunfire from Allied warships that went near shore to blast German tanks. Following this success Patton's men began to knife inland, fighting their way to the northern shore. To the east the British and Canadian forces pushed forward along the east coast but met a stone wall, for the moment, at Catania. Here the Axis defense line was supported by towering Mt. Etna, from which guns could command the Catanian plain below. After eight days of fighting, more than 3000 square miles had been conquered, 200 miles of coast cleared, and 30,000 prisoners taken. In a brilliant maneuver General Patton's army cut Sicily in two and captured Palermo, the island's capital, on the northern coast. All Axis troops to the west were now cooped in a small area. Leaving adequate forces to mop up these nests of resistance, the American army then drove east along the north coast, with Messina as the objective. Resistance of the Italians and Germans was confined to the northeastern tip of Sicily, with Italy only two miles behind them across a narrow strait.

The Sicilian catastrophe had a chilling effect on Italian morale. It grew worse after a mass raid on Rome's transportation system was carried out on July 19 by 500 U. S. planes.

Fall of Mussolini. In desperation Mussolini and Hitler conferred about Italy's plight. Taking advantage of Italian discouragement and war weariness, President Roosevelt and Prime Minister Churchill offered peace, declaring: "The time has come for you to decide whether Italians shall die for Mussolini and Hitler—or live for Italy, and for civilization." On July 25 a startled world heard the news that Mussolini had been removed from office by the king and that Marshal Pietro Badoglio had been appointed premier. A long string of defeats—in Greece, Abyssinia, Libya, and Sicily—had finally toppled the "Sawdust Caesar" who had prated so long about the nobility of war. The fall of Mussolini and the disbanding of the Fascist Party set off peace demonstrations all over Italy, but Badoglio declared that Italy would continue to resist alongside Germany.

Meanwhile the Sicilian campaign drew to a close. The British Eighth Army captured Catania and edged around the slopes of Mt. Etna. Finally on August 17 Messina was captured by American troops, joined shortly by their British comrades.

The Sicilian balance sheet showed a victory over 300,000 Axis troops and the conquest of 10,000 square miles of territory. Of these troops an Italian army of 225,000 had been captured or destroyed; of the 75,000 crack German soldiers some 40,000 had managed to escape to Italy. A huge amount of booty had been captured; a superb fighting machine of some 300,000 Americans, British, and Canadians had gained a fighting efficiency unsurpassed in this war. Furthermore the Mediterranean was now virtually an Allied lake. Transports and supplies en route to the Near and Far East could now ply its waters, which also could be used for amphibious operations against the Fortress of Europe.

Tables turned in Russia. Meanwhile on the Russian front decisive action was coming. In previous summer drives the Germans had just fallen short of victory. In the summer of 1941 Moscow had almost fallen; in the summer of 1942 Stalingrad and the Caucasus had nearly been overwhelmed. The summer of 1943 was likely the last opportunity for a victory drive against Russia. In June the Soviet army was told by its leaders, "The hour of decisive events is approaching"; but they were not discouraged. They were encouraged, in fact, for their air squadrons had begun to achieve supremacy during the savage air fighting in May and early June. Offensive action was undertaken by the Nazis in several areas during June, but as we have seen, it was not until July 5 that their real summer drive was opened on a 165-mile front between Orel and Belgorod.

This battle has been referred to as the greatest tank battle in history. The German forces made a few gains, but after ten days they were halted; the Russians assumed the offensive. The great Nazi defense bastion of Orel was captured on August 5, and on the same day Belgorod was entered. It was then evident that a great Soviet offensive was in progress on a 450-mile front. The next objective was Kharkov, and this likewise was captured, two weeks later. The sledge-hammer blows had so far been aimed at the middle and southern sections of the long battle line. A third attack was directed against Smolensk, in the north; but to attain this objective the Russians had first to storm the vital center of Bryansk. By August 17, Soviet forces were only 15 miles from this stronghold. They had shown that the *Wehrmacht* was no longer the strongest single force in Europe.

The German drive had been halted and forced into reverse gear. The Russians' month-old offensive had resulted in the recapture of 5000 square miles of territory, control over the vital Moscow-Kharkov railroad, and a possibility of encircling German troops along the Sea of Azov. These facts, together with the results of the Sicilian campaign, meant that the offensive in Europe had definitely passed to the United Nations.

Allied air offensive. In the Churchill-Roosevelt conference of May 1943, it was decided that Allied air power was great enough to permit an all-out air blitz. The first crippling blow in the air attack against the Axis came that same month when a specially trained group of British Lancaster bombers made a night attack on three key dams in the German Ruhr district. The results were disastrous. Towns were inundated, power stations flooded, and industry halted. During June the tempo of air attack was stepped up, with the British attacking at night and American squadrons during the day. The growing power of the United Nations in the air was also shown in June by bombing raids over Axis targets in Greece.

What was referred to as "the third front against the Axis," that is, the air offensive, was carried on during the first half of July and reached a new intensity in the final days of that month. Hamburg, the Reich's second city and most important port, attacked night and day, was hit with 10,000 tons of bombs. This was more than had been dropped on London in an entire month by the *Luftwaffe* during the Nazi blitz of 1940. Hamburg was practically destroyed and thousands of its people buried under a mass of rubble. Berlin was next to feel the shock of Allied bombs. In several consecutive night raids thousands of tons of bombs were dropped on the Reich capital. The final city to be pulverized as August ended was Nuremberg, the site of important industry and a key railroad center for communication with Italy. Far to the east in the Balkans a serious air blow was delivered against the center of Rumania's oil industry.

The Allied third front required the services of British and American personnel on a huge scale. The bombing of Hamburg, for example, was equivalent to fighting a full-scale land battle in Germany. For one raid on this target over 5000 men to man the planes, 100,000 ground technicians, and some fifty air fields were necessary. It was estimated that one such air attack inflicted damage equal to the work of 77,000 Germans for one month.

Showdown in the Solomons. Early in the spring of 1943, when the Tunisian campaign was monopolizing attention, there were signs of another showdown in the South Pacific. Following their failure to hold Guadalcanal, the Japanese tried to build up air strength in New Guinea and in the central Solomons.

To smash Japanese strength in the Solomons and at the same time to seize air fields as future springboards against Japanese bases north of the Solomons, United States forces carried out the biggest offensive to date in the South Pacific. The attack began on the night

of June 29. One force landed in Japanese-held territory not far from Salamaua. Another convoy landed unopposed on two groups of islands lying between Guadalcanal and southern New Guinea. To the northeast another force captured the island of Rendova after brief but sharp fighting, and troops landed under heavy fire on the southern tip of New Georgia Island.

The objective of the Solomons push was the capture of an important Japanese air base, Munda, 200 miles northwest of Guadalcanal. The fighting on New Georgia was as fierce as the battle for Guadalcanal, but now Allied troops were experienced jungle fighters clad in splotched green-yellow coveralls for protection against Japanese snipers. The fighting continued for two months until, late in August, the remnants of the Japanese garrison fled to a nearby island still in their hands. At the same time savage fighting was taking place as Allied troops advanced toward Salamaua.

As important as the land fighting in the central Solomons were the American victories on the sea and in the air. The most serious Japanese loss was in ships.

Occupation of Kiska gets under way, with each member of the landing party doing a specific job. To help landers avoid sharp underwater rocks, the earthen ramp was extended from the rock-covered beach into the water.

Securing the Aleutians. In the North Pacific Kiska was bombed and shelled continuously during the summer. On August 15 American forces landed unopposed on the island to discover the flight of several thousand Japanese troops under cover of darkness and heavy fog. From the Aleutians American air power began to reach out in the direction of Japan proper.

The Quebec Conference. In August 1943 Churchill and Roosevelt had their sixth meeting, in historic Quebec. Here the two leaders of the English-speaking world with their Chiefs of Staff took stock of the global war and made plans for the fifth year.

Despite China's success in halting recent Japanese drives it was apparent in the summer of 1943 that the naval blockade and the cutting of the Burma Road were beginning to have deadly effect on Chinese resistance. The leaders at Quebec, fully aware of the gravity of the situation, created a new military southeast Asia command based in India and Ceylon. Direction of this new post was given to Lord Louis Mountbatten, a naval officer who had won distinction as leader of the British Commandos. It was generally believed that Mountbatten's objective would be to drive the Japanese out of Burma in order to reopen the Burma Road.

As a result of the Conference the French Committee of National Liberation was recognized, partially by the United States and Britain, fully by Russia. Following the conquest of North Africa acrimonious disputes had taken place between General de Gaulle's Free French organization in London and General Henri Giraud, the head of French administration in North Africa. Differences had finally been reduced and the two factions had merged. After much regrettable controversy, the united participation of Frenchmen in the cause of the United Nations seemed assured.

During the summer of 1943 there were numerous rumors of misunderstandings and rivalries between Russia and her two great allies. These tales seemed to be confirmed when Stalin did not attend the Quebec Conference.

Russia, longing for relief from her great struggle and looking for unquestionable expression of good faith from her capitalistic allies, continued to urge Britain and America to open a second front in western Europe. In answer to criticism, the United States and Britain could point out that while Russia had

The leaders of the Quebec Conference in a jovial mood. That is the Earl of Athlone, Governor General of Canada, on President Roosevelt's left. Mackenzie King, Canada's Prime Minister, is standing to the right of Winston Churchill with the omnipresent hat and cigar.

a single foe to contend with, they had not only Germany but Japan. This required diversion of men and supplies to the Pacific area which might otherwise have been sent to the European theater. Even so, great quantities of food and military supplies had been sent to Russia, appreciatively acknowledged in a message from Stalin: "Our friends who are participating in the manufacture of the ammunition and supplies of provisions are rendering great support in the fight against our common enemy." If Britain and the United States for their part were reluctant to open a premature second front across the English Channel, Russia herself was equally reluctant to open another front by providing air bases for American bombers to use in the war against Japan. Also, while Russia found her enemy on her own soil, the United States in particular was forced to transport men and material thousands of miles to the war areas. The truth seemed to be that Russia on one hand, and Britain and the United States on the other, each had certain distinctive problems which dictated their military strategy. The contribution of the British and American strategy became more evident in the fall of 1943 when the first major phase was successfully concluded (see page 216).

Meeting in Moscow. In September the world began to hear more and more about a forthcoming meeting of British, American, and Russian representatives. Late in October Secretary Hull and Foreign Minister Eden flew to Moscow for sessions with Foreign Minister Molotov. The conference, with the Chinese ambassador to Russia participating—and large staffs of diplomatic and military experts—surprised the world with results that seemed to promise the solution of such problems as the second front, the conduct of the war, and the nature of the peace. (See page 224.)

The submarine war. In the "silent war" against the Nazi submarines, gratifying results had been achieved by September 1943. From January to October 1942 the undersea craft had been so dangerously successful that energetic measures were introduced against them in the fall of 1942. Convoy methods were improved, more ships were built, and vessels were better armed. In particular, the use of air power checkmated the undersea menace. Long-range reconnaissance planes from shore bases scoured the sea lanes and small "flat tops"—carriers—were used to afford convoys air protection even when in mid-Atlantic. As a result of these measures it was announced in September that no ship had been sunk by submarine in the North Atlantic during the past four months.

The air offensive (continued). Air power was not only instrumental in defeating the submarines; it was also increasingly utilized as a major destructive weapon against the German Fortress of Europe. During the fall of 1943 strategic centers and industrial establishments were bombed night and day by the R.A.F. and the U.S. Eighth Air Force. On October 10 they penetrated the continent as far as East Prussia and Poland; five days later another force flew deep into Germany to bomb an important ball-bearing industry. In this last raid 60 bombers were lost with their crews, estimated at 593 men dead or captured. This was a high price to pay, but evidence was accumulating that the steady air war against the Third Reich was undermining German morale and seriously curtailing production. These raids were also forcing the Nazis to withdraw air power from the fighting fronts. The air offensive was therefore of tremendous assistance to the Russian offensive, ensuring Russian supremacy in the air on the eastern front.

Russian gains. Most spectacular of the military operations was the progress of the Russian summer offensive. Hurled as a counterattack against a faltering Nazi offensive begun in July, the Soviet drive gained momentum late in August and in September.

In the south, along a fringe of the northeastern coast of the Black Sea, German troops fought desperately to maintain their bridgehead in the Caucasus, but were finally driven out in October. Farther north the Russian forces had retrieved the rich industrial Donets Basin and had taken the city of Dnepropetrovsk, site of Russia's greatest dam, which in 1941 had fallen a victim of the scorched-earth policy. These advances meant that the entire Ukraine was rapidly being recaptured. Early in October Soviet armies surrounded the historic Ukrainian capital of Kiev. By November they had captured it.

Some 700 miles north of the Black Sea the "Gateway to Moscow" had been taken from the Germans in the recapture of Smolensk. This advance brought Russian armies close to the old Latvian border and threatened to cut off Nazi forces in a pocket around Leningrad. The Nazi High Command hoped to be able to make a stand at the Dnieper. Since July 12, 1943, Soviet armies had reconquered 195,000 square miles.

The surrender of Italy. Meanwhile Italy was going through a tragic ordeal of retribution for its unprovoked attack upon France and Great Britain in the spring of 1940. Two weeks after the conquest of Sicily, Montgomery and his Eighth Army, protected by air power, landed in southern Italy opposite Messina. One of the most dramatic events of the war came the evening of September 8 when General Eisenhower announced over the Algiers radio that Italy had been granted a military armistice, effective immediately. An hour later Premier Marshal Pietro Badoglio announced over the Rome radio, "Italian forces will cease all acts of hostility against the Anglo-United States forces. . . . They will, however, oppose attack from any other quarter."

The desperate position of Italy was frankly admitted in a message sent by Badoglio to his former Axis allies, which ended: "In order to avoid complete ruin, Italy is therefore obliged to ask her enemies for an armistice."

The armistice carried thirteen provisions, the most important of which were: the end of all Italian resistance, the surrender of United Nations prisoners held in Italy, transfer of the Italian fleet, use of the Italian mer-

Like that of Sicily, the invasion of the Italian mainland was largely an amphibious one. Eager Yanks, pouring from landing craft at Salerno, are met by enemy fire—fire that was to become heavy, cause many casualties, threaten the success of the operation. Note the machine guns trained skyward.

chant marine if necessary, and free use of ports and air bases in the fight against Germany.

The Nazis quickly proceeded to make Italy a vassal state. German troops occupied the main cities, especially Genoa, Rome, Milan, and Naples, and sporadic fighting ensued between Nazi forces and Italian soldiers. To prevent the Germans from consolidating their hold over central Italy, a second amphibious attack was directed by General Mark Clark's Fifth Army just south of the great port of Naples. Landing on the beaches took place on the morning of September 9. In the meantime the British Eighth Army was punching its way north from the toe and heel of Italy.

The fight for Naples was one of the fiercest yet experienced by American troops. For two days they and the British Allies enlarged their bridgehead. But counterattacks followed. Nazi tank units drove the Allied forces back, in some instances almost to the sea. After six days of savage fighting, the Fifth Army held and was soon joined by the British Eighth coming up from the south. In the next two weeks the combined armies forced their way through the German lines, and on October 1, the once beautiful, now war-torn port city was entered.

In accordance with the armistice terms, units of the Italian navy left port and made their way to Malta and other Allied ports.

While en route the great Italian battleship *Roma* was sunk by German bombs.

The sinking of the *Roma* and the determination of the Germans to make Italy their battlefield brought a dramatic transformation in Italo-German relations, and on September 20 Badoglio announced to the Italians: "We are cooperating side by side with the Anglo-Americans, who are now accepting our assistance in the task of driving the Germans from the country." The situation was further complicated by the "rescue" of Mussolini by Nazi troops. Il Duce was thereupon made the head of an Italian puppet régime by his Nazi masters. While the status of Italy, which had signed an unconditional surrender, remained for a time obscure, it was quite apparent that at least she was more than a mere conquered ex-foe. Since Italy had turned against the Germans there were references to her as a "co-belligerent," and on October 13 Badoglio formally stated Italy was at war with Germany.

Elsewhere in the Mediterranean Hitler's outposts of the *Festung Europa* fell: Sardinia, Corsica, and several eastern Mediterranean islands.

The surrender of Italy had repercussions favorable to the United Nations everywhere in the global struggle: (1) Conquest of the Mediterranean shortened lines of communication to the Near and Far East. This meant more tools of war to Russia, to North Africa, and to India. (2) With the surrender of the Italian fleet, considerable British and American naval forces were freed for action in the Bay of Bengal and the Pacific. (3) Possession of important air bases in Italy brought eastern Germany and Austria within more effective bombing range. (4) The invasion of Italy opened up the way for Allied fleets in the Adriatic. These could bring badly needed supplies for the heroic Yugoslav guerrillas or perhaps even convoy an Allied invasion force to open up a Balkan front. (5) The collapse of Italy naturally was a great psychological help to the Allied cause throughout the world.

Pacific operations. While the world's attention was centered on the dramatic events in Italy and Russia, there were marked advances in the Pacific battle. In September the United States Navy defied the Japanese high seas fleet by raiding the Japanese island base of Marcus, only four hours from Tokyo by air. There was a fourth air attack against Paramoshiri, nearest Japanese base to the Aleutians. The most important operation in the South Pacific early in the fall of 1943 was the offensive against Japanese bases in central New Guinea and further advances in the Solomons. By the use of paratroopers and amphibious landing operations, Salamaua and Lae were cut off,

partially destroyed, and eventually captured. The important position held by the Japanese at Finschhafen in New Guinea was also surrounded, and in October it was taken. Later air and sea attacks in the direction of Rabaul and Truk gave promise of new advances.

Position of neutrals. The cumulative effect of Axis reverses was plainly marked in the behavior of the European neutrals who previously, willingly or not, had danced to whatever tune Hitler played. In 1943 neutral countries basically sympathetic to the Allied cause adopted a more independent attitude. Sweden, for example, forbade the transit of German troops across its territory to Norway, and Portugal turned over valuable naval and air bases in the Azores to Britain. While there was little for Switzerland to do except hope for a German defeat, there were increasing signs that Turkey was more committed to the Allied cause. As for Fascist Spain, its dictator, Franco, viewed the prospect of Nazi defeat with unmitigated dismay. During the high tide of German victory, Franco had cooperated to the full with the Nazis. Spain was a hotbed of Nazi espionage; and during the Tunisian campaign the Spanish government maintained menacing concentrations of troops in Spanish Morocco. Allied successes at least made Fascist Spain more discreet and less able, if still willing, to do Hitler's bidding.

Cairo and Teheran: New Unity

Hopes for progress. Late in November and early in December came the most dramatic meetings of the war, two of the most momentous in history. The long hoped-for conferences between Churchill, Roosevelt, and Chiang Kai-shek, and between Churchill, Roosevelt, and Stalin, finally materialized, and at last the world seemed on the way to becoming one world.

Agreement at Cairo. In Cairo Britain, the United States, and China pledged themselves to the complete defeat of Japan and to the reduction of her empire to the small islands with which it had begun fifty years ago. In particular, it was agreed that "in due course" Korea is to be given her independence, the territories which Japan has stolen from China, including Manchuria and Formosa, are to be restored. The official report of the meeting made no mention of the states in southeast-

ern Asia or of Japan's strategic holdings in the South Pacific, but the conference results seemed a basis for the assumption that there was potential if not present enlightened agreement on these questions too; perhaps parts of these areas would be placed at least for a time under some kind of international direction.

The promise of Teheran. In Teheran, in ancient Persia (Iran), while the whole modern world watched and waited, Churchill and Roosevelt met Stalin, whose first trip outside the borders of his country in thirty-one years could be taken as a further token of the return of Russia from isolation. The Anglo-American leaders presumably secured Stalin's endorsement—if they did not already have it—of the results of the Cairo meeting; more direct participation than this on the part of Russia could hardly be expected since Russia and Japan still were not at war. Then launching a four-day session, the "Big Three" proceeded to cover all phases of the European war, military and political. It soon became apparent that a new unity was being forged, that there was agreement even on the question of a second front. The declaration of Teheran that came out of the conference was short, and at first disappointing to those who had hoped for the announcement of immediate political offensives (such as the formation of a United Nations executive council and an ultimatum to the German people), but on further examination observers began to see that the settlement of the long and threatening second-front debate was in itself a tremendous event, and that the additional words of Churchill, Stalin, and Roosevelt were at least full of promise— the promise of unity and victory, the promise of understanding and cooperation in a peace that would "banish war for many generations."

As the new year approached, the people of the United Nations hoped that the new declarations would soon be followed by great actions—the formation of a United Nations council; possibly the entry of Turkey into the war and an Allied invasion through the Balkans; when the time was ripe, a direct appeal to the German people; and a major attack on the long-awaited second front.

Checks on optimism. But the war was by no means over. Although the Russians had recaptured two thirds of their lost territory, the Germans in December were counter-attacking with some gains on the Ukrainian front, they were fighting effectively against the Allied-American Fifth and the British Eighth Armies trying to reach Rome, and in Berlin and elsewhere they were standing up—at least the Gestapo was forcing them to stand up— under bombings more terrible, more destructive, than anything the warring nations had previously known. Berlin was finally getting the blasting that the Allies had promised, that Goering and Goebbels had said would never come; the German home front, however, was yet to be crushed. In the Pacific the Japanese, as the month-clock turned to 12, exacted a heavy toll of American Marines for the capture of the small Gilbert islands, Tarawa and Makin—especially at Tarawa, which would go down in history as one of America's most heroic victories. While a great Allied drive might be developing in the direction of Southeast Asia and the adjacent waters of the Pacific, Japan was still threatening the heart of free China. Early in December the Japanese were able to carry a new attack in central China's "rice bowl" area as far as Changteh, important highway junction only 300 miles east of Chungking.

Summary

In September 1943 the Second World War entered its fifth year. For the first three years the Axis powers had enjoyed the military initiative and in June 1942 had begun a world-wide offensive which was to fall just short of success. This was the high mark of totalitarian strength. With the turning point of Stalingrad the United Nations emerged in growing military might and started on a series of outstanding victories.

Allied forces cleared the Aleutians of the Japanese. In the South Pacific they eliminated the Nipponese from central New Guinea and all of the Solomons. In North Africa and the Mediterranean region striking successes were achieved. Sicily was conquered; Mussolini was overthrown and Fascism discredited. Italy turned against Germany. The long-heralded German offensive had backfired, and the Russians were making substantial gains all along the eastern front. While the Allies pointed toward Europe proper in the west, Germans at home were for the first time experiencing the horrors of war; the savage air blitz of the British Isles carried out in the fall and winter of 1940-1941 was being turned back on Germany with ample interest. On every front there were signs of Axis weakness and imminent further offensives by the United Nations. With meetings at Moscow, Cairo, and Teheran, the Allies appeared to have established a new and promising unity.

The United States

1942	Huge all-out war effort	Increase in production
	Fight against inflation	Taxes; rationing; price and wage ceilings
1943	Coal miners' strikes	John L. Lewis, leader
	Further measures against inflation	Subsidies on important food commodities
	Congress vs. Roosevelt	Overriding of veto on Smith-Connally anti-strike bill; repeal of salary ceiling
	Participation in postwar planning	Fulbright, Connally resolutions
	Race riots	

Great Britain

1942	Vast social revolution	Lessening of class feeling
	Increase in production	Intensive mobilization of manpower
	Agricultural revolution	Government subsidies; large labor front
1943	Mobilization of women in industry	
	Economic transformation	Cooperative economy favored

Canada

1939-1942	Industrial Revolution	Most ambitious industrial program
	Control of inflation	Price control, rationing, victory loans
	British Commonwealth Air Training Plan	
1943	Leader at United Nations Food Conference	
	Quebec Conference	
	U. S.-Canadian cooperation	Permanent Joint Board on Defense
	Political swing to left	Importance of new Labor Party
	Problem of English-French relations	

Other British Dominions

1942-1943	Australia creates Manpower Directorate	
	Election of Labor government in Australia	Headed by Premier John Curtin
	Pro-war government in South Africa	General Smuts, head
	Conversion program in South Africa	Governmental planning
	Social and Economic Council in South Africa	Postwar reconstruction plans

Latin America

1942-1943	Good Neighbor Conference in Rio de Janeiro	
	All except Argentina break with Axis	Proclaimed List of Blocked Nationals
	Economic importance	Supplies for war and peace time
	Political upheaval in Argentina	Revolt against government of Castillo

Russia

1941-1942	Industrial trek to the East	Women play major role in industry
1943	Reconstruction of demolished areas	Rebuilding of Kharkov
	Second front question	
	Abolition of Comintern	Aids friendlier international atmosphere

China

1943	Treaties with U. S. and Britain	Extraterritorial rights abrogated
	Chiang Kai-shek appointed President	
	Development of democracy	People's Congress to replace one-party government; *hsien* system
	Growth of light industry	Chinese Industrial Cooperatives

Axis Countries

1943	Fall of Mussolini; Italy joins Allies	Badoglio appointed successor
	Third Reich undergoes heavy bombing	Berlin bears brunt
	Japan prepares for long war	Decentralization of industry

CHAPTER 8

On the Home Fronts

As no other war in history, the Second World War has broken down the old lines of demarcation between the firing and home fronts. For this is total war—war involving total populations. Not only is it total war because civilian populations have faced new dangers, but because the very nature of modern warfare demands the closest integration of domestic and military interests. Every country, Allied or Axis, has been concerned about the proper allocation of manpower: to the farm, the factory, and the firing front. This section, therefore, although it emphasizes the impact of the war upon the civilian populations, desires to set up no false boundary between soldier and civilian. They are in it together. And together after the war they will face the problem of constructing a durable peace.

The United States

The arsenal of democracy. The United States has built up in the Second World War a production machine whose size surpasses anything in the world's history. The output of American mines, blast furnaces, shipyards, mills, and plants has been in figures which are almost beyond comprehension. For example, steel production in 1943 is estimated at more than 90,000,000 tons, almost twice as much as the best year in the First World War, and more than that of all the rest of the world put together. Five ocean-going ships were slid-ing down the ways every twenty-four hours in 1943. Whereas in the First World War the United States turned out 80 tanks, by the end of the first year alone of the Second World War the nation had produced 20,000. In 1943 the goal of 10,000 war planes a month—scoffed at by the Axis—was sighted. Every month in 1943 the munitions plants were making almost 2,000,000,000 small-arms cartridges, 18,000,000 artillery shells, 66,000 machine guns, and 2500 75-mm. field guns.

In June 1943 Donald Nelson could report

to the President: "The record certainly makes it clear that the American industrial system can be justifiably proud of an astonishing display of economic muscle. In the main, the productive achievement of the American war economy in 1942 met the requirements of our war strategy; and the prospects for 1943 are for a quantity and quality of production that will realize to the full the tremendous potential of American industry."[1] Mr. Nelson's confident views were fortified by convincing statistics. Whereas the overall military program in 1942 amounted to $59,000,000,000, the program for 1943 was set at $106,000,000,000—an increase of 80 per cent.

But these results did not come overnight, nor were they unaccompanied by serious problems and domestic dissension. Like her English-speaking allies, the United States did not comprehend the full gravity of the war for the first six months or more. A series of stinging defeats in the Pacific was needed to awaken the man in the street to the perilous military situation. Then, despite the complacency of the average citizen and the confusion of overcrowded Washington, the country in 1942 converted its industries in a huge all-out effort. While the armed forces expanded from two million men to seven million, industrial centers began to change. Millions of war workers poured into cities to find ready jobs and ready money—but not ready houses in which to live. New factories rose on the outskirts of towns and operated on a twenty-four hour schedule, so that "swing shift" and "graveyard shift" became nationally understood terms.

Danger of inflation. Serious shortages soon developed in materials and manpower. Manufacturers frantically sought the highest priori-

ties at Washington, and industry and agriculture argued with the army and navy about the indispensability of workers. Civilians found that the war was something more than repeating "Remember Pearl Harbor."

As shortages in civilian goods became more acute the nation's purchasing power increased. Incomes for 1944 were expected to be over twice the figures for 1940. With unprecedented amounts of money in circulation and less civilian goods available, the cost of living rose to a point roughly estimated as 25 per cent above that of 1939. Strict governmental controls in the forms of higher taxes, more stringent rationing, and effective price and wage ceilings became necessary measures in the battle against inflation.

President Roosevelt had called on Congress to assist the Office of Price Administration by limiting wages, farm prices, and profits and by passing a fiscal program to drain off surplus purchasing funds. By the end of 1942, stabilization measures had saved the government and the American consumer many billions of dollars. Price control measures, though, however beneficial to the nation as a whole, often proved irksome to the public and unprofitable to some pressure groups. The result was that the OPA lost favor in Congressional circles, and price controls sagged in effectiveness. As the country embarked on its 1943 course, the danger of inflation mounted.

There was an insistent voice in the cost-of-living struggle, a voice which could not be ignored. It belonged to organized labor, which in 1943 complained unceasingly that the Administration was in effect "freezing" wages, yet allowing the cost of living to mount alarmingly. Labor had held pretty well to its no-strike pledge (99.95 per cent compliance according to one source[2]), but its dissatisfaction with wage ceilings, corporation profits, executive salaries, and constantly rising prices resulted in more than one dramatic outburst. The most spectacular strikes in 1943 centered about John L. Lewis' demands for portal-to-portal payments for his coal miners, wage increases which he maintained were necessary if the miners were to cope with the rise in living costs.

The War Food Administration and the Office of Price Administration were directed in September 1943 to proceed with the payment of roll-back subsidies on important food com-

OUR CHIEF PRESSURE GROUPS

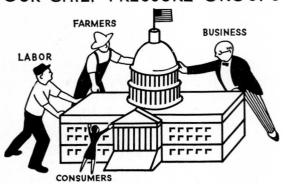

LABOR   FARMERS   BUSINESS   CONSUMERS

modities. This program, estimated to cost $1,000,000,000 yearly, was depended upon to lower living costs between 4 and 5 per cent. It was a step in the Administration's commitment to reduce living costs to the level of September 15, 1942. However, the program to hold down the cost of living by the payment of subsidies, successful in Britain and Canada, faced strong Congressional opposition, with the farm bloc especially emphatic in its disapproval of ceilings on foodstuffs.

In 1943, then, perhaps the most serious domestic economic problem was that of inflation, involving as it did the increase in national income, the decrease in consumer goods (with the natural result of greater willingness to pay more for a commodity), the freezing of wages in certain quarters, and a cost of living which had risen in the United States far more than in Britain or Canada. However, toward the end of the year, Price Administrator Prentiss Brown (prior to resigning) voiced his belief that the danger of inflation had been halted. Later developments left the issue in doubt.

The public debt. Meanwhile the war was costing the United States the greatest amounts in the world's history. In the fiscal year 1942, expenditures for war activities amounted to 26 billion dollars. In 1943, the figure jumped to 75 billion. According to the President's statement in July 1943, on the summation of the 1944 Federal budget, war expenditures for the fiscal year just starting would come to approximately 100 billion.[3] By June 1943, monthly war expenditures had risen to 7.7 billion.

Concomitant with the increase in war expenditures was the rise of the public debt. According to the President's figures, at the beginning of the 1942 fiscal year, the public debt stood at 48 billion. In 1943 it had risen to 72 billion. At the beginning of the 1944 fiscal year (June 30, 1943) the direct public debt (excluding obligations of government corporations) amounted to 137 billion dollars, and Roosevelt warned that unless additional tax legislation was enacted, the debt would increase to 206 billion dollars by June 30, 1944.[3]

The President and many Congressional leaders anxiously urged the immediate adoption of "a truly stiff program of additional taxes, savings, or both." It was maintained that individual tax rates in 1943, much lower than in Britain and Canada, had not advanced with the increase in incomes, and also that many American corporations were still making huge profits, compared with British and Canadian companies, subject to a 100 per cent tax on excess profits. To end war profiteering, Congress passed the Contract Renegotiation Act in April 1942, giving power to four executive agencies to renegotiate contracts and subcontracts whenever excessive profits would otherwise result. This Act was not ineffective. In 1943, however, pressure was being exerted in some Congressional quarters for repeal, or at least strong modification, of the Renegotiation Act, on the grounds that postwar reconversion necessitated the setting aside of large reserves which should be included as costs. Advocates of the Act replied that war industries were already guaranteed against postwar losses and, furthermore, that corporations had set aside by the end of 1943 war years' reserves which amounted to almost four times the total accumulated reserve for the 1936-1939 period. A special 1943 study of 29 large corporations showed that 23 of them had at least doubled their normal peacetime profits in 1942—after taxes were paid.[4]

Politics within. On the domestic political front, both major parties were jockeying into position for the 1944 presidential election. The more conservative Congress elected in 1942 was much less sympathetic toward the New Deal and much more independent of the President. During 1943 Congress showed not too gentle concern for Mr. Roosevelt's program for controlling the cost of living, and overrode his veto of the Smith-Connally Anti-Strike Bill. Congress also lifted the $25,000 salary ceiling which the President favored; abolished such agencies as the NYA (June), WPA (June), CCC (April), and the National Resources Planning Board (August); and appropriated for the Farm Security Administration funds which the President's supporters deemed "ridiculously inadequate." Lack of concerted action by the executive and legislative branches was heightened by cleavages within the ranks of the President's own party—cleavages that made clear-cut legislation difficult, and at times drove the country's allies to worry over the apparent lack of political policy.

Search for a foreign policy. On the question of foreign policy, the issues in 1943 appeared at times dangerously confused. True enough, Roosevelt and Churchill had met again at Quebec in August, and reported that all was going well with the war. But there was growing criticism in many circles that these conferences were not satisfactory: (1) because China and the Soviet Union were not co-participants; (2) because they featured an Anglo-American pattern for the postwar era; and (3) because they seemed—at least to some critics—to show an inadequate understanding of the sociological and ideological problems of the peoples of Europe.

The defeat of Italy in 1943 brought the problem into prominence. Critics contended that while all through the Mussolini régime there had existed a strong democratic underground opposed to Fascism, the American government appeared less interested in supporting this people's movement than in "playing ball" with the House of Savoy and Marshal Badoglio, who, despite his coolness toward Il Duce in former days, had nevertheless led the Fascist forces into Ethiopia. American liberals were worried. They had been disturbed earlier by the sometimes cordial relations with Franco's Spain and Pétain's Vichy France, and by the apparently unsatisfactory relations with the Soviet Union. The State Department was emphatic in maintaining that American-Russian relations were excellent, but in the summer of 1943 its critics remained unconvinced.

To add further to the political confusion in the autumn of 1943, as we have seen, was the still burning question of a second front. (See page 215.) In October, however, new hopes for a solution of this and related problems were born. Accompanied by diplomatic and military experts, the foreign ministers of the United States, Britain, and Russia met in Moscow and after twelve days of conferences came forth with what promised to be historic new patterns of collaboration. Among the Moscow decisions, in which China was represented too, were the agreements to act together in the war; not to conclude a separate peace; and to establish as soon as possible an international organization of all peace-loving nations. The three countries, in addition, set up a European council and a Mediterranean council (in which France was to have a place) to make studies and recommendations on future political questions; called for the establishment of democratic government and principles in Italy; laid down a pattern for the salvation of Austria and, presumably, other countries; warned Axis leaders and followers that those guilty of atrocities would eventually be punished as war criminals.

Then came the meetings in Cairo and Teheran, which, as we have seen in the preceding chapter (page 218), established a still stronger unity of action among the Allies.

The year 1943 had been marked by divergent views as to the postwar role America should play. "Neo-isolationist" groups in the Midwest and certain newspaper chains had strongly opposed "foreign entanglements." More than one important voice was heard suggesting what some said would be American imperialism, involving a favored position in Latin America, a five-ocean navy, and ownership of air bases from Asia to Greenland and Dakar. Leaders like Willkie and Wallace advocated complete international participation. The Congress went on record as favoring participation.

The declarations at Moscow, Cairo, and Teheran, however, were bold, clarifying strokes. The United Nations appeared to have embarked on a new era of cooperation; the United States seemed committed to a broadened foreign policy.

Race problems at home. While discussion of the United States foreign policy continued, a grave social problem flared to ugly dimensions within the country itself in 1943. This was the race problem, conspicuous for a time in Los Angeles and Detroit especially. As a result of expanded war production with its accompanying high wages, many classes of Americans found themselves with more money than they had ever possessed before. With the improved financial status came a conscious or unconscious demand for greater social recognition than they had hitherto received.

In Los Angeles the race problem involved a portion of the Mexican population, known (because of the exaggerated garb they wore) as "zoot-suiters." Mexican youths became embroiled in street brawls with members of the armed services. Probably blame must be apportioned to both sides. That the officials involved acted with legal impartiality was debated throughout the country, however. Significantly enough, some psychologists made the analysis that the "zoot-suiters" by their costume and acts were expressing an inner drive to break free of the inferiority complex caused by an unhealthy social and material environment; the war and its new social pattern afforded them that chance.

Much more serious was the bitter race riot

in Detroit. That city had become dangerously overcrowded and ill-housed, and long hours at production lathes did little to improve the people's tempers. Furthermore, the offer of lucrative jobs attracted thousands of workers from the South—both Negroes who had earned little, if any, hard cash before, and "poor whites," almost as poverty-stricken, many of whom were imbued with a deep Negro animosity. Both classes found themselves thrown into the same depressed neighborhoods, with more money than they needed. Out of the complex of old hatreds, new money, bad living conditions, and sultry summer days and nights suddenly flared the worst race riots in modern American history. The entire nation was shamed. The full causes of the riot were the subject of much debate, but one thing appeared tragically certain in 1943: little had been done apparently to cure the evil.

Looking over America in 1943, one could see indications that many people were not yet taking a sufficiently profound and sober view of the war and its larger meanings. How the country would handle the great social and political problems still before it, remained to be seen. Observers found it disturbing, for example, that Congress debated so long over the soldier vote bill. But of this there could be no doubt—the natural resources, the skilled labor, the inventive genius, the will to win the war were all present, indeed were all in action.

Great Britain

Social revolution. It is commonplace to describe the significance of the Second World War with the words "vast social revolution." Whatever may be the case for other countries, that term applies clearly for Great Britain. The British people have been in the struggle since September 3, 1939, and deep in it. One home in every five has been damaged or destroyed; whole areas have been obliterated.

Class stratification has been fundamentally shaken by the war. There is agitation from many quarters for a new education "deal"—one which will do away with the evils of social discrimination inherent in two distinct school systems, the public school and the private school. In the past the majority of top-ranking positions in British society were held by the "old school tie"—those fortunate persons to whom the accident of birth had bequeathed title or wealth. All Parliamentary parties are now agreed that British education must be broadened to give every group a longer and more adequate schooling, and that educational opportunity must be based on ability rather than social status. Another significant educational development has been the strong emphasis placed upon adult education in the armed forces. American observers in Britain have remarked that, although the American doughboys stationed there are better clothed, better fed, and better entertained than the British Tommies, they lack the latter's political and ideological training. In other words, the British soldier has a good idea of what he's fighting against and what he's fighting *for*—and it is this factor which may help revolutionize postwar Britain.

The blitz bombings and the stringent food rationing have proved blessings in some ways. Many of the slums of London, Glasgow, and the Lancashire cities—slums which nineteenth-century industrialism begot—were blown or burned up when the Nazis tried to smash the industries which the slums encircled. England has been planning a housing system even vaster than the prewar building program, which saw 60,000 slum dwellings demolished every year. Decentralization of industry and the creation of model "garden cities" in the countryside have already been started. The British people in 1942 were healthier than before the outbreak of war; the birth rate was up and the death rate down. And this encouraging condition prevailed despite the strict rationing of foodstuffs. For Britons in 1942 were enjoying more balanced diets with more dairy products and vegetables. However, in 1943 experts saw the cropping up of dietary deficiencies and a certain lowering of health levels.

The cultural life of the British people was at a new high in 1943, if adult education classes, discussion groups, and interest in literature and the arts were at all indicative. The CEMA—Council for the Encouragement of Music and the Arts—brought concerts, plays, and art exhibitions to villages and war factories, and the finest stage talent was enlisted. Civilians and soldiers have also turned out by the scores of thousands for the traveling shows in which Ministry of Information films provide entertainment of an educational nature.

Every available economic and human resource has been mobilized. Characteristics of prewar business—the leisurely pace, the long weekend, the complacent attitude, the sharp social stratification, the "old school tie" leadership—have largely had to go. To get the maximum results, the National Service Act has absolute control over manpower. Consequently, at least two out of every three persons between the ages of 14 and 65 are working full time in the armed forces, industry, or civil defense. The age limit in the armed forces had been raised to 51 by 1943. An important aspect of present-day British life has been the mobilization of women in industry; by May 1943, over 7,000,000 women were engaged steadily in the war program, while millions more (such as housewives) were working part time. Also, seven out of every ten girls and boys between 14 and 17 were doing war work.

The British people know that there is no going back to the England of prewar days. This fact was emphasized by the American historian Commager upon his return from an extended visit in 1942. The British also realize that their postwar plans are contingent upon the victory aims of the United States.

Production increases. The intensive mobilization of manpower in Great Britain has enabled the country to challenge the industrial might of Germany. Aircraft production, three times as great in 1942 as in 1939, has shattered all previous records. Shipping has always been Britain's lifeline, and never have the people relaxed in constructing both naval and merchant craft. Up to March 1943, they had completed and added to the Royal Navy over 900 ships, thus making the fleet stronger, despite its heavy losses, than at the outbreak of war. Merchant tonnage was already twice as great by 1941 as in 1939. The British people did not intend to starve because of shipping losses in this war as they came so perilously close to doing in the last conflict. Britain has been a huge tank arsenal for the Allies, turning out by the middle of 1942 some 257,000 tanks and mechanical vehicles a year—or more than five times the number produced during the dark days of Dunkirk. Army supplies and stores kept pace with this swift armament expansion, so that toward the end of 1943, artillery and ammunition were being turned out in twice the quantities of the preceding year.

Important progress has also been made on the agricultural front. Prior to the war, British farming was in a bad way, with decaying farmhouses and neglected fields. Britain's agriculture was able to support only a third of her population. But the war brought radical changes, for the shipping strain had to be reduced by all possible means. As the Minister of Agriculture put it in 1942, the plan was to convert the island "from a mainly grazing to a mainly arable country, to save a round voyage for a ship with every 10,000 tons of food we could grow."[5] The government paid substantial subsidies for the plowing up of untouched grasslands, for draining and ditching, and for the making of tools. Markets were assured by the Ministry of Food, and national minimum wages for farm workers were laid down. By the end of 1942 some 6,000,000 more acres were under cultivation than in 1939, and a record harvest resulted. Britain was now not one-third but two-thirds self-sufficient.

Two factors had much to do with the record production. One was the tremendous increase in the use of tractors, so that in 1943 British agriculture had become the most highly mechanized in the world. The second factor was the creation of a large farm labor front including notably the Women's Land Army and the use of the armed forces to help with the harvesting. Italian prisoners of war were also employed in draining and reclamation projects, while hundreds of thousands of city dwellers had their own gardens or went out to the countryside to work at harvest time. British agriculture is today in a healthier condition than it has been for decades.

The economic transformation. The war has proved a heavy financial obligation to the British people. In 1940 the cost of running the war was £5,000,000 a day; in 1943 it had risen to £15,000,000. The national debt has reached astronomical proportions. Because the government has been a strong advocate of pay-as-you-go, the British taxpayer has had to carry a load unsurpassed by any of his allies. For example, the income tax is fixed on the standard rate of 10 shillings on the pound (20 shillings), while the maximum rate of tax runs as high as 19 shillings, sixpence. Excess profits are taxed 100 per cent, while the Purchase Tax—a sales tax on consumers' goods—ranges from 12 to 50 per cent on retail prices.

But personal savings have increased during the war because of the rationing of goods, the high peak of employment, and the cutting down of pleasure spending. The country in 1943 had over 300,000 Savings Groups compared with 45,000 in 1939. An important result will be apparent in the postwar era when, to quote Prime Minister Churchill, "there will be seven or eight million people in the country with two or three hundred pounds apiece."

That postwar Britain is in for striking economic changes can be deduced from existing conditions. Naturally such problems as reconversion of expanded industry to peacetime production, absorption of fighting personnel into agriculture and industry, women workers, and a huge national debt must affect Britain and her allies alike. But there are problems of a particularly national significance. One is the matter of foreign investments. Prior to the war British investors owned valuable assets in every nook and cranny of the world—rubber plantations in Malaya, oil fields in Rumania, and railroads in South America. Axis occupation destroyed British investments in many lands, at least temporarily, and it is problematical whether the *status quo ante bellum* will be restored. But even British investments in Allied nations have altered drastically. To pay for vast military supplies from the United States and Canada, for example, Britain sold hundreds of millions of dollars' worth of securities pertaining to those countries. In the postwar era Britain will not have this investment income once so important in her economy.

Britain's lucrative carrying trade has changed considerably also. At one time British ships carried most of the world's commerce; after the war they will have to compete with huge merchant fleets of the United States, Canada, and the Soviet Union. Nor will British shipyards be able to maintain their former virtual monopoly.

Foreign markets are yet another vital problem. The United Kingdom lived by its sale of manufactured goods to Canada, Australia, South America, China, and other countries. After the war, Canada and Australia will be much more industrially self-sufficient, and already Britain's position in the markets of South America, in comparison with that of the United States, has suffered considerably. In fact, some economists feel that Britain's great-

Air raid warnings did not keep this newsman from supplying the people with news. With a tin hat for security, he sticks to his post. Determination to "get on with it" has been a marked characteristic of the English during four years of war.

est postwar economic problem is that of exports; she must export manufactured products if she is to exist. This may help explain why the country as a whole was apparently quite willing in 1943 to embark upon new economic developments, involving international cooperation.

Too alarming a picture of Britain's future economic life should not be painted; the country has access to vast resources, and its industry will make adjustments needed to cope with world conditions. British economists are well aware of the sweeping economic changes in store. Furthermore, the British people anticipate these changes and are already prepared to go a long way. The direction they favor is to the left (though not along Marxist lines), toward a cooperative international order, and toward a progressively cooperative economy.

However, despite an unmistakable approval of the postwar objective of social reconstruction, there was no certainty in 1943 how the basic pattern would look. Great numbers of landowners and industrialists favored social concessions sufficient to weather the postwar storms but not radical enough to alter Britain's basic capitalistic and nationalistic institutions. Articulate elements of labor, especially the trade union groups, were warning of the dangers of what they called a "Tory victory." They pointed out, for example, that although every party in the House of Commons had paid lip service to the principles of the Beveridge Report, the Conservative-dominated government had flatly refused to put any of those principles into law during the war.

And labor groups, while endorsing the uncompromising war program of Churchill, have reported that they will want a dissolution of the present agreement between Conservatives and Labor once the war has been won. For they continue to believe that Churchill is the man to win the war—but apparently fear that he may not be socially constructive enough to win the peace.

British morale in 1943 was stronger than at any time since the outbreak of war. Gone were the foreboding days of Dunkirk and the heavy air raids; victory appeared inevitable. But the home front, in the conflict since the first day, refused to be unrealistic about the length of the war. The British worker and farmer preferred to say, "Let's get on with it," meanwhile paying the greatest attention to postwar planning. In 1943 Britons believed—as perhaps no other people except the Russians— that they were fighting a "people's war."

Canada

From complacency to action. Madame Chiang Kai-shek, speaking before the House of Commons in Ottawa in June 1943, stated that Canada's war effort was the greatest per capita among the United Nations.

Canada entered the war in September 1939, but its industrial mobilization did not become immediately effective. Following the typical history of the democracies, the country basked in the complacency of the "sitzkrieg," satisfied with sending Great Britain and her allies increased supplies of raw materials and agricultural products. But with the fall of France in June 1940, Canada went to work in earnest.

Canada's Industrial Revolution. Prime Minister Mackenzie King has pointed out that during the first three years of the Second World War the Dominion underwent an Industrial Revolution. Instead of concentrating upon the export of wheat, nonferrous metals, wood products, and fish, as in the past, Canada embarked upon one of the most ambitious industrial programs in modern history.

First there had to be rapid expansion of capital equipment. At the same time the government had to check all inflationary tendencies caused by this expansion and restrict specific commodities in domestic consumption. By March 1941, however, the newly constructed factories were beginning to turn out their war products in sizable quantities, and in the war years which followed, Canadian production, employment, and wages mounted to unprecedented heights. The Second World War has brought swift maturity to the country.

Canada in 1943 was the fourth largest producer of war supplies among the United Nations. More than 50 per cent of the mechanized transport used by the British army in North Africa was manufactured in Canada.

The shipbuilding industry shows expansion as great as that of the automotive industry. At the outbreak of war Canada was constructing virtually no ships at all. As of June 1943, there were in various stages of production 167 cargo ships of the 10,000-ton category, and 15 ships of the 4700-ton class. In addition, Canadian shipyards are turning out corvettes and frigates in a steady stream for the all-important convoy duty of the R.C.N. Before the war, Canada's aircraft industry employed only 1000 people, who turned out 40 planes a year. In July of 1943 almost 100,000 workers had built about 10,000 planes since the outbreak of war.

Food exports. In the last war Canada's great contribution to her allies was in agriculture, especially the export of wheat. In this war there is more emphasis upon the shipment of cheese, eggs, bacon, and pork. In addition the entire 1942 catch of salmon and herring went to the United Kingdom. Food objectives for 1943 call for a 22 per cent increase in hog production and a 29 per cent increase in eggs, and an 18 per cent decrease in wheat acreage because of a wheat surplus of almost 800,000,000 bushels beyond domestic needs—a surplus which will nevertheless be valuable to Europe in the postwar reconstruction years. Canadian delegates took an active part at the United Nations Food Conference held at Hot Springs,

Virginia, from May 18 to June 3, 1943. The importance of Canada in the international food situation was given full recognition.

Financing the war. How is the Second World War affecting the Canadians from a financial point of view? Some of the features of Canada's financial plans have been closely analyzed by American economists.

Government expenditures for 1943-1944 are estimated at approximately eleven times as much as the average of the years just before the war. Naturally, such heavy expenditures mean heavy obligations for the taxpayer. Both direct and indirect taxes have been increased steadily since the outbreak of the war. When rates of taxes paid by the average man in the United States, Britain, and Canada are compared, it will be seen that the Canadian consistently paid in 1943 half as much again as the American, and about as much as the Englishman.[6] Income taxes, on a pay-as-you-owe basis, are deducted from pay envelopes or collected in quarterly installments. Part of the sum is a compulsory saving to be refunded after the war, with 2 per cent interest. Exponents of the plan maintain that this arrangement not only reduces civilian purchasing power and combats inflation but also sets aside for the taxpayer funds which will be welcomed during the trying postwar period. Corporation and luxury taxes were also at a record high in 1943.

In spite of the heavy taxation, the national debt rose from $3,152,000,000 in 1939 to $4,045,000,000 in 1942, and economists estimate that it will jump to $9,215,000,000 in 1944. To meet this condition, the government has relied primarily on borrowing through Victory Loans.

Control of inflation. To prevent inflation, the Wartime Prices and Trade Board introduced price ceilings on November 30, 1941. The ceiling decided upon was the level of retail prices between September 15 and October 11, 1941. To keep prices from rising despite increased consumer purchasing power and mounting production costs, the Canadian government has consistently paid subsidies.

Price control and rationing have worked well. During the first war, when prices were unchecked, they rose 57.6 per cent above the prewar level. In World War II the cost-of-living index by December 1941 had risen but 14.7 per cent—and since the enforcement of price ceilings it has mounted only another 1.5

per cent. Canadian economists look with apprehension at American difficulties with price controls. For, if inflation should have its way in the United States, it must inevitably cross the boundary, so closely interdependent have the economies of the two countries become.

Other wartime controls include the National War Labor Board, which both regulates wages and administers cost-of-living bonuses so that wages will not lag behind wartime price levels.

The Air Training Plan. In some ways Canada's most spectacular military contribution—and certainly one out of all proportion to its population—has been its air force and air training plan. The British Commonwealth Air Training Plan is jointly the project of Canada, Great Britain, Australia, and New Zealand, but is administered by the R.C.A.F. This training scheme, which on May 1, 1943 involved 150,-000, grew up soon after the outbreak of the war in 1939. Huge airfields and training schools mushroomed across the entire length of Canada, and young recruits from all over the Empire reported for duty. Each month has seen an increase in the number of air crew personnel graduated and sent overseas. Sixty per cent of the Plan's graduates are Canadians, and the Dominion has paid about the same proportion of its cost and upkeep.

This aerial revolution in Canada portends a strategic postwar role in aviation. Thousands of skilled fliers and technicians, superb new facilities and aircraft manufacturing plants, huge military bases on both coasts, and especially the new airfields in the Northwest promise an important future in commercial air travel along the great northern route to Europe and Asia. Well aware of postwar possibilities, the government has officially stated that the development of Canadian aviation will not be left to chance or the plans of rival commercial companies, but will be fostered and supervised mainly by the government.

Canada comes of age. The growing stature of Canada as a nation is reflected in its relations with other members of the United Nations. The country is no longer an acquiescing, timid stepchild of Great Britain. To Ottawa go the diplomatic and economic representatives of a score of countries to deal with the government on a new plane of parity. To Quebec went Roosevelt and Churchill in August 1943. In both war and postwar plans Canadians show frankness and independence.

Demonstrating United States-Canadian cooperation and solidarity, Canadian builders hand over this sleek corvette, adorned with the American flag and goodwill messages, to the United States Navy.

Canadian-American relations have always been a model of international amity and co-operation. The war has, if anything, strengthened them; the two nations have pooled their resources and planning initiative, especially in the Permanent Joint Board on Defense.

Canada's economic relations with Great Britain have assumed an unprecedented importance. The mother country has had to make heavy purchases in the Dominion, and the Canadian government entered into various arrangements to facilitate payment by Britain. Then in 1942 the Dominion made an outright gift of $1,000,000,000 in materials, munitions, and foodstuffs to the United Kingdom. This gift was followed by the passage on May 20, 1943, of the United Nations Mutual Aid Bill, providing for the distribution to Canada's allies of material, foodstuffs, and equipment worth $1,000,000,000. These supplies are not being sold but contributed, for Canadians agree that postwar debts among nations will only lead to grave international friction.

Debit and credit. But the national picture is not without its discordant elements. Canadians did the usual grumbling about rationing, the various black markets, the coal shortage—especially as much-needed shipments of hard coal from the United States were threatened by the coal situation there—and manpower difficulties. There was strong criticism in various quarters that too much manpower has been allowed to continue in the less essential industries, while many indispensable industries suffered from a dearth of labor.[7]

Labor's reaction to the manpower problem in 1943 was emphatic. Canadian labor had a record of few strikes, but it maintained that this existed in spite of inadequate representa-

In November 1943 the first United States-Alaska land route formally opened. Faster and less vulnerable than the old water route, the 1500-mile Alaska Highway has strategic importance now and postwar industrial value for the Western Hemisphere.

tion in Ottawa's wartime administration. Some labor groups were convinced that Selective Service had been a means of "freezing" workers at their posts and depriving them of better wages. By and large, Ottawa's handling of the manpower situation could bear favorable comparison with conditions in Great Britain and the United States; but there was enough dissatisfaction among the working groups to explain the results of the August 4, 1943 provincial election in Ontario. The new labor party, the C.C.F. (Cooperative Commonwealth Federation), jumped from a no-seat group to almost a majority group in the legislature. This election had peculiarly national implications because Premier King had personally endorsed the incumbent Ontario government—which was almost obliterated at the polls. The political temper throughout Canada in 1943 was an unmistakable swing to the left, with the C.C.F. and its policy of national planning and public ownership forging ahead in nearly every province. In fact, a Gallup poll taken in the fall of 1943 indicated that the C.C.F. then slightly led the Liberals and Progressive-Conservatives in popular favor. C.C.F. critics of the government charged that the government's production policy was all to the advantage of large financial and industrial groups. They warned that unless steps were taken, Canada after the war would be the victim of big business monopolies.

One problem, which troubled Canada in the last war also, has been English-French relations. The problem is highly complex, because the tensions which have developed over decades are at once social, political, economic, and religious. The French-Canadians are exceedingly loyal in their love of Canada, but their conditioning has tended to make and keep them strongly isolationist. The result is that a foreign war has little appeal for Quebec, even though the rest of the Dominion maintains that the security of Canada—and therefore of Quebec itself—depends upon an Allied victory overseas. The government, wishing at all costs to avoid the unfortunate misunderstanding in French-English relations during World War I, has compromised on certain basic issues. One of these is conscription. Conscription of all eligible males for military service was in force in 1943, but only those soldiers who volunteered for general service needed to serve overseas. This system satisfied the Quebec element, but appeared to be highly distasteful to the rest of the Dominion, who insisted volubly that conscription must be both universal and complete. Actually, the vast majority of Canadian soldiers have volunteered for general service, but the presence of many French-Canadians among the trainees called up only for home defense has created a delicate situation.

There were still other issues which gave rise to anxiety among various groups, but, when a national balance is struck, Canada's domestic condition appeared very sound. The Canadian people had no Utopian ideas about the reconstruction years; but already they were trying to plan a postwar social and economic order of plenty—for their country had come of age.

Australia, New Zealand, South Africa

Australia. Unlike the First World War, during which the enemy was 10,000 miles away, the Second World War has brought the fearful possibility of invasion and national annihilation to Australia's very doorstep. It has been the most critical period of the nation's history. Statistics show that every other man between the ages of 18 and 45 is in the fighting services. Altogether 800,000 men have been inducted—the equivalent of more than 15,000,-000 Americans in uniform. Australian feats in the Second World War live up to the proud record of 1914-1918, "Cobbers" having distinguished themselves in Libya, Egypt, Syria, Greece, Crete, Malaya, the Netherlands East Indies, and New Guinea.

The home front had to overcome grave handicaps to meet the threat from abroad. Since Australia has a population of only 6½ million, the foremost handicap was manpower. To create a proper balance between the fighting and production fronts, the government established a Manpower Directorate.

Another handicap was that prior to this war Australia was primarily an agricultural country, relying heavily upon manufactured imports. After 1939 the country had to set its energies to turning out the tools and munitions of war.

Australia saw the danger of concentrating her industries in two or three large cities on the east coast as the threat of Japanese bomb-

As the war advanced, even the very young were doing their part for the home front. These small members of an Australian "Cub Pack" are obviously pleased with their collection of scrap metal.

ing grew greater. Much of industry was therefore decentralized and spread out into the interior; at the same time use of more local labor and resources became possible. The conversion of the country's industry from a peacetime to a wartime economy has been the special job of the Department of War Organization of Industry.

As in other Allied countries, the surplus purchasing power created by consumer restrictions was checked by a heavy increase in taxation and by government loan programs. In spite of action taken early in the war, living costs in Australia have risen sharply, but it was felt in 1943 that the adoption of the Canadian principle of paying subsidies to producers of war essentials to maintain price ceilings would do much to check inflation.

Australian workers are enthusiastic trade unionists and as such enjoy a strong economic and political bargaining power. The trade unionists were largely instrumental in electing a Labor Government under Premier John Curtin in 1941, and they have accepted the drastic government action to step up the total

war effort. The special regulations passed in February 1942 were designed to peg wage rates in all industries, freeze all workers in their jobs, suspend all holidays, and impose penalties on absenteeism. In the general election held August 21, 1942, Curtin's government won a smashing victory, capturing about two thirds of the 75 seats in the House of Representatives, and all 19 Senate seats, for which voting took place.

In 1943 American soldiers filled the streets of Sydney; American planes filled the skies of "Down Under." Doughboys were marrying Australian girls in surprising numbers, and Yankees and "Cobbers" vied with each other in outlandish slang, beer drinking, and a mania for betting on anything and everything. The fighting qualities of each nation were fully approved by the other, and the Aussies were cooperating splendidly with General MacArthur. American men and materials had been transported many thousands of miles to the Australian war theater, and the Commonwealth was deeply appreciative of America's Lend-Lease aid.

What we may not realize is that Australia was repaying this aid with a reciprocal aid program of her own. At the end of 1942, American forces had received 30 million pounds of meat and 50 million pounds of vegetables and fruits from the Australian government, which provides rations for every American soldier stationed on its soil. Likewise the government provided camp accommodations, services, hospitals, and large quantities of army and civilian stores. It is said that on a population basis, Australian aid was approximately seven times as great as United States aid to Australia.[8] Australia promises to come out of the war stronger and more united, more industrialized, and more aware than ever of her responsibilities in the family of nations. The cooperation demonstrated by Australia and the United States was a portent of the kind of world that democratic action could create.

New Zealand. Within a matter of minutes after Britain's declaration of war on September 3, 1939, New Zealand's cabinet unanimously followed suit. Since that day, this country of but 1,640,000 inhabitants has made a military contribution on an all-out scale, and her men have distinguished themselves on battlefronts the world over. A New Zealander was the first Allied war ace, and the New

Zealand cruiser *Achilles* helped to destroy the *Graf Spee* in the battle of the River Plate.

In normal times New Zealand's prosperity is largely based on the export of great quantities of butter, cheese, meat, and wool, its best customer being the United Kingdom. Faced with the possibility of invasion and the cutting of her supply lines, New Zealand simply had to embark upon a rapid industrial program, even though she must import all her steel. What plant facilities there were had to be converted, and workers trained to do precision work unknown in the Dominion before. By 1943 an industrial transformation had resulted, and armored vehicles, Bren gun carriers, mortars, and ammunition were swelling the supplies of the United Nations. In the words of one New Zealander, addressing American readers: "It isn't much to set beside your giant factories. But remember we start from scratch—and the more we can produce here the less is the strain on your shipping."[9]

New Zealanders and Americans stationed in the Dominion in 1943 were establishing a basis for greater cooperation in the postwar era. It was not impossible that returning doughboys would help spread news of the progressive quality of the social security program of New Zealand—"the test tube of the democracies."

South Africa. In September 1939, one outstanding leader of South Africa, General Hertzog, held that since the Dominion was a sovereign independent state not bound to participate in a war simply because Britain was involved, it should adhere to a policy of benevolent neutrality. But General Smuts, who maintained that in this crisis the destinies of all democracies were inseparably linked, carried the day and formed a new pro-war government. Pro-war leaders had 84 seats in the House of Assembly against the 66 seats mustered by the anti-war forces. The difference constituted a fairly comfortable working majority, and with it General Smuts began a vigorous policy of war participation.

Nevertheless, the opposition continued to give voice to its strong disapproval of South Africa's foreign policy. And so, on July 7, 1943, a general election was held, with the war as the principal issue. Interest ran high throughout the Union, and about 75 per cent of the eligible population voted. Ballots were sent to the soldiers scattered in North Africa, Britain, India, and elsewhere, and then flown

New Zealand soldiers fought—and fought well— alongside their allies in the North African campaign. Here New Zealanders man slit trenches in the Battle of Egypt.

back for tabulation. The results were an overwhelming victory for the pro-war parties, so that they then held 107 seats in the House of Assembly to the anti-war groups' 43.

South Africa's war effort has been valiant. The Union has a white population of only 2,230,000, yet has more than 200,000 well-equipped "Springboks" under arms. The industrial front has made rapid strides. At the outbreak of the war, South Africa had but three factories capable of producing military materials; after two years, she could boast of more than six hundred.

The Dominion's conversion program was the result of efficient governmental planning, largely directed by a special civilian agency known as the War Supplies Board. The production of steel was rapidly stepped up, as was the mining of coal. It became possible to manufacture indispensable military tools. An entirely new and important machine tool industry has been created. In 1943 the workshops of the state-controlled South African Railways and Harbors, the largest organization in the Dominion, were turning out armored cars, troop-carrier bodies, airplane hangars, electric generators, gun sights, and precision instruments. The country's shoe and textile industries were not only fulfilling all their own army's needs but making large deliveries of boots and blankets to Britain and other Allies.

On June 13, 1942 was held the inaugural meeting of the Social and Economic Planning Council, created to handle postwar reconstruction plans. A fundamental postwar problem is that of the status of the colored population. The British and Boers are far outnumbered by the Negroes and the latter have virtually no say in the government. Articulate Negro ele-

ments have been increasingly persistent in demanding for their people greater educational facilities, a higher economic status, and more political representation. The democratic ideals to which the war aims of the Union are pledged demand, observers point out, an eventual settlement of this complicated question.

In 1943, then, the political horizon was not without clouds, but, as in its sister Dominions, Canada and Australia, the Union's swiftly growing industrialization had brought a new maturity and promise.

Latin America

Good **Neighbor cooperation.** The twenty-one sovereign republics of the Western Hemisphere have a total population of some 270,000,000. The problems which they share in common—hemispheric defense, health and education, standards of living, trade, and mutual understanding—necessitated the creation of special machinery. Thus, since 1923, inter-American conferences have been held every five years, and three special meetings have been called since 1939—at Panama in 1939, Havana in 1940, and Rio de Janeiro in 1942.

The last conference recommended that the American nations sever relations with the Axis powers (which all Latin American republics with the exception of Argentina have now done), and it set up an Inter-American Defense Board as well as an Emergency Advisory Committee for Political Defense to stamp out fifth-column activities. United States Lend-Lease has assisted many republics in buying army and navy equipment; and the State Department has enforced the regulations of the Proclaimed List of Blocked Nationals—a blacklist of 3000 Axis firms, and firms operating with the Axis, in Latin America.

Economic importance. Since the loss of southeastern Asia to Japan, the United Nations have had to rely almost entirely on South American sources for shipments of natural rubber, tin, quinine, antimony, and other needed war materials. Besides these products, they depend on Latin America for a diversity of goods, ranging from sugar to iron. To coordinate the production and distribution of these vital war materials swiftly and effectively has been a large job. After the conference at Rio de Janeiro, the United States concluded agreements with various South American coun-

tries to furnish them with machinery and financial and technical assistance in return for their products. Necessary loans are made through the Export-Import Bank and the Reconstruction Finance Corporation. Transportation of the products to the United States is under the cooperative direction of various Washington agencies, such as the State Department, the War Production Board, and the War Shipping Administration.

Thus, even though from a military point of view the Latin American countries have played to date a purely defensive role, patrolling their shores, events in the Pacific war theater and the technological demands of modern combat have combined to make the South American economy especially important and strategic. The Axis powers realized the economic significance of Latin America long ago. For years prior to 1939 all three nations—Germany, Italy, and Japan—were busily engaged in pouring money and nationals into the southern continent in an effort to gain a stranglehold over its economic and political life. Today their economic power is virtually annihilated, and Axis political influence is being combated. Meanwhile, the Allies have become increasingly aware of the role Latin America can play now and in the postwar era.

Latin American difficulties. The present economic condition of the republics to the south is not a simple one of progress and prosperity. Distressing problems confront the Good Neighbors, and a solution to some of them must be discovered soon.

The cost of living in almost all the Latin American countries has been mounting steadily, and from 1941 has risen alarmingly. For example, taking the cost of living index in

Good Neighbor policy in action at the conference table in Rio de Janeiro. The United States representative, Sumner Welles, then Undersecretary of State, is seated at the far right.

Brazil as 100 for 1929, in 1938 it was 125, and by March 1943 had soared to 163 in Rio de Janeiro. Wages have not kept pace with the inflation of prices; so a progressively reduced standard of living has resulted. The story is similar for most of the other republics, and in Bolivia the situation has already become highly critical. There the cost-of-living index for the capital city, La Paz, jumped from 100 in 1931 to 1497 in December 1942. Many of the countries have created special price controls to aid in stabilization, but apparently these measures have not been successful.

The shipping shortage has been acute and has brought in its wake pressing economic problems. Brazil has accelerated its industrial development in steel, aluminum, rayon, and chemical products, but this entire development depends upon shipments of petroleum and coal from the United States. Limited shipping space meant a limitation in imports and a serious threat to Brazil's war effort.

The shipping problem affects almost all the other republics as well. Chile has had a shortage of needed petroleum, while in 1942 Colombia could not fill its coffee quota as established in the Inter-American Coffee Agreement, even though production was sufficient. Uruguay's construction industry, employing a large proportion of the industrial population, has been held back because it has not been possible to import sufficient iron and steel. Venezuela's oil production has been curtailed drastically because of a shortage in tankers; unemployment in this important industry has increased markedly. Cuba could not export all its 1942 sugar crop. The "banana republics," unable to ship their chief product abroad, have suffered sharp economic reverses.

The war has cut off important European and, to a lesser degree, Asiatic markets; some countries have been hit hard. In 1942 Argentina's imports were by volume less than half those of 1938, while its exports were also less, although slightly greater in actual value. Since cereals can no longer be exported as formerly, the government has had to pay continued subsidies to their growers.

A significant feature of South American trade at present is the growing importance of the United States' position. Naturally, the war has decimated the lucrative commerce enjoyed by Germany and Italy, and the United States has been by all odds the chief gainer, even in comparison with Britain. With probably no exception, every Latin American republic has shown the ascendancy of the United States in its trade. It will be interesting to see whether the United States continues to enjoy this favorable economic position.

Despite the many difficulties, the Second World War is helping to industrialize Latin America; this development in turn holds forth the promise of a higher standard of living. Much remains to be done, however, before the vast majority of the people south of the Rio Grande enjoy anything like a proper economic existence. Dietary deficiencies, nutritional diseases, lack of sanitation, illiteracy, and abject poverty have to be attacked vigorously. In this vast socio-economic struggle, the United States is contributing its exports and resources. In Peru, for example, the American government has authorized an Export-Import Bank loan of 25 million dollars, and is rendering financial and technical assistance for a cooperative sanitation and health program. An American mission is planning a cooperative food production program for the country. In Costa Rica, American money and technical aid are helping to complete the Pioneer Road, which will link finished sections of the Pan-American Highway. A health program has been inaugurated to accompany the road building. These Good Neighbor contributions bode well for the future of the Western Hemisphere.

Political Latin America. By and large, the political front in Latin America has shown both stability and solidarity. Perhaps the most prominent political upheaval in 1943 was the Argentine revolt of June 4 against the government of President Ramon S. Castillo, who had pursued an appeasing policy of "prudent neutrality." It was hoped that the revolt would result in the formation of a more pro-Allied government, but the first cabinet appointed by Ramirez appeared to be strongly nationalist and included leaders with pro-Axis leanings. The present political struggle is being closely followed by the United States and the Argentine's neighbors.

The balance sheet shows that Latin America as a whole is linked to the United Nations and their cause. Eleven republics have declared war on the Axis powers, seven have severed relations with them, and two have assumed a nonbelligerent position, allowing the Allies—but not the Axis—to use their ports. Pan-American relations were further cemented in 1943 by the special trips of Latin American Presidents for conferences and negotiations in Washington and by Vice-President Wallace's extensive tour of every South American republic. Wherever he went, Mr. Wallace received heartfelt ovations, which could be taken as evidence of the growing approval of American foreign policy.

Russia

Meeting the crisis. The position of Russia in 1943 amazed the world. That the country did not capitulate from economic necessity and psychological despair after the Nazi invasions will go down in history as a tribute to the tenacity of the Russian populace. That the Russians were able to drive the Germans back beyond the Dnieper by fall seemed almost miraculous. Certainly part of the success was due to the Soviet leaders' foresight and planning.

On July 3, 1941, eleven days after the Nazis poured across the borders, Stalin declared: "To the enemy must not be left a single engine, a single railway car, not a single pound of grain or a gallon of fuel."[10] The world expected that this now-famous "scorched-earth" policy would result in the systematic destruction of all factories and installations. What the world did not expect was the wholesale removal of entire plants. For example, the Russians removed to new foundations a thousand miles eastward in the Urals the tractor works of Kharkov, the farm implement factory of Rostov, the aircraft plants of Taganrog, and huge armament works. The great industrial trek to the East, involving hundreds of large and small plants, was accompanied by the transfer of an estimated million workers with their families. Prewar planning by Stalin and his engineers made the trek possible; because of it the USSR was able to catch its second wind. The transfer of industry held important postwar implications as well. The Urals and western Siberia are fabulously rich in mineral resources, the twin-peaked Magnet Mountain, for example, being an almost solid mass of magnetite, 60 per cent pure iron. Lenin long foretold the industrial potentialities of this vast hinterland. The words of ex-ambassador Joseph E. Davies are significant:

" . . . I saw great cities—boom cities, laid out in squares like our prairie towns, dotted with factories, huge plants and chimneys all over the place—one small Pittsburgh after another. . . .

The impression of power, innate strength, vigor, and pioneer energy, which one gets from this great section, is extraordinary."[11]

The efforts of the industrial workers, whose output has increased daily, have been matched by the farmers, despite loss for a time of all the Ukraine and the fertile Don region. Some 5,000,000 acres of uncultivated land were made productive to compensate for the millions of acres lost to the Nazis. Soviet agriculture has faced dangerous shortages in manpower, machines, and animals as well. The sowing and harvesting were taken over principally by women, men too old for military service, and hundreds of thousands of school children and students. The country suffered but averted the starvation which Hitler must undoubtedly have relied upon.

A marked characteristic of the Russian home front in 1943 was the growing proportion of women in industry. Even before the war the world saw pictures of Soviet women driving locomotive engines, tractors, and subway trains, performing operations, welding, bricklaying, or unloading ships. The socialist philosophy stresses complete equality of the sexes. By 1943 there were 15,000,000 women in industry, and of course women were playing an unprecedented role of importance in Soviet agriculture. In addition a half million women were serving in the Red Cross and Red Crescent Societies at the front. Nor have Americans forgotten meeting in 1942 the mild-mannered young lady who, as one of many women snipers, had accounted for 309 Nazis.

Putting finishing touches on ammunition for the Red Army, these Soviet women typify the unprecedented role of women in industry on all home fronts.

The war brought serious social problems to the country. Untold numbers of civilians in overrun territory had been slain or left to starve. As the Red armies drove victoriously westward in 1943, the government had to grapple with the tremendous job of reconstructing areas of desolation. For example, the city of Kharkov was left burning by the retreating Germans, the streets blocked by piles of broken glass, bricks, and twisted iron. The Ukrainian Academy of Sciences had developed plans—while the city was still occupied by the Nazis—for the reconstruction of Kharkov, utilizing the best available materials, making provision for subways and a new drainage system. In 1943 these plans had already begun to take form.[12]

Also in 1943, as the southern regions of the Soviet Union were liberated, the collective farmers began to repair the destruction wrought by German occupation. Since almost all farm machinery and buildings had been demolished, the government at once sent in about 11,000 specialists and hundreds of tractors and other machines. Agricultural research is being resumed.[13]

These liberated areas have required not only the services of engineers but those of doctors, educators, and social workers. The invasion necessitated the stepping up of hospital facilities and medical personnel. Although there were 160,000 doctors in 1940 (as contrasted with 20,000 at the time of the Revolution), the needs of the war forced the medical schools to speed their graduation rate from 12,000 yearly to an estimated 42,000 for the first sixteen months of the war. With the liberation of Russian territory came Russian doctors and nurses to aid the sick.

One poignant aspect has been the problem of war orphans. Whenever land has been reconquered, the government has immediately set aside special stores of foods, medicines, and school supplies, and has established special homes and nurseries for orphaned children. A popular movement has been the adoption of orphans by citizens living all over the Soviet Union. But, like Britain, Russia faces a large problem in readjusting psychologically thousands of these young minds, scarred by the terrors of modern warfare.

The national budget. In a socialistic state the annual budget naturally must be reckoned in tremendous figures. The Soviet budget in 1941, for example, reached 216 billion rubles. The 1931 budget was 19 billion rubles. That the war has been a heavy burden on the Russian people is shown by the fact that in 1931 less than one billion rubles were appropriated for the army, whereas in 1941 the appropriation came to 70 billion, or about one third of the annual budget. No doubt the critical years, 1942 and 1943, have witnessed a still greater percentage set aside for military operations. A breakdown of the 1941 budget affords other interesting insights into the country's economic condition. Of the 216 billion total, 33 per cent was appropriated for capital construction in industry, agriculture, and transportation. Government operations, police and court administration, social security reserves, and emergency funds required about 12 per cent. However, despite the critical foreign situation with its heavy demands on defense preparations, the 1941 budget called for appropriations amounting to 22 per cent to be spent on the nation's educational system, health program, and scientific research.[14] Budget statistics like these help explain what the Russian people were fighting for as they met Hitler's challenge.

In 1943 the government allotted over 67,000,000 rubles to the People's Commissariat of Education to restore and reëquip schools in liberated regions. It was pointed out in an article in *Izvestia* that of 18,000 schools in twelve liberated areas, 10,500 had already been restored.[15] However, it will be a long time before the losses suffered by schools and libraries are fully replaced.

Political differences. As has been indicated, the world in 1943 was unstinting in its praise of Russia's military accomplishments and resiliency of its economic and social institutions. But Russia's allies were more hesitant when it came to evaluating the Soviet's foreign policy and political frame of mind. What was Russia's real postwar objective? What was Russia's true evaluation of her allies?

Because until November there was no closely knit program of political activity among the four principal United Nations, there seemed little possibility in 1943 of getting definitive answers to these questions. But it is important to bear in mind that in 1943 the Russian people were also troubled by the same questions: what were the true postwar objectives of Britain and the United States?

The principal source of trouble in 1943 was the second front which the Russians were asking the Allies to establish. (See pages 215 and 224.) Similarly, in the fall of 1943 many Americans were asking aloud what Russia was going to do about Japan. They felt that she could at least provide bases in Siberia for her Allies. Roosevelt was of the opinion, however, that Soviet policy regarding Japan was dictated by purely practical reasons; in 1943 her hands were tied in the west.

In other matters also, on the political and diplomatic fronts, Soviet leaders in 1943 were not seeing eye to eye with the British and Americans. Washington and London gave partial recognition to the French Committee of National Liberation; Moscow recognized it fully. London and Washington seemed interested in plans suggested by Polish leaders for a postwar East European Federation (to be made up of Poland, Czechoslovakia, Hungary, Rumania); Moscow came out flatly against this. *War and the Working Class*, a new semiofficial Moscow periodical, perceived in the whole idea an unfriendly move by Polish reactionaries and warned about trying to establish another "cordon sanitaire" against Russia.

At the same time government-approved groups in Moscow were supporting a Free Germany Committee. Some observers abroad saw in this new movement a Soviet desire either to bring about a negotiated peace with Germany or to pave the way for the eventual establishment of bolshevism in German territory. Defenders of the movement replied that it was designed to encourage and aid the strong anti-Hitler underground forces in Germany to throw off the Nazi leadership; that its objectives were similar to those of the French Committee of National Liberation and of Roosevelt and Churchill regarding Italy, i.e., encouragement of anti-Fascist governments which would bring about the regeneration of the countries.

Promising signs. The conferences at Moscow and Teheran, as we have seen (pages 224 and 218), promised much for more complete understanding and cooperative action among the Allies. Another step toward creating a friendlier international atmosphere was the abolition of the Comintern by Stalin. With the historic termination of this world-wide organization for the propagation of communism, Russia's allies had further evidence that she was not trying to sabotage their capitalistic institutions.

Meanwhile, the smashing victories on the front were celebrated with cannon salutes in Moscow and fireworks. Victory seemed at last in sight. The people at home had no abundance of food, but there was no famine—and no inflationary increase in the cost of living, and no war profiteering. The theaters were more widely patronized than ever, although many of Russia's finest theater and ballet companies were spending most of their time entertaining the soldiers at the front. Sports contests were widely held and well attended. The Archbishop of York, visiting Moscow in September, reported publicly that he found complete freedom of religion there, that antireligious propaganda had ceased, that fifty to sixty churches were open in the Moscow area alone.

Russian people presumably had their differences of opinion, their domestic conflicts, their great problem of providing a high degree of individual liberty within a way of life regulated by the state. But they stood before the world as a unified people throwing back an aggressor.

China

After twelve years. On September 19, 1931, Japanese troops marched into Manchuria and set in motion a train of events culminating in the Second World War. On September 19, 1943, the Chinese people looked back over twelve heart-breaking years of fighting Japanese aggression. On them had fallen a tremendously heavy yoke. In those twelve years the richest regions of the land—the teeming seaports and industrial cities, the fertile river valleys—had been occupied by the Japanese, millions of Chinese soldiers and civilians had perished, and the supplies promised by China's allies, on which the nation's fate depended, were in the fall of 1943 still only trickling in between the Japanese-held areas. The gravity of China's position had not gone unnoticed abroad; the Quebec Conference drafted plans for an ambitious campaign in southeastern Asia, and later in Cairo Churchill and Roosevelt joined Chiang Kai-shek in pledging the complete defeat of Japan. But China's burden was heavily trying.

Three-point program. Yet in one of China's darkest hours, Madame Sun Yat-sen, the widow of the nation's great modern reformer, had set forth a three-point program for the future: (1) China must attain political, economic, and cultural equality with other nations; (2) the Japanese must be forced out of Chinese territory; and (3) China must become a true democracy by the national election of a People's Congress to replace the one-party government of the Kuomintang.[16]

Toward Madame Sun Yat-sen's first goal, historic action was taken simultaneously in Washington and Chungking on January 11, 1943. In the former capital, the United States and China signed a treaty ending the special rights enjoyed by the United States in certain Chinese cities, including special courts at Shanghai for the trial of Americans.[17] At Chungking British and Chinese officials signed a similar treaty abrogating the extraterritorial rights and privileges of the British Empire. Thus ended a century of political humiliation for China. In addition the Chinese government in February 1943 unilaterally abrogated the treaty of 1899, by which France had leased Kwangchowwan on China's southern coast.

The second goal, as expressed by Madame Sun Yat-sen, was perhaps brought a little closer in 1943 as the Chinese won minor battles against the Japanese. Dr. T. V. Soong, China's Foreign Minister, was explicit regarding his country's attitude toward the regaining of lost

Camouflaged Chinese troops ford a river near the front, as the Japanese are held at China's "back door."

areas, stating that China had no territorial ambitions and claimed no special privileges. He expected Manchuria and Formosa to be returned to China, but thought Korea ought to be independent.[18]

China's struggle toward democracy—the third goal—was marked during 1943 by both disturbing and promising developments. Another dangerous rift appeared between the Central Government and the Chinese Communists. The Central Government strongly opposed the Communists' possession of an autonomous government, army, currency, and taxation system in the border provinces. The Communists, on the other hand, have for years criticized what they deem the inefficiency and half-heartedness of the Central Government's war against the Japanese. Furthermore, the Communists wanted full recognition as a political party, but were afraid to give up their military organization until their political aims were granted. Actual clashes broke out in the summer of 1943, the official Central News revealed.

But this serious internal crisis seemed likely to be satisfactorily settled by the Kuomintang and Generalissimo Chiang Kai-shek. On August 1, 1943, the venerable and respected President of China, Lin Sen, died. In September, the Central Executive Committee of the Kuomintang selected Chiang Kai-shek as Lin Sen's successor, thus legalizing Chiang Kai-shek's position as the military and political leader of China. Chiang told the Central Executive Committee to maintain a "policy of leniency and forbearance" toward the Communists, and stated that the problem "should be solved by political means."[19]

The new President went farther, encouraging the Central Executive Committee to pass a resolution stating that a People's Congress to adopt a constitution must be held within a year after the war. The Kuomintang was responding to the note struck in Chiang's new book, *China's Destiny.* Though in the past China's fate depended on foreign policy, now "it depends on our ability to secure inner political unification and concentration of national power. China stands at the watershed of her fate."[20]

Economic and political developments. The Kuomintang's Central Executive Committee also passed a 16-point resolution blueprinting China's postwar economic aims. The resolution allowed for both private and public enterprise. Those industries which are inherently monopolistic and public utilities are to be owned by the state. On the other hand, "industry which may be entrusted to individuals or which will be less suitable for the state to operate shall be privately operated."[21]

In addition to the democratic economic planning, a new system of self-government, known as the *hsien* system, has developed widely in Free China during the war. "These *hsien* governments are very close to the people, . . . and are giving the farmers an increasing share in the running of local affairs."[22]

The ability of the Chinese to keep fighting the aggressor has been due largely to the removal of strategic industries into the still-free regions, as in Russia. With government help, 450 private factories with their personnel have been moved despite the appalling transport difficulties. Hundreds of thousands of farmers and their equipment and most of China's student body have also moved inland.

The government has played an important role in establishing and subsidizing new industrial enterprises and regulating prices, wages, credit, and foreign trade. Light industry— for instance, textiles and medical supplies— with emphasis upon decentralization and high mobility, has been fostered by the Chinese Industrial Cooperatives. Only a few years old,

these cooperatives numbered 1700 in 1941, and they promised to play an increasingly important role in postwar China.

Critical domestic condition. Nevertheless, China's domestic condition was extremely critical in 1943. The Japanese blockade was proving all too effective; shortages of food and necessary medical and military supplies in Free China were becoming alarming. Transportation facilities in Free China were so bad that it required superhuman efforts to ship food from one region to another. China's coastal and river shipping dropped from 1,500,000 or 2,000,000 tons, before the war, to 110,000 tons.[23] In order to keep the troops fed at all adequately, many of China's armies were forced to grow their own rice, wheat, and vegetables. Milk and medicine were even scarcer, and the people as a whole were suffering from serious undernourishment. The acute shortage in Free China of everything from munitions to milk resulted in the skyrocketing of prices, adding to the woes of the people.

Yet in 1943 the Chinese spirit still seemed indomitable. The universities which they had transported hundreds of miles upstream into Free China still carried on. A further indication of China's age-old veneration for learning was the announcement in March 1943 that the *Encyclopaedia Britannica* was about to be translated *in toto* into Chinese.

Italy

Grievances of the people. From 1922 to July 25, 1943, Mussolini had been the absolute head of the Italian people substituting for the democratic tradition a Machiavellian philosophy based on aggression, state absolutism, and the subordination of individual rights. By 1943, however, his attempt to construct a new Roman Empire had brought Italy to the point of national exhaustion, war weariness, and bankruptcy. World-shaking changes were inevitable—and Il Duce went out, and Badoglio came in.

Italy's natural resources are relatively poor, and the country is not equipped to be a first-rate military power, though superficially it might appear to be. Yet for years Mussolini had been forcing his people in an unnatural attempt to dominate the Mediterranean. The Italian people were given only the most glowing accounts of victories. Finally, as Italy's mili-

tary prestige sank lower and lower, the impotent rage of the masses against the leader who had so tragically misled them reached new peaks of intensity.

The Italian people nursed other grievances at home as well. Mussolini had linked his fate irrevocably with Hitler's, resulting in what from the historical point of view must be considered an unnatural alliance. However, it was not an alliance of equals, but of master and servant.

Hundreds of thousands of Italian workers, as well as shipments of agricultural products needed by the underfed populace in Italy, were sent to Germany. In April 1943 reports from Switzerland, Russia, and Britain indicated that the Italian diet was poor compared with that of the Germans. For example, the normal bread ration in Italy was 37 ounces per week as contrasted with 80 ounces in Germany; the normal adult meat ration was 5-7 ounces weekly as against the Nazis' 12½ ounces.[24] The Italians knew that they were vastly worse fed than their "blood brothers" and they bitterly resented further exporting of foods. Meanwhile, much-needed imports from Germany fell far below expectations in 1943, the Nazis, for example, admitting their inability to supply Italy's war industries with the 1,000,000 tons of coal per month that agreements called for. Thus in 1943 the raw materials and food situation grew desperate. Added to this was an inflationary rise in prices and a widespread black market which harmed the poorer classes especially. Long before the summer of 1943 the Italians had come to the realistic conclusion that whether the Allies or Germany won, they had lost.

The political struggle. Therefore, when military desperation forced the resignation of Mussolini (and his subsequent flight to Germany), the Italian masses gave vent to their feelings by spontaneous demonstrations of enthusiasm in the large cities. This spirit had already been manifested when the Allies conquered Sicily and the boot of the peninsula. All Fascist insignias disappeared; workers in the northern cities went on strike in the war factories; demands arose for the rededication of Italy to democratic principles of government.

From Germany the fallen Duce proclaimed the formation of a new Fascist Republican State. In a radio speech he exhorted "loyal" Italians to take up arms again on the side of Germany and Italy, to reorganize the armed forces and militia, to eliminate the "traitors" collaborating with the Allies, and to reëstablish Fascist order.

The Italian people had no desire to heed Mussolini's exhortations. They had a new government, led by Badoglio, who clamped down strict censorship on the press and put the railway, postal, radio, and telegraph operators under military control. They had to worry about the problems attending "unconditional surrender" and the terms of the armistice. They were now battling their former Axis partners in the streets of Naples and Rome, and soon the southern half of the peninsula was aflame. The Italians were caught between two fires.

They were caught between other fires as well, republican and monarchial, revolutionary and reactionary. Throughout the Fascist régime a strong underground had persisted in the northern industrial centers. Composed of workers who had seen Fascism destroy ruthlessly the rights of labor and murder its leaders, this underground came to the surface immediately upon Mussolini's fall. The movement favored a clean break not only with Germany and all vestiges of the old Fascist order, but also with the House of Savoy and the group around Badoglio. It called for a popular front, democratic elections, and favored collaboration with the United Nations.

The American and British governments, however, announced (in the words of Churchill), "We certainly do not seek to reduce Italian life to a condition of chaos and anarchy, and find ourselves without any authority with whom to deal." There were many in high governmental circles in Washington and London who saw in the popular movement the danger of a communist revolution. The House of Savoy was commended (by General Eisenhower) for getting rid of Mussolini, and active support was given Badoglio in establishing government and order. The Marshal favored a government recognizing all shades of political thought, and intimated that his own views were those of a moderate. In October 1943 Italy joined the Allies as a cobelligerent, declaring war on its former ally.

However, Italian progressives in exile like Count Sforza and Professor Salvemini decried the maintenance of so many of the old Fascist régime, including petty party bureaucrats; they doubted whether the regeneration of the country could come at the price of so much compromise. For it was well known that Badoglio's own record was in almost direct contrast to the avowed purposes of the democracies; "Since 1936 he had been a member of the Fascist Party. He had acted as the unofficial leader of its right wing. He had paid public tribute to the Duce, master-minded the Fascist victory in Spain, defeated the Ethiopians and accepted from the grateful Mussolini the title of Viceroy and Duke of Addis Ababa."[25] Many Laborites in the British House of Commons deplored what appeared to them a "deal" made with Italian Quislings, and American liberal journals declared that Anglo-American policies were thwarting the democratic ambitions of the Italians.

But the upholders of the official Allied attitude toward the House of Savoy and Marshal Badoglio were quick to point out that much British and American blood had been saved. Italian soldiers and workers, they said, would relieve Allied troops for combat by unloading ships, guarding railways, building roads. The Italian fleet had come over almost intact to the side of the Allies, without firing a shot. The State Department and Foreign Office appeared reasonably satisfied that the promise of Badoglio to work out a democratically constructed government seemed hopeful —and certainly worth a trial.

Germany

Propaganda and facts. Reports leaking out of the Reich in July 1943 gave credence to the joke current there: "We'd better enjoy the war while we can. The peace is going to be terrible."[26] Whether apocryphal or not, the story was apt in that it pointed up the people's realization that for them the war had shifted from a victorious offensive to a bitter defensive. The German population had come to think of the Russian campaign as a living nightmare. To steel home-front resistance, the propaganda agencies drummed into the minds of the people the alleged barbarities of Communist life and the merciless fate awaiting a defeated Germany at the hands of Stalin. In a somber speech in May 1943 the Fuehrer neither minced words nor predicted victory; to lull the German populace by soft words at that stage might prove fatal. Emphasis was placed upon a new propaganda word: *Notgemeinschaft*, unity because of necessity.

The havoc wreaked by the *Luftwaffe* on European cities and historic shrines had been returned ten-fold by 1943—to virtually obliterate Hamburg and many great industrial Ruhr towns, and even begin the destruction of Berlin itself. Hitler in the prewar years continually glorified war; but the temper of the German home front was expressed by one Cologne newspaper after that city had been bombed over a hundred times: "Anyone who lives in a district threatened by air raids experiences a feeling of physical disgust when he meets a comrade who today still glorifies war."[27] Eyewitness accounts relayed from Stockholm and Berne agreed that the destruction wrought in the large industrial areas was well-nigh unbelievable; that families by the thousands were destitute, homeless, and without food; that the transportation and production systems of the Reich were critically shaken.

In addition to the effects of the boomeranging Russian campaign and the Allied aerial offensive, the German people in 1943 were hard hit by the defection of Italy. For months Hitler had maintained a strict silence, but the psychological effects of the collapse of Italy necessitated his reporting to the home front. He attempted to minimize from a military standpoint the withdrawal of Italy from the Axis. He also tried to minimize the fact that the German people were nearly alone in their struggle by maintaining that they could now proceed "free of all burdensome encumbrances."[28] It is interesting to recall his remarks to the Reichstag in 1940: "We could not allow Italy to be defeated. We know that if Fascist Italy were to go down it would be the end of Nazi Germany." To keep the home front in order, Hitler in August 1943 formally appointed Heinrich Himmler (Chief of the Gestapo) both Minister of the Interior and Chief of the Reich Administration. As head of the powerful black-uniformed SS (Schutz-Staffel) troops since 1929, the new home-front "czar" was expected to be able to take care of any possible trouble in his usual efficient, ruthless fashion.

Working conditions inside Germany. The German people were spending long hours in factories during 1943, turning out vital supplies amid the crash of block-busters. They were faced by a serious manpower shortage; the heavy losses on the eastern front necessitated scouring the bottom of the manpower barrel for all possible recruits. By inducements and force the Nazis brought many workers from occupied countries. According to one report, in September 1943, some 30 per cent of all labor forces in Germany were composed of foreigners.[29] Without a doubt this vast labor army freed able-bodied Germans to fight in the armed services. However, forced labor could scarcely be expected to work enthusiastically, and the setbacks of the "master race" in Russia and Italy undoubtedly contributed to a further decline in this foreign labor's will to work. Certain classes of the recruited workers were being treated decently, but other classes were not so fortunate. For example, the *International Labor Review* reported that the Nazis systematically maintained their "discriminatory racial policy against the millions of Soviet workers placed in German industry and agriculture," that the Soviet workers were housed in special barracks, given only limited medical care, were isolated from other groups, and grossly underpaid and overworked.[30] Much of Germany's forced labor was existing in a state of near-slavery.

The German home front did not suffer from an acute food shortage in 1943, although certain commodities (soap, for example) were very scarce. The Nazis had commandeered food supplies from occupied countries to make sure that the needs of the German population were met first. Germany's farm crop prospects in 1943 appeared normal. The first priority on food was held by the armed forces, followed by hospitals, people in bombed areas, children, expectant mothers.

Germans in face of defeat. Allied capitals in the fall of 1943 were rife with rumors that Germany might be closer to capitulation than military experts would admit. In November and December Berlin was subjected to bombings of the intensity which had practically destroyed Hamburg, and the meeting of Stalin, Churchill, and Roosevelt was to bring additional strains on German morale. But experts had to assume that the German armies would fight bitterly to build and maintain a wall of steel around their fatherland. German home production was still at an exceptionally high peak, and the output was good both in quantity and quality. The German worker and farmer were at once hard-working and patient, and their tenacity was further strengthened by their deep dread of a victorious Russia—and by the specter of a flaming revolt of the peoples in Europe. Furthermore, during most of 1943 the German home front hoped that dissension and cross-purposes among its major enemies would yet allow the Reich to win. The Moscow Conference and the Teheran Conference did much to challenge that hope.

Japan

Military and economic consolidation. For the Japanese the question in 1943 was whether they could retain their recently occupied territories long enough to consolidate their military position, at the same time exploiting the resources of the new lands to a degree sufficient to make the war economy at home virtually impregnable. In large measure it was a race against time, because the naval and military offensive had passed to the United Nations.

On the home front the chief objective was to step up war production to the maximum level before the vast arsenal of the United States hit its full stride. In the spring of 1943 the Japanese Diet passed bills centralizing unprecedented power in Tojo. He was given authority to take over any Cabinet Minister's duties pertaining to "labor, materials, motive power and capital,"[31] to centralize those Japanese economic resources not already absorbed by the military socialism long developing in Japan. In October 1943 the industrial subsidiaries owned by the House of Mitsubishi were ordered to double their capital and sell half their stock to the government.[32] Observers in Washington assumed that this step paved the way for government control of the other large Japanese financial and industrial houses also. The Mitsubishi interests included shipbuilding, aircraft production, and steel—three "Achilles heels" to Japan. Without adequate ships, aircraft, and steel she was bound to lose the war—and in all three she had serious shortages in 1943.

Production difficulties. The very existence of the Japanese Empire clearly depended upon ships—ships to carry the raw materials of Malaya, the Philippines, the Dutch East Indies to the mother country, and to take back the finished products of Tokyo and Osaka, and ships to transport and provision the Emperor's armies. At the outbreak of war, Japan was estimated to have 6,300,000 tons of cargo shipping. With further construction and the seizure of vessels, the Japanese brought their shipping total to about 7,500,000 tons. However, on September 3, 1943, Secretary of the Navy Knox announced that of this 7,500,000 total, some 2,500,000 had been sent to the bottom.[33] The Japanese had done everything to overcome this heavy damage, including the construction of wooden ships, but the shipping shortage in 1943 seemed a problem which neither the naval nor the industrial chiefs were able to eliminate.

One of the reasons for the shipping shortage lay in the lack of adequate supplies of iron and steel. Whereas the United States in 1943 was producing around 95,000,000 tons of steel, Japan could only turn out some 8,000,000 tons. In a desperate effort to step up production, Tojo's economic planners attempted the expansion of production facilities in Manchuria, Korea, China, and Japan proper, but it was reported that difficulties were encountered in building blast furnaces. Prior to the outbreak of hostilities Japan fed her war machine to an important extent on the scrap iron purchased from the United States, and the countries which she has overrun have been systematically stripped. One of these sources of supply was now entirely cut off, while another possessed only limited iron and steel.

Before Pearl Harbor the world underrated the power and effectiveness of Japan's air force. The Zero fighter plane and its skilled pilot necessitated a change of attitude. Nevertheless American airplanes proved to be better armed and better protected, and Japanese planes were shot down in 1942 and 1943 in great numbers. The country's air force declined seriously, and it was evident in the fall of 1943 that the aircraft factories of Nagoya and Kobe could not begin to match the output of their enemies. The United States alone was producing many times the maximum Japanese output. Allied experts, after having studied Japan's industrial potential, agreed that a drastic shortage of machine tools would hinder any important increase in Japan's productive capacity in 1944.[34]

The home front had more to worry about than just the construction of airplanes. The country's heavy industry was highly concentrated along a narrow southern coastal belt extending south some 600 miles from Tokyo to Nagasaki. The ability of the island empire to wage war depended upon the continuous-producing capacity of these industrial centers. The cities are largely of the "tinderbox" construction, and hence very inflammable. The Japanese had long realized their vulnerability. Accounts seeping through censorship indicated in 1943 that the Japanese population greatly feared repetition of the bombing raid carried out by Doolittle's men. Knowing the potency of the psychological as well as the military factor involved, many persons in the United States pressed for more and heavier

bombings of Japan's principal cities. The Japanese were aware that they would presently be subjected to attack from bases in China, and the Philippines, and from aircraft carriers, whatever the stand of Russia on the use of her far-eastern bases. As a result, Tojo's planners have been engaged in working out a decentralization program for industry, and some of Japan's vital factories have been moved to Manchuria and China.

The Japanese were working much longer hours, and their living costs had at least doubled. All classes and ages were being drafted either for military purposes or essential war work. Students formerly exempted from the draft had their deferments canceled, and reports maintained that even Koreans and Formosans, hitherto regarded as untrustworthy, were to be conscripted. Many occupations were open to women only. Yet, despite the growing severity of wartime restrictions and sacrifices, and the admissions by high-ranking politicians and militarists that the war had entered a critical stage, the Japanese people apparently showed little or no signs of cracking.

Preparing for a long war. The enemies of Japan were forced to realize in 1943 that with her gains Japan was no longer a "have-not" nation. True, the Japanese war machine was handicapped by shortages in copper and nickel. But now the resources of Japan had been powerfully augmented by the rice of Indo-China and Thailand, sugar and chrome from the Philippines, lead and zinc from Burma, oil from the Dutch East Indies, antimony from China, and the prospect of nickel from the Celebes. Furthermore, Japan had at her command a potential slave labor force of a billion people, whom she was exploiting ruthlessly, but not without disguise. Every day the peoples of East Asia were bombarded by the constant refrain of "Asia for the Asiatics," by reference to Occidental imperialism before the war, by the promise (however hypocritical) of "co-prosperity" and "co-administrative" rule, and by the establishment in occupied lands of native puppet governments.

As 1944 approached, the "Co-Prosperity Sphere of Greater Asia" had scarcely been attained—but neither was Japan yet defeated. The Allies' attempts to wrest back their lost possessions island by island were about to be replaced by larger naval air operations against Japan proper and land operations via southeastern Asia and China. The Japanese guessed this and were preparing for a long war. And in this struggle they were fanatical in the divine mission of their cause. Their whole conditioning and environment had made them unswerving, loyal subjects of the Emperor— and therefore of the military caste and industrial hierarchy which directed the policies of the Emperor. In the opinion of Ambassador Grew and others familiar with Japan, the Japanese would not crack until the bitter end. And it would be well to remember that they were always buoyed up by the proudest of national traditions: Japan had never lost a war. But she had never fought a first-class foe— certainly not a coalition of first-class foes.

Summary

In reviewing events on the home fronts during 1942 and 1943, the fact that this has been a total war stands out in bold relief. True, the visitation of death and destruction has fallen upon particular peoples. But—and this is important in the broad historical perspective—all the peoples of the world have been subjected to the crucible of war.

Certain socio-economic trends can be discerned in all countries. One is the vast expansion and stepping-up of industrial processes. Thus, for example, veritable industrial revolutions have been taking place in the British Dominions, the Soviet Union, and China, while the United States, Great Britain, Germany, and Japan have expanded their facilities almost beyond recognition. To thoughtful students everywhere this worldwide industrialization posed serious questions. If the prewar world suffered from technological unemployment, what is to happen in the postwar world where industrial facilities have been almost doubled? At the same time, no one doubts that. if properly handled, this unprecedented expansion makes possible a postwar standard of living capable of giving every man, woman, and child throughout the world a decent way of life.

Another unavoidable trend has been the growing importance of government controls and enterprise. In Allied and Axis lands alike, the state has been forced either to regulate basic industries and utilities, or to take them over outright. Many far-reaching decisions confront the people after the war as to their permanent disposition. For example, American taxpayers have paid out billions of dollars for plant expansion. Will those government-built facilities be maintained by the people, will they be turned over to private enterprise, or will there be some sort of joint management? This is symptomatic of a fundamental issue confronting every country after the war—the relative merits of economic individualism and collectivism.

A further interesting change in the industrial field has been that of decentralization. The whole trend has been toward spreading factories—and cities too—throughout the countryside. The Soviet Union, China, and Japan have made remarkable shifts of industry to prevent destruction from enemy bombs. Modern industrial life has demonstrated surprising mobility. One beneficial social result will probably be the continued growth of suburban and "garden" towns, and a more healthful environment for factory workers.

The exigencies of modern warfare have made for an intensification of the goal of national self-sufficiency. But this situation guarantees some serious postwar problems.

More than one student is wondering whether the trend toward self-sufficiency does not carry with it the seeds of unbridled nationalism as well.

The problems which civilian populations have faced are to an unusual degree universal. Perhaps this is all to the good; for with the end of the war, all the peoples of the earth will have to learn to cooperate in building a new world society. The sacrifices which they have shared in common will motivate them toward a new understanding—without which even the most striking military victory must result only in social defeat.

Transition problems	Problem of treaties	
	Preliminary Treaty	Imposed; take care of insistent conditions
	Final Treaty	Negotiated; long-range problems
	Relief and rehabilitation	
	Joint Wheat Council	In charge of relief pool of wheat
	United Nations Conference on Food and Agriculture	Freedom from want
	UNRRA	Relief for war victims in areas controlled by United Nations
	Restoration of governments	
	Occupation and policing of Axis territory	
	Shift from war to peace economy	
	Committee on Economic Development	
	N.R.P.B. research	
	Churchill's Four-Year Economic Plan	
	Roosevelt's demobilization plans	
Long-term problems	Reduction of the hazard of war	
	Political determination	
	Treatment of Axis countries	
	Hemispherists' plan	Hemisphere solidarity
	Geopoliticians' plan	Balance of power favorable to U. S.
	International organization plans	Cooperative machinery to maintain peace
	World federation	Streit, Culbertson, Stassen
	Regional federation	World Commonwealth plan
	Perfection and encouragement of democracy	In the democracies; in other countries
	Advancement of colonial peoples	Colonial Charter; colonial pool
	Freedom from want	
	Laissez-faire capitalism	Minimum governmental control
	Collectivism	State-owned, state-planned, state-directed production
	Middle road economy	Profit motive and individual enterprise within fabric of governmental control
	The Beveridge plan	Minimum of subsistence from "cradle to grave"
	N.R.P.B. plan	Social security
	The Wagner plan	Extension of social security benefits
	International economic cooperation	
	Cancellation of Lend-Lease obligations	Mutual benefits
	Free movement of world trade	
	Migration and Settlement Commissions	Ease strain of overpopulation
	Development Commissions	Administer international funds for public works
	The White plan	International treasury and international monetary unit
	The Keynes scheme	

CHAPTER 9

Preparing for Tomorrow

UNTOLD numbers of men and women in the United Nations ponder why two horrible world wars have occurred in less than thirty years. They are considering what may be done to lessen the danger of such periodic catastrophes and what can be accomplished toward general economic and social reform. Beyond victory they seek a way of life worth all the blood, sweat, and tears of the agonizing war years.

The First Steps

Peace agencies. Numerous agencies have been set up to study postwar problems, even among the handicapped refugee governments in London. In the United States at least 150 groups have been active, such as the Commission to Study the Organization of Peace, the Harvard-Radcliffe Bureau of International Research, the Institute of Pacific Relations, the Universities Committee on Postwar International Problems, and the Foreign Policy Association. In American business circles the Committee on Economic Development was set up in 1942 to study the gigantic problem of switching America's war industries to a peacetime economy. In the Federal Government the National Resources Planning Board, the Federal Reserve Board, the Treasury, and the State Department also carried on studies relating to the establishment of a lasting peace.

Outstanding in importance has been the work of the Church—Protestant, Catholic, and Jewish—in studying postwar problems. For example, the Protestant Federal Council of Churches of Christ has met twice and, with fourteen nations represented, produced the "Six Pillars of Peace," a specific program of collaboration for the postwar period.

New forces after the war. Wars are not detached military episodes significant only on the battlefield and unimportant as instruments of change in human affairs. They release new forces, accelerate the development of emerging ideas and institutions.

"Wars . . . sweep away the half-rotted structure of an old social and political order, and lay the foundations of a new. New trends germinating unseen beneath the surface are brought to a sudden maturity in the forcing-house of war. War begets new needs and new

"A platform is no good without steps" is the title of this cartoon by Bishop. Each must be strong, and there must be enough of them, to insure peace.

loyalties which help to determine social and political forms for the coming century."[1]

These words of the English historian E. H. Carr do not mean that war necessarily brings only desirable results, or that of itself it solves existing problems. The "new loyalties" and the "new trends" may contain serious negative qualities. The truth is that great conflicts leave behind them a complex pattern of results both good and bad, permanent and ephemeral. The important thing to keep in mind is that whether good or bad the consequences of war mean considerable modification of the traditional forms of society. As the British economist R. H. Tawney wrote: "The crisis confronting the world is not a mere interlude from which it can turn, when the last bomb has been dropped, to re-knit, with a sigh of relief, the broken threads of its existence."[2]

On the debit side of war there is the staggering expenditure of money for purely destructive purposes. The human cost in misery, lives lost, bodies maimed, and homes uprooted cannot be estimated. And with peace will come additional problems: the demobilization of soldiers, the scrapping or conversion of the huge war industrial installations, the resumption of world trade, the emergence of subjugated peoples' long-smoldering hatreds against their totalitarian oppressors—these and other problems.

But war has its credit side too. The horrors of total war have brought about in the minds of many men and women a new appreciation of the importance of international law and some cooperative way of enforcing it. Also in many lands the totalitarian menace to democracy has removed some of the complacency and obscurity regarding the aims of democracy. New bonds of neighborliness and mutual aid have brought people closer together. Above all, the war has given impetus to plans for social and economic reform: stabilized employment, adequate housing, and provision for medical care and educational services.

In scientific and technological realms, the influences of the war have been revolutionary. There has been notable progress in medicine; air transport has made unbelievable strides; the war has brought about rapid progress in radiotelephony, as seen in the "walkie-talkie," and in television; the war boom in transparent plastics and plywood will lead to many startling applications in furniture, automobile body design, and home building; the need of housing for war workers has accelerated experimentation in prefabrication; radar, the detector so vital in wartime, will in peacetime keep airplanes from flying blindly into mountains and keep ships from colliding; and finally processes of food concentration have been advanced.

The war, then, is both the means of self-protection and the opportunity for self-improvement. What can be gained from it depends upon the vision and purpose of the victors. More specifically, it depends upon their having a conscious desire to be prepared for the task of reconstruction. Mental unpreparedness for war almost fatally handicapped the Allies when Axis aggression came; unpreparedness for peace could prove even more disastrous, paving the way for future conflicts. On this point President Roosevelt has declared:

"In the process of our working and fighting for victory, we must never permit ourselves to forget the goal which is beyond victory. The defeat of Hitlerism is necessary so that there may be freedom; but this war, like the last war, will produce nothing but destruction unless we prepare for the future now."

The Period of Transition

Immediate and long-range aims. Most students of postwar conditions visualize a settling-down process after the war in two distinct stages. The first, a relatively brief period of from three to ten years, will be concerned largely with the problems of disarming the Axis powers, evacuating them from conquered countries, policing their territory, punishing war criminals, returning refugee governments and prisoners to their countries, and bringing relief to millions of needy people all over the world. The second, growing out of the first period, will be concerned with setting up healthy trade relations throughout the world, rehabilitating industry and agriculture in war-devastated areas, cooperating with liberal and peace-desiring elements in the vanquished countries in order to establish stable governments, and, above all, building up the international machinery to reduce the factors which have led to war in the past and, if necessary, to coerce nations which break the peace and embark on aggression.

Kinds of treaties. Some authorities believe two types of treaties should be arranged.[3] The first would be a Preliminary Treaty imposed on the Axis countries, and would take care of insistent conditions: disarmament, demobilization, relief, and provisional boundaries. The Final Treaty, drawn up at an International Congress, would be not imposed but negotiated with the defeated powers. Boundaries would be definitely fixed; specific conditions laid down for the return of defeated powers to full nationhood; long-range plans made for international cooperation in trade, emigration of peoples, and access to raw materials. At this congress steps would also be taken to set up some form of league, federation, or alliance to enforce the Final Treaty. This two-stage treaty process would have a distinct advantage over the procedure in 1919, when all problems regardless of their short- or long-time character were settled in one conference.

Problems of the Transition. Whatever treaty plan is followed, the Transitional Period will be concerned with the following major problems: (1) relief in war devastated areas; (2) restoration of legal governments in Axis conquered lands; (3) occupation and policing of Axis territory; and (4) transition from a war to a peace economy in all nations.

Relief and rehabilitation. The problem of relief and rehabilitation following the war will be the most acute in the history of the world. During the first two years of war the Axis powers overran thirty-five countries with a population of more than half a billion people. The Chinese have suffered worse than the people of the South Pacific battle areas, who may rely on jungle products and who do not need warm clothing; but the Europeans have suffered worst of all.

In Europe raw materials have become an acute problem, because of the stoppage of imports and the Nazis' demands. Factories have been dismantled by the Germans for scrap and machinery to be used in making armaments. Whole districts, once good farmland, have been out of cultivation, for the farm workers have been sent as forced labor to Germany. Agricultural machinery has rusted or been taken to Germany. Livestock has been slaughtered to provide meat for the Nazi army. In July 1943 Herbert Lehman wrote, "Never before has the world witnessed so ruthless a despoliation of so many in so short a time."[4] Malnutrition in Europe is universal. Thousands have already died of disease and lingering starvation. Unless provision is made for the immediate distribution of food, clothing, and medical supplies, a horrible period of famine and plague seems likely.

It will be recalled that in 1941 representatives of eleven Allied countries approved the Atlantic Charter, agreeing "That it is their common aim to secure that supplies of food, raw materials, and articles of prime necessity should be made available for the postwar needs of the countries liberated from Nazi oppression."[5] The conference created an Inter-Allied Relief Committee. The entry of the United States into the war, and behind it the resources of the entire Western Hemisphere, accelerated the relief movement inaugurated in London. During the summer of 1942, members of the Committee conferred with American officials in Washington. The next step was the creation of a Joint Wheat Council, consisting of representatives of the great wheat countries—the United States, Canada, Australia, and Argentina. It has been given charge of a relief pool of one hundred million bushels.

SOME JOBS FOR THE UNITED NATIONS RELIEF ORGANIZATION

Late in 1942, President Roosevelt created a special agency to take over plans for relief, the Office of Foreign Relief and Rehabilitation (abolished in September 1943, its functions being shifted to a newly-created Foreign Economic Administration). In May 1943 he further advanced postwar relief plans by convening a United Nations Conference on Food and Agriculture. This Conference, held at Hot Springs, Virginia, was attended by over 500 delegates representing 45 nations. While immediate postwar needs were considered, the Food Conference dealt with more fundamental and long-range problems concerning freedom from want. It was emphasized that many peoples of the world do not have sufficient food even in peace time, that a world agricultural policy is essential.

The planning for a United Nations Relief and Rehabilitation Administration was heartening. The agency was to provide "food, fuel, clothing and other basic necessities, housing facilities, medical and other essential services" for victims of war in any area under United Nations control.

The UNRRA, as the agency is called, would consist of a Director General, a Council, and a Central Committee. Representatives of all interested nations would make up the Council, dealing largely with matters of policy. The Central Committee, consisting of representatives of the United States, Great Britain, China, and Russia, would represent the Council when that body was not in session.

The agency was definitely formed when representatives of 44 nations signed an agreement in Washington and on November 12 convened at Atlantic City.

There are some people who criticize proposals to feed the hungry abroad on the basis that "charity begins at home" and that the United States should hardly be expected "to give away" her own food and clothing. Others agree with Herbert Lehman:

"If we have learned anything from the decades just behind us it is this: that we cannot, even if we would, make ourselves secure in a world in which millions of men, women, and children are dying of want or epidemic.

. . . If the United States is to have any hope of lasting peace and a stable world economy, it must help see to it that the liberated peoples of the world are restored as rapidly as possible to a self-sustaining basis."[6]

Restoration of governments. The second major problem of the Transitional Period is the restoration of government in lands freed from Axis rule. The majority of these countries already have exile governments which have adhered to the principles of the Atlantic Charter, kept in constant touch with underground movements in their occupied lands, and contributed substantial amounts of money and men in the common cause. The exile governments of Poland, Czechoslovakia, Yugoslavia, Belgium, the Netherlands, Luxemburg, Greece, Norway, and France have been recognized by the Big Four (the United States, Britain, Russia, and China). Will such governments be acceptable to the people, who perhaps have developed new leaders and new ideas about government during the period of Axis domination? Such exile governments as have been recognized by the Big Four may be restored with their aid until the wishes of the people have been determined. In the interim it is likely that some form of United Nations occupation will be sought to maintain order, administer relief, and supervise the creation of a legitimate government acceptable to the majority of people. Where the political desires of a people are complicated and rent with factionalism, this work will be difficult.

Following World War I, there was a tendency of the newly-formed central European states to defy or ignore recommendations made in the general peace. Minor wars ensued and territorial arrangements were set aside. It has been suggested that the exile governments be restored "only in accordance with (1) their acceptance throughout the period of transition of the supreme authority of the United Nations; (2) their willingness to get along with their neighbors; (3) their acceptability to their people and their chances of keeping order."[7]

Administering Axis territory. The occupation and administration of Axis territory will be a third major task during the Transition. Disarmament of the Axis powers as described in the Atlantic Charter would be impossible without successful policing of this territory.

Following World War I, Allied troops of occupation were stationed in the German Rhineland district until 1930, and certain Allied commissions operated in Germany until 1927. It is likely that occupation forces will cover a much wider area in Germany after this war. In addition there will be Japan, if not Italy, to consider. The U. S. Army School of Military Government at Charlottesville, Virginia, has trained a large number of officers for this work. The British Army has a Civil Affairs Service whose personnel also is prepared to take over this job of administration.

A preview of AMG (Allied Military Government) was given in Sicily. Within a week of the British-American amphibious invasion of Sicily, the system was established on this island. It was a combined American and British régime, secretly planned long before the invasion took place. The proclamation setting up the new administration assured Sicilians that rule was to be benevolent, that when possible, administration would be through the peoples' own officials, although all Fascist officials would be removed from office. It also promised the people food, rationed by AMG. It is worth while noting additional provisions:

"Freedom of religious worship will be upheld and the position of the Catholic Church and all religious institutions will be respected.

All laws which discriminate on the basis of race, creed, or color will be annulled.

Physical symbols of the culture of true Italy, buildings, libraries, monuments, archives, and works of art will be protected from damage.

Within military necessity free press and free speech will be promulgated.

Those accused of crimes against the Allies will be tried by Allied military courts under AMG."

Mediterranean operations have been an all British, Canadian, and American performance and AMG reflects this fact. In the administration of Germany, however, conditions will be different. As it became likely that Soviet forces would conquer and occupy larger areas of at least eastern and central Europe than would American and British forces, there was raised the question of whether the system of military occupation will vary from area to area depending on what United Nations force is in occupation, or whether agreement among all the United Nations will result

Italian citizens of Sicily are interested in the proclamation put up by the AMG.   The Italians are being assured of good treatment if Allied orders are obeyed.

in a common system of administration over all territories.

Transition to a peace economy. Success in the Transitional Period will depend largely upon how soon and how smoothly the economy of the world is shifted from production for war to production for peace. There can be little assistance to the rest of the world if the United Nations, especially the United States, have millions of demobilized soldiers and former war workers unemployed in their own countries.

Broadcasting to the British Empire and the United States in the spring of 1943, Churchill proposed a Four-Year Economic Plan for the period of transition and reconstruction. Numerous organizations in Britain, such as the Association of British Chambers of Commerce, the Federation of British Industries, and the National Institute of Economic and Social Research, have also made specific recommendations to ensure speedy return to a healthy economic condition after the war.

The problem of economic transition will be most difficult in the United States, however, where the largest industrial resources in the world were geared and expanded. In midsummer 1943, it was estimated that 60 per cent of

the United States industrial capacity was devoted to war needs, and that despite the millions of men in the armed services, employment figures for men and women reached 52 million.

The United States, like Britain, has been looking ahead to these problems. There are, for example, the peace agencies already mentioned (page 249). There are also many far-seeing business executives who are laying plans for the changeover from weapons to refrigerators, automobiles, radios, helicopters, and other consumer goods of peace.

Perhaps the most comprehensive study of postwar economic problems in the United States was that made by the National Resources Planning Board. In the spring of 1943 the findings of the N.R.P.B. were sent to Congress in two reports. These dealt with the general topic of social security and the role government should take in the postwar economic situation. The most controversial aspect of the Board's recommendations was that the federal government should consider various types of partnership in such war-expanded industries as aluminum, shipbuilding, aircraft, and magnesium. In the fall of 1943 it was not clear how Congress would finally act on the

Board's proposals, but the Congress of 1943 had voted against a continuation of the Board.

Considerable attention was also given to President Roosevelt's recommendations for the demobilization of the U.S. armed forces, made in a nation-wide broadcast on July 28, 1943:

1. Mustering-out pay to every member of the armed forces and merchant marine when he or she is honorably discharged, large enough to cover a reasonable period of time between his discharge and the finding of a new job.

2. In case no job is found after diligent search, then unemployment insurance if the individual registers with the United States Employment Service.

3. An opportunity for members of the armed services to get further education or trade training at the cost of their government.

4. Allowance of credit to all members of the armed forces, under unemployment compensation and Federal old-age and survivors' insurance, for their period of service. They should be treated as if they had continued their employment in private industry.

5. Improved provisions for the hospitaliza-

tion of the armed forces and merchant marine.

6. Sufficient pensions for disabled members of the armed forces.

Many students of economics urge that some of the war agencies and wartime controls should not be disbanded immediately following peace. To do so would invite the sudden dislocation of a complex system of production and distribution. It is likely, therefore, that the United Nations will continue cooperatively to control shipping, foreign exchange, and the allocation of certain raw materials. Within each of the victorious nations it is possible that rationing and price ceilings will be kept for a limited period.

Relief in the war areas, restoration of governments, occupation and policing of Axis territory, shift from a war to a peace economy—these are the immediate problems of the Transitional Period. Beyond these, observers say, lie at least five long-term aims: (1) reduction of the hazard of war, (2) perfection and encouragement of democracy, (3) advancement of colonial peoples, (4) achievement of freedom from want, (5) economic cooperation.

Reduction of the Hazard of War

First aim of the United Nations. The question of boundaries and political self-determination, the treatment of Axis states, and the establishment of some form of international cooperation to preserve peace constitute the crux of the first postwar aim of the United Nations—reduction of the hazard of war.

Boundary questions. The map of the world will show many changes involving more than a mere return to the status quo before 1939. In certain cases there will be little difficulty for the boundary fixers. For example, the historic outlines of Norway, Denmark, Holland, Greece, Belgium, and France will probably be re-created. But there are many areas where clear-cut decisions will be difficult to make. Undoubtedly an independent Czechoslovakia will emerge after the war; but will the German-speaking Sudeten region be joined to the Czech state as it was in 1919? In Poland it seems likely that Russia may claim the eastern portions taken in the summer of 1939 when the Nazis overran the country from the west. This claim would be based on certain historic and racial factors. Again—will Austria remain with

Germany or will it prefer to be set up anew as an independent state? Here perhaps a plebiscite might be resorted to in settling the problem. The status of the Lilliputian Baltic states—Lithuania, Latvia, and Estonia—is at present confused. The Soviet Union after ejecting the German armies may well wish to absorb these states into the Union rather than see them return to their precarious independence of 1919-1940. The ghost of the Polish Corridor will also rise at the Peace Conference. Poles have historic arguments for such a corridor as well as the logic of immediate economic needs; on the other hand a corridor between eastern and western Prussia would be objectionable to the Germans.

The problems involved in determining the dimension and the status of nations are most complex in Europe, but a global war raises similar problems all over the world. Manchuria, it has been promised, will be given back to China after the dozen or so years of Japanese rule. But how about Hong Kong? The Chinese government may not urge its immediate cession to China by Great Britain following the ejection of the Japanese, but the gradual liquidation of British control over this Chinese island seems inevitable. After over a quarter century of Japanese rule, the Koreans are more than ever resolved to be free and masters of their own destiny. An independent Korean state, according to the Cairo Conference, will join the family of nations after victory.

Political determination. Changes in political status will occur in what may be termed the Colonial World. The United States has pledged itself to underwrite a free Philippine Commonwealth; Britain has promised to give India independence after the war; and Ethiopia will continue to be free of Italian Fascist rule. Certain strategic islands in the Pacific mandated to Japan in 1919 after the First World War may well be taken from her to be administered by members of the United Nations. The future of Italy's African colonies, Tripoli, Libya, Somaliland, Eritrea, remains uncertain; their disposal may be left primarily to Great Britain and the United States, the powers most responsible for ridding Africa of Axis rule. As for such Axis-conquered colonies as Burma, British Malaya, the Dutch East Indies, and Dutch-Australian New Guinea, it appears to be taken for granted by the former imperial powers that victory will see their colonial rule reëstablished. The question of colonies is further examined on page 260.

Treatment of the Axis countries. While there is wide acceptance of unconditional surrender, disarmament, and punishment of war criminals as factors in the treatment of defeated nations, there is much disagreement over many other issues. Germany usually has been singled out as the most serious problem. Even before the events of September 1943, Italy was not generally regarded as a menace. Comparatively little has been said about what should be done to Japan, though she is considered the most fanatical. Perhaps this is because the great powers of the West naturally regard as most dangerous the aggressive tendencies of a state among their own number. Probably they feel, also, that a victorious Russia and a constantly more progressive China can easily keep Japan in check. Furthermore, they know that in industrial potential, Japan—unless she is permitted to utilize the great resources of her new colonial empire—is far behind Germany, Russia, Britain, and the United States.

On the treatment of Germany, opinion is divided. There are two main schools. The first believes that the Germans' astounding rise to political and economic power from 1870-1914 made them a "bumptious, conceited, aggressive people"; and that long before the Nazis came along a philosophy had taken root, compounded of the master-race idea, the decadence of democracy, the nobility of war, and the rightness of ruthlessness for a chosen people to achieve its "destiny." This school believes further that: (1) the Germans should be defeated on their own soil; (2) disarmament must be complete; (3) a system of policing must prevent rearmament; (4) all property stolen or destroyed by the Germans must be restored; (5) liberated peoples should be fed first, before Germany; (6) Germans accused of crimes must be tried and punished if found guilty.[8] (A blacklist of 4000 Nazi criminals has been prepared; it is based on evidence obtained by the Polish underground and smuggled into London.) In effect, in the words of Bernadotte Schmitt, "The only sensible course is to give the Germans a strong dose of their own medicine. . . . We cannot bribe the Germans to behave. They must learn, from hard and bitter experience, that their political philosophy leads them only to misery and disaster."[9]

The second school, while not eliminating retribution and punishment where merited, supports a moderate treatment. It believes that Germany was led to war by a relatively small clique that bullied and hypnotized the masses. The German nation, it is argued, should not be partitioned; pernicious elements within it must be destroyed, but for the bulk of the people there should be the opportunity to participate with other great nations in the common tasks of civilization.

Supporting this moderate approach to the German problem, the English historian E. H. Carr has written: "The modern world is not so richly endowed with ability and resourcefulness that it can light-heartedly cast out from its midst as irredeemably bad, a nation possessing, in combination with many grave defects, so many valuable attributes."[10] Even Joseph Stalin has declared that the aim of Russia is the destruction of the Hitlerite state and its leaders only, and he adds, "It is impossible to destroy Germany, just as it is impossible to destroy Russia."

The second school believes that the principle of monetary payments, which after World War I placed a tremendous burden on Germany, should be abandoned for one utilizing German labor and technical facilities in rebuilding the war-torn areas of Europe. Above all, the United Nations should carry on "the most stupendous experiment for reëducation the world has ever witnessed."[11] The task would be "to encourage the work of groups and individuals in Germany who share the ideas of the United Nations and can advance them in terms understandable to the German people."[12] It should be explained to the Germans that as soon as they proved they no longer followed the Nazi ideology, ample opportunity would be offered to join the United Nations on a basis of equality. This view seems to be held by the majority of Englishmen.

Some observers advocate the fragmentation of Germany. Other students point out that the splitting up of Germany would seriously disrupt the economic unity of Central Europe.

The problem seems well-nigh insoluble. European peace apparently demands a weak, divided Germany, but the reconstruction and future prosperity of the continent is dependent in large measure upon the industry of a strong, united Germany. The solution may well be the strengthening of liberal elements, as mentioned above. Perhaps the best approach does not involve so much emphasis upon Germany's territorial extent but upon Allied supervision of Germany's industrial potential. German business could be prevented from serving war and could be directed to constructive purposes for the greater benefit of the German people.

The demarcation of boundaries and the solution of German and Japanese problems have direct bearing on the prospects of peace. The most challenging question, however, is what political arrangements for national security and world peace should be made.

The Hemispherists' plan. The Hemispherists repudiate any allegiance to a re-created League of Nations. They believe that security for the United States will be achieved best by a policy of hemisphere solidarity, of building up and maintaining the armed forces of the United States and securing common defense arrangements with the Latin American republics as well as Canada. At the same time the peace of the world would be served by the Americas' non-interference in the great regional political systems set up elsewhere for the same purposes.

The Geopoliticians' plan. Opposed to the Hemispherists' plan, the Geopoliticians believe that American foreign policy must be predicated on a broader geographical basis than the Western Hemisphere. In a world compressed by modern invention, the United States must seek its friends and thwart its enemies all over the globe. The primary purpose would be the maintenance of a balance of power throughout the world favorable to the United States. Alliances would be made with any nation whose interests paralleled our own, and following the war care would be taken not to make China or Russia too strong. Thus N. J. Spykman observes: "The danger of another Japanese conquest of Asia must be removed, but this does not inevitably mean the complete elimination of Japan and the surrender of the Western Pacific to China or Russia."[13]

The Geopoliticians side with the Hemispherists, however, in repudiating membership in any world organization. "If the foreign policy of a state is to be practical," asserts Spykman, "it should be designed not in terms of some dream world but in terms of the realities of international relations, in terms of power politics. The international community is without government, without a central authority to preserve law and order, and it does not guarantee the member states either their territorial integrity, their political independence, or their rights under international law."[14]

Plans for international organization. In contrast with the ideas of the Hemispherists and Geopoliticians there are the plans which insist upon the creation of some form of international organization with cooperative machinery to maintain world peace. Interest in such a program has been widespread. The Atlantic Charter pledged the United States and Great Britain to work for "the establishment of a wider and permanent system of general security." In the Moscow Conference of October 1943, representatives of Russia, China, England, and the United States expressed their approval of a world organization. On October 6, leaders of the Protestant, Catholic, and Jewish faiths in the United States united in a statement of seven main principles, advocating international collaboration.

The adherents of international organization for peace condemn Nazi Germany for plunging the world into war in 1939. But they place the blame, more fundamentally, on the perpetuation of the national state system, in which the states do not have to answer for their acts to a higher body representing the collective interests of mankind. It is argued that the real responsibility for the Second World War is shared by men and women in all lands, who failed to create an effective system of collective security after the first war, allowing the Axis powers to terrorize the world. The lawbreaker bears the most obvious responsibility, but behind it is the absence of cooperative effort to limit lawlessness.

Plan to revive the League. Among the various plans for the establishment of some form of world organization, one proposal calls for the resuscitation and strengthening of the old League of Nations. In spite of handicaps imposed by the war this organization still continues its valuable work on a diminished scale. A skeleton staff of about eighty remains at Geneva to keep up the records. One department has been removed to Princeton and another to Montreal, where they are working on postwar economic problems. The League of Nations is, then, very much alive; forty-five members still pay their annual dues. In the 1942 *Report* of the Acting Secretary-General of the League, it was stated that the various agencies of this body are "ready at the appropriate moment to take their respective parts in the reconstruction of the world or to serve as the foundations on which the new order can be built."[15]

Although there are strong supporters for a revived League, majority opinion among those advocating international organization seems to be opposed to it. In place of its loose system of sovereign states which failed to achieve united action in the face of emergency, a more binding system is desired. This calls either for world federation outright or at least for regional federation with the machinery of each geographical unit loosely tied to some international body.

Plans for world federation. One of the outstanding publicists of federation has been Clarence Streit. In *Union Now*, published in 1939, he advocated the federation of fifteen democracies—the democracies of Europe, the members of the British Commonwealth, and the United States. After Nazi Germany's conquests in Europe in 1940-1941, Mr. Streit in *Union Now With Britain* urged the immediate union of the United States with the British Commonwealth as a nucleus for a wider union after the war. In these federal plans the member states definitely cede powers relating to citizenship, defense, trade, currency, and some powers of taxation to the federal government consisting of a two-house legislature, a five-man executive board, and a high court.

More ambitious is the plan of Ely Culbertson, which would set up a super-federal government for the entire world. In it eleven regional federations, such as American, British, Latin-European, North European, Middle Eastern, are suggested. These would then be a part of a World Federation made up of a Legislature, a World Supreme Court, a World Court of Equity, and a World Police Force.

Another scheme for federalism on a global scale was advanced by Harold E. Stassen while Governor of Minnesota. This calls for the continuance of the present alliance of the United Nations and its expansion into a United Nations of the World. In his words:

"Through a gradual development over a period of years, we should reach a point eventually where a United Nations government of limited powers would function in seven major fields: (1) temporary administration of Axis, backward, or disputed territories; (2) maintenance of a police force; (3) regulation of international airways; (4) supervision of sea gateways; (5) stimulation of trade; (6) promotion of health and literacy; and (7) enforcement through a court of a basic code of justice."[16]

Plans for interlocking regional federations. Less ambitious than outright world federation are the plans for regional federation which envisage groups of states in an interlocking association in preference to a single league or union. One such proposal, called the World Commonwealth plan,[17] would set up (1) an Inter-American System; (2) the Soviet Union; (3) Europe; (4) a Far Eastern Association consisting of China, Japan, India, and an Indonesian Union (the Philippines, Burma, Dutch East Indies, British Malaya, Thailand, and Indo-China); (5) perhaps a Mohammedan League in the Near East; and (6) a possible British Commonwealth System in which Great

Britain would to some extent withdraw from the European System. Such groupings would be represented in an international organization. This would consist of an Assembly and World Court, together with various other bodies dealing with international economics, human welfare, colonies, and scientific and cultural cooperation. The regionalists depend upon each regional federation to maintain peace within its own political orbit. Each federation, therefore, would have a central governmental body empowered to enforce its will in stipulated matters over its member states. No provision is made for an international police force with authority over the member federations. The hope would be that consultations and negotiations between the various federations in the international Assembly would discourage war between regional groupings.

Plans have been advanced especially for the federation of Europe. Some of these proposals call for the complete federation of the entire continent. While these are only paper schemes as yet, already definite steps have been made by some European states in the direction of limited European regional federation. In 1942 the Polish and Czechoslovakian governments in exile drew up a plan for confederation in Central Europe; and in the Greek-Yugoslav agreement made in the same year, plans were also drawn for a Balkan Union.

Dominance of the Big Four. In the planning for postwar political organization there is general agreement on one point. Postwar international politics will begin with the dominance of the leading powers of the United Nations: the United States, Russia, China, and Britain. After disarmament and occupation of Axis countries, power in the world will be in their hands. Some observers, then, believe future world organization should grow out of the hegemony of the United Nations. In *U. S. Foreign Policy: Shield of the Republic*, Walter Lippmann asserts the interests of the United States and the peace of the world can best be served by the formation of a "nuclear alliance" between Britain, China, Russia, and the United States.

Anthony Eden and other British statesmen have pointedly stressed that the Big Four mean to hold the peace after victory. At the same time it is agreed that as soon as possible other states must be allowed to play their part, the dominance of the Big Four thus giving way to an expanded international system.

Some contend that it may be wiser, though not so spectacular, to follow this policy of gradualism. Payson S. Wild expresses it thus:

"Out of the links now connecting the United Nations may be forged firm bonds for permanent collaboration. International government created in this unspectacular fashion may lack the glamour that might be associated with a great charter or a solemn covenant, but it should be remembered that international arrangements developing in an *ad hoc* manner may prove stronger and have a far sounder basis for the future than a special new edifice created at one stroke of the pen."[18]

Already the United Nations have established an amazing structure of international collaboration in shipping, military strategy, standardization of military equipment, and monetary policy. Plans for postwar economic collaboration have also been laid down in the various Lend-Lease agreements made by the Allies.

It is argued on the other hand that the situation of the world today may be parallel to the situation of America in 1787, when the loosely joined states—finally realizing their great need for a strong union—assembled in convention, argued out their differences (including questions of "sovereignty"), and within a relatively brief period created the system of federal government embodied in the American Constitution.

On the whole, the trend of public opinion in both the British Commonwealth of Nations and the United States appears to be in favor of association with some international organization rather than a return to isolationism or the operation of power politics. Isolationism, so long entrenched in United States philosophy, has not of course been one hundred per cent superseded. But Gallup Polls; the polls of *Fortune* and the National Opinion Research Center of the University of Denver; the developments in the Republican Party (which in 1919 opposed United States entry in the League); and Congressional action, in particular the adoption by overwhelming majorities of the strengthened Connally resolution in the Senate and the Fulbright resolution in the House—all indicate support of the United States' adherence to a world system of collective security.

Perfection and Encouragement of Democracy

Second aim of the United Nations. The United Nations' second aim, to perfect and encourage democracy, is closely related to the first—the prevention of war. Only when we have ultimately a universal democracy protecting all individuals and groups will we have an enduring world state and lasting peace.

Democracy, like everything else in life, can suffer from complacency. In the 1920's and early 1930's the democracies of the world were severely criticized for their lack of leadership, for the apathy of the electorate, for putting politics above patriotism, for giving democracy a too narrow definition, or for their lack of dynamic political faith. Such accusations were true in greater or less degree in many of the countries possessing representative institutions.

The future of democracy at home and abroad depends upon the answers given to the following questions: (1) What can be done to strengthen and perfect democracy at home? In particular what can be done to extend economic democracy along with political democracy? (2) What can be done to encourage the growth of democratic institutions in the Axis countries? (3) What can be done to foster self-government among the so-called backward and colonial peoples of the world? The latter question will be taken up in the general discussion of the advancement of colonial peoples.

Democracy in the democracies. The Second World War has done much to quicken a new respect for democratic government among those people who have been fortunate enough to retain their representative institutions and among those conquered people who look to the day when such governments can be restored. Democracy has therefore to a large extent been revitalized and has met the challenge laid down by one of its champions, the eminent German novelist, Thomas Mann, who declared: "It should put aside the habit of taking itself for granted, of self-forgetfulness. It should . . . renew and rejuvenate itself by again becoming aware of itself."[19]

Renewal of faith is fundamental, but important too is a determination to broaden the definition and improve the techniques of democracy. The democratic way of life cannot be static but must be prepared to adapt itself to the demands of a rapidly changing world. In one country this may mean working for a better civil service, in another higher pay for legislators, in another greater protection of minority groups, in another new techniques to interest the electorate in governmental issues. As Charles E. Merriam expressed it, "Democracy is not merely something to be defended and preserved . . . but an ideal to be developed and enriched, a constant approximation to higher standards of living and higher levels of the good life."[20]

Democracy for other countries. Should the United States, following victory, attempt to universalize democratic government? It is argued that the world is too small for totalitarianism and democracy to exist side by side, and that one or the other will have to go. However, it is admitted that every people should have the right to choose its own form of government and that no democratic country should force its own way of life upon unwilling peoples, that the object of universalizing democracy does not necessarily involve coercion. Much can be done by assisting liberal elements everywhere and by showing that the democratic system is the way of the richer and more abundant life.

Advancement of Colonial Peoples

Third aim of the United Nations. The third basic aim toward which the United Nations are working is the protection and advancement of the world's colonial peoples. The question of self-government for these peoples has been raised in the discussion of democracy. While the Allies fight to free subjugated peoples from Axis imperialism, it is natural that a great deal of criticism should be leveled against any form of empire in which colonial subjects are denied the right of self-government. From many quarters there has come the demand that imperialism of any sort must go.

As has been said, India and the Philippines have been promised self-government. There are other colonial areas where self-government may soon be possible, as in Ceylon and Burma.

In British Malaya, however, 37 per cent of the population are Malays, 42 per cent are Chinese, and 13 per cent are Indians. In this area the question would be: self-government for whom and according to which set of ideas? A similar mixed racial situation exists in other colonial areas. In Fiji the native people are outnumbered by the Chinese and Indians. In Africa, the native populations of the tropical colonies are split into dozens of tribes with no tradition of cooperation to hold them together. Would self-government mean independence for each of these many tribes? Furthermore, such tribes are only just emerging from a primitive culture and are utterly unable to cope with the complexities of the modern world now.

Except in the more advanced areas, then, supervision and protection of colonial areas must be continued in some form. Such colonies could be pooled and placed under the control of some supervisory body connected with a world organization. Or the colonial powers could continue the administration of their colonies but in cooperation with some international agency.

Colonial Charter. An influential body of opinion in Britain has advocated the creation of a Colonial Charter to be formulated and agreed to by all members of the United Nations. The Charter would stipulate that (1) colonies should be administered on the basis of benevolent guardianship; (2) the people should be trained for eventual self-government where possible; (3) the colonies should be developed economically both for the interests of the native people and for the world in general; and (4) the principle of the Open Door should permit economic equality for all nations in such colonial areas. The important consideration is to ensure that control and administration are free from exploitation.

The principles of the Colonial Charter are not entirely new. They were contained in the machinery of colonial mandates set up by the League of Nations in 1919. However, the League did not possess sufficient supervisory power over such mandates, though it provided that "There should be an annual examination of the mandatory by the Mandates Commission."

Colonial trusteeship has been developed independently, too, especially by Britain. In 1923, for example, Britain refused to grant local self-government to the British settlers in the African colony of Kenya because the members of the British government "regard themselves as exercising a trust on behalf of the African population, and they are unable to delegate or to share this trust, the object of which may be defined as the protection and advancement of the Native races."[21] British colonies are no longer regarded as "possessions." Increased attention has been given to native education, agriculture, and medical needs for which the Colonial Development Fund provides. The system of Indirect Rule has been successful in providing natives with increased responsibilities in self-government.

The future of colonies constitutes one of the great basic contemporary problems. If an effective and truly international league with a colonial pool fails to eventuate with the peace—the ideal solution for colonies not yet prepared for the responsibility of self-government—the alternative is the perpetuation of colonial systems administered by nation states. If such powers progressively expand the principle of colonial trusteeship or the technique of a Colonial Charter underwritten by all members of the United Nations, the tutelage of colonial peoples will be benevolent and their prospects for ultimate equality in the family of nations certain.

Freedom from Want

Fourth aim of the United Nations. Postwar political relationships both within and between nations have been considered so far. Of comparable importance is the improvement of the economic structure, within countries and between countries. Thus the fourth and fifth basic objectives of the United Nations are freedom from want and improvement of international economic cooperation.

The Second World War has accelerated the process of inquiry and reform in economic systems. From every side have come appeals to eliminate or reduce economic evils. Pope Pius XII, speaking to the world on Christmas Day, 1940, urged that every state be given "the medium necessary for insuring the proper standard of living for its own citizens of every rank."[22] Mr. Eden, the British statesman, has said, "Never again must we tolerate chronic unemployment, extremes of wealth and poverty, slums, and the lack of opportunity for so many which disfigured our national life in the past."[23] Vice-President Henry A. Wallace has declared, "The peace must mean a better standard of living for the common man";[24] and President Roosevelt's Four Freedoms include "freedom from want" for his own and as far as possible for all peoples.

The laissez-faire approach. There are three main types of plans to eliminate poverty and unemployment. The first would leave the capitalist system more or less as it is at present, and perhaps even eliminate recent innovations interfering with the laissez-faire principle, which calls for the very minimum of governmental control. It is asserted that governmental supervision and regulation of business results in capricious and uninformed bureaucracy; that the taxation of the ambitious and successful elements in society for the provision of economic security has a dangerous tendency to subsidize the shiftless and penalize the efficient and productive; that anything beyond certain minimum governmental controls slows down initiative and results in bureaucratic centralization menacing individual freedom. The kernel of argument is the so-called Fifth Freedom—"To be free, men must choose their callings, bargain for their own services, save and provide for their families and old age. And they must be free to engage in enterprise just so long as each does not injure his fellow man."[25]

The collectivists' approach. At the other extreme is the collectivist plan, which would substitute for individual capitalistic enterprises a state-owned, state-planned, state-directed system of production and distribution. It is argued that the people would have the final control through democratic elections; that ultimately the individual would have more real expression and liberty than he can have under a set-up which permits uncontrolled concentrations of power; that only by all-out planning and elimination of wasteful competition can a nation achieve a full standard of living. The collectivists have little faith in international organization as a means of discouraging war as long as capitalism is allowed to operate. For "capitalism is itself the general underlying cause of war."[26] In the words of one of its advocates, collectivism "is the only alternative to capitalism. It is the transfer of the national economy to the ownership and control of the entire people, incorporated into the working class."[27]

The "middle road." There is another road leading to economic improvement. Those who advocate following it emphatically deny that collectivism is the only alternative to capitalism. This may be thought of as a middle road economy between pure laissez-faire doctrine and collectivism. Walter Lippmann has called it a "compensated economy," and it is referred to by the editors of *Fortune* as a new "democratic capitalism—a synthesis of the conflicting elements in our recent past."[28] It seeks to perpetuate the profit motive and individual enterprise within a fabric of governmental control and support. The chief objects are (1) the restriction of activities by business elements, whether employers or employees, deemed injurious to the public good; (2) the support by governmental action of the economic structure when necessary in order to maintain full and continuous employment for all; and (3) the guarantee to all of basic economic and social essentials, such as medical care, education, housing, accident compensation, unemployment insurance, and old-age pensions.

Social security. Although the principle of social security usually plays an important part in the middle road solution, it is by no means the exclusive possession of this school of economic thought. In Britain it is supported by Churchill and by the traditionally conservative newspaper, the *Times.* And in the United States, support is found in labor circles, among important employer groups, and in the press from union weeklies to *Fortune.* This is not to say that a majority of people in the United States have come to believe in a comprehensive system of social security. The issue is still hotly debated. But the principle has already been accepted widely enough to make it one of the major possibilities in postwar society.

The Beveridge plan. In Great Britain a Committee on Social Reconstruction headed by Sir William Beveridge presented a noteworthy report to Parliament in December 1942. A plan was submitted guaranteeing the British people a national minimum of subsistence "from the cradle to the grave." The program was a considerable expansion of already existing social services and caught the imagination of the people. The Beveridge report overnight became a "best seller."

Some of the specific recommendations were: (1) $11.20 a week unemployment insurance for an indefinite period; (2) $11.20 a week for nonindustrial disability; (3) $8 a week for old age pensions; and (4) a comprehensive medical service for all citizens.[29] Support for the Beveridge report came from all sections. The *Times*, for example, declared it was "A momentous document which should and must exercise a profound and immediate influence on the direction of social change in Britain."

Canada also was tendered a kind of Beveridge plan—the Marsh plan—in the spring of 1943 when a committee appointed by the Canadian Prime Minister, W. L. Mackenzie King, submitted two reports on a national social insurance plan.

The N.R.P.B. report on security. In the United States, interest in social security was accelerated by the report of the National Resources Planning Board presented to Congress in March 1943. The Board, while covering economic questions (see page 254), examined the limited social security measures which have existed in the country during the past ten years and made recommendations for their expansion. These were based on the socio-economic philosophy that it should be the policy of the national government:

"To underwrite full employment for the employables:

To guarantee a job for every man released from the armed forces and the war industries at the close of the war, with fair pay and working conditions;

To guarantee and, when necessary, underwrite:

Equal access to security.

Equal access to education for all.

Equal access to health and nutrition for all.

Wholesome housing conditions for all."[29]

The Wagner plan. In June 1943 the so-called Wagner plan was introduced into both Houses of Congress. This plan went much farther than the report of the N.R.P.B., extending social security to 15 million persons now excluded from such benefits in the United States. Like the Beveridge plan the Wagner program calls for payments both from the employer and the employee to help finance the system. The proposed plan, in the words of its creator, "covers broadly the major economic hazards of average people throughout their lifetime—loss of income in unemployment, sickness, temporary and permanent disability, and old age."[30]

Improvement of International Economic Cooperation

Fifth aim of the United Nations. The problem of raising standards of living and guaranteeing economic security for the average man cannot be managed entirely within domestic fields. Equally important are matters relating to trade and monetary relations between nations. All proposals for postwar organization, therefore, emphasize a fifth objective—the improvement of international economic cooperation. Wendell Willkie has pointedly declared: "Political internationalism without economic internationalism is a house built upon sand. For no nation can reach its fullest development alone."[31] Technological progress has made the nations so interdependent that no nation can cavalierly adopt economic policies without reference to the effect upon its neighbors.

War debts. It is now believed by many economists that following the First World War, healthy world trade and harmonious economic relations between nations were obstructed by the legacy of war debts. These deranged and confused the monetary and trade structure of the world.

Under Lend-Lease agreements the United States has sent to its allies, principally the British Empire and Russia, billions of dollars of war supplies and food. Lend-Lease is not a one-way affair; the Allies have contributed large quantities of material to the United States armies. In the final analysis, however, the major measurable contribution in the Lend-Lease system will be made by this government. Even so, "there must be an all-round cancellation of obligations in respect to Lend-Lease goods actually consumed in war effort, on the theory that each of the United Nations will have contributed, to the best of its ability, to the common effort and, having given of its best, will owe nothing to the others."[32]

Trade and currency. To facilitate economic cooperation between nations, the majority of political plans for international organization provide for agencies which would remove obstacles to the free movement of world trade, such as unreasonably high tariffs, quotas, ruthless competition for markets, and the manipulation of currencies. Advocated also are Migration and Settlement Commissions to ease the strain of overpopulation in certain areas and Development Commissions to administer international funds for public works.

In March 1943 appeared two important plans designed to secure stable exchange rates in the world's monetary system, to help free world trade, and to encourage fiscal cooperation. The White plan was the work of an official of the United States Treasury, and the Keynes scheme was devised by Lord Keynes, adviser to the British Treasury. Both would set up an international treasury to control the fluctuation of currencies in the world and establish a new international monetary unit.

The whole subject of international trade and currency becomes highly technical; the important thing to understand is that there is growing agreement among the world's best economic thinkers that no machinery devised for political cooperation can succeed unless at the same time it provides for comparable economic cooperation. Economic nationalism has been a prolific cause of international disputes and war in the past. Yet the world's business is not something to be fought over by various national units but a common task and opportunity leading toward benefits for all.

Summary

The most perplexing and difficult postwar problems have to do with long-range attempts to ensure the kind of world the people of the United Nations are seeking. Such a world has been described in general terms in the Atlantic Charter and in the speeches of statesmen of the United Nations. The United Nations seek five ideals for the postwar world, three of them political and two economic: (1) reduction of the hazard of war—freedom from aggression means freedom from fear; (2) perfection of democracy in every way possible at home; encouragement and expansion of democracy abroad; (3) protection and advancement of the so-called backward or colonial peoples; (4) achievement of the highest possible level of individual economic prosperity and security in all countries; (5) realization of a high degree of economic cooperation between nations.

The United Nations may not succeed in bringing about a painless and an entirely smooth transition from war to peace. But apparently the basic needs and problems have been recognized and plans to meet them have been set in motion. Whether in the end these will amount to a people's peace depends, in the final analysis, on the people.

Aids to Further Study

Chart of Contemporary Events   266

Bibliography and Acknowledgments   270

General Index   281

Chart of Contemporary Events

Occasional reference to this chart from the chronological tables at the head of each chapter will indicate the parallelism of events throughout the world.

Year	India, China, Japan, Oceania	North and South America	Russia	Smaller European Countries	Italy	Germany	France	England and The British Empire
1870	Japan westernized; Indian National Congress formed; Sino-Japanese War; Treaty of Shimonoseki; Foreign concessions in China		War with Turkey over Balkans; Alliance with France; Social Democratic Party organized	Leopold of Belgium claims Congo	Joins Triple Alliance; Defeat in Abyssinia	Three Emperors League; Congress of Berlin; Large areas claimed in Africa	Third Republic; Control over Indo-China	Gladstone, Disraeli, prime ministers; Boer War
1900	Open Door Policy; Boxer Rebellion; Morley-Minto reforms; Japan annexes Korea	First Pan-American Conference; Venezuela dispute; Gentleman's Agreement, U. S. and Japan; Panama Canal opened	War with Japan; Peasant revolt; Trans-Siberian railway	Austria annexes Bosnia-Herzegovina; Portuguese republic; Balkan wars	War with Turkey; Tripoli acquired		Separation of Church and State; Algeciras Conference; Moroccan protectorate	Australian Commonwealth; Triple Entente; Union of South Africa formed
1918	Japan's Twenty-One Demands on China	U. S. enters war; Wilson's Fourteen Points	Communist Revolution; Czar murdered	FIRST WORLD WAR	Italy joins Allies	Republic established		
1919	Treaty of Sèvres with Turkey; Rowlatt Acts in India	Eighteenth amendment in U. S.; Social reform in Mexico; U. S. refuses to join League or World Court; Nineteenth amendment in U. S.; Rise of middle class in Mexico	Civil war between Reds and Whites	LEAGUE OF NATIONS — Poland recreated; Czechoslovakia and Yugoslavia formed; Finland independent; Aland dispute settled by League; Masaryk president of Czechoslovakia	Fiume seized by D'Annunzio	Treaty of Versailles; Reparations imposed; Weimar Constitution	National Bloc government	
1920	Gandhi's civil disobedience campaign		War Communism period	Horthy dictator in Hungary; Irish Free State	Treaty of Rapallo with Yugoslavia	Hitler organizes National Socialist Party		Brief economic boom
1921	Sun Yat-sen president in China		New Economic Policy		Fascist party formed			Postwar depression
1922	Greco-Turkish war	Fordney-McCumber Tariff Act in U. S.	U. S. S. R. created	Austria receives financial aid from U. S.; Rivera, Spanish dictator	Mussolini assumes government	Reparations payments stopped	Little Entente; Alliance with Poland	Bonar Law, premier
1923	Earthquake in Japan; Treaty of Lausanne revises Sèvres; Ataturk, dictator	Teapot Dome oil scandal in U. S.			Corfu dispute with Greece	Inflation, financial collapse; Hitler's Munich Putsch	Occupation of Ruhr	Leadership of Baldwin
1924		Johnson Immigration Act in U. S.	New constitution; Death of Lenin; Stalin wins over Trotsky as leader		Murder of Matteoti	Dawes plan; Hitler begins *Mein Kampf*	Alliance with Czechoslovakia; Evacuation of Ruhr; Left Cartel ministry	MacDonald, first Labor prime minister; Conservative government takes over
1925	Death of Sun Yat-sen; Manhood Suffrage Bill in Japan	Coolidge, U. S. president			Fascist Party supreme	LOCARNO TREATIES	Dangerous monetary policy	General strike; Imperial Conference
1926	Chiang Kai-shek dictator in China			Pilsudski dictator in Poland	Syndicalism established in economic structure		Pact with Rumania; National Union government	
1927								Trade Disputes Act

(Annotations across Smaller European Countries / Italy columns: NINE — POWER — TREATY)

266

	England and The British Empire	France	Germany	Italy	Smaller European Countries	Russia	North and South America	India, China, Japan, Oceania
1928		Treaty with Yugoslavia				First Five-Year Plan	McNary-Haugen bill in U. S. Hoover, president Pan-American Conference	
1929	MacDonald heads Labor government	Poincaré's retirement	Young plan				Stock market crash in U. S. Strict immigration act in U. S.	Simon Commission tours India
1930	London Naval Conference						Smoot-Hawley Tariff Act in U. S.	
1931	Off gold standard National Coalition under MacDonald Statute of Westminster		Hoover Moratorium	National Council of Corporations set up	Carol reascends Rumanian throne Abdication of Alfonso		Wickersham Report in U. S.	Round Table conferences in London Manchuria invaded by Japan
1932	Free trade abolished Ottawa Imperial Economic Conference International Economic Conference				Salazar dictator in Portugal			Japan puts puppet ruler in Manchukuo
1933		Stavisky scandal Paris riots National Union government	Withdrawal from League Reichstag fire Enabling Act makes Hitler dictator Anti-Jew boycott Blood purge of Nazi leaders Non-aggression pact with Poland			Second Five-Year Plan Decreased illiteracy	Pan-American Conference U. S. abandons gold standard Good Neighbor policy	T'ang-ku Truce Japan leaves League
1934				Reorganization of Corporate state	Assassination of Alexander of Yugoslavia Civil war in Austria Boris' dictatorship	Joins League	Export-Import Bank established Platt Amendment abrogated by U. S.	Tydings-McDuffie Act for Philippines
1935	Baldwin, prime minister	Laval, premier Hoare-Laval agreement over Abyssinia		Conquest of Abyssinia	New Polish constitution legalizes dictatorship		Social Security Act in U. S. Neutrality law in U. S.	Government of India Act
1936		Popular Front under Blum Socialist legislation	Four-Year Plan Rome-Berlin Axis Anti-Comintern Pact Rhineland remilitarized		Metaxas dictator in Greece Fascist revolt in Spain	New democratic constitution Treason trials	Pan-American Conference, Buenos Aires	Kidnaping of Chiang Kai-shek
1937	Chamberlain, prime minister	New conservative government	Demand for Lebensraum	Withdrawal from League Mussolini visits Hitler Adheres to Anti-Comintern Pact Chamber of Fasces and Corporations formed				Reopening of Sino-Japanese war Fall of Nanking
1938			Niemoeller in concentration camp Nazi purge Invasion of Austria		Carol dictator in Rumania	Third Five-Year Plan	Pan-American Conference at Lima	Fall of Canton Japan declares "New Order in Asia"

KELLOGG-BRIAND PACT

WORLD ECONOMIC DEPRESSION

Date	England and The British Empire	France	Germany	Italy	Smaller European Countries	Russia	North and South America	India, China, Japan, Oceania
1939			Jewish persecution; Non-aggression pact with Russia; Invasion of Poland *(MUNICH AGREEMENT)*		Sudetenland occupied; Final victory of Franco; Czechoslovakia capitulates	Pact with Germany	Revision of U. S. neutrality law; U. S. fleet to Pacific	
1940	Retreat from Dunkirk; Churchill, premier; Battle of Britain	Nazi invasion and conquest; Vichy government	Occupation of Denmark and Norway; Low Countries invaded *(SECOND WORLD WAR)*	War declared against France; Invasion of Greece; Defeat in Africa	Rumania dismembered		Selective Service Act in U. S.; Third term for Roosevelt	Japan dominates Indo-China; Burma Road closed, reopened
1941	Atlantic Charter; Pact with Russia; Occupation of Syria; Nazis routed in Africa; Fall of Hong Kong	Cooperation with Nazis	Military alliance with Japan, Italy; Submarine warfare; Revolt engineered in Iraq; Invasion of Crete		Bulgaria joins Axis; Yugoslavia attacked; Greece overwhelmed	Nazi blitzkrieg; Invasion of Iran	Lend-Lease Bill; Atlantic Charter; Repeal of neutrality	Thailand under Japanese control
1942	Air raids on Germany		Drive in Egypt			Nazi advance to Caucasus oil	Fall of Philippines, Wake, Guam; Rio Conference; Coral Sea, Midway Battles; All-out production *(PEARL HARBOR)*	Cripps Mission to India; Java, Burma fall
July	Social revolution; Second front question	DeGaulle in England	Submarine campaign	Fascism doomed	Underground organizations	Nazi conquest of Crimea; Nazis threaten Voronezh and Caucasus	18 nations against Axis	Japanese in Solomons, New Guinea, Aleutians; Constant Japanese stabs in China
Aug. Sept.	Agricultural production doubled		Rommel halted at el Alamein; New Nazi offensives in Africa and Russia			Assault on Stalingrad begins	First Allied Pacific offensive, in Solomons	Battle for Guadalcanal begins
Oct.	Offensive in North Africa							
Nov.	Attack and counter-attack in Tunisia	Morocco, Algeria invaded; Germany occupies all France	Rommel in retreat	Italians take Corsica		Russian offensives at Stalingrad, Rzev, Voronezh, Leningrad, and in Caucasus	Troops landed in Africa; Naval strength in Solomons shifts to U. S.	Allied air offensive in New Guinea
Dec.	Beveridge report							
1943				British take Tripoli, last of Italian empire		Stalingrad: first German catastrophe	Casablanca Conference	Allies take Buna, Gona; Allied raids on Burma; U. S. and British special rights in China ended
Feb.							Americans gain Guadalcanal	

Month	England and The British Empire	France	Germany	Italy	Smaller European Countries	Russia	North and South America	India, China, Japan, Oceania
Mar.	Keynes plan					German offensive held along Donets	N. R. P. B. report and White plan	
Apr.	Climax of Tunisian campaign							China's economy stunned by Japanese blockade
May			Wholesale surrender in Tunisia				Allies take Bizerte, Tunis; Allied victory on Attu; Churchill-Roosevelt meeting at Washington	
June			U-boat campaign blocked; Allied air offensive	Surrender of Pantelleria; Allies invade Sicily; Mussolini's dictatorship ended				
July					Unrest in Balkans	German offensive reversed		Allies thwart Japanese air effort in South Pacific
Aug.	R.A.F. nightly raids in Europe; AMG in Sicily		Steady retreat in Russia	Messina captured: end of Sicilian campaign	Sweden forbids transit to Germans	Russians capture Orel, Belgorod, Kharkov, Taganrog	U. S. troops take Munda; Allied capture of Kiska clears the Aleutians; Quebec Conference	Americans on New Georgia
Sept.		U. S., Britain, Russia recognize French Committee of National Liberation	Labor 30% foreign	Badoglio asks Allies for an armistice; Mussolini proclaims new Fascist government	Yugoslav guerrilla warfare	Novorossiisk, Bryansk captured		Salamaua and Lae fall to Allies; Democratic planning in China
Oct.				Naples captured by Allies; Badoglio declares war on Axis; Allies take Sardinia, Corsica	Heavier Allied bombing of strategic industries; Portugal allows Allies to use Azores as bases	Russians regain Smolensk, Dnepropetrovsk; Russian front at Dnieper; Moscow Conference	Crisis in Argentine government	Finschhafen captured by Allies; Offensive and counter-offensive in China; Central Solomons cleared
Nov.			Berlin heavily bombed			Russians retake Kiev; Ukraine freed	UNRRA meeting at Atlantic City; Cairo Conference; Teheran Conference	
Dec.								
1944								

Bibliography and Acknowledgments

1: Explosion in Europe

Specific References

1. H. A. L. Fisher, *A History of Europe*, Houghton Mifflin Company, 1936, p. 1114.
2. Quoted by R. J. Sontag, *European Diplomatic History, 1871-1932*, D. Appleton-Century Company, 1933, p. 213.
3. Quoted by Hermann Foertsch, *The Art of Modern Warfare*, Oskar Piest, 1940, p. 3.
4. J. Salwyn Schapiro, *Modern and Contemporary European History*, rev. ed., Houghton Mifflin Company, 1934, p. 687.
5. From C. J. H. Hayes, *A Political and Cultural History of Modern Europe*, 1937, II, p. 774. By permission of The Macmillan Company, publishers.
6. *Ibid.*, p. 776. By permission of The Macmillan Company, publishers.
7. *Ibid.*, p. 778. By permission of The Macmillan Company, publishers.
8. Royal Institute of International Affairs, *Political and Strategic Interests of the United Kingdom*, London, Oxford University Press, 1939, p. 14.
9. J. W. Swain, *Beginning of the Twentieth Century*, W. W. Norton & Company, 1933, p. 377.
10. From W. C. Langsam, *The World Since 1914*, 3rd ed., 1937, p. 38. By permission of The Macmillan Company, publishers.
11. S. E. Morison and H. S. Commager, *The Growth of the American Republic*, Oxford University Press, 1937, II, pp. 453-454.
12. Quoted by L. M. Hacker and B. B. Kendrick, *The United States Since 1865*, 3rd ed., F. S. Crofts & Co., 1940, p. 520.

General References

The treatment of this complex and controversial subject had to be general without benefit of the mass of material found in many historical monographs. The authors found the following surveys terse and accurate: J. E. Gillespie, *Europe in Perspective*, Harcourt, Brace and Company, 1942; B. E. Schmitt, *Triple Alliance and Triple Entente*, Henry Holt and Company, 1934; G. P. Gooch, *History of Modern Europe, 1878-1919*, Longmans, Green & Co., 1923; Erik Achorn, *European Civilization and Politics Since 1815*, Harcourt, Brace and Company, 1933; J. W. Swain, *Beginning the Twentieth Century*, W. W. Norton & Company, 1933; and R. J. Sontag, *European Diplomatic History, 1871-1932*, D. Appleton-Century Company, 1933. More specialized works consulted on specific problems were: S. B. Fay, *The Origins of the World War*, 2 vols. in 1, rev. ed., The Macmillan Company, 1930; H. E. Barnes, *The Genesis of the World War*, Alfred A. Knopf, 1929; B. E. Schmitt, *The Coming of the War*, 2 vols., Charles Scribner's Sons, 1930; and G. Lowes Dickinson, *The International Anarchy*, D. Appleton-Century Company, 1926. A penetrating interpretation of the period from 1870 to 1914 was obtained in Benedetto Croce, *History of Europe in the Nineteenth Century*, especially chap. 10, "International Politics, Activism, and the World War," Harcourt, Brace and Company, 1933. A moderate, scholarly account of the German side was found in Erich Brandenburg, *From Bismarck to the World War*, Oxford University Press, 1927. A brief excellent account of Balkan nationalism was W. M. Gewehr, *Nationalism in the Balkans, 1800-1930*, Henry Holt and Company, 1931. The costs of the war were fully treated in E. L. Bogart, *Direct and Indirect Costs of the War*, Oxford University Press, 1920. A dramatic, well-written account of Great Britain at war was furnished by Winston Churchill, *The World Crisis*, Charles Scribner's Sons, II, 1923, and III, two parts, 1927. For the United States the following were consulted: T. A. Bailey, *A Diplomatic History of the American People*, F. S. Crofts & Co., 1940; Walter Millis, *The Road to War*,

Houghton Mifflin Company, 1935; and C. H. Grattan, *Why We Fought*, Vanguard Press, 1929. For a general study of military affairs C. R. M. F. Crutwell, *History of the Great War*, Oxford University Press, 1936; and C. J. H. Hayes, *A Brief History of the Great War*, The Macmillan Company, 1920, were indispensable guides. For a discussion of action at sea H. J. Newbolt, *A Naval History of the War*, Hodder & Stoughton, 1920, was consulted.

2: A Quest for World Order

Specific References

1. From W. C. Langsam, *The World Since 1914*, 3rd ed., 1937, p. 111. By permission of The Macmillan Company, publishers.
2. Quoted by Erik Achorn, *European Civilization and Politics Since 1815*, Harcourt, Brace and Company, 1934, p. 470.
3. From Karl Lowenstein in *Governments of Continental Europe*, ed. by J. T. Shotwell, 1940, p. 400. By permission of The Macmillan Company, publishers.
4. Quoted by Achorn, p. 473.
5. S. E. Morison and H. S. Commager, *The Growth of the American Republic*, Oxford University Press, 1937, II, p. 497.
6. League of Nations Document C. 77. M. 37. 1939. VII., quoted in "The United States and World Organization During 1938," *International Conciliation*, Carnegie Endowment for International Peace, September, 1939, No. 352, pp. 390-391.
7. F. Lee Benns, *Europe Since 1914*, rev. ed., F. S. Crofts & Co., 1934, p. 312.
8. *Ibid.*, p. 314.

General References

The most useful treatment of postwar diplomacy was G. M. Gathorne-Hardy, *Short History of International Affairs*, Oxford University Press, 1938. For Great Britain and France much reliance was placed upon Arnold Wolfers, *Britain and France Between Two Wars*, Harcourt, Brace and Company, 1940. A brief and lively discussion of international affairs was given in William A. Orton, *Twenty Years' Armistice*, Farrar & Rinehart, 1938. Of special value in linking diplomacy with economic factors was F. H. Symonds and Brooks Emeny, *The Great Powers in World Politics*, American Book Company, 1937. R. Palme Dutt, *World Politics, 1918-1936*, Victor Gollancz, 1936, was characteristic of the school which blames world strife mainly upon capitalism. The following were also consulted: W. C. Langsam, *The World Since 1914*, The Macmillan Company, 1937; J. E. Gillespie, *Europe in Perspective*, Harcourt, Brace and Company, 1942;

and F. Lee Benns, *Europe Since 1914*, rev. ed., F. S. Crofts & Co., 1934. Simplified accounts whose summary of international economic and political trends was most helpful were: Varian Fry, *The Peace That Failed*, 1939; Varian Fry, *Bricks Without Mortar, the Story of International Cooperation*, 1939; and Thomas Brockway, *Battles Without Bullets, the Story of Economic Warfare*, 1939—all three published by The Foreign Policy Association. For the conference of Paris and the Peace Treaties the following works were consulted: René Albrecht-Carrié, *Italy at the Peace Conference*, Columbia University Press, 1938; R. S. Baker, *Woodrow Wilson and World Settlement*, 3 vols., Doubleday, Page & Company, 1922. One of the most penetrating studies of the Paris Peace Conference was found in Harold Nicolson, *Peacemaking*, Houghton Mifflin Company, 1933. E. M. House and C. Seymour, Eds., *What Really Happened At Paris*, Charles Scribner's Sons, 1921, was also consulted. A valuable recent study of the Treaty of Versailles was Paul Birdsall, *Versailles Twenty Years After*, Reynal & Hitchcock, 1941. Valuable also were: S. P. H. Duggan, Ed., *The League of Nations: the Principle and the Practice*, Little, Brown & Company, 1919; J. S. Bassett, *The League of Nations*, Longmans, Green & Co., 1928; G. N. Barnes, *History of the International Labor Office*, Williams and Norgate, 1926. A good account of the peace settlement and the fight for the League in the United States was given in Thomas A. Bailey, *A Diplomatic History of the American People*, F. S. Crofts & Co., 1940, chaps. 39 and 40. Used in preparing the economic sections of this chapter were: H. G. Moulton and Leo Pasvolsky, *World War Debt Settlements*, Brooklings Institution, 1926; J. M. Keynes, *The Economic Consequences of the Peace*, Harcourt, Brace and Company, 1920; and S. B. Clough and C. W. Cole, *Economic History of Europe*, D. C. Heath and Company, 1941. Consulted for the problem of disarmament were: J. W. Wheeler-Bennett, *Disarmament and Security Since Locarno*, The Macmillan Company, 1932, and Salvador de Madariaga, *Disarmament*, Coward-McCann, 1929.

3: *New Patterns in Statecraft*

Specific References

1. From Michael T. Florinsky, in *Governments of Continental Europe*, ed. by James T. Shotwell, 1940, p. 816. By permission of The Macmillan Company, publishers.
2. *Ibid.*, p. 817. By permission of The Macmillan Company, publishers.
3. Quoted by W. N. Loucks and J. W. Hoot, *Comparative Economic Systems*, 1938, p. 240. Reprinted by permission of Harper & Brothers.
4. From Florinsky, p. 855. By permission of The Macmillan Company, publishers.
5. Samuel N. Harper, *The Government of the Soviet Union*, D. Van Nostrand Company, 1938, pp. 169-170.
6. *Ibid.*, p. 170.
7. Quoted by Vera M. Dean, *Russia At War*, The Foreign Policy Association, 1942, p. 71.
8. Based on Florinsky, p. 838.
9. Joseph E. Davies, *Mission to Moscow*, Simon and Schuster, 1941, p. 94.
10. From *Soviet Russia Today*, November, 1937, quoted in Loucks and Hoot, p. 485. Reprinted by permission of Harper & Brothers.
11. R. T. Bye and W. W. Hewett, *Applied Economics*, F. S. Crofts & Co., 1934, p. 642.
12. H. E. Barnes, *The History of Western Civilization*, Harcourt, Brace and Company, 1935, II, p. 1019.
13. Dean, p. 56.
14. Earl R. Sikes, *Contemporary Economic Systems*, Henry Holt and Company, 1940, p. 370.
15. Cf. A. R. Williams, *The Soviets*, Harcourt, Brace and Company, 1937, p. 309.
16. From Arnold J. Zurcher, in *Governments of Continental Europe*, p. 613. By permission of The Macmillan Company, publishers.
17. *Ibid.*, p. 610. By permission of The Macmillan Company, publishers.
18. F. Lee Benns, *Europe Since 1914*, rev. ed., F. S. Crofts & Co., 1934, p. 356.
19. From Walter C. Langsam, *The World Since 1914*, 1937, p. 373. By permission of The Macmillan Company, publishers.
20. Sikes, p. 430.
21. From Langsam, p. 401. By permission of The Macmillan Company, publishers.
22. *Ibid.*, p. 401. By permission of The Macmillan Company, publishers.
23. From Zurcher, p. 748. By permission of the Macmillan Company, publishers.
24. From Karl Lowenstein, in *Governments of Continental Europe*, p. 403. By permission of The Macmillan Company, publishers.
25. *Ibid.*, p. 406. By permission of The Macmillan Company, publishers.
26. Quoted by G. M. Gathorne-Hardy, *A Short History of International Affairs, 1920 to 1934*, London, Oxford University Press, 1934, p. 252.
27. From Lowenstein, p. 473. By permission of The Macmillan Company, publishers.
28. Max Ascoli and Arthur Feiler, *Fascism For Whom?*, W. W. Norton & Company, 1938, p. 207.
29. Sikes, p. 509.

General References

The general framework of this chapter is based on F. Lee Benns, *Europe Since 1914*, F. S. Crofts & Co., 1930, and W. C. Langsam, *The World Since 1914*, The Macmillan Company, 1937. In addition "New Dictatorships and Old Democracies" in H. A. L. Fisher, *A History of Europe*, London, Edward Arnold and Company, 1936, was most helpful. Also good in providing interesting items were: *Ambassador Dodd's Diary*, W. E. and Martha Dodd, Eds., Harcourt, Brace and Company, 1941; W. L. Shirer, *Berlin Diary*, Alfred A. Knopf, 1941; and John Gunther, *Inside Europe*, Harper & Brothers, 1938. The discussion of Nazi Germany was written only after a careful study of Hitler's *Mein Kampf*, unabridged ed., Reynal & Hitchcock, 1939. One of the best summaries of postwar Germany is given in F. L. Schuman, *Germany Since 1918*, Henry Holt and Company, 1937; and in V. L. and M. H. Albjerg, *From Sedan to Stresa*, chap. 27, D. Van Nostrand Company, 1937. Henri Lechtenberger, *The Third Reich*, Greystone Press, 1937, an objective study by a French scholar and noted student of German life and culture, was especially helpful. Other works consulted were: K. Heiden, *A History of National Socialism*, Methuen and Company, 1934; and by this same authority on Nazism, *Hitler*, Alfred A. Knopf, 1934; Stephen A. Roberts, *The House That Hitler Built*, Harper & Brothers, 1938, especially good for the characterization of Hitler and his lieutenants; E. A. Mowrer, *Germany Puts the Clock Back*, rev. ed., William Morrow & Co., 1939; F. L. Schuman, *The Nazi Dictatorship*, Alfred A. Knopf, 1939; and Calvin B. Hoover, *Germany Enters the Third Reich*, The Macmillan Company, 1933, particularly good on the early phases of National Socialism.

H. Powys Greenwood, *The German Revolution*, George Routledge & Sons, 1934, represented a certain section of English society that admired Nazism in its early phases. Special obligation is expressed to Karl Lowenstein for his informative section on Germany in *Governments of Continental Europe*, ed. by J. T. Shotwell, The Macmillan Company, 1940. For the general trend of developments in Italy the authors express their indebtedness to Benns, Langsam, and Albjerg, all cited above. Benito Mussolini, *My Autobiography*, London, Hutchinson & Co., 1939, was an interesting approach to a complex personality. Much reliance was placed upon Arnold J. Zurcher's section on Italy in *Governments of Continental Europe*, cited above. H. A. Steiner, *Government in Fascist Italy*, McGraw-Hill Book Company, 1938, gave many details on the emergence of Fascism. Useful in the appraisal of the Fascist movement was Hugh Quigley, "Fascism Fails in Italy," *Current History*, Events Publishing Co., June, 1934. The economic structure of Italian Fascism was ably presented by Earl Sikes, *Contemporary Economic Systems*, Henry Holt and Company, 1940. M. T. Florinsky's study of Soviet Russia in *Governments of Continental Europe*, cited above, was helpful for all phases. Joseph E. Davies, *Mission to Moscow*, Simon and Schuster, 1941, containing reports to the United States Department of State, presented useful material. An excellent condensation of Soviet Russia was Vera M. Dean, *Russia at War*, The Foreign Policy Association, 1942. The best succinct treatment of the economics of Communism was in W. N. Loucks and J. W. Hoot, *Comparative Economic Systems*, Harper & Brothers, 1938. Other sources were: H. E. Barnes, *The History of Western Civilization*, II, chap. 25, Harcourt, Brace and Company, 1935; A. R. Williams, *The Soviets*, Harcourt, Brace and Company, 1937; W. H. Chamberlain, *Collectivism: A False Utopia*, The Macmillan Company, 1937; R. T. Bye and W. W. Hewett, *Applied Economics*, chap. 29, F. S. Crofts & Co., 1934.

4: *Democracy on Trial*

Specific References

1. Quoted by W. C. Langsam, *Major European and Asiatic Developments Since 1935*, 1938, p. 15. By permission of The Macmillan Company, publishers.
2. *Ibid.*, p. 17. By permission of The Macmillan Company, publishers.
3. W. P. Hall and W. S. Davis, *The Course of Europe Since Waterloo*, D. Appleton-Century Company, 1941, p. 745.
4. From J. T. Shotwell, Ed., *Governments of Continental Europe*, 1940, p. 1036. By permission of The Macmillan Company, publishers.
5. F. Lee Benns, *Europe Since 1914*, rev. ed., F. S. Crofts & Co., 1934, p. 481.
6. *Cmd. 2768* (of 1926), London, p. 14. Quoted by Sir J. A. R. Marriott, *Modern England, 1885-1932*, London, Methuen and Company, 1934, p. 466.
7. Carl Wittke, *A History of Canada*, F. S. Crofts & Co., 1941, p. 400.
8. Quoted by W. C. Langsam, *The World Since 1914*, 1937, p. 752. By permission of The Macmillan Company, publishers.
9. S. F. Morison and H. S. Commager, *The Growth of the American Republic*, Oxford University Press, 1937, II, p. 531.
10. Carleton Beals, *America South*, J. B. Lippincott Company, 1937, p. 359.
11. J. F. Rippy, *Historical Evolution of Hispanic America*, F. S. Crofts & Co., 1940, pp. 539-540.
12. From *A New Doctrine for the Americas*, pp. 93-94. Copyright 1941 by Charles Wertenbaker. By permission of The Viking Press, Inc., New York.
13. Rippy, p. 541.

General References

The framework of the discussion of postwar United States was based upon the following standard historical surveys: John D. Hicks, *The American Nation: A History of the United States from 1865 to the Present*, Houghton Mifflin Company, 1941; F. L. Paxson, *Recent History of the United States: 1865 to the Present*, Houghton Mifflin Company, 1926; A. M. Schlesinger, *Political and Social Growth of the American People*, The Macmillan Company, 1941; and S. E. Morison and H. S. Commager, *The Growth of the American Republic*, II, Oxford University Press, 1937. Also helpful were: D. L. Dumond, *Roosevelt to Roosevelt: The United States in the Twentieth Century*, Henry Holt and Company, 1937; Charles and Mary Beard, *America in Midpassage*, The Macmillan Company, 1939; D. W. Brogan, *U. S. A.: An Outline of the Country, Its People and Institutions*, Oxford University Press, 1941; and Sir Walter Citrine, *My American Diary*, George Routledge & Sons, 1941. The study of Great Britain after World War I owes much to the excellent survey in Sir John Marriott, *Modern England, 1885-1932*, London, Methuen and Company, 1934; to the comprehensive discussion in J. A. Spender, *Great Britain, Empire and Commonwealth, 1886-1935*, Cassell & Co., n. d.; and to the concluding chapter in W. P. Hall and R. G. Albion, *A History of England and the British Empire*, Ginn and Company, 1937. For developments in the British Empire the following sources were consulted: Sir Arthur Willert, B. K. Long, and H. V. Hodson, *The Empire in the World*, Oxford University Press, 1937; A. E. Zimmern, *The Third British Empire*, 3rd ed., Oxford University Press, 1934; and R. Coupland, *The Empire in These Days*, The Macmillan Company, 1935. For the British Dominions the concluding chapters of Carl Wittke, *A History of Canada*, F. S. Crofts & Co., 1941, were particularly helpful. A brief but penetrating interpretation of modern Canada was found in B. K. Sandwell, *The Canadian Peoples*, Oxford University Press, 1941. Readable and scholarly was A. L. Burt, *A Short History of Canada for Americans*, The University of Minnesota Press, 1942. The following works were frequently consulted for Australasia: E. Scott, *Short History of Australia*, Oxford University Press, 1927; W. P. Morrell, *New Zealand*, London, Ernest Benn, 1935; and *The Cambridge History of the British Empire*, VII, two parts, *Australia* and *New Zealand*, Cambridge University Press, 1933. The discussion of South Africa owes much to the standard history by E. Walker, *History of South Africa*, Longmans, Green & Co., 1939, and to the popularly written but reliable survey by J. H. Hofmeyr, *South Africa*, London, Ernest Benn, 1931. The discussion of Latin America was based upon the fol-

lowing authorities: A. C. Wilgus, *The Development of Hispanic America*, Farrar & Rinehart, 1941; S. G. Inman, *Latin America, Its Place in World Life*, Willett, Clark & Company, 1937; J. Fred Rippy, *Historical Evolution of Hispanic America*, F. S. Crofts & Co., 1940; C. E. Chapman, *Republican Hispanic America: A History*, The Macmillan Company, 1937. For social and economic trends the following work was especially provocative: Carleton Beals, *America South*, J. B. Lippincott Company, 1937. Many facets of Latin American culture were explored by various authorities in the admirable *Modern Hispanic America*, ed. by A. Curtis Wilgus, The George Washington University Press, 1933. Inter-American relations were discussed with penetration by Charles Wertenbaker, *A New Doctrine for the Americas*, The Viking Press, 1941. In tracing European developments after 1919 the following works were consulted: A. J. Zurcher, *The Experiment With Democracy in Central Europe*, Oxford University Press, 1933; R. L. Buell, *Poland: Key to Europe*, Alfred A. Knopf, 1939, the best short survey in English; W. J. Rose, *Poland*, Middlesex, Penguin Books, 1939; J. H. Jackson, *Finland*, London, George Allen & Unwin, 1938, the standard work in English; M. W. Childs, *Sweden, The Middle Way*, Yale University Press, 1936, an excellent discussion of Swedish cooperatives; E. C. Bellquist, *Some Aspects of the Recent Foreign Policy of Sweden*, University of California Press, 1939; R. J. Kerner, Ed., *Czechoslovakia, A Record of Two Decades*, University of California Press, 1940; Salvador de Madariaga, *Spain*, Charles Scribner's Sons, 1930; Louis Pierard, *Belgian Problems Since the War*, Yale University Press, 1929; A. J. Barnouw, *The Dutch: A Portrait Study of the People of Holland*, Columbia University Press, 1940.

5: *The Orient Astir*

Specific References

1. See C. F. Remer, *Foreign Investments in China*, The Macmillan Company, 1933, p. 406.
2. *Ibid.*, p. 397.
3. *Ibid.*, p. 636.
4. As of 1942, according to J. Anton de Haas, *Our Allies! The Netherlands East Indies*, London, Oxford University Press, 1942, p. 6. But for 1940 figures, consult Amry Vandenbosch, *The Dutch East Indies*, 2nd ed., University of California Press, 1941, p. 5.
5. Vandenbosch, p. 28.
6. Cf. Remer, pp. 338, 407, 553.
7. Harold M. Vinacke, *A History of the Far East in Modern Times*, 4th ed., F. S. Crofts & Co., 1941, p. 478.
8. From Kenneth S. Latourette, *The Chinese, Their History and Culture*, 2nd rev. ed., 1934, I, p. 487. By permission of The Macmillan Company, publishers.
9. T. A. Bisson, *Shadow Over Asia*, The Foreign Policy Association, 1941, p. 60.
10. From Remer, p. 76. By permission of The Macmillan Company, publishers.

11. Bisson, p. 69.
12. Quoted by Claude A. Buss, *War and Diplomacy in Eastern Asia*, 1941, p. 54. By permission of The Macmillan Company, publishers.
13. Quoted by Buss, p. 118. By permission of The Macmillan Company, publishers.
14. Vinacke, p. 585.

General References

The authors are indebted to Harold M. Vinacke for his excellent survey *A History of the Far East in Modern Times*, 4th ed., F. S. Crofts & Co., 1941. Also consulted for its survey value was G. Nye Steiger, *A History of the Far East*, Ginn and Company, 1936; while appropriate chapters in K. S. Latourette, *The Chinese, their History and Culture*, 2 vols. in 1, 2nd ed. rev., The Macmillan Company, 1934; and Walter C. Langsam, *The World Since 1914*, 4th ed., The Macmillan Company, 1940, were found valuable. Of particular value in connection with the Netherlands Indies was Amry Vandenbosch, *The Dutch East Indies*, 2nd ed., University of California Press, 1941. T. A. Bisson, *American Policy in the Far East, 1931-1940;* Irving S. Friedman, *British Relations with China, 1931-1940;* and Hugh Borton, *Japan since 1931*, all three published by the Institute of Pacific Relations, 1940, proved valuable in their fields. An excellent and authoritative study of the strength of European, American, and Japanese economic interests in China was C. F. Remer, *Foreign Investments in China*, The Macmillan Company, 1933. A short but reliable account of the rise of militant Japan was found in T. A. Bisson, *Shadow Over Asia*, The Foreign Policy Association, 1941.

The authors made use of Claude A. Buss, *War and Diplomacy in Eastern Asia*, The Macmillan Company, 1941, for an over-all picture of the relative positions and strength of the major powers in the Pacific area, and also examined W. D. Pulestan, *The Armed Forces of the Pacific*, Yale University Press, 1941. They consulted for treaty stipulations, Harley F. MacNair, *Modern Chinese History, Selected Readings*, Shanghai, Commercial Press, 1923. Numerous articles in such journals as *Far Eastern Survey, Pacific Affairs, Amerasia,* and *Asia* were helpful. For political conditions and developments in India from 1914 to 1939, A. B. Keith, *Constitutional History of India, 1600-1935*, London, Methuen and Company, 1936, was valuable. E. Thompson and G. T. Garratt, *The Rise and Fulfilment of British Rule in India*, The Macmillan Company, 1934, was also consulted. In economics the following were especially helpful: V. Anstey, *Economic Development of India*, Longmans, Green & Co., 1937, and D. M. Bucchanan, *The Development of Capitalist Enterprise in India*, The Macmillan Company, 1935. One of the best surveys of politics, economics, and social life was found in the *Indian Statutory (Simon) Commission Report*, I, London, 1930. The constitutional reforms of 1919 were discussed at length in E. A. Horne, *The Political System of British India*, Oxford University Press, 1922. For the nationalist movement the following were especially useful: C. H. Van Tyne, *India in Ferment*, D. Appleton-Century Company, 1923; Sir V. Lovett, *History of the Indian Nationalist Movement*, London, John Murray, 1921; E. J. Thompson, *Reconstructing India*, Dial Press, 1930.

6: A World Divided

General References

The authors placed main reliance upon the following works: F. L. Schuman, *Europe On the Eve: the Crisis of Diplomacy, 1933-1939*, Alfred A. Knopf, 1939; E. H. Carr, *The Twenty Years' Crisis, 1919-1939*, The Macmillan Company, 1939; D. E. Lee, *Ten Years*, Houghton Mifflin Company, 1942, a clear and objective synthesis of diplomacy from 1930 to 1942; Sir John Marriott, *The Tragedy of Europe*, Glasgow, Blackie & Son, 1941, a suggestive interpretation of prewar trends in Europe; William Orton, *Twenty Years' Armistice: 1918-1938*, Farrar & Rinehart, 1938, a popular account but helpful in giving "a rapid view of the period as a whole." R. P. Dutt, *World Politics, 1918-1936*, Victor Gollancz, 1936, highly critical of the foreign policy of

British conservatives. One of the best surveys of international affairs is the standard work by G. M. Gathorne-Hardy, *A Short History of International Affairs, 1920-1938*, Oxford University Press, 1938. A penetrating examination of foreign policy was Arnold Wolfers, *Britain and France between Two Wars*, Harcourt, Brace and Company, 1940. W. C. Langsam, *The World Since 1914*, The Macmillan Company, 1937, with a supplement *Since 1939: A Narrative of War*, The Macmillan Company, 1941; and F. Lee Benns, *Europe Since 1914*, F. S. Crofts & Co., 1934, with supplement *Europe's Return to War*, F. S. Crofts & Co., 1941, constitute a reliable survey of international developments. The most comprehensive study dealing with the immediate background and causes of the war was

F. L. Schuman, *Night Over Europe: The Diplomacy of Nemesis, 1939-1940*, Alfred A. Knopf, 1941, a brilliant treatment. A good example of the German viewpoint was found in Alfred von Wegerer, *The Origins of World War II*, Richard R. Smith, 1941. Among the many personal accounts dealing with the coming of the conflict, Sir Nevile Henderson, *Failure of a Mission, Berlin 1937-1939*, G. P. Putnam's Sons, 1940, was found to be one of the most significant. The official British explanation of the outbreak of war is contained in *Documents Concerning German-Polish Relations and the Outbreak of Hostilities between Great Britain and Germany on September 3, 1939*, London, H. M. Stationery Office, 1939. The course of the war was clearly outlined in Edgar McInnis, *The War: First Year*, Oxford University Press, 1940, and *The War: Second Year*, Oxford University Press, 1941. Of much assistance also were the various bulletins of the governments of the United Nations. The *Yale Review*, Yale University Press and *Foreign Affairs*, Council of Foreign Affairs, contained articles by eminent scholars and publicists on various aspects of the Second World War. One of the most useful expositions of the strategic situation in the Pacific was Captain W. D. Puleston, *The Armed Forces of the Pacific*, Yale University Press, 1941. The his-

torical background to the Pacific conflict was presented effectively in F. R. Dulles, *America in the Pacific*, Houghton Mifflin Company, 1942. The various factors behind the attack on Pearl Harbor are explained in W. C. Johnstone, *Why Japan Chose War*, Oxford University Press, 1942. The treatment of the foreign policy of the United States and the reaction of public opinion to the blitzkrieg in Europe was based on a study of current American periodicals and press notices, as well as books. The isolationist view was capably presented in General Hugh S. Johnson, *Hell-Bent for War*, Bobbs-Merrill Company, 1941. The much discussed book of Anne M. Lindbergh, *The Wave of the Future*, Harper & Brothers, 1940, also belongs in the isolationist category. R. H. Markham, *The Wave of the Past*, University of North Carolina Press, 1941, is an answer to the latter work. A good consensus of the interventionist viewpoint was found in William A. White, Ed., *Defense For America*, The Macmillan Company, 1940. The effect of Hitler's victories on American opinion is well treated in W. H. Shepardson and W. O. Scroggs, *The United States In World Affairs, 1940*, Harper & Brothers, 1941. H. R. Luce, *The American Century*, Farrar & Rinehart, 1941, is a stirring appeal for intervention.

7: Since Stalingrad

Specific References

1. *Statement published by the Government on the Congress Party's responsibility for the Disturbances in India, 1942-1943*, London, 1943, p. 5.
2. *Ibid.*, p. 4.
3. See *Time*, Dec. 28, 1942, p. 21.

General References

Most of the data for the military narrative of 1942-1943 came from military communiqués, as reported in the *New York Times* and other newspapers. The authors are indebted also to Edgar McInnis, *The War: Third Year*, Oxford University Press, 1942, a scholarly and compact survey. The account owes much to the splendid reports of correspondents in the field, as found in *Time, Newsweek*, and the more important newspapers. At all times the articles of Major George Fielding Eliot and Hanson Baldwin were consulted with profit. For the military story from July 1942 to the winter of 1943 main reliance was of course upon periodical literature and government press releases. Many recently published books may be suggested for fur-

ther reading: Hilary St. George Saunders, *Combined Operations*, The Macmillan Company, 1943, valuable for an account of the British Commandos; Henry C. Cassidy, *Moscow Dateline, 1941-1943*, Houghton Mifflin Company, 1943, a description of Russia at war, good for military developments; Vincent Sheean, *Between the Thunder and the Sun*, Random House, 1943; and John T. Whitaker, *We Cannot Escape History*, The Macmillan Company, 1943. The following first-hand accounts of fighting in various war theaters offer vivid descriptions of global military operations: Lt. John Mason Brown, *To All Hands*, Whittlesey House, 1943, dealing with the invasion of Sicily; Howard Handleman, *Bridge to Victory*, Random House, 1943, fighting in the Aleutians; Captain Ralph Ingersoll, *The Battle Is the Pay-Off*, Harcourt, Brace and Company, 1943; Richard Tregaskis, *Guadalcanal Diary*, Random House, 1943; G. H. Johnston, *The Toughest Fighting in the World*, Duell, Sloan, and Pearce, an account of operations in New Guinea; A. B. Austin, *We Landed at Dawn*, Harcourt, Brace and Company, 1943, dealing with the Dieppe incident; Ira Wolfert, *Battle for the Solomons*,

Houghton Mifflin Company, 1943; Russell Hill, *Desert Conquest*, Alfred A. Knopf, 1943, the story of the British Eighth Army; Ernie Pyle, *Here Is Your War*, Henry Holt and Company, 1943, an intensely human story of American troops under fire; Ian Hay, *Malta Epic*, D. Appleton-Century Company, 1943.

Other books bearing on various aspects of the global conflict are: A. A. Michie, *The Air Offensive Against Germany*, Henry Holt and Company, 1943; Raoul Aglion, *The Fighting French*, Henry Holt and Company, 1943; Reynolds and Eleanor Packard, *Balcony Empire*, Oxford University Press, 1942; J. B. Jansen and Stefan Wyl, *The Silent War: The Underground Movement in Germany*, J. B. Lippincott Company, 1943; Johannes Steel, *Men Behind the War*, Sheridan House, 1942, some seventy brief biographical sketches; Alexander G. Clifford, *The Conquest of North Africa, 1940-1943*, Little, Brown and Company, 1943.

8: *On the Home Fronts*

Specific References

1. Office of War Information Release, No. 2022, p. 1.
2. See Julius Hochman, "Let's Look at Labor," VII, "The Opportunity for Leadership," *Nation*, Sept. 11, 1943.
3. See *New York Times*, Aug. 1, 1943.
4. See Helen Fuller, "The Rich Get Richer," *The New Republic*, Sept. 20, 1943. See also *Survey of Current Business*, U.S. Department of Commerce, Sept. 1943, p. 57.
5. *Home Front Handbook*, Q2227, British Ministry of Information, April 1943, p. 4.
6. See *Canada at War*, Ottawa, Wartime Information Board, June 1943, p. 54.
7. See Editorial, *Toronto Globe and Mail*, June 28, 1943.
8. See *The Job Australia Is Doing*, Australia News and Information Bureau, 1943, p. 13.
9. *Meet New Zealand*, distributed by New Zealand Legation, 1943, p. 24.
10. Quoted by Albert Rhys Williams, *The Russians*, Harcourt, Brace and Company, 1943, p. 128.
11. Joseph E. Davies, in *Soviet Russia Today*, Aug. 1943, p. 9.
12. See *Information Bulletin,* Embassy of the USSR, Sept. 14, 1943, p. 7; and *Information Bulletin*, Sept. 18, 1943, p. 8.
13. See *Information Bulletin*, Sept. 14, 1943, p. 8.
14. See Williams, pp. 162 and following.
15. See *Information Bulletin*, Aug. 24, 1943, p. 7.
16. See *Time*, Feb. 15, 1943, p. 34.
17. See *New York Times*, Jan. 12, 1943.
18. See *Ibid.*, Aug. 5, 1943.
19. See *Ibid.*, Sept. 13, 1943.
20. See *Time*, Sept. 20, 1943, p. 27.
21. *Ibid.*, p. 27.
22. Editorial, "Democracy in China," *The New Republic*, Sept. 27, 1943, p. 412.
23. See Brooks Atkinson, to *New York Times*, from Chungking, July 8, 1943.
24. See *New York Times*, April 23, 1943.
25. *Time*, Aug. 2, 1943, p. 25.
26. "Nazi Desperation Reflected by Switch of Propaganda Line," *Newsweek*, July 12, 1943, p. 46.
27. William L. Shirer, in *Montreal Standard*, from London, July 3, 1943.
28. See *New York Times*, Sept. 11, 1943.
29. See *Ibid.*, Sept. 26, 1943.
30. See *International Labor Review*, Montreal, Canadian Press, May 2, 1943.
31. See *Time*, April 5, 1943.
32. German Transocean Agency broadcast, reported in *Chicago Tribune*, Oct. 17, 1943.
33. See *New York Times*, Sept. 4, 1943.
34. See A. T. Steele, to *The Chicago Daily News*, from New Delhi, Oct. 29, 1943.

General References

The contemporaneous nature of this chapter necessitated a heavy reliance upon American daily, weekly, and monthly publications, and also upon the publications of the war information bureaus of the United Nations governments. Verbatim reports of important domestic and international events were found, for example, in the *New York Times* and *Herald-Tribune;* summaries of the swift-changing pattern of world events were gathered from such weekly magazines as *Time, Newsweek;* while articles of opinion were read in publications such as *Harper's, The Atlantic Monthly, Fortune, Yale Review, American Scholar, The Nation,* and the *New Republic.* The publications of the Allied governments' information bureaus were invaluable, especially for statistical evidence of progress in home front production, but the slanting of these publications for propaganda purposes made necessary a constant scrutinizing of their conclusions. In addition, recently published books indicated to the authors new trends of thinking on the part of American and foreign writers—trends which are helping to re-shape the culture pattern on the home fronts. Works by Wendell Willkie, Henry Wallace, and Herbert Hoover cannot be ignored. Nor can we overlook the criticism of the Occident as presented by Dr. Lin Yutang in *Between Laughter and Tears*, The John Day Company, 1943; the incisive analysis of present-day political and economic thought in Edward H. Carr, *Conditions of Peace*, The Macmillan Company, 1942; the challenge to American attitudes in Walter Lippmann, *U. S. Foreign Policy: Shield of the Republic*, Little, Brown and Company, 1942; and the blunt warnings of Canada's ex-minister to the United States, W. D. Herridge, in *Which Kind of Revolution?*, Little, Brown and Company, 1943. For the discussion of the United States the following were consulted also: bulletins and releases of the Office of War Information, especially Release Number 2022, summarizing Donald M. Nelson's "Report on War Production for 1942 with prospects for 1943"; the monthly issues of the Department of Commerce, *Survey of Current Business*—especially for August, September, October, 1943; the *Monthly Labor Review*, Bureau of Labor Statistics; and E. A. Bogan, *Handbook of War Production*, McGraw-Hill Book Company, 1942. For the preparation of material on Great Britain, the Ministry of Information kindly supplied various publications, including its *Home Front Handbook*. Also consulted was the "Review for 1942," in the *London Times*, January 2, 1943. A clear idea of trends in social thinking was gained through a full examination of Sir William Beveridge's much-discussed Report, with its numerous recommendations regarding social security in the postwar era. Among the official publications consulted for the material on Canada were the "Reference Papers" and the monthly bulletin, *Canada at War*, of the Wartime Informa-

tion Board; the *Labour Gazette*, Canadian Federation of Labour; *Hansard*, King's Printer; and *The Canada Year Book*, King's Printer, 1942. Important daily newspapers, such as the *Montreal Standard*, the *Toronto Star*, and the *Toronto Globe and Mail*, helped gauge Canadian trends more accurately. The Marsh Report was consulted as the Canadian counterpart of the Beveridge Report. The publications of the Canadian Association for Adult Education proved invaluable in helping to visualize the problems most vital to Canadians in 1943. For the section on Latin America, material was gathered largely from reports and pamphlets furnished by the Office of the Coordinator of Inter-American Affairs, from articles appearing in such journals as *Harper's* and *Atlantic Monthly*, from reports printed in the *New York Times*, and from such newly published works as Graham H. Stuart, *Latin America and the United States*, revised edition, D. Appleton-Century Company, 1943, invaluable as a study of diplomatic and commercial relations. For material on Russia, besides making use of the Soviet Embassy's *Information Bulletin* and the monthly magazine *Soviet Russia Today*, the authors made extensive use of Joseph E. Davies, *Mission to Moscow*, Simon and Schuster, 1941; Albert Rhys Williams, *The Russians*, Harcourt, Brace and Company, 1943; and Williams' earlier book, *The Soviets*, Harcourt, Brace and Company, 1937. Among the works on China consulted were H. D. Fong, *The Postwar Industrialization of China*, National Planning Association, 1942; Chiang Kai-shek, *Resistance and Reconstruction*, Harper & Brothers, 1943; Creighton Lacy, *Is There Democracy in China?*, The John Day Company, 1943; Agnes Smedley, *Battle Hymn of China*, Alfred A. Knopf, 1943; Hubert Freyn, *Free China's New Deal*, The Macmillan Company, 1943; and numerous articles in the *New York Times, Asia and the Americas*, and the *New Republic*.

9: *Preparing for Tomorrow*

Specific References

1. E. H. Carr, *Conditions of Peace*, 1942, p. 3. By permission of The Macmillan Company, publishers.

2. R. H. Tawney, *Why Britain Fights*, London, 1941, p. 45. By permission of The Macmillan Company, publishers.

3. See for example Herbert Hoover and Hugh Gibson, *The Problems of Lasting Peace*, Doubleday, Doran and Company, 1942, chap. 14;

and Harold Nicolson, *Why Britain Is at War*, Penguin Books, Ltd., 1939, pp. 148-149.

4. Herbert H. Lehman, *Relief and Rehabilitation*, Foreign Policy Reports, July 15, 1943, p. 102.

5. See "Allies Chart Post War Plans," *Inter-Allied Review*, Oct. 15, 1941, p. 1.

6. Lehman, p. 105.

7. "The United States in a New World," IV, "Relations With Europe," *Fortune*, May 1942, p. 10.

8. See Bernadotte E. Schmitt, *What Shall We Do With Germany?* Public Policy Pamphlets, No. 38, The University of Chicago Press, 1943, pp. 16-20.

9. *Ibid.*, p. 21.

10. Carr, p. 221.

11. See Robert Ergang, "Subjugate or Conciliate Germany," *Current History*, Events Publishing Company, Feb. 1943, p. 473.

12. V. M. Dean, *What Future For Germany*, Foreign Policy Reports, Feb. 1, 1943, p. 295.

13. N. J. Spykman, *America's Strategy in World Politics*, Harcourt, Brace and Company, 1942, p. 460.

14. *Ibid.*, p. 447.

15. Quoted by R. L. Buell, "Draftsmen of the New World," *Fortune*, Feb. 1943, p. 152.

16. Harold E. Stassen, "We Need a World Government," *The Saturday Evening Post*, May 22, 1943, p. 41.

17. See P. E. Corbett, *Post-War Worlds*, Farrar and Rinehart, 1942, pp. 189-190.

18. Payson S. Wild, *Machinery of Collaboration between the United Nations*, Foreign Policy Reports, July 1, 1942, p. 106.

19. Thomas Mann, *The Coming Victory of Democracy*, Alfred A. Knopf, 1938, p. 14.

20. Charles E. Merriam, *On The Agenda of Democracy*, 1941, p. 14. Reprinted by permission of the President and Fellows of Harvard College.

21. CMD, 1922, *Indians in Kenya*, London, 1923.

22. See *Toward a New World Order*, Foreign Policy Reports, May 15, 1941, p. 54.

23. Quoted from H. P. Whidden, *As Britain Sees the Post-War World*, Foreign Policy Reports, Oct. 15, 1942, p. 192.

24. Henry A. Wallace, *Free World Victory*, L. B. Fischer, 1942, p. 19.

25. Hoover and Gibson, p. 209.

26. Earl Browder, *The Way Out*, International Publishers, 1941, p. 15.

27. *Ibid.*, p. 106.

28. See "The United States in a New World," III, "The Domestic Economy," supplement to *Fortune*, Dec. 1942, p. 17.

29. Details of the Beveridge and the N.R.P.B. plans were taken from a convenient summary in *Bulletin of the Commission to Study the Organization of Peace*, May-June, 1943.

30. Quoted from *Christian Science Monitor*, June 4, 1943, p. 1.

31. Speech before *New York Herald-Tribune* Forum, Nov. 17, 1942.

32. J. B. Condliffe, *Implications of Lend-Lease*, Foreign Affairs, April 1943, p. 501.

General References

For material on postwar planning and reconstruction the following were found very valuable: Clarence Streit, *Union Now*, Harper & Brothers, 1939, and *Union Now With Britain*, Harper & Brothers, 1941; Vera M. Dean, *Toward a New World Order*, in the *Foreign Policy Reports*, May 15, 1941, and *The Struggle For World Order*, Foreign Policy Association, 1941; P. E. Corbett, *Post-War Worlds*, Farrar & Rinehart, 1942; W. B. Curry, *The Case for Federal Union*, Middlesex, Penguin Books, 1939; H. G. Wells, *The New World Order*, Alfred A. Knopf, 1940; *The United States in a New World*, No. I., *Relations With Britain* from *Fortune*, May, 1942, Time Inc.; W. P. Maddox, *European Plans for World Order*, American Academy of Political and Social Science, 1940; W. Ivor Jennings, *A Federation for Western Europe*, The Macmillan Company, 1940; Herbert Hoover and Hugh Gibson, *The Problems of Lasting Peace*, Doubleday, Doran and Company, 1942; and *The World's Destiny and the United States*, World Citizens Association, 1941. One of the most significant contributions to the study of postwar problems is E. H. Carr, *Conditions of Peace*, The Macmillan Company, 1942. The article by R. L. Buell, "Draftsmen of the New World," *Fortune*, Feb. 1942, contains suggestive material. Much valuable material was also obtained from the British Library of Information and the United Nations Information Office. A brief but splendid exposition of a program for dynamic democracy is outlined in Charles E. Merriam, *On the Agenda of Democracy*, Harvard University Press, 1941. Postwar democracy is discussed in the address of Vice-President Henry A. Wallace, "The Price of Free World Victory," published by L. B. Fischer, 1942. Another helpful discussion is to be found in Carl Becker, *Modern Democracy*, Yale University Press, 1941. The publications of the Commission To Study the Organization of Peace are helpful in suggesting specific postwar problems. The periodical *New Europe and World Reconstruction*, largely the channel for the expression of views of émigré European scholars, presents much valuable material as do publications of the United Nations governments, such as the *Inter-Allied Review* and *Bulletins from Britain*. The colonial problem is well treated in W. C. Langsam, *In Quest of Em-*

pire, The Problem of Colonies, Foreign Policy Association, 1939, and more extensively in Royal Institute of International Affairs, *The Colonial Problem,* Oxford University Press, 1937. The rôle of the United States in the postwar world is provocatively treated by Nicholas John Spykman, *America's Strategy in World Politics,* Harcourt, Brace and Company, 1942. Economic trends in America are covered in the popular but suggestive brief volume: Stuart Chase, *The Road We Are Travelling, 1914-1942,* Twentieth Century Fund, 1942. Additional readings of value are: Allan Nevins, *This Is England Today,* Charles Scribner's Sons, 1941; J. B. Priestley, *Out of the People,* Harper & Brothers, 1941; C. H. Pegg and others, *American Society and the Changing World,* F. S. Crofts and Company, 1942; H. E. Barnes, *Society in Transition,* Prentice-Hall, 1939; Sir George Schuster and G. Vint, *India and Democracy,* The Macmillan Company, 1941; *Winning both the War and the Peace,* The Annals of the American Academy of Political and Social Science, 1942; Liston Pope, *Religious Proposals for World Order,* The Church Peace Union and World Alliance, 1941; H. G. Wells, *The New World Order,* Alfred A. Knopf, 1940; Carl Wittke and others, *Democracy Is Different,* Harper & Brothers, 1941; pamphlets prepared by the Universities Committee on Post-War Problems; Bulletins of the Commission to Study the Organization of Peace; *War and Peace Aims of the United Nations,* compiled and edited by L. W. Holborn, World Peace Foundation, 1943, indispensable aid in studying plans for the postwar period; Norman Angell, *Let the People Know,* The Viking Press, 1942, from the pen of a famous worker for international peace; Michael Straight, *Make This the Last War,* Harcourt, Brace and Company, 1943; J. C. Smuts, *Plans for a Better World,* London, Hodder & Stoughton, 1942, collected speeches of the distinguished South African statesman; Ely Culbertson, *Summary of the World Federation Plan,* Garden City Publishing Company, 1943; Walter Lippmann, *U. S. Foreign Policy: Shield of the Republic,* Little, Brown and Company, 1943; Wendell Willkie, *One World,* Simon and Schuster, 1943, an absorbing little volume designed to stimulate the "world-view" in America; Sumner Welles, *The World of the Four Freedoms,* Columbia University Press, 1943, twelve important speeches by the former Under-Secretary of State; R. M. MacIver, *Towards an Abiding Peace,* The Macmillan Company, 1943. The following Foreign Policy Reports offer pertinent material: C. Grove Haines, *What Future For Italy,* Oct. 1, 1943; L. K. Rosinger, *What Future for Japan,* Sept. 1, 1943; V. M. Dean (already mentioned); H. P. Whidden, *As Britain Sees the Post-War World,* Oct. 15, 1942; *What Americans Think about Post-War Reconstruction,* Oct. 1, 1942 and Jan. 15, 1943; and Owen Lattimore, *Asia in a New World Order,* Sept. 1, 1942. The following studies are important also: T. A. Raman, *Report On India,* Oxford University Press, 1943; Harold Laski, *Reflections on the Revolution of Our Time,* The Viking Press, 1943; G. Salvemini, G. La Piana, *What To Do With Italy,* Duell, Sloan, and Pearce, 1943.

General Index

Suggested pronunciations for difficult or unusual words are respelled according to the table below, which is repeated in simplified form at the bottom of each right hand page of the *Index*. The mark ⁄ is placed after a syllable with primary or strong accent; the mark ' shows a secondary or light accent, as in **civilization** (siv′i-li za′tion).

The local pronunciations of many foreign words are too unusual for persons untrained in linguistics, and the aim has therefore been to provide pronunciations commonly acceptable in unaffected, educated American speech.

a	hat, cap	j	jam, enjoy
ā	age, face	k	kind, seek
ã	care, air	l	land, coal
ä	father, far	m	me, am
		n	no, in
b	bad, rob	ng	long, bring
ch	child, much		
d	did, red	o	hot, rock
		ō	open, go
		ô	order, all
e	let, best	oi	oil, voice
ē	equal, see	ou	house, out
ėr	term, learn		
		p	paper, cup
f	fat, if	r	run, try
g	go, bag	s	say, yes
h	he, how	sh	she, rush
		t	tell, it
i	it, pin	th	thin, both
ī	ice, five	ŦH	then, smooth

u cup, butter
ů full, put
ü rule, move
ū use, music

v very, save
w will, woman
y you, yet
z zero, breeze
zh measure, seizure

ə represents:

a in about
e in taken
i in pencil
o in lemon
u in circus

FOREIGN SOUNDS

Y as in French du. Pronounce ē with the lips rounded as for English ü in **rule**.

œ as in French peu. Pronounce ā with the lips rounded as for ō.

N as in French bon. The N is not pronounced, but shows that the vowel before it is nasal.

H as in German ach. Pronounce k without closing the breath passage.

A

Abd-el-Krim (äb′del krim′),   101

Abyssinia, conquered by Italy,   154-155; *m.* 160. *See also* Ethiopia.

Africa Corps (af′rikə kôr),   188, 197, 201

Agadir,   16; *m.* 17

Agriculture, U. S. problems of,   109-110

Air offensive, Allied, in North Africa, 204; in the Pacific, 207, 208; in Western Europe, 213-214, 216, 219

Aland Islands,   43-44; *m.* 35

Albania,   boundary dispute with Jugoslavia, 44, *m.* 48-49; war with Italy, 169

Aleutians,   187, *m.* 178-179, 195; American offensive in, 209; Attu, Kiska invaded, 209, *m.* 209; fall, 209

Alexander, General Harold,   197

Alexander, King of Yugoslavia,   98

Alexandria,   188

Alfonso, King,   102

Algeciras,   16; *m.* 17

Algeria,   202; *m.* 202

Allied Military Government,   253

Alsace-Lorraine,   32, 33; *m.* 35

America First Committee,   174

Andaman Islands (an′də man),   187

Ankara,   80; *m.* 48-49

Anschluss (än′shlůs),   37, 98

Anti-Comintern Pact,   147, 157

Argentina,   112, 113, 185, 234, 236

Assembly of League of Nations,   39

Atlantic Charter,   **175**, 176, 185, 251, 253, 257

Attu Island,   209; *m.* 209

Auchinleck, General (ô′chin lek),   181, 188, 197

Australia,   decentralization of industry in, 232; development after World War I, 106; Japanese threat to, 184-185, 199, 231; Labor government in, 232; Manpower Directorate, 231; relations with United States, 232

Austria,   annexation by Germany, 157-158; Balkan interests, 13; financial collapse in, 45; and peace settlement, 37, *m.* 35; postwar government, 98-99; reaction to peace settlement, 46

---

hat, āge, cãre, fär; let, ēqual, tėrm; it, īce; hot, ōpen, ôrder; oil, out; cup, půt, rüle, ūse; ch, child; ng, long; th, thin; ŦH, then; zh, measure; ə represents a in about, e in taken, i in pencil, o in lemon, u in circus.

Austria-Hungary, dismemberment, 37; at Peace Conference, 32; *m.* 35
Avenol, Joseph, 40
Axis. *See* Rome-Berlin Axis.
Axis countries, and democracy, 260; occupation and administration of, 253-254; treatment of, 256-257
Azaña, Manuel (ä thän′yä, mä nwäl′), 102

B

Badoglio, Marshal Pietro (bä dō′lyō, pyä′trō), 212, 216, 217, 224, 242
Balance of power, after First World War, 38
Baldwin, Stanley, 103, 104, 157
Balilla (bä lē′lä), 79
Balkans, 11-14, *m.* 12, 17; proposed union of, 259
Bank for International Settlements, The, 56
Bataan, 184, 187; *m.* 178-179
Belgium, investments in China, 131; peace settlement, 33, *m.* 35; German invasion in Second World War, 166; postwar development, 101
Belgrade, 171
Benes, Eduard (be′nesh), 47, 97, 158, 161
Bennett, Richard B., 106
Bentham, Jeremy, 38
Berlin, Congress, 13; bombing of, 219
Beveridge Plan, 262-263
Bizerte (bē zärt′), 203, 204; *m.* 202
Black Shirts. *See* Fascism, in Italy.
Blum, Léon, 96
Bolsheviks, 64, 65
Boris, King of Bulgaria, 100
Borneo, 184
Borodin, Michael (bôr′ə din′), 136
Bosnia-Herzegovina, 13; *m.* 12, 17
Bosporus, 12. *See also* Straits.
Boxer Rebellion, 134, 139
Brazil, 112
Brest Litovsk, Treaty of, 37, 66
Briand, Aristide (brē än′, ä rēs tēd′), 47
British Empire. *See* Great Britain and England.
British Imperial Conference, 105
Bulgaria, acquires Rumanian territory, 169-170; and Balkan Wars, 13-14, *m.* 12; and peace settlement, 37, 46, *m.* 35; and postwar dictatorship, 100; Treaty of Neuilly with, 37
Burma, 107; Japanese conquest of, 186; *m.* 178-179
Burma Road, 182, 185, 186, 210; *m.* 210

C

Cairo, 168, *m.* 178-179; Conference, 218
Canada, Dominion of, and Air Training Plan, 229; conscription in, 231; control of inflation in, 229; cooperation with United States, 230; development after First World War, 105; economic relations with England, 230; English-French relations, 231; food exports of, 228-229; Industrial Revolution in, 228; labor relations in, 230-231; maturation of, 228, 229; Sicilian invasion, 212; social security in, 263; and United Nations Food Conference, 228; war expenditures of, 229
Canton, 135, 144; *m.* 133
Capitalism, 58, 59
Carol II, King, 99, 100, 169
Caroline and Marshall Islands, 132; *m.* 178-179
Carr, E. H., 250, 256
Casablanca Conference (kä′sə bläng′kə), 210; *m.* 194, 202
Castillo, Ramon S. (käs tē′ lyō, rä mōn′), 236
Caucasus, 177, 196, 205, 207; *m.* 178-179
Celebes, 184
Central Corporative Committee, 78
Central Europe Confederation, 259
Ceylon, 107
Chamberlain, Neville, 157-158, 159, 161, 167
Chamberlain, Sir Austen, 47
Chavez, Carlos (chä veth′, kär′lōs), 116
Chelyabinsk (chel′yä binsk′), 71; *m.* 48-49
Chennault, Brigadier General Claire L., 198, 210
Chiang Kai-shek (ch y äng′ kī′shek′), Communists subdued by, 138, 144; head of Nanking government, 137; kidnapping of, 144-145; President of China, 240
Chiang Kai-shek, Mme., 210, 228
Chile, 112, 185
China, abrogation of extraterritorial rights in, 239; Boxer Rebellion, 134; capture of Hangchow-Nanchang Railroad, 198, *m.* 210; Chiang Kai-shek, 137-138, 240; Communism in, 137; economic and social change, 138-139, 240-241; investments in, 128; Japanese invasion, 143, 145; loss of Changteh, 219, *m.* 210; political development, 241; renewed Japanese offensive, 189, 198; struggle for democracy, 240; Sun Yat-sen, 135-136; three-point program, 239; trade with Germany, 130-131; Twenty-One Demands, 140-141; and United States Air Force, 198, 210; and western exploitation, 133; *m.* 133
Chinese Eastern Railway, 133
Church, The, and postwar planning, 249, 257
Churchill, Winston, 167, 169, 185, 218, 227, 254
Civilian Conservation Corps, 111
Clayton Anti-Trust Act, 108
Clemenceau, Georges (klə mäN so′), 32, 94
Collective farming, in Russia, 71
Colonial Charter, 261
Committee to Defend America by Aiding the Allies, 174
Committee on Economic Development, 249
Committee of National Liberation, 215, 238
Communism, in China, 138, 144-145; comparison with Fascism, 78; in France, 96; in Hungary, 98; in Germany, 81; in Russia, 67-74; threat of in Italy, 76
Communist Party, 69
Connally Resolution, 259
Conscription, in Canada, 231; in Great Britain, 161; in United States, 174
Constitution, in India, 1935, 124; in Russia, 1924, 67-68; in Russia, 1936, 68-69; Weimar, 81
Coolidge, Calvin, 109
Cooperatives, in Scandinavia, 100
Cooper, Alfred Duff, 160

Coral Sea, Battle of, 187; *m.* 178-179
Corfu incident, 44; *m.* 48-49
Corporate state, 77-78
Corporations, and finance capitalism, 59
Corregidor (kôr eg′i dôr), 184, 187
Cortes (kôr′tez), 102
Costa Rica, 112
Council of League of Nations, 39-40
Council of Nationalities, 68-69
Council of People's Commissars, 69
Council of Ten, 33
Covenant of League of Nations, 33, 39, 41, 50
Credit Anstalt Bank (kre dēt′ än′sht ält bängk *or* bangk), 57
Crete, invasion of, 171-172; *m.* 178-179
Crimean peninsula, 180; *m.* 48-49
Cripps, Sir Stafford, 125, 187
Croatia-Slavonia, 98
Croats, 98
Croix de Feu (krwä de fœ′), 96
Culbertson, Ely, and world federation, 258
Curtin, John (kèr′tin), 232
Czechoslovakia, alliance with France, 47; *m.* 48-49; composition of, 97; creation of, 96, *m.* 35; Munich Agreement, 159; Sudeten problem, 158-160; total capitulation, 161

D

Dairen, 133; *m.* 133
Daladier, Edouard (dä lä dyä′), 159, 161
D'Annunzio, Gabriele (dä nün′tsi ō, gä brē el′), 74
Danzig, 34, 42, 45, 162; *m.* 35, 160
Dardanelles, 12, 20, 21. *See also* Straits.
Darlan, Admiral (där läN′), 202
Davies, Joseph E., 72, 237
Dawes Plan, 54
Denmark, German invasion of, 165; history after World War I, 100-101; and peace settlement, 33; *m.* 35.
Development Commissions, 264
Dieppe, Commando raid on (di ep′), 201
Disarmament, proposals for, 50-51; provided for in League Covenant, 41-42
Dnieper River (nē′pər), 180, 206; *m.* 48-49, 206
Dnepropetrovsk (d nye′prō pye trofsk′), 71, 216; *m.* 48-49, 206
Dollfuss, Engelbert, 99, 157
Don River (don), 180, 188, 195; *m.* 196, 206
Doumergue, Gaston (dü märg′), 95
Drummond, Sir Eric, 38
Duce, Il (dü′chā, ēl). *See* Mussolini.
Duma, 65
Dunkirk, 166; *m.* 178-179
Dutch East Indies. *See* Netherlands East Indies.
Dutch Harbor, 187; *m.* 178-179

E

East Indies. *See* Netherlands East Indies.
East Prussia, 34, 42; *m.* 35
Ebert, Friedrich, 81
Eden, Anthony, 185, 259, 261-262
Egypt, 107, 168-169, 171; *m.* 178-179
Eire. *See* Irish Free State.
Eisenhower, General Dwight, 202, 204, 216
Enabling Act in Germany, 87
England. *See* Great Britain and England.
Estonia, 45, 100, 164-165, 180; *m.* 35
Ethiopia, 43, 168. *See also* Abyssinia.
Export-Import Bank, 118
Extraterritoriality, 132; abrogation of, in China, 239

F

Fascism, definition of, 77; beginning of, in Italy, 75-76; in Belgium, 101; comparison with Communism, 78; education and, 78-79; in France, 167; government, 76-77; and nationalism, 78; in Spain, 155-157
Fascist Grand Council, 77
Federal Farm Loan Board, 110
Federal Housing Administration, 111
Ferdinand, King of Bulgaria, 100
Ferdinand, King of Rumania, 99
Finland, and Aland Island dispute, 43-44, *m.* 35; government after First World War, 100; war with Russia, 164-165
First World War. *See* World War, First.
Fiume, 37; *m.* 35
Five-Year Plan, first, 70-72; second, 72; third, 72
Flandin, Pierre Etienne (fläN daN′), 96
Foch, General (fosh), 27
Fordney-McCumber Tariff Act, 55-56, 108
Formosa, 133; *m.* 133
Four-Power Treaty, 141
Fourteen Points, 33
Four-Year Economic Plan, 254
Four-Year Plan, 88
Franco, General Francisco, 155-157
France, attitude in Italo-Abyssinian War, 154-155; exploitation of China, 133, *m.* 133; invasion of Ruhr, 54; investments in eastern Asia, 128; Kwangchow leased, 133, *m.* 133; monetary policy, 94; Munich Agreement, 159; non-intervention in Spanish Civil War, 156; and Rhineland remilitarization, 155; **World War I:** desire for postwar security, 46, *m.* 48; postwar alliances, 47, *m.* 48-49; postwar governments, 94-96; postwar position, 38; **World War II:** 162, 166; Committee of National Liberation, 215, 238; fall of, 166; German invasion, 166, 202; scuttling of fleet, 202-203; Vichy government, 167
Free French, 181, 202, 215, 238

---

hat, āge, cãre, fär; let, ēqual, tèrm; it, īce· hot, ōpen, ôrder; oil, out; cup, pút, rüle, ūse; ch, child; ng, long; th, thin; ᵺ, then; zh, measure; ə represents *a* in about, *e* in taken, *i* in pencil, *o* in lemon, *u* in circus.

Free Trade, abandonment of, 55
French Indo-China. *See* Indo-China.
Führer, der (fY′rər, dər). *See* Hitler.
Fulbright Resolution, 259

G

Gamelin, General (gäm laN′), 157, 164, 166
Gandhi, Mohandas K., civil disobedience campaign, 123, 199; demand for Indian independence, 198; life of, 122-123; and pacifism, 198-199
Gaulle, General Charles de (də gōl), 181, 203
Geneva, 38; Conference, 52
Gentlemen's Agreement, 109
Geopoliticians, and postwar planning, 257
George, King of Greece, 171
German Workers' Party, 84
Germany, acquisitions in China, 133, *m.* 133; Anti-Comintern Pact, 147; Austria annexed, 157-158; bombing of, 213-214, 216, 219, 243; comparison with Japan, 146; control of Kiaochow Bay, 133, *m.* 133; Czech capitulation to, 161; eastern Asia interests, 130-131; foundations of dictatorship, 83; Hitler's dictatorship, 85-88; intervention in Spanish Civil War, 155; League of Nations membership, 43, 50, 82; and Locarno Pacts, 47, 50; Munich Agreement, 159; Nazism's rise, 85; Pact with Poland, 162; and reparations, 53-55; Rhineland reoccupied, 155; Rome-Berlin Axis, 147, 217, 243; Russian Pact, 163; Sudetenland annexed, 158-159; trade with China, 131; with Latin America, 114; Versailles Treaty imposed upon, 46; and war guilt, 36; Weimar Republic, 81-83; withdrawal from League, 155; working conditions in, 243-244; **World War I:** at Peace Conference, 32; peace settlement, 36; postwar inflation, 54, 81; territory lost, 33-34, *m.* 35; **World War II:** assault on Stalingrad, 196; battle of Naples, 217; gains in Ukraine, 213; North African campaign, 196-198, 201-205; Poland invaded by, 163; retreat in Russia, 205-207, 213, 216; Russia invaded, 177; summer offensive in Russia, 195-196; treatment of postwar, 256-257; youth movement in, 88
Giraud, General Henri, 215
Gold standard abandoned, 57-58
Good Neighbor policy, 117-118, 234
Gorki, Maxim (gôr′ki), city named for, 71; *m.* 48-49
Government of India Act, 124
Graziani, Marshal (grä′zi ä′ni), 168-169
Great Britain and England, agricultural progress, 226; all-out German bombing, 168; appeasement policy, 157; attitude in Italo-Abyssinian War, 154; Cairo Conference, 218; conscription in, 161; currency devaluation, 57; Dunkirk retreat, 166; economic cooperation, 263-264; economic transformation of, 226-227; empire after First World War, 105-107; exploitation of China, 133, *m.* 133; free trade abolished, 57; gold standard abandoned, 58; Greek retreat, 171; Hong Kong acquired, 133, *m.* 133; India problem, 107, 122-126, 187, 198-199; industry in, 226;

international cooperation, 257, 259; investments in Far East, 126-128; joint supply boards with U. S., 185; Mesopotamian oil dispute, 44; Munich Agreement, 159; National Service Act, 226; non-intervention in Spanish Civil War, 156; and Polish crisis, 162-163; and position in Pacific, 145; and Rhineland remilitarization, 155; Russian Pact, 180; social revolution in, 225; social security, 262-263; Teheran Conference, 218; **World War I:** postwar attitude toward Germany, 103; postwar governments, 102-105; postwar isolation, 46; **World War II:** African campaign, 169, 201, 203-205; battle of Naples, 217; entry into, 162-163; labor and postwar economy, 227-228; postwar imperialism, 256; and Sicilian invasion, 212-213; and surrender of Italy, 216-218
Greco-Turkish War, 45
Greece, Corfu incident with Italy, 44; German conquest of, 171; Italian invasion repulsed, 169
Grotius, Hugo, 38
Guadalajara (gwä′dä lä hä′rä), 156; *m.* 160
Guadalcanal, Battle of, 200-201, 207; *m.* 200
Guam, 132, 184; *m.* 178-179

H

Hacha, Emil (hä′chä), 161
Hague, The, 40
Haile Selassie, Emperor (hī′li sə las′i), 154
Hainan, 182
Haiti, 117
Harding, Warren G., 108
Havana, 117
Hawaiian Islands, 132
Hay, John, 133
Heimwehr (hīm′vär′), 99
Helen, Princess, 99
Hemispherists, and postwar planning, 257
Henderson, Sir Nevile, 163
Herriot, Edouard (e′ri ō′), 94, 95
Hertzog, General, 233. *See also* South Africa, Dominion of.
Hess, Rudolf, 84, 86
Himmler, Heinrich, 86
Hindenburg, Paul von, 82, 85, 86
Hinduism, 125, 126
Hindus, 125
Hitler, Adolf, chancellor, 85; dictator, 86; early life, 83-84; and Italian surrender, 243; Munich *Putsch*, 81; organizes National Socialist party, 84; party purge, 86-87; personal command of army, 180. *See also* Germany.
Holland, German invasion of, 165-166; government after First World War, 101; policy in East Indies, 129
Hong Kong, 182, 184
Hoover, Herbert, 110
Hoover Moratorium, 57
Horthy, Admiral, 98
House, Colonel, 33
Hughes, Charles Evans, 52

Hull, Secretary of State, 118, 173

Hungary, acquires Rumanian territory, 170; dictatorship in, 98; financial collapse in, 45; government after First World War, 98; joins League, 43; reaction to peace settlement, 46; and Treaty of Trianon, 37, 46; *m.* 35

Hu Shih, Dr., 139

I

Immigration, Johnson Act, 109; restriction of, in United States, 109

Imperialism, in China, *m.* 133; economic, 10; Fascist Italy and, 78; Great Britain and, 256; after Second World War, 260-261; United States and, 256

India, and Burma, 210, *m.* 210; constitution of 1919, 122; constitution of 1935, 124; Cripps mission, 125, 187; demand for self-government, 107, 122-126, 198-199; economic life, 125; languages, 125; Morley-Minto reforms, 122; population, 125; social conditions, 125; and World War I, 122; and World War II, 198-199

Indian Congress Party, 198-199

Indian National Congress, 124

Indo-China, 126, 133, 182

Indonesians, 128

International Economic Conference, 58

International Labor Conference, 40-41, 43

Inter-Allied Relief Committee, 251

Iran, 181; *m.* 48-49

Iraq, 34, 169, 171, 180; *m.* 34, 48-49. *See also* Mesopotamia.

Irish Free State, 43; *m.* 48-49

Iron Guard, 100

Italy, conquest of Abyssinia, 154-155; Corfu incident, 44; corporate state, 77; fall of Mussolini, 212, 241, 242; government after First World War, 75; government under Badoglio, 212, 216, 217, 242; grievances of the people, 241-242; and imperialism, 79; intervention in Spanish Civil War, 155; Munich Agreement, 159; Near East interests, 131; and peace settlement, 37, 47, 74; relations with Austria, 157; relations with Germany, 217; Treaty of London, 37; Treaty of Rapallo, 74; and the underground, 242; war with France, 166; withdrawal from League, 147; **World War II:** armistice agreement, 216-217; battle of Naples, 217; surrender of, 216-218

J

Japan, Aleutians invaded, 209; Anti-Comintern Pact, 147; capture of Changteh, 219, *m.* 210; checked in New Guinea, 208-209; comparison with Germany, 146; conquest of Philippines, Wake Island, Guam, Hong Kong, Singapore, Java, Burma, 184-186; control over Indo-China and Thailand, 182; earthquake of 1923, 142; economic and military consolidation in, 244; economic power in China, 140; economic progress, 141; exclusion of emigration to U. S., 109, 148; Gentlemen's Agreement, 109; Hainan seized, 182; imperialism in China, 139-141; invades New Guinea, 199; Manchurian campaign, 142-143; Marcus Islands raided, 218, *m.* 195; new offensive in China, 189, 198; Paramoshiri attacked, 218; *m.* 209; Pearl Harbor attack, 184; position in Pacific in 1939, 146; position after World War I, 38; production difficulties of, 244-245; Russian War, 139-140; and Solomons, 200-201, 207, 214, 217; southwest expansion, 106; at Washington Conference, 141

Java, 128, 186; *m.* 178-179

Jesuits, dissolution in Spain, 102

Jews, persecution of, 161

Jinnah (ji nä′), 199

Johnson Act, 171

Johnson Immigration Act, 109

Joint Wheat Council, 251

K

Kalinin (kä lēn′in), 65

Kamenev (kä′myen yef), 65

Kant, Immanuel, 38

Kellogg-Briand Pact, 50, 52-53

Kemal Ataturk (kə mäl′ ä′tä tʏrk′), 37; life of, 79-80; reforms of, 80; takes over government, 80-81

Kenney, General, 208

Kerenski, A. F., 65

Kharkov, 180, 206, 213; *m.* 48-49, 196, 206

Kiaochow Bay (kyou′chou′), 133; *m.* 133

Kiev (kē′ef), 180, 216; *m.* 48-49, 206

King, Mackenzie, 228, 231

Kiska Island, 209, 215; *m.* 209

Korea, 133, 139; *m.* 133

Kuang Hsu (kwäng′ shü′), 134

Kuibyshev (kwē′bi shef′), 180

Ku Klux Klan, 108

Kulaks, 67, 71

Kun, Bela, 98

Kuomintang, 136, 239, 240

Kurusu, Saburo (kü′rü sü), 183

Kursk, 188

Kwangchow, 128, 133; *m.* 133

L

Labor Party, 103

Lansing-Ishii Agreement, 141

Latin America, art of, 116; Church in, 115; development after World War I, 112-118; economic importance of, 234; and Good Neighbor policy, 234; illiter-

hat, āge, cãre, fär; let, ēqual, tėrm; it, īce; hot, ōpen, ôrder; oil, out; cup, pu̇t, rüle, ūse; ch, child; ng, long; th, thin; ᴛʜ, then; zh, measure; ə represents *a* in about, *e* in taken, *i* in pencil, *o* in lemon, *u* in circus.

acy in, 115; mounting inflation in, 234-235; and Pan-Americanism, 117, 176; race fusion in, 116; relations with Axis, 234; revolt in Argentina, 236; Rio Conference, 185; and shipping problems, 235; and United States, 234, 236

Latvia, 100, 165, 180; *m.* 35

Lausanne, Treaty of, 37; Conference, 57

Laval, Pierre, 96

Law, Andrew Bonar, 103

Lebensraum (lā′bəns room′), 157

League of Nations, Abyssinian appeal to, 154; Aland Island dispute, 43-44; Chinese appeal to, 143; Corfu incident, 44; Covenant of, 33, 39; Danzig, administration of, 34; and International Labor Conference, 40-41; and Manchurian invasion, 143; mandate system, 34, *m.* 34; membership of, 43; organization of, 38-41; plan for, 33; purposes of, 41-42; revival of, 258, 261; and Russo-Finnish War, 164-165; sanctions against Italy, 155; withdrawal of Germany, 147, 155; withdrawal of Italy, 147; withdrawal of Japan, 143; and World Court, 40

Left Cartel, 94, 95

Lehman, Herbert, 251, 252-253

Lend-Lease Bill, 176, 180, 181, 185, 263

Lenin, Nikolay, 64-66; *coup d'état*, 65-66; life of, 66; death of, 67

Leningrad, 180, 181, 205, 207; *m.* 48-49, 206

Leopold, King of Belgium, 166

Lewis, John L., 222

Ley, Robert (lī), 87

Liaotung peninsula, 133; *m.* 133

Libya, 168, 188; *m.* 178-179

Liebknecht, Karl (lēp′kneнt), 81

Lippman, Walter, 259, 262

Lithuania, 34, 100, 165, 180; *m.* 35

Litvinov, Maxim (lit vē′nôf), 158, 163

Lloyd George, David, 32, 37, 103

Locarno Treaties, 47, 50

London, bombing of, 168; Naval Conference, 52, 111; Treaty of, 37; World Economic Conference in, 57

Luftwaffe (lúft′väf′ə), 157, 164, 168, 169, 213

Lupescu, Magda, 99

Luxemburg, 32, 165; *m.* 35

Luxemburg, Rosa, 81

Lytton Commission, 111, 143

M

Macao (məkä′ō), 131; *m.* 133

MacArthur, General Douglas, 184, 186, 187, 199, 208

Macassar Strait, 185; *m.* 178-179

MacDonald, James Ramsey, 103, 104

Madagascar, 187; *m.* 178-179

Madrid, 156; *m.* 160

Maginot Line, 164, 166, 167

Magyars (mag′yärz). *See* Hungary.

Malaya, 184, 185

Manchukuo, 130, 143-144; *m.* 127, 178-179

Manchuria, 129, 139, 142, 143, 144. *See also* Manchukuo.

Manchus, 134-135

Mandates, 34; *m.* 34

Manhood Suffrage Bill, 142

Manila, 184

Mannerheim Line, 165

Mareth Line, 201, 203, 204

Marsh Plan, 263

Marx, Karl, 65

Marxian Socialism, in Russia, 64

Masaryk, President Thomas (mä′sä rēk), 47, 97

McNary-Haugen Bill, 110

Mein Kampf (mīn kämpf′), 84-85, 157

Mensheviks, 64

Mesopotamia, 44

Messina, 212, 213; *m.* 211

Metaxas, General John, 100

Mexico, 43, 112; relations with Axis, 185; social change in, 114-115

Midway Islands, 187; *m.* 178-179

Migration and Settlement Commissions, 264

Millerand, 94

Minorities, in Czechoslovakia, 97, *m.* 39; in Europe after First World War, 38, *m.* 39; in Poland, 97, *m.* 39; in Russia, 74; in Rumania, 99; *m.* 39

Molotov, Foreign Commissar V. (môl′ə tôf), 188, 216

Monroe Doctrine, 53

Montgomery, General Bernard, 201, 203, 216

Morley-Minto reforms, 122

Morocco, 16, 101, 155, 202; *m.* 17, 202

Moscow, 177, 180, 181, 206, 215-216, *m.* 48-49, 206; Conference, 215-216, 224, 257

Moslem League, 199

Moslems, 125

Mountbatten, Lord Louis, 215

Munda Island, 214; *m.* 200

Munich Agreement, 159

Mussolini, colonial demands, 161; and Corfu incident, 44; fall of, 212, 241, 242; head of puppet régime, 217; invades Abyssinia, 154-155; life of, 75; Munich Agreement, 159; takes over government, 76; war on France, 166-167. *See also* Italy.

Mustafa Kemal (mús′tä fä kə mäl′). *See* Kemal Ataturk.

N

Nanking government, 137; *m.* 133

Naples, Battle of, 217; *m.* 202

Narvik, 165

National Council of Corporations, 78

National Defense Advisory Board, 174

Nationalism, economic, 56-58; and Fascism, 78-79; and First World War, 11

National Labor Relations Board, 112

National Resources Planning Board, abolition of, 255; and economic problems, 254; and social security, 263

National Socialist Party, 84

Nazi Party. *See* National Socialist Party.

Nazism, in Austria, 99; economics of, 88; and persecution of Jews, 87; power gained by, 85; propaganda and education, 88; and religion, 87; rise of, 85; ter-rorism, 86-87. *See also* Hitler, Germany.

Nehru, Jawaharlal (nä′rü), 124, 126, 199

Nelson, Donald, 221-222

Netherlands. *See* Belgium and Holland.

Netherlands East Indies, Dutch rule of, 126; invasion of, 184; investments in, 128-129; Japanese pressure on, 182

Neuilly, Treaty of (nœ yē′), 37

New Caledonia, 132; *m.* 178-179

New Deal, 58, 111-112, 223

New Economic Policy, 67

New Guinea, 184, *m.* 178-179, 195; capture of Lae, Salamaua, 218, *m.* 200; fall of Finschhafen, 218; invaded by Japan, 199; Japan checked in, 208-209

New Order in Asia, 145, 157

New Zealand, Dominion of, development after First World War, 106; industrial program of, 233; Second World War, entry into, 232; social security in, 233; and United States, 233

Nicaragua, 117

Nicholas, Grand Duke, 65

Niemoeller, Reverend Martin (nē′mœ l′ər), 87

Nine-Power Treaty, 111, 141

Nippon. *See* Japan.

North Africa, Allied invasion of, 202; battle for Egypt, 196-198; fall of Bizerte, Tunis, 204, *m.* 202; fall of Tobruk, 201, *m.* 202; repercussions of invasion of, 202-203; Tunisian campaign, 203-205

Norway, development after First World War, 100; German invasion of, 165

Novorossiisk (nov′o ro sēsk′), 196; *m.* 195, 206

Nye, Senator Gerald, 172

O

Oceania, 131-132

Office of Foreign Relief and Rehabilitation, 252

Open Door Policy, 133-134

Opium, in Manchukuo, 144

Oran, Battle of, 167-168; *m.* 178-179

Orozco, José Clemente (ō rōs′kō), 116

Ottawa Imperial Economic Conference, 57

P

Paderewski, Ignace (pä′də ref′ski), 97

Palermo, 212

Palestine, German threat, 172; mandate of, 34, 37, 107; *m.* 34

Pan-Americanism, 117, 176, 234; Rio Conference, 185

Pan-Slavism, 13

Pantelleria (pän tel′ä rē′ä), surrender of, 210

Paris, fall of, 167; Peace Conference, 32-37; riots in, 95

Patton, General George, 212

Paul, Prince of Yugoslavia, 98, 170

Peace Conference, principle of self-determination at, 38; after World War I, 33

Pearl Harbor, 183-184; *m.* 178-179

Peiping (pā′ping′). *See* Peking.

Peking, 136, 145; *m.* 133

Penn, William, 38

Permanent Court of International Justice. *See* World Court.

Persia. *See* Iran.

Pétain, Marshal (pā taɴ′), 167, 181, 202

Peter, King of Yugoslavia, 170

Peter of Rumania, 98

Philippines, bill for independence, 130; exports to U. S., 130; independence after Second World War, 256; Japanese invasion, 184

Pilsudski, Józef (pil sůt′ski), 97

Platt Amendment, 118

Plekhanov, George (ple kä′nof), 64

Poincaré, Raymond (pwaɴ kä rä′), 54, 94, 95

Poland, alliance with France, 47; German conquest of, 163-164; German demands on, 161-163; minorities in, 97; and peace settlement, 34, *m.* 35; recreation of, 97; war with Russia, 1920, 41

Polish Corridor, 33-34, 161-162; *m.* 35, 160

Politburo (po lit′bu rō), 67, 68

Popolo d'Italia, Il (pō′pō lō dē tä′lyä, ēl), 75

Popular Front, 96

Population, of Canada, 105; of India, 125; of Poland, 97; of Rumania, 99

Port Arthur, 133; *m.* 133

Portinari, Cândido, 116

Portsmouth, Treaty of, 140

Portugal, government after First World War, 100; port in China, 131

Postwar aims, 251. *See also* Postwar planning.

Postwar planning, administration of Axis territory, 253-254; advancement of colonial peoples, 260-261; collectivism, 262; "compensated economy," 262; demarcation of boundaries, 255-256; freedom from want, 261-263; the Geopoliticians and, 257; the Hemispherists and, 257; international economic co-operation, 263-264; international organization, 257-258; laissez-faire, 262; peace agencies, 249; perfection and encouragement of democracy, 260; political determination, 256; reduction of hazard of war, 255-259; regional federation, 258-259; relief and rehabilitation, 251-253; restoration of governments, 253; revival of the League, 258; social security, 262-263; transition to a peace economy, 254-255; treatment of Axis countries, 256-257; world federation, 258

Q

Quebec Conference, 215, 229

Quiros, Cesáreo Bernaldo de (kē rōs′), 116

Quisling, Vidkun, 165

hat, āge, cãre, fär; let, ēqual, tèrm; it, īce; hot, ōpen, ôrder; oil, out; cup, pùt, rüle, ūse; ch, child; ng, long; th, thin; ᴛн, then; zḅ, measure; ə represents *a* in about, *e* in taken, *i* in pencil, *o* in lemon, *u* in circus.

R

Radar, 250
Radich (rä′diн) *or* (rad′ich), 98
Ramirez (rä mēr′es), 236
Rapallo, Treaty of, 74
Rasputin, 64
Reciprocal trade agreements, 118
Reichstag, fire, 86
Reparations, 34-35, 53-56, 57
Revolt in Argentina, 236
Rexist movement, 101
Reynaud, Paul (re nō′), 166, 167
Rhineland, 155
Ribbentrop, von, 86, 158, 163
Rio de Janeiro Conference, 234
Rivera, Diego (ri vär′ä, dyä′gō), 116
Rivera, Primo de (ri vär′ä, prē′mō dä), 102
Roehm, Captain Ernst (rœm), 87
Rome-Berlin Axis, 147, 157, 217; *m.* 160
Rommel, General Erwin, 181, 188, 197, 201
Roosevelt, Franklin D., 111, 172, 173, 174, 176, 177, 218-219, 250, 252, 255, 262
Rostov, 180, 205, 206; *m.* 196, 206
Round Table Conferences, 123-12
Rowlatt Acts, 122
Royal Air Force, 168, 216
Ruhr, invasion of, 54; *m.* 35
Rumania, alliance with France in 1926, 47; dismemberment, 169-170; German puppet, 170; government after First World War, 99-100; intervention in Hungary in 1919, 98
Russia, abolition of Comintern, 239; acquisitions in China, 133; assault on Stalingrad, 196; Balkan ambitions, 12-13; communism in, 64-65; Communist Party in, 69; Constitution of 1936, 68-69; Dairen and Port Arthur leased, 133, *m.* 133; economic planning in, 72; education in, 73-74; Finland conquered by, 164-165; Five-Year plans, 70-72; and Free Germany Committee, 238-239; German invasion of, 177; German summer drive of 1942, 195-196, *m.* 196; great offensives of, 205-207, 213, 216; illiteracy in, 74; intervention in Spanish Civil War, 156; Japanese War with, 139-140; joins League, 43; minorities in, 74; Moscow Conference, 215-216, 224, 239; pact with Germany, 163; pact with Great Britain, 182; Polish territory acquired, 1939, 164; Polish War in 1930, 41; position in eastern Asia, 131; position in Pacific, 146; relations with China, 131; relations with Japan, 131; relations with United Nations, 238; religion in, 73, 239; Revolution of 1917, 35; and second front, 215, 238; social problems of, 237-238; "scorched earth" policy, 236-237; and Teheran Conference, 218; treason trials of 1936, 70; Treaty of Brest Litovsk, 37, 66; Treaty of San Stefano, 13; importance of women in industry, 237
Russian Socialist Federated Soviet Republic, 67
Russo-Finnish War, 164-165
Russo-Japanese War, 139-140
Ruthenians, 161

S

Saar Basin, 33, 42, 45; *m.* 35
St. Germain, Treaty of, 98
Sakhalin (sä′kä lēn′), 140; *m.* 178-179
Salazar, Dr. Antonio de Oliveira (sä′lä thär′), 100
Sanctions, 41, 155
San Stefano, Treaty of, 13
Sarajevo, 17; *m.* 17
Scheidemann, Philipp, 46
Schleicher, General von (fon shlī′нər), 87
Schleswig (shles′wig), 33, 42; *m.* 35
Schlieffen Plan (shlē′fən), 20; *m.* 21
Schmitt, Bernadotte, 256
Schuschnigg, Kurt, 158
Second front, 201, 215, 219, 224
Second World War. *See* World War, Second.
Secretariat of League of Nations, 39-40
Securities Exchange Commission, 112
Selective Service Act, 174
Serbia, 13, 17; *m.* 12
Serbs, 98
Sevastopol, 180, 188
Sèvres, Treaty of, 37, 80
Seyss-Inquart, Dr. Arthur (zīs′in′kwärt), 158
Shanghai, 137; *m.* 133
Shantung peninsula, 133; *m.* 133
Shimonoseki, Treaty of, (shē′mō nō sä′ki), 133, 139
Sicily, AMG in, 253; amphibious invasion of, 212; capture of Palermo, 212; fall of Messina, 213; *m.* 202, 211
Siegfried Line, 163
Silesia, 34, 42, 44
Simon Commission, 123
Singapore, 184, 185; *m.* 178-179
Smith, Alfred E., 110
Smoot-Hawley Tariff Act, 56, 110
Smuts, General, 33, 37, 233. *See also* South Africa, Dominion of.
Social Democratic Party, in Russia, 64
Socialism, in Austria, 98-99
Social Security Act, 112
Soldiers' Bonus Bill, 109
Solomons, battle of Cape Esperance, 200; battle of Santa Cruz Islands, 201; capture of Munda, 214, *m.* 200; Japan turned back in, 207-208; struggle for Guadalcanal, 200-201; *m.* 200
Somaliland (sō mä′li land′), 168
Soong, Mei-ling (süng′, mä′ling′), 137. *See also* Chiang Kai-shek, Mme.
South America. *See* Latin America.
South Africa, Dominion of, election of 1943, 233; and postwar planning, 234; Second World War, effort in, 233-234; entry into, 233
Soviet Russia. *See* Russia.
Soviets, organized in Petrograd, 65; place in constitution, 67-68
Spain, Civil War, 155-157, *m.* 160; Nazi espionage in, 218; republic of, 102
Spartacists, 81

Spykman, N. J., 257

Stalin, Joseph, 65; and abolition of Comintern, 239; conference with Anthony Eden, 185; life of, 67; position in government, 68; and "scorched earth" policy, 236; and Teheran Conference, 218; and treatment of Germany, 256

Stalingrad, 196, 205, 206, 207; *m.* 194, 196, 206

Stambuliski, Alexander (stäm´bü lēs´ki), 100

Stassen, Harold E., 258

State and the Revolution, The, 65

Stilwell, General Joseph, 186

Stimson Doctrine, 142-143

Stimson, Secretary of State, 117

Storm Troops, 84

Straits, 12, 37; *m.* 17

Strasser, Gregor, 87

Streit, Clarence, 258

Stresemann, Gustav, 47, 82

Strikes, 59; at beginning of Russian revolution, 65; in England (1926), 103; in India, 123; in U. S., 107, 222

Submarine war, 216

Succession States, 96; *m.* 35

Sudan, 168

Sudetenland, 158-159

Suez Canal, 168; *m.* 17

Sun Yat-sen, life of, 135; death of, 136; philosophy of, 135-136; president of Canton government, 136

Supreme Court, of U.S.S.R., 69

Supreme Soviet of U.S.S.R., 68-69

Swaraj (swə räj´), 123

Sweden, and Aland Islands dispute, 43-44; development after First World War, 100; sympathy with United Nations, 218

Switzerland, democracy in, 101

Syndicalism, 77

Syria, mandate of, 34, 37, 171, 181; *m.* 34

T

Tangier, 16; *m.* 17

T'ang-ku Truce (täng´kü´), 143

Taranto, 169; *m.* 178-179

Tarawa, Battle of (tä rä´wä), 219; *m.* 195

Tariffs, in Great Britain, 57; in U. S., 55-56

Tawney, R. H., 250

Teapot Dome, 109

Teheran Conference (te rän´), 218-219

Tennessee Valley Authority, 112; *p.* 111

Thailand (tī´lənd), 127, 183

Third Reich 87

Three People's Principles, 136-137

Timoshenko, Marshal (tim´ō sheng´kō), 187-188

Tobruk (tō brúk´), 197, 201; *m.* 202

Tojo, General (tō´jō), 183

Toulon (tü lōɴ´), 202; *m.* 202

Trade, rivalry in Latin American, 113-114

Trade Disputes Act, 103

Transcaucasia, 67; *m.* 48-49

Trianon, Treaty of, 37, 98

Triple Alliance, 14; *m.* 17

Triple Entente, 15-16; *m.* 17

Trotsky, Leon, 65, 66-67

Tunisia, 202, 203-205; *m.* 202

Turkey, alliance with British, 162; Balkans controlled by, 11; Balkan Wars, 13; German threat to, 171; Kemal Ataturk's dictatorship, 79-81; Mesopotamian oil dispute, 44; at Peace Conference, 32, *m.* 35; and peace settlement, 46; republic of, 80; Straits, control of, 12; Teheran Conference, 218; Treaty of Lausanne, 37; Treaty of Sèvres, 37; war with Russia, 12-13; westernization, 80

Twenty-One Demands, 140

Tydings-McDuffie Act, 130

Tyrol, south, 37; *m.* 35

Tzu-Hsi (tsü´shē´), 134

U

Ukraine, 67, 177, 206; *m.* 48-49

Underwood Tariff Act, 55, 108

Union Congress of Soviets, 68

Union Now, 258

Union Now with Great Britain, 258

Union of Soviet Socialist Republics, 67. *See also* Russia.

United Nations, 185, 189; basic peace aims of, 255-264; dominance of in postwar politics, 259; and economic cooperation, 263-264; Food Conference of, 252; and international collaboration, 259; and Lend-Lease, 263; and occupations policy, 253; and relief problems, 251-253; treaties with defeated powers, 251; unity among Big Three, 219

United Nations Conference on Food and Agriculture, 228, 252

United Nations Relief and Rehabilitation Administration, 252

United States, action in New Guinea, 199, 208-209, 218; all-out war effort in, 221-222; and Cairo Conference, 218; conscription in, 174; currency devaluation, 57; development after First World War, 107-112; domestic political front, 223; economic transition in, 254-255; fight against inflation, 222-223; fighting in Aleutians, 209, 215; foreign policy of, 223-224; French North African invasion, 202; gold standard abandoned by, 58; Harding administration, 108-109; and hemispheric solidarity, 257; immigration laws, 109; and imperialism, 256; isolationism, 172; Italian surrender, 216-218; Japanese relations, 147-148; joint shipping and supply boards, 185; labor problems in, 222; and League of Nations, 42-43; and Manchurian conquest, 142-143; and Moscow Conference, 224; naval bases acquired, 173; neutrality acts, 171, 172, 173, 176; New Deal, 111-112, 223; Open Door Policy

hat, āge, cãre, fär; let, ēqual, tèrm; it, īce; hot, ōpen, ôrder; oil, out; cup, pùt, rüle, ūse; ch, child; ng, long; th, thin; ᴛʜ, then; zh, measure; ə represents *a* in about, *e* in taken, *i* in pencil, *o* in lemon, *u* in circus.

of, 133; and peace settlement, 37; Pearl Harbor, 183; policy in Near East, orient, 129-130; position after First World War, 39; and postwar planning, 224; public debt, 223; race riots in, 224-225; rearmament, 174; Second World War, entry into, 184; Sicilian invasion, 212-213; social security in, 263; Solomons campaign, 200-201, 207, 214, 218; stock market crash, 57; and Teheran Conference, 218; Tunisian campaign, 203-205; and war debts, 54-55

U.S. Foreign Policy: Shield of the Republic, 259

U.S.S.R. *See* Russia.

V

Versailles, Treaty of, 36-37, 155
Vichy government, 167, 202; *m.* 178-179
Vienna, 98; *m.* 48-49
Vila-Lobos, Heitor (vē′ä lō′bos), 116
Völkische Beobachter (foel′kish ə bā ō′baʜ tər), 84
Voronezh (vo ron′yesh), 195-196, 205; *m.* 196, 206

W

Wagner Plan, 263
Wake Island, 184; *m.* 178-179
Wallace, Henry A., 262
Warsaw, 164; *m.* 48-49
Washington Conference, 51-52, 111, 140, 210
Wavell, General Archibald, 169, 210
Weihaiwei (wā′hǐ′wā′), 133; *m.* 133

Weimar, Constitution of, 81
Welles, Sumner, 118, 173
Westminster, Statute of, 105
Weygand, General (vā gäɴ′), 166
White army in Russia, 66
Wild, Payson S., 259
Wilhelmina, Queen, 166
Willkie, Wendell L., 263
Wilson, Woodrow, 32-33, 42-44
Woman suffrage, in U. S., 108
World Commonwealth Plan, 258-259
World Court, 40, 104, 172
World Economic Conference, 57
World federation, 258
World War, First, 9-27; *m.* 17, 21, 27
World War, Second, 164-190, 193-219, *m.* 194-195; postwar planning, 249-264

Y

Young China Party, 135
Young Plan, 56
Yuan Shih-kai, General (yü än′ shē′kǐ′), 136
Yugoslavia, 37; alliance with France, 47; boundary dispute with Albania, 44; invasion of, 170-171; problems after First World War, 98; Treaty of Rapallo, 74

Z

Zamora, Alcala (thä mō′rä, äl′kä lä′), 102